The Life, Art, and Transcendence of
ALICE COLTRANE

COSMIC MUSIC

Andy Beta

First published in the US by Da Capo Press an imprint of Grand Central Publishing

First published in Great Britain in 2026 by White Rabbit,
an imprint of The Orion Publishing Group Ltd
Carmelite House, 50 Victoria Embankment
London EC4Y 0DZ

An Hachette UK Company

The authorised representative in the EEA is Hachette Ireland,
8 Castlecourt Centre, Dublin 15, D15 XTP3, Ireland (email: info@hbgi.ie)

1 3 5 7 9 10 8 6 4 2

Copyright © Andy Beta 2026

The moral right of Andy Beta to be identified as
the author of this work has been asserted in accordance
with the Copyright, Designs and Patents Act of 1988.

All rights reserved. No part of this publication may be
reproduced, stored in a retrieval system, or transmitted
in any form or by any means, electronic, mechanical,
photocopying, recording, or otherwise, without the
prior permission of both the copyright owner and the
above publisher of this book.

A CIP catalogue record for this book is
available from the British Library.

ISBN (Hardback) 978 1 3996 2621 7
ISBN (Ebook) 978 1 3996 2624 8
ISBN (Audio) 978 1 3996 2625 5

Printed in Great Britain by Clays Ltd, Elcograf, S.p.A.

www.whiterabbitbooks.co.uk
www.orionbooks.co.uk

To God

For Theresa, Dorothy, Cecilia

Susan, Vanessa, Bessa

Contents

xi   *Author's Note*

xxiii   *Prologue*

Part 1: Alice McLeod

3   Chapter One
      Hellfire in Paradise Valley

17   Chapter Two
      Motor City Music

33   Chapter Three
      Only God Can Make a Tree

45   Chapter Four
      Graduation

59   Chapter Five
      Three Guys and a Doll

73   Chapter Six
      April in Paris

87   Chapter Seven
      Soulsphere

101   Chapter Eight
      Always

Part 2: Alice Coltrane

117	Chapter Nine **Your Lady**
135	Chapter Ten **Song of Praise**
147	Chapter Eleven **Expression**
173	Chapter Twelve **Seraphic Light**

Part 3: Turiya

181	Chapter Thirteen **Manifestation of Cosmic Energy**
195	Chapter Fourteen **IHS**
207	Chapter Fifteen **Mantra**
219	Chapter Sixteen **Journey on the Ship of Satchidananda**
237	Chapter Seventeen **Universal Consciousness**
255	Chapter Eighteen **Galaxy in Turiya**
273	Chapter Nineteen **Angel of Sunlight**

Part 4: Swamini Turiyasangitananda

287	Chapter Twenty	**A Prophetic Song**
301	Chapter Twenty-One	**Monument Eternal**
313	Chapter Twenty-Two	**Highest Song of Bliss**
323	Chapter Twenty-Three	**Turiya Sings**
333	Chapter Twenty-Four	**A New Sun**
343	Chapter Twenty-Five	**Each Second an Eternity**
353	Chapter Twenty-Six	**The Coltrane Legacy**
363	Chapter Twenty-Seven	**The Divine Fragrance of a Dedicated Life**
373	Chapter Twenty-Eight	**Going Home**

385 *Epilogue*
393 *Acknowledgments*
395 *Notes*
433 *Index*

Author's Note

For Purusha Hickson, he was busy busing tables at a temple in San Francisco when he first experienced Alice Coltrane's music; instantly, he knew that she *knew*. For Shankari Adams, she attended an Alice Coltrane show in Northern California, waiting for a postconcert comedown that never came. Grad student Franya Berkman lay in shavasana—corpse pose—after a sweaty yoga class in Brooklyn when Alice Coltrane's music first washed over her. These three have all written their own books about her.

For myself, it was Alan—working in vitamins and supplements—who introduced me to Alice Coltrane's music in the 1990s. When he wasn't talking about the health benefits of shark cartilage, ginkgo biloba, and crystals in the aisles of Whole Foods Market with customers, Alan recorded gentle tapes of New Age music in his spare time. I worked in the kitchen, my music blasting out of a tiny boom box. I was a teenager who grew up in the suburbs of Texas, weaned on grunge, hip-hop, punk, electronic, and other furious types of music.

And I had just tentatively dipped my toes into jazz. A friend's dad made him a mixtape and one of the most astonishing moments was a song that opened with tabla, sitar, bird chirps, and wicked electric growls, before it turned into a funky breakbeat, though one filled with handclaps, whistles, and what sounded like a downed power line whipping around. It was credited to famous jazz trumpeter Miles Davis, from an album called *On the Corner*. It was hard to believe that this bewildering matrix of sound could be jazz. Was there even a trumpet in there?

Similarly, a stylish punk band with a sharp graphic design on their CD had featured a lowercase *i* followed by an exclamation point. So when I saw the bright orange spine of a CD with that same *i!* I took it to be a beacon and purchased *Om*, by John Coltrane. By that point of high school I may have already been dimly aware of the Eastern concept of *om* as the first sound of the universe, but I was not at all prepared by what was unleashed when I first pressed play. A slushing of bells, a chant about "clarified butter," and then the most fiery and unhinged scream of haunted sound that I had ever come across, like a spume of lava erupting from the manicured lawns of Central Texas and turning everything in its path to ashes. *This* is what jazz sounds like???

The only thing I knew was that Alice had been John Coltrane's wife. But a CD reissue of Alice Coltrane's 1971 album *Journey in Satchidananda* had recently appeared, and Alan told me I had to check it out. "It's some of the most beautiful music in the universe," he softly said. I took it home but couldn't make heads or tails of it. I detected some similarities between it and this music of Miles Davis and John Coltrane. There were those droning Indian elements, a steady pulse of bass, the unfettered cries of a saxophone. Atop it all were the strums of Alice Coltrane's harp, a sound associated with dream sequences and fantasy in films and television. In my narrow purview, I could imagine that Indian instrumentation belonged in jazz, but why a harp? That didn't make much sense. And rather than the hectic, chaotic tumult of *On the Corner* and *Om*, there was a peacefulness to *Journey in Satchidananda* that soared right over and passed me by.

Weirder still, my mind instantly got lost in this music. I would remember the start of it, that tamboura buzzing like a gate opening wide, the slow amble of the bass, the accrual of other instruments, the kaleidoscopic swirl of Coltrane's harp, and then...it all drew down to a close. What had happened? How long was this first song, "Journey in Satchidananda"? Had I just not been paying attention? I could follow lyrics, hooks, chord changes, beats, the building and release of tension at the chorus, but there was a slippery quality to this music that just baffled me. It could feel like those few moments after a nap, not quite sure what was a remnant of dream and what was reality. Or like those times I played in the ocean as a kid, swimming and then suddenly realizing I was a hundred feet away from where my parents were. The music acted like the underlying current, subtly lifting me and transporting me elsewhere. I had never experienced anything like it.

As to the title referencing Satchidananda, it would be many years before I understood its true meaning. As a fan of the Beatles and their story, I knew well the story of their time spent in India with Maharishi Mahesh Yogi and could see any number of such Indian figures popping up on the album covers of other classic rock figures, from George Harrison and Pete Townshend to Santana and John McLaughlin. But it didn't occur to me that the name Satchidananda itself referred to a guru, taking it at first as some far-off destination in India that Alice must have traveled to at that time. And since he didn't appear on either of the multi-album set documenting the Woodstock Festival of 1969 (and he's only briefly glimpsed in the original film), I didn't make the connection that the man who gave the blessing and benediction to over three hundred thousand wide-eyed kids at the most iconic rock festival of the 1960s was the same man being name-checked on this album.

It took me a few other forays into the canonical albums of Davis and Coltrane like *Kind of Blue* and *A Love Supreme* before I realized that these entry points into jazz were far away from what was considered to be jazz and that most critics, players, and listeners had long ago written off albums like *On the Corner*, *Om*, and *Journey in Satchidananda*. But in the intervening decades, other outliers in music had caught up to these misunderstood works. By the time I happened upon these albums in the 1990s, electronic dance music and techno had dug into the tape loops, electronic processing, and rhythmic focus of Miles's electric era. Thanks to the example of Sonic Youth, Nirvana, and other guitar bands—not to mention European free improv musicians who used standard jazz instrumentation but deployed in decidedly more extreme ways—that had also done away with such structures and instead embraced noise, feedback, screams, and the types of sound that lay between notes and scales, something like John Coltrane's *Om* was a prime example of what true freedom might sound like. *Journey in Satchidananda* seemed to have resisted such acceptance and assimilation, though.

How many more years passed before I even realized that Alice Coltrane had released more than one album? Although she released ten albums on major labels, just three of those albums saw domestic release on compact disc. Only in the twenty-first century—over thirty years after it was first released—did that finally start to change, mostly because European and Japanese demand led to the rest of her catalog finally being more readily available. Which meant I could load albums like *Universal Consciousness* and *Lord of Lords* onto a second-generation iPod and take this enigmatic music with me when I traveled to Southeast Asia a few years later.

I would listen to these albums on the long bus or boat rides through these countries. Even with a decade of listening to *Satchidananda*, much of Alice's music slipped out of my grasp. It was exotic, dreamy, immersive, but also turbulent, harrowing. It could be calm as a lake, yes, but also white-knuckled as roaring rapids. It reminded me of looking out at the dense jungles as they blurred past my window, dense and unknowable. Yet there would then be quick glimpses of majestic golden temples, of some otherworldly beauty mixed into it, gone in a blink but still vibrant in my mind. I kept returning to this music.

In 2010, I found myself in a small house tucked into a narrow hillside in Echo Park in Los Angeles belonging to Steven Ellison, better known as electronic music producer Flying Lotus. Lording over the cramped living room was a giant five-foot-tall canvas in vibrant black and gold of his great-aunt, Alice Coltrane. He regretted not being able to have her play harp on his album. I knew that she had instead turned away from public life and founded her own ashram, becoming a guru and nurturing a small community of followers, but I didn't quite understand the lasting impact she had on her family and that community. In the public realm, she was Alice Coltrane, but to the devotees that followed her to her ashram in the rustic countryside of Agoura Hills in California, she became known as Swamini Turiyasangitananda. Her eight-syllable name translates from Hindi as "the Transcendental Lord's highest song of bliss."

There's a long history of musicians turning toward spirituality and deepening their faith, but something about Alice Coltrane felt decidedly different in that regard. Jazz musicians might adopt the faith of Islam, rock stars might sit at the foot of a guru or else be born again, singers might spend time in a monastery. Few turned away from their ego entirely and abandoned the material trappings of their fame and fortune. As far as I knew, no one had become fully realized, a guru themselves.

At the end of 2011, I traveled to India for a friend's wedding in Kolkata and decided to stay in the country for another two months. Before I left, a few DJs for Los Angeles's local internet radio station Dublab informed me that while Alice Coltrane had indeed turned away from recording for the public in the late 1970s, she had continued to make music with her congregation, self-releasing a series of cassette tapes in the early 1980s. She would play organ and synthesizer and the members of her ashram would chant and sing bhajans, a type of devotional hymn whose roots stretch all the way back to India's Vedic era, circa 1500–500 BCE. On one particularly resonant yet haunting tape, titled *Turiya Sings*, I could hear her deep, devout singing voice for the very first time. I loaded nearly four hours of this devotional music on an iPod and took it with me overseas.

After the wedding, I spent the winter traveling around India: Varanasi, Shantiniketan, Mumbai, Kerala, and elsewhere. It was arduous travel. India overwhelms the senses in every sense of the word. I saw stunning golden spires but also abject poverty and suffering. The smell of rot and death intermingled with wondrous spices, fragrant flowers, and incense. But there was no way to separate these extremes. Many nights I regretted such a long trip and wished I could leave the next day. I decided to undertake a two-week silent meditation retreat in rural India, and when I emerged at the end of it, India was not transformed; instead it was my self that had changed. As someone put it to me during my travels: "There's a reason why incense and meditation was invented in India thousands of years ago."

Another feature story on Ellison a few years later led me back to L.A., and we spent more time together and talked at length about his "auntie." He talked about going out to the ashram every Sunday, the feeling of the place. He pulled out a photo of him as a newborn, his auntie dressed in vivid saffron robes, blessing him. The old photo was bent in such a way that it looked as if a ray of light was beaming down on the young baby. And there was the time he accompanied his auntie to India in the 1990s, taking video of her in the city of Puttaparthi, a small remote municipality in the Indian state of Andhra Pradesh. There, strangers and beggars would drop down in the street at the sight of her so as to kiss and touch her feet in reverence. He had never seen her in such a light before.

Although Alice Coltrane had passed away in January 2007, I learned that there were still families living on the ashram and tending to the grounds. It was closed to the public, save for on Sunday, when visitors could come to the mandir and participate in the kirtan or singing of bhajans. I wondered if Ellison might go with me out to the ashram as part of the feature story. He demurred. But my curiosity led me to make the drive myself one Sunday.

To reach the Sai Anantam Ashram, I had to drive the entire length of the San Fernando Valley, across the Santa Monica Mountains, and toward the Pacific Ocean. As the misty morning gave way to a brilliant and bright afternoon, I turned down a road that wound through Agoura Hills, the land brown and red with tufts of white and green brush. The scrub brush gave way to vineyards and an equestrian center, until the dirt road ended at the ashram gates. For four hours each Sunday, these gates were open to the public. The grounds were almost silent.

I walked into a room off to one side that featured a face I instantly recognized from my days at Whole Foods Market, perusing the aisle of self-help books and boxes of Nag Champa incense: Sathya Sai Baba.

His portrait was garlanded with flowers as was a beatific photograph of Swamini Turiyasangitananda, her profile aglow and her eyes turned up toward heaven.

I was no stranger to attending a religious service far different from the upbringing I had in the Catholic Church. I had been to temples in Thailand, in India, up in Harlem. On those occasions, I would slip into a pew or cushion in the back of the sacred space and take part in ritual as best I could, all while keeping my tall, innocuous self out of sight as much as possible. Sometimes I would slip back out the door before services had concluded, before it was time to shake hands with a member of the congregation, walking back out those doors and returning to my regular way of life.

That was not possible here. Only eight people were at the Vedantic Center's service that day. Plastic patio chairs lined the walls of the unadorned room and marigold throw pillows were scattered atop a very plush royal-blue carpet. Led by an organist situated between garlanded portraits of Sathya Sai Baba and Swamini Turiyasangitananda, music soon filled the room.

The devotees, clad all in white, sat still yet sang the bhajans with great fervor. The bhajans as heard on *Turiya Sings* had a haunting quality about them, but they were vibrant and alive in that room, a joyous celebration. The gathered sang more than a dozen hymns, accompanied by the organ and the hand drums, bells, and rattles that the devotees played themselves. The bhajans segued into one another. Curiously, these Indian hymns seemed to have a Pentecostal gospel feel to them, the blues coursing through each mesmerizing movement so as to suggest a place where Southeast Asia and the Deep South of America met. I sang the Hindi text as best I could and clapped along.

After the two-hour service concluded, the small congregation gathered for fellowship. Since the Swamini had passed on January 12, 2007, only seven people still lived at the ashram. I went to the small gift shop and the organist, a woman named Radha Botofasina, helped me as I purchased Alice's self-published memoir *Monument Eternal* and other privately issued tapes of bhajans that Alice had also recorded. I asked questions and she wondered aloud if she was "being interviewed."

Over carrot-raisin bread and paper cups of strawberry lemonade, the remaining devotees of Turiyasangitananda discussed the upcoming anniversary of their Swamini's passing. The word *death* was never uttered. One member says that they should no longer call it a *memorial*, as that word lingered in the past. Another offered up a suggestion: The anniversary should be called an *ascension*, as a way to keep the blessed Swamini Alice Coltrane Turiyasangitananda forever in the present.

The goal of this book is to serve a similar purpose, to keep Alice Coltrane Turiyasangitananda's work in the present. The previous books on her—luminous, insightful, deeply personal works written by Hickson, Adams, and Berkman—are either self-published or academic in nature. For *Cosmic Music*, my goal is clarity and understanding, to trace the biographical and musical events that transformed Alice McLeod into Swamini Turiyasangitananda.

It was not an easy task. Even at the height of her fame in the world of jazz, the critics were skeptical at best, at least when their misogyny wasn't just blatant on the page. And after she receded from public view in the 1970s, there was little that appeared in the public record. The stories that would emerge foregrounded John Coltrane instead, a stance which she herself nurtured. Ever the devoted wife, Alice Coltrane was more than happy to stay out of the spotlight herself, to give all praises due instead to John Coltrane—whom she often referred to as "Ohnedaruth" or "The Father"—or, in her later life, to Sai Baba.

As I dug into the research, I blanched at the dearth of material to be found in various libraries. There was not much to be found in books on jazz history, in newspapers, or magazines. There was never a review of any of her albums in the *New York Times* or in magazines like *Rolling Stone* during her recording career. (The only time she warranted ink in the *Times* was by proxy, as Alvin Ailey's *Cry* [which featured Alice's music on its soundtrack] was mentioned many times over the years.) There was never a full print feature on her in jazz periodicals like *Down Beat*.

Any archival recording of her late husband would garner the lead review in that magazine, while her own work was relegated much farther back. What was then written about her was even more abysmal. The lack of research material was daunting, in that I fretted about how to trace Alice Coltrane's trajectory without much of a paper trail. But on the flip side, it also meant that there was a finite amount of interviews and reviews. Even visiting a major library like the New York Public Library for the Performing Arts, I could get through their entire archive of pertinent material in a matter of hours.

In 1987, a *New York Times* feature by Robert Palmer discussed the continuing influence of John Coltrane on rock music, citing the likes of Eric Clapton, the Byrds, Santana, and featuring quotes from the biggest rock band in the world at that time, U2, with Bono enthusing about his music. Alice talked about her and her late husband's shared vision of "cosmic music," calling it "a mosaic of sound and energy…an expression of the colors and varieties of sound, and how they interweave and complement each other. A number of people were quite confused by that, but if the same people look at paintings with a variety of colors and textures, they're pleased." In her own recordings, the confines of "jazz" fell away and instead I heard a continuation of her husband's quest, how she utilized an exquisite range of colors, timbres, and textures to realize this vision.

The last ten years have brought about a sea change in understanding her own "cosmic music." Every generation appears to find its own lost musician to exhume and exalt. In the 1960s, the biggest white rock stars championed the nearly forgotten blues guitarist Robert Johnson. In my own generation, there was reverence for singer-songwriter Nick Drake. At the start of the twenty-first century, I watched as Arthur Russell went from a curio known only by a few obsessive record collectors to a beloved cultural touchstone. Albums that once seemed outlandish and off-putting, like Miles Davis's *On the Corner* and John Coltrane's *Om*, can decades on sound like a transmission from the future.

Even five years ago, it seemed unlikely that *Journey in Satchidananda* and the music of Alice Coltrane could ever be acknowledged or accepted by a wider audience. Yet with each passing year, the album—and Alice herself—seems to only grow in stature and influence. A feature I wrote about Alice's spiritual transformation for influential music website Pitchfork in 2016 became one of the most read pieces on the site. The next year, a compilation of the bhajans she had recorded in Agoura Hills in the early 1980s was being prepared for reissue on David Byrne's Luaka Bop imprint. I was asked to interview one of the children who had grown up in the ashram and was now working in a bustling restaurant in Midtown Manhattan, a long way from the pastoral acreage of Agoura Hills. His name was Surya Botofasina, the son of Radha. Our conversation became a part of the package of *The Ecstatic Music of Alice Coltrane Turiyasangitananda* reissue.

Members from the ashram toured the world, singing these bhajans to huge crowds, with Surya in the role of bandleader. (These days, you can catch him playing keyboards in André 3000's jazz group, a wonderful update on the spiritual jazz tradition, abetted no doubt by a direct connection to one of its guiding spirits.) In 2021, *Journey* was finally ranked on *Rolling Stone*'s "500 Greatest Albums of All Time," the lone jazz album by a woman to make the list. That same year, WNYC celebrated the album's fiftieth anniversary and I found myself as a guest on *The Brian Lehrer Show* discussing the album's timelessness.

Yet I'm reluctant to classify Alice Coltrane as an example of a beloved artist going from obscurity to belated discovery. The stars are always above us, but the conditions on Earth must be right in order to fully glimpse their splendor. In that sense, Alice's "cosmic music" was always there, waiting for that moment when a new generation would be ready to hear its message, aware and openhearted to "the most beautiful music in the universe."

Before its incarnation the soul is sound.
It is for this reason that we love sound.

—Hazrat Inayat Khan

Particular sounds and scales are intended to produce specific emotional meanings…But what are these pieces and what is the road to travel to attain a knowledge of them, that I don't know. The true powers of music are still unknown. To be able to control them must be, I believe, the goal of every musician.

—John Coltrane

When art is done as an offering to God, it is not common entertainment. It is divine.

—Swami Satchidananda

Everything I do is an offering to God—that's the truth.

—Alice Coltrane

Prologue

The spark came to life on a beautiful November afternoon in 2018 at a Southern California Edison substation. A former rocket engine testing and nuclear power research facility nestled into the low rocky mountain range of Simi Valley, the old Santa Susana test lab had witnessed the most fantastical of human inventions: rocket propulsion for moon landings, nuclear reactors, the launching of GPS satellites into outer space. It was shut down in 2006, but the ground still bore the scars of its nuclear waste and contaminants. Most of the remaining buildings belonged to Boeing.

Just that past June, three fire departments had convened and trained together in the Santa Susana area to prepare for such a wildfire, which seemed to be not an *if* but a *when* event. The surrounding land was prime kindling for the state's seasonal wildfires. At first, the surrounding rocks prevented the gusting 100-mph Santa Ana winds from reaching the small spark. But with one breath, that spark became a fire. A plume of smoke stood out on that clear day and it wasn't alone.

The Camp fire had started in Northern California the same day at 6:33 a.m. Less than fifteen miles to the west of Santa Susana, another blaze called the Hill fire was already gathering speed and strength, straining the resources of every firefighter in the area. In fifteen minutes, that fire had grown to one hundred acres in size, moving from the arid mountainsides and rolling down toward the 101, gathering in power as it threatened homes on the other side of the freeway. Some four hundred firefighters were sent that direction.

Then the Santa Ana winds touched that new flame, nudged and nurtured it at a brisk 37 miles per hour. Soon, the Woolsey fire began to grow and spread. First responders arriving in the valley struggled during those early-afternoon hours. Cell phone service faltered in the hills, radio calls dissolved into static, and there was a lack of water reserves stored at Boeing. Air tanker support had already been diverted farther west to fight the Hill fire. The Los Angeles County Fire Department, the Ventura County Fire Department, and the Los Angeles Fire Department had mutually agreed to work together to handle new wildfires the moment they were spotted. But there was no clear plan of attack.

By five p.m., aided by the Santa Ana winds, the Woolsey fire revealed its true power and ferocity, having grown to 750 acres in size. By midnight, the fire was 4,000 roaring acres and insatiable. The winds doubled to 70 miles per hour, rendering air drops futile. In the wee hours of November 9, the fire doubled once again in size, a maw now encompassing 8,000 acres and nearly fourteen miles wide. An hour before sunrise, the Woolsey fire jumped the 101 freeway, raced down between the San Fernando Valley and the Conejo Valley and then whipped through the Santa Monica Mountains, before marching down to Malibu, a wall of destruction roaring toward the Pacific Ocean.

"In my thirty years of experience, I've never seen a fire that explosive," LAFD Deputy Chief Trevor Richmond told a reporter. "Seeing how quickly that fire traveled to Agoura Hills and Oak Park and Thousand Oaks and jumped the freeway the next morning, and in four hours, it's burning kelp beds in the Pacific Ocean—that's pretty incredible. This one was the big one."

If one wanted to understand the temporality of this world, to truly grasp the concept that the most solid of structures are ultimately fated to turn back to ash, you could do worse than follow in the wake of this fire. Previously, the biggest fire in the area occurred in 1933 when 38,000 acres burned. In one night, Woolsey scorched over 100,000 acres. Some 1,500 structures were incinerated in the span of a single day. Groves of California sycamores and coast live oaks became instant cinders. A town called Paradise burned like hell. Trailer parks and the sprawling mansions of Neil Young, Miley Cyrus, and movie stars were now handfuls of dust. As the ocean waters began to boil, its path of destruction was complete. It was as if the entire California coastline—its mountains, forests, mansions—were offered up as yajna, a religious sacrifice consecrated in flame.

Somewhere in the char, nineteen miles from that initial spark, fifty acres in Agoura Hills burned in the night, the surrounding sage and chaparral shriveled into black. On that land stood a simple white structure reflecting all the brilliance of the California sun, its understated exterior as bright and magnificent as the clouds overhead. A fire worthy of Shiva devoured the structure entirely as if an offering of oblation, the burnt offering itself being consumed by the flames. The wide white stone steps that had previously ushered its handful of devotees to services at the mandir every Sunday were now steps leading up to meet the empty sky.

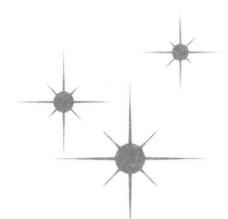# PART 1

Alice McLeod

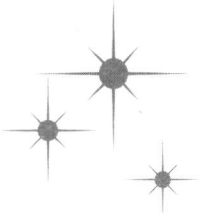

CHAPTER ONE

Hellfire in Paradise Valley

FIVE CHILDREN PERISH IN FIRE

So the headline screamed in bold print—well above the *Detroit Tribune* eagle clutching a banner that read *Leading Negro Weekly of Michigan*—on April 16, 1949.[1] The tragedy happened down in Birmingham, Alabama, overnight, but the heat and grief was felt thousands of miles north. Five "motherless children" were left at home alone, their father working overnight, and defective wiring in their four-room frame dwelling led to a blaze while they slept. The children ranged from two years old to the eldest daughter, Gloria, age eleven.

Some eight pages in, in a section of the *Tribune* headed "Detroit Schools," another eleven-year-old appeared. In the upper right corner, next to drawings of the Phi Delta Kappa sorority triangle and a diligent young man with a cap and diploma resting nearby, was a photo of a beaming eleven-year-old sixth grader who had just won the city's spelling bee. Her name was Alice L. McLeod. The caption read: "She out-spelled Eunice Boyton, an eighth grade student of Russell School to qualify her for the district's representative to compete in the finals." A seven-paragraph story detailing the spelling championship was faded and overexposed to the point of indecipherability, save for this fragment: "Alice, daughter of Mr. and Mrs. Solon McLeod of 644 East Farnsworth is, according to her principal O.D. Moore (Trowbridge School) an outstanding student with a winning personality and is liked by her fellow students. She is a music lover and plays the piano for the Mt. Olive Baptist Church Sunday school each week, according to her teacher."[2]

Two weeks later, the *Tribune* printed another item about the spelling bee, detailing how nineteen of the twenty-one children were eliminated within the first hour, but the two girls continued on well into a third hour. Only then did the eighth grader Boynton stumble (on the word *rouge*), leaving McLeod the winner. Some seventy-plus years of fading newsprint has done little to diminish the wattage of Alice's smile.

ALICE LUCILLE MCLEOD WAS BORN ON AUGUST 27, 1937, IN DETROIT, Michigan. It was a clear and bright summer day, the heat assuaged by the balmy breeze that carried off the nearby Detroit River. A little after five p.m., the fifth child of Solon and Ann McLeod came into the world. In that last stretch of labor, Ann McLeod gripped the doorframe for support as the third daughter in the family and Ann's second child born in Detroit arrived.[3] Her half brother Ernest Farrow, half sister Margaret Farrow, brother Jackie, and sister Jo-Anne (sometimes spelled JoAnn) all welcomed the new baby. Less than two years later, her baby sister Marilyn would arrive.

Ann K. Johnson (in various documents her name also appears as Anna, Anne, or Annie) grew up in Athens, Alabama, about a hundred miles due north of Birmingham. Ann's father was a writer, lecturer, and teacher associated with the Tuskegee Institute of Alabama. Her mother lent her talents as a singer and pianist to their church and was an active member of the community.

Such service and Christian belief was instilled in Ann as a child. She's described as having a lovely alto voice that could be heard during Sunday service, resounding throughout the church. Just how or why Ann Johnson arrived in Huntington, West Virginia, in her twenties is not exactly clear, but by October 27, 1927, she was married to Harold Clifford Farrow. Farrow was born March 5, 1900, and was raised in Huntington, where he served as musical director at a local church. Just over a year later, Mr. and Mrs. H. C. Farrow welcomed their first son, Ernest, born November 13, 1928. On October 12, 1930, Margaret Ouida arrived. Sometime between 1930 and 1934, the Farrows and their young family uprooted from Huntington and arrived in Detroit, Michigan, Mrs. Farrow now some seven hundred miles from her family back in Athens.

In this, the Farrows were not alone, but one small family in this heaving northward emigration, joining the swells of millions of other Black families who would comprise the Great Migration. What started as a trickle during World War I swelled to dam-bursting between the wars. In the 1920s, the Black population in Detroit tripled from 40,000 to 120,000.[4] Black populations in Philadelphia might be composed of families from other parts of the mid-Atlantic, but most of Detroit's incoming population came from the rural parts of Mississippi, Alabama, and the like. Trains winding through the Deep South seemingly arrived every hour on the hour at Michigan Central Station. Black passengers were immediately dumped into Black Bottom, a crammed, filthy eastern neighborhood wedged between the train tracks and the banks of the Detroit River, one of the few areas in which Black people were allowed to reside. If family fortunes ticked up a notch, they might squeeze in a few streets to the north in Paradise Valley. (The upwardly mobile and middle class could afford to cross over Woodward Avenue and be considered West Siders.) Connecting these two Black neighborhoods was Hastings Street.

The city could barely keep up with the influx of arriving families and was far less inclined to do so to accommodate Black families, even as the city's famous automobile factories were ramping up production and employment. Even Black families long since settled in Detroit could find themselves on the move to get a better opportunity. Having arrived from Georgia in 1922, Berry Gordy II settled on the west side of Detroit, raising his family there. In the late 1920s, his seventh child, Berry Gordy III, was born. When he was nearly seven years old, Gordy's father bought a two-story property at the corner of Farnsworth and St. Antoine Streets and moved the family across Woodward Avenue to the east side of Detroit.[5]

The Gordys were perched near the uppermost part of Paradise Valley, just above E. Warren and near the Wayne State University campus. Look to the east and a young Gordy would have just been able to make out the Romanesque high-rise truss tower of the Maccabees Building on Woodward Avenue. Turn south and the din of construction from the Brewster-Douglass Housing Projects cut through the city noise. Spread across the city block between St. Antoine and Hastings Streets, the Brewster houses were inaugurated by the First Lady herself, as Eleanor Roosevelt had broken ground on the project in 1935 and construction would continue for the next two decades.

The Gordy family lived in a flat above the storefront. On street level was a beauty shop, a barber shop, and a laundry with *Delaney's Cleaners* painted on the big plate glass window. The Gordy family's newest business endeavor was a grocery store, named for famous Black educator Booker T. Washington. But Woodward Avenue was a clear demarcation for Black and white residents alike. The West Side was more affluent and residential, while the Black population on the East Side was rougher and almost everyone living there struggled financially. Gangs owned those streets and if you weren't careful, you could get roughed up in an instant. Moving from west to the east was jarring, as Gordy recalled:

> Coming to the Eastside was like moving from the country to the city—there was action all the time. There were so many different kinds of people—all hustlers in their own way. There was the street kind: pimps, gamblers and numbers men. I had always heard that the Eastside was where all the bad people lived. The two worst places there were Hastings Street, where you could easily be killed by drunk people, and Black Bottom, a place near the Detroit River, where you would just disappear and never be heard from again. Suddenly, I found myself living there, one block from Hastings Street. I was scared. There were the dirtiest

rat-infested alleys you ever saw running behind our house. Strange old white men with black hats and long white beards came down them on horse-driven carts—searching through trash and garbage, picking up stuff that had been thrown out.[6]

For as tough as Detroit could look right outside his front door, Gordy soon realized that was also where the action was:

The minute you'd step outside our building, the mouthwatering aroma of smoldering ribs would hit you in the face. Directly across the street from our front door was CT's, a busy little storefront barbecue joint where all day long a steady stream of people were coming and going... I quickly learned that... CT's was headquarters for the numbers, the illegal lottery, a way of life in our neighborhood. Everybody played them.[7]

Even more so than the West Side, your friends and neighbors always kept an eye on you on the East Side, the sense of community and support tactile. And as his was the only family to own a commercial building in the neighborhood, he also realized that his family had a little bit of weight in the hood. What was frightening became enlivening once you could negotiate the bustling sidewalks and all the characters out on parade. Reaching Hastings Street was like cranking open a fire hydrant, a gusher of sound and sensations that overwhelmed the young boy's senses. He remembered it vividly:

The infamous Hastings Street turned out to be exciting and colorful, changing my fear into awe. There were bars and pawn shops, five-and-ten-cent stores, the little Warfield Theater and greasy spoons that made the most delicious chili hot dogs in the world. When I'd gone exploring for the first time and stepped over a wino sitting on the sidewalk drinking out of a paper bag, I remember feeling a strange desire to talk to him and find out why he was there.[8]

The Farrows were on the same stretch of Farnsworth as the Gordys, though they weren't quite the Farrows any longer. Soon after arriving in Detroit, H. C. Farrow became the choirmaster and musical director at Mt. Olive Baptist Church, situated less than a block from the family's front door. But somewhere along with the family settling into their new home of Detroit, Ann Farrow made the acquaintance of another Mt. Olive parishioner, Solon McLeod.

McLeod was born April 10, 1900, in Clayton, Alabama, but was raised in Birmingham. He served under General John Pershing in World War I as a private in the 528th Engineer Battalion who rose to the rank of corporal and fought in France in the last years of the war. Even in his civilian years after, he volunteered as an air raid warden in Detroit. McLeod stood over six feet tall, dark, solidly built, with what his daughter Alice would later describe as "clear bright eyes. He was an excellent father—civic-minded and generous. He often donated whatever he could to charity, even if his resources were scarce."[9] Whether they met during Sunday services at Mt. Olive Baptist or elsewhere, soon Ann had taken up with Solon instead of H. C., and that was that. A son named Jackie McLeod arrived in 1934, and daughter JoAnn McLeod not long after. A divorce was finally filed with the City of Detroit on July 8, 1938, when Alice was almost a year old. About a month after that, Ann was pregnant with her sixth child, Marilyn.

It was nothing if not an amicable divorce, as Ann still played keyboard every Sunday and Farrow remained choirmaster at Mt. Olive Baptist Church. The extended Farrow-McLeod family—Ernie, Margaret, Jackie, JoAnn, Alice, and Marilyn—were seated in the pews not just every Sunday, but three times a week.

In the *Michigan Chronicle*, under the headline DIRECTOR ENTERTAINED, one can catch a glimpse of Mrs. McLeod, member of the senior choir. She clasps her right hand with her left, a neutral expression on her face.[10] It's in this photograph that one can discern a beautiful, serious face graced with high cheekbones, a tapered jawline, and what Alice would sometimes describe as her mother's fine Native American Indian features. Ann's great-grandfather was said to be Chief Running Fox, and when Alice was a young child, her grandfather would regale her with tales of seeing his grandfather dressed in full chieftain attire. In her later years, Alice would sit in meditation and describe how her great-great-grandfather would sometimes materialize before her, "always fully attired in deer and buckskin clothing and wearing his eagle-winged chieftain headdress." The feathered headdress would remind her of an image from her study of ancient Indian religions, of the thousand-petal lotus fanned out around the crown of the head.[11]

Solon McLeod drove a truck while Ann McLeod stayed at home with her six children, rarely taking on outside work as domestic help unless the extra money was needed during the holidays. In the eyes of young Alice, her mother was the definition of strength and fortitude:

> My mother was an incredible woman with unbelievable energy, and she could fix or restore practically anything. At the same time, she was also the most spiritual person I ever knew. She had a highly developed level of intuition, and, somehow, she could anticipate future events before they even happened. She was tireless, as she endlessly worked both in the home and at church. She even took in, fed, and clothed refugees—often better than her own children. During those early years, I believed, without a doubt, that our mother was invincible.[12]

Life on Farnsworth for the McLeods was simple and working class, centered wholly around the church. H. C. Farrow was still very much a part of his children's lives while Ann spent whatever hours she wasn't at home at the parish, doing whatever the small church needed. The McLeods—all eight of them—were squeezed into a two-room apartment. There was a living room, a bedroom, a little kitchen area, and a bathroom. The six kids piled onto bunks in the bedroom while Solon and Ann slept in the living room. One relative remembered that "everybody was always welcome" at the McLeod household, and even Berry Gordy would come over to the house and "eat out the pot," partaking in whatever Ann had made for evening supper, with everybody else.

Descriptions of Alice's parents center mostly on them being extremely spiritual people living simple, devotional lives, deeply ensconced in their faith and the calendar at Mt. Olive Church. There was a beautiful altar in the living room and the family would gather around it multiple times a day to say their prayers.

Sunday was the biggest day of the week for the McLeods. Ernie, Margaret, Jackie, JoAnn, Alice, and Marilyn would get ready in their Sunday best to attend morning worship, which would stretch from late morning until the afternoon hour. Ann would teach Sunday school and sing in the senior choir, and Solon would often assist the chaplain and walk the aisles with the woven offertory basket. The family would then return home to a big dinner, before walking back to Mt. Olive a few hours on to take in the evening services. As Marilyn recalled: "Our participation at church was never a chore. We always enjoyed it."[13]

Ernest, the eldest, inherited his mother's musical talents and played in the church band. As the eldest daughter, Margaret helped with many of the household chores and also assisted her mother with planning the Sunday school lessons. During the week, while her mother was at the church, she would make sure her younger siblings took care of their homework and prep dinner. Like her mother, Margaret also lent her fine singing voice to the church choir and worked diligently for the church and in the community for most of her adult life. No doubt she had to keep an eye on young Jackie, the mischievous and adventurous one in the family. Precocious from a young age, Alice always helped her mother when she was preparing to read a sermon and give a presentation to the church or community.

JoAnn, only one year older than Alice, suffered a serious injury as a young child and spent roughly five years of her early childhood at the Children's Hospital of Michigan. Her brothers and sisters—still too young to visit inside the hospital—were relegated on family visiting hours to waving and smiling at their sister through the window. When she had fully convalesced and was back at home, she too took to singing in the choir. As Marilyn would later describe it: "We had wonderful times together and a great family life. Our parents taught us to share and care about one another, both in good and difficult times."[14]

The church was foundational to most Black families of the era. Gordy recalled how "three times a week and all day Sunday, [our parents] would herd us off to one of the storefront churches in our neighborhood." While he might have been bored and fidgety while sitting in the pews in his itchy "Sunday best," the young Gordy was nevertheless magnetized by the men leading the congregation, hanging on every word of their sermons. The more dynamic and forceful the delivery, the stronger the impression it made on him and the other parishioners: "The preachers were the stars; dynamic, moving and emotional, they wielded great power and influence. Their words were solid, strong, repetitious and infectious; they could send the congregation into a frenzy."[15]

Far from the tidy spiritual messages of Sunday sermons, there was just as much learning to be had on the streets of his hood and on the air, and Gordy was equally attuned to all of that. At home, Gordy and his family would gather around a little upright piano or the radio, tuning in for shows like *Ghost Stories*, *Amos 'n' Andy*, *The Lone Ranger*, and Eddie "Rochester" Anderson—a rare Black voice on the air in the late 1930s—on *The Jack Benny Show*.

The cruel nuances of real estate redlining of Detroit in the early twentieth century may have gone over the young kids' heads, but the wonders of childhood were undiminished for the most part in Black Bottom and Paradise Valley. "I thought the whole world was black except for Santa Claus," Gordy recalled. "I thought the few white people who came to our neighborhood were accidents of nature." Never mind that at Trowbridge Elementary, he realized that while most of the kids were Black, all of the teachers were white (and not Santa Claus). The chant he heard on the playground stuck with him: "If you're white, you're all right. If you're yellow, you're mellow. If you're brown, you can stick around; but if you're black—get back."[16]

While there was news of war from overseas, America was still far from the horrors of Europe and the Far East. But by the summer of 1941, they were facing their own conflicts in every major urban center, as racial tensions began to reach their boiling point, especially in Detroit. The Detroit Housing Commission was struggling to erect enough adequate housing for the continued influx of Black people fleeing from the Jim Crow South. And the federal government was still doing its best to ignore their plight. One housing project plan—to be erected at the corner of Dequindre and Modern Streets in the heart of the 7 Mile & Fenelon neighborhood—was proposed for Black people until the government halted work. And when the Sojourner Truth Projects (named for the famous abolitionist and women's rights pioneer who lived the last years of her life in Battle Creek to the west of Detroit) did finally start construction on September 29, 1941, it wasn't long before tensions flared.

Just over a year later, with the first twenty-eight units finished and ready for occupancy, a cross was stuck into the frozen ground near the projects and set aflame. Overnight a hundred white picketers convened with the purpose of preventing *any* of the approved Black tenants from moving into the project. By morning, that crowd had swelled to over a thousand. As author/historian Herb Boyd recounted:

> The Sojourner Truth riot erupted the next morning when two cars driven by blacks crashed through a line of white picketers. The bold action sparked a bombardment of bricks from whites. Blacks retaliated from the opposite side of Ryan Road. Only after the police placed the blacks under protective custody was the riot halted.[17]

Moving Black families into their new homes was halted until April, when Detroit's Mayor Edward Jeffries then deployed over a thousand police and 1,600 National Guardsmen to protect the families moving in.

But racial violence continued elsewhere through the city. As America was drawn deeper into World War II, Detroit's mighty auto industry ramped up production. Almost overnight, the Motor City became an integral cog in the American military-industrial complex, earning another nickname in the process: "The Arsenal of Democracy." Ford, Packard, Dodge, Murray Body, and other automobile manufacturers began to switch from rolling out cars for American consumers to producing tanks to ship overseas. That level of mobilization meant more workers were needed and the city swelled with another five hundred thousand migrants in the early 1940s. Between 1940 and 1943, the Black population doubled.[18]

But whenever Black workers, no matter their qualification level, were given promotions on the factory floor, their white co-workers would protest. The promotion of two Black polishers led approximately 250 white workers to stage a sit-down strike. A similar strike followed at Hudson Motor Company. Even with the country turning its attention and labor force to fighting fascism and empire overseas in Europe and Asia, white workers back home still had plenty of vitriol in reserve to protest their Black neighbors getting ahead or merely getting by. And the Black population, crammed into miserable conditions in Black Bottom and Paradise Valley, was sick and tired of being second-class citizenry while also providing the labor for the war effort. They were drafted to fight Hitler overseas only to return home and now have to fight the Ku Klux Klan. Something had to give. As a *Life* magazine article titled "Detroit Is Dynamite" put it in 1942, "the city can either blow up Hitler or blow up the U.S."

In April 1943, Detroit listed toward the latter. The National Association for the Advancement of Colored People (NAACP) teamed up with the United Auto Workers with an organized rally that convened over ten thousand people. Later that month, when three Black workers were finally promoted at the Packard plant, over twenty-six thousand white workers walked out.[19] The NAACP printed a pamphlet listing the multiple work stoppages that white factory workers enacted over a three-month period. Issues for walkouts might have varied: demand for separate sanitary facilities; colored help placed in the production department; hiring of colored plant guards; and so on. But they all shared a common theme. Tensions were not defused. And as the summer came on, the temperatures on the Detroit streets and in the minds of its citizenry reached the boiling point.

One hot, humid day in June, as the mercury topped ninety degrees, hundreds of thousands of Detroiters made their way across the MacArthur foot bridge to Belle Isle. A popular getaway for city dwellers looking to absorb some of the breeze coming off the Detroit River and get some relief from the hot asphalt, the park and its beach beckoned. Black and white crowds jostled for space, and the flare-ups that had previously taken place at housing construction sites, on factory floors, and in the wee hours of bars around Detroit now spilled out into public space during the daytime.

Boyd writes about a young Black man named Charles "Little Willie" Lyon, who had been jumped a few days earlier by a group of young white men as he tried to enter Eastwood Amusement Park out by 8 Mile Road. His cuts and bruises still fresh, now Lyon stalked Belle Isle with a group of his friends, intent on exacting vengeance:

> Willie and friends broke up family picnics, beat up some boys, and started a melee on the bridge connecting isle to city. Fights broke out all over the island. From the playground to the bus stops, blacks and whites were ripping into each other ferociously. Several white sailors from a nearby armory, who were angry about a previous incident in which blacks had attacked one of them, went to the bridge and fueled the furor. Like a wildfire, the riot and rumor spread beyond the island into the city, coiling dangerously around Black Bottom and Paradise Valley.[20]

This human wildfire, gobbling up generational racial animosity like so much fuel, roared through the city. And like the accompanying smoke, rumors and misinformation moved just as swiftly through the streets, obfuscating things further. At one club, the Forest Club, a patron yelled that white mobs had killed a Black woman and thrown her baby over the bridge, which led to even more people pouring out into the streets. Black people would assault any white person they came across on the streets of Paradise Valley and elsewhere.

And as Detroit police raced onto the scene, their badges and sense of civic duty gave way to their own tribal affiliations. White cops began to nightstick and punch any Black person within arm's reach, beating adults and teens indiscriminately. Those farther out of reach were likely to be shot instead. Police violence was like gasoline sprayed on this wildfire. Black anger turned next to the businesses nearby, with people breaking store windows and looting shops all along Hastings Street, with particular acrimony paid to the white and Jewish-owned businesses in the area. The National Guard was called in and violence continued well into the June night and the next day and the day after that. Atrocities became commonplace. A woman watched as a National Guardsman nearly sawed a Black man in half with bullets as he ran with an armful of clothes from a pawn shop. As Boyd wrote of one of the worst race riots in the history of our country:

> Two days of mayhem produced thirty-four corpses, twenty-five of them African American, seventeen killed by the police. These deaths, the police claimed, were justifiable homicides because the victims were looting the stores on Hastings Street. In addition, nearly two thousand people were arrested, the majority of them black, and an unknown number were severely wounded, most of them black. Not one white person was convicted of any crime committed during the riot.[21]

It required President Franklin Delano Roosevelt deploying over six thousand army troops to the streets of Detroit (rather than to the battlefields in Europe) to finally quell the rioting. Property damage topped $2 million. The vibrant economical heart of Paradise Valley, Hastings Street, was strewn with broken glass, burnt storefronts, dead bodies, and unwanted merchandise scattered everywhere. Black Bottom was in even worse shape. Cars were overturned and set on fire in the middle of the street. Buildings were damaged, burnt out, and in serious need of repair. City officials, however, viewed these slums and dilapidated old buildings as not being worth saving. Here the bitter disharmony between the neighborhoods' impoverished Black residents and the white property owners who benefited from their business was laid bare:

> Nowhere were the Jewish merchants more devastated than on Hastings St. This street was densely populated by blacks and was, in the opinion of the Urban League's John Dancy, a veritable cesspool of filth and squalor but it also "contained a number of small businesses operated by… mainly Jewish merchants. They began to stone and destroy these shops; the destruction spread until practically all the white-owned businesses in the Negro section had been attacked."[22]

What a six-year-old Alice McLeod could have seen or heard outside her apartment window and how her family weathered those three days can't really be known, save the thought that hell—as it was depicted every Sunday in church, in Sunday school, and in the Bible—couldn't be much different than what transpired a block from their home.

CHAPTER TWO

Motor City Music

Long after services had ended, Mt. Olive's sacred music seemed to follow Alice home and linger, never quite lifting, even when Sunday night turned into Monday morning. It wasn't just that she heard these hymns as they were played on organ in the parish and felt them resonate inside her chest, but how the senior choir delivered that powerful message of God. Even during church services, she could always discern her mother's beautiful alto, soaring above the chorus.

Ann was fond of religious singing, humming as she did chores, her voice carrying from the kitchen or in the other room. She was emulating the role model she had in her own mother. During the week, Ann might not only lead the choir in rehearsal but also accompany them on piano. According to Franya Berkman, the McLeods' neighborhood church featured a standard repertoire for that era: from spirituals that stretched back to the slavery days to eighteenth-century Calvinist hymns to the songs that arose out of the Second Great Awakening, a Protestant religious revival that swept the United States starting in 1850.[1]

And much like the way that their faith was founded on the Holy Bible and the stories from both the Old and New Testaments, the music of Mt. Olive Baptist Church was deeply rooted in two key hymnals. There was former slave Richard Allen and his 1818 collection, *The African Methodist Pocket Hymn Book*, which was modeled on *The Methodist*

Pocket Hymn Book and contained 314 hymns. And then there was *Gospel Hymns and Sacred Songs*, first compiled by Dwight Lyman Moody and Ira David Sankey in 1875.

Mt. Olive Baptist Church featured several choirs, common during an era when the Black church and its stirring sound echoed through Detroit. As in other Baptist and Methodist parishes, they featured different choirs singing different repertoires. There was a senior choir, which Ann was a key member of, which would sing the hymns from the European-American tradition, while the gospel choir featured a slightly more updated songbook more closely aligned with what could be heard in Pentecostal and the little Church of God in Christ storefront churches scattered around Paradise Valley.

There was also the youth choir. The year 1921 brought forth a new book of hymnals. *Gospel Pearls* was small, just 7½ by 5 inches and containing just over 160 compositions, but it became one of the most popular hymnals of the early twentieth century, presenting simple Protestant and gospel hymns (as well as patriotic fare like "The Star Spangled Banner" and "Battle Hymn of the Republic," the latter a lifelong favorite of Alice's) that were readily adapted by churches around the country.

While her sisters also liked to sing in the choir, Alice's oldest brother, Ernest Farrow, stood apart in his love of music. Nine years her senior, Ernie was the oldest sibling with the most responsibilities, including keeping his younger charges out of trouble and intimidating anyone who tried to mess with them. The violence to be encountered out in Paradise Valley and Black Bottom was no joke, but Ernie could also be fun, playful, and funny, making his brothers and sisters belly laugh.

And he was dead serious about the music, whether it was coming from the church or down the street. The tall, lanky Ernie loved music down to the core of his being and had found the instrument to match his large frame, the bass violin. He studied music at school and was intent on mastering its deep, bellowing resonance. He dragged his bass violin everywhere with him; he was also intent on keeping up its appearance so that the thick strings were always in tune and the wood gleamed. It had to look sharp. And when he heard jazz, he took up the alto saxophone and began to learn how that worked as well.

Some days, Alice could hear a mellifluous sound of piano emanating from somewhere in their tenement building. It was like the music of Sunday services but with a moving sense of freedom to it. While the hymns in church would hover in place and repeat each chorus, this was a piano music that seemed to blossom and grow, expanding and revealing new melodies until it reached a thrilling finale. If the hymns of Mt. Olive were a pond, then this cascading sound was a river flowing toward the ocean.

By age seven, Alice knew that she wanted to play piano just like her mother and study music just like her older brother (now almost sixteen years old and keenly focused on alto sax), and she knew just who to ask for lessons. One day, she mustered up the courage to knock on her neighbor and fellow parishioner Hellen Philpot's door and asked for his wife, Ruby Philpot. Touched by the request, the forty-year-old Mrs. Philpot explained that while she did play piano, she had never given—much less offered—piano lessons before.

"I was hesitant to say that I would like for her to teach me," Alice said. "But I approached her, and she obliged, and it was great, starting out with little scales and simplistic solos." Every Saturday, Alice would knock on their door and continue her lessons with Mrs. Philpot.[2]

Alice proved to be an apt piano student and a quick study. Soon after, she had mastered her scales and sight reading so that Mt. Olive's congregation agreed to sponsor her for a year of study at a nearby community music school. But there was still the matter of the McLeods not having the necessary funds to purchase a piano for their own home. When she couldn't practice with Mrs. Philpot or at the church, Alice would resort to pressing her fingers on the kitchen table, imagining what that sound might be.

Ernie's longtime girlfriend, Terry Pollard, was a young pianist who also lived in the neighborhood. Six years older than Alice, she was as devout in her study of her instrument as Ernie was with his and no doubt saw in the young McLeod not only a little sister but a kindred musical spirit. Seeing how intent Alice was with her piano practice in the first year delighted her, so when Pollard upgraded the piano in her own home, she gifted her old upright piano to the McLeod family.

From that point on, Alice really was at the piano every single day. When she would come home from a long day of study at Trowbridge, she would immediately head to that upright. She thrilled at how the ivory keys would respond to her every touch. There was a joy in how her eyes and hands could move together, translating the black dots on the sheet music into pure notes. These notes would sound and she could just imagine the Mt. Olive choir lifting the melody and spiritual message even higher. Shankari Adams recounted Alice's level of dedication:

> One day when her sister, Margaret, reminded her to first hang up her coat, Alice said most seriously, "I cannot do that now, because I have to practice." Each day, while neighborhood children played outdoors, they could hear Alice methodically practicing the scales, finger exercises, and basic melodies, as she prepared for her Saturday morning piano lessons.[3]

That year with Mrs. Philpot instilled the tenets of classical music in Alice as she learned to read sheet music and understand the concepts of melody and harmony. And the scholarship for private lessons that Alice received from Mt. Olive soon bore fruit. By the time she was nine, Alice began to play for the Sunday school. And she found herself in a prominent new role at the church, leading the Young People's Choir. In a short span of time, her acumen at the keys led to new responsibilities every Sunday:

> Her increased keyboard dexterity enabled her to serve as pianist and organist for the Mount Olive Baptist Church. There she accompanied the senior choir, the pastor's chorus, and general, congregational services. Alice also played for numerous other churches in the Detroit

area, for weddings, funerals, and religious programs. The awe-inspiring tone and grace of her organ playing produced powerful divine sounds of praise and evoked feelings of glorification to God.[4]

Looking back on that time in her childhood, she recalled with fondness playing for the church's three choirs:

> For the young people, there were all the written musical pieces that I would play for them to sing. There wasn't as much rhythmical involvement there. Senior Choir was very nice, sort of strict, leaning toward the European anthems; a number of them were beautiful hymns from the hymn book. There was not a great deal of additional work needed other than being able to read...but when you are playing in the Pastor's chorus, you have to play in a different kind of way. The Pastor's chorus sounds like gospel. You have the gospel songs, from a book called *Gospel Pearls*, if you can find it. Beautiful songs.[5]

She considered her musical education at Mt. Olive Baptist Church to be "a gradation or graduation of sorts" giving her a solid foundation for a life of music ahead. In the gospel portion of Sunday service, the songs—while seemingly simple—are constructed so that the call-and-response builds and builds, the emotional intensity ratcheting up as pastor and the assembled reach the point of catharsis and sweet, God-affirming release. And Alice's piano and organ helped to lift everyone in the pews up to that particular vibratory state and keep them aloft for as long as possible. As Berkman noted:

> Elements of musical performance such as dramatic shifts in timbre and register, highly syncopated rhythm, and flexible improvisational structures are tailored to the emotional peaks of the ritual and support this purpose of spiritual transformation. In retrospect, one can see how these musical skills came to serve Alice in a variety of improvisational contexts outside the church. In a very practical sense, her church training

provided her with many of the requisite skill for life as a professional jazz musician: she was required to sight read, arrange spontaneously from a lead sheet, and listen and respond intently.[6]

The church wasn't the only place where music was happening. "The blues emanated from every keyhole and peephole on Hastings," Boyd said.[7] At the street level in Paradise Valley, it seemed like the blues radiated from just about every barbershop, major intersection, open (or shuttered) door, theater, church, sewer grate, and alleyway in Detroit. The post-riot cleanup wasn't even finished (or much begun) and already that music was back on the street, the blues like the mosses and lichens that grow back first in the wake of a forest fire. Walk with a certain gait up and down the streets and the bricks and cement seemed to just quiver with the sound. Berry Gordy reminisced that "at night Hastings lit up like a Christmas tree. You could always hear shouting Blues songs blasting out of the bars, and exciting women standing out front with nothing to do. I liked it."[8]

He wasn't the only one. Who knows if finger-picking guitarist Arthur "Blind" Blake was actually from Detroit or just passing through. But he certainly shouted out Paradise Valley, first 169 Brady Street ("wonder what is on Brady / must be something then *very* marvelous, *mmm-mmm*") and then Hastings on a 1920s nimble Piedmont-style blues titled "Hastings Street."

And a young sharecropper reared on religious fare down in Tutwiler, Mississippi, also fell under Hastings Street's spell as soon as he arrived in 1943. When John Lee Hooker wasn't working by day at the Ford Motor Company, he was taking in the sound of the boogie-woogie piano blaring out of every establishment on Hastings, especially the Henry Swing Club. A few years later, he would pay tribute to that raucous, roiling sound (by then already on the decline because of deteriorating conditions) when he plugged in an electric guitar—thumbing his bass strings so as to replicate that undeniable urban churn—to cut a shellac 78 titled "Boogie Chillen."

Foundational as John Lee Hooker would be for the blues in the decades ahead, the postwar electric blues of Detroit had nothing on its jazz scene. With its large middle-class Black families and plenty of paying jobs, there was a huge and sophisticated audience to be had, and the economic ecosystem feeding into the scene made it one of the most formidable outside of the major coastal cities. In the wake of the Great Depression, Detroit had rebounded in a major way, thanks in no small part to the automobile industry becoming America's arsenal during the war.

The grand ballrooms of yore were no longer viable (and no longer hip), but when night fell in Paradise Valley, one could duck into any number of black-and-tan nightclubs (emulating the kind of mixed-race venues that could be found in Harlem) and feel—for an evening at least—that the color line had been erased. Whites patronized and mingled at Black-owned clubs like the Flame Show Bar and Club Harlem, catching popular singers of the day like Ella Fitzgerald, Pearl Bailey, or the Ink Spots. Duke Ellington was booked to inaugurate the Paradise Theater when it opened in 1941, followed by the likes of Louis Armstrong, Dizzy Gillespie, and Billie Holiday. Local jazz orchestras and traveling bands might pull in to make the crowds dance at venues like the Plantation and the Chocolate Bar. That white audience fell off precipitously in the wake of the Belle Isle Riots, but the Black audiences still had their hard-earned wages burning a hole in their pockets come payday.

By the end of spring 1945, it looked as if the end stages of World War II were finally here. The Third Reich fell in May, while war in the Pacific raged on. Just two months later, tragedy struck the family. On August 6, 1945 (while the *Enola Gay* was en route to Hiroshima), H. C. Farrow, Ann's ex-husband and the former musical director at Mt. Olive, was killed. In the early-morning hours that Monday morning, he stepped out at the intersection of Trumbull and Michigan, crossing against a red light, and was struck by a car, dying instantly.[9]

Hitler defeated, the Empire of Japan still burning in horror and surrender, the troops were finally coming back. But the hundreds of thousands of Black soldiers returning to the States still faced an enemy back home. Now that they had seen life in other countries, without segregation, with a sense of equality, being back was a brutal reminder of the repression they still faced on every street corner.

If you weren't frequenting the uptown clubs of New York City, you might not have known much about the revolution in jazz that was already afoot. The American Federation of Musicians' recording ban—which had stretched from 1942 to 1944—finally lifted and jazz groups were racing to put their new ideas, long in foment, down on shellac. For years, there had been an incubator of ideas cooking every week: down in Midtown at the clubs clogging a few blocks of 52nd Street (with Birdland just a few steps above 52nd Street at 1678 Broadway) and farther uptown after-hours at a spot called Minton's Playhouse on West 118th Street in Harlem. If you didn't make it to the Big Apple, much less up that flight of stairs to catch the Monday night jam sessions at Minton's (that could stretch into the daylight hours), it was only when a series of sides cut in 1945 by alto saxophonist Charlie "Yardbird" Parker and trumpeter John Birks "Dizzy" Gillespie hit the airwaves that the new sound could finally be heard. The big band sound and swing era came to a screeching halt; bebop had arrived.

"Bird and Diz played this hip, real fast thing, and if you weren't a fast listener, you couldn't catch the humor or the feeling in their music," Miles Davis said. "Bird and Diz were great, fantastic, challenging—but they weren't sweet."[10] Bebop hit you in the head rather than your feet, moving at the speed of (benzedrine-fueled) thought. Melodies were downright dizzying at times, and their harmonies were equally complex. Bebop took beloved if shopworn standards and flipped them on their heads, stripping out well-known chord progressions for altered or extended new chords, making the familiar more Frankenstein. The more byzantine and aslant it got, the better. And all of it came at its listeners at fast tempos suited for highways, what writer Albert Murray called "the velocity of celebration."[11] Fittingly, the Motor City players could get with such speed and they were ready.

The next generation of Detroiters flipped out, not only on Bird and Diz but the other players as well. There were formidable drummers like Max Roach and Kenny "Klook" Clarke, the jagged mosaic piano of Thelonious Monk and Bud Powell, the teenage Juilliard-educated trumpeter Davis. If they listened closer, they could hear the underlying message in this bustling new music: Sure, maybe the white jazz players got the money, fame, and accolades from other (mostly white) critics, but could they really keep up with *this?*[12] "White people back then liked music they could understand, that they could *hear* without straining," Davis said:

> Bebop didn't come out of them and so it was hard for many of them to hear what was going on in the music...A lot of people didn't like what was going on on 52nd Street. They didn't understand what was happening with the music...them white motherfucking critics hated what we were doing. They didn't understand the music...and hated the musicians. Still, the people were packing into the clubs to hear the music.[13]

In New York, the myths surrounding Bird and his earthly appetites—heroin, booze, blowjobs, fried chicken (to name just a few of his all-consuming vices)—spread. Young players began to think that the only way to play like Bird was to fly as high as him, while outsiders perceived the jazz world as being inhabited by nothing but junkies, fallen women, and drug dealers as their audience. Jazz was a scourge in some corners of polite American society. While Black soldiers had their minds widened by the war in Europe, they came home to the same narrow stereotypes.

The next generation of musicians to come out of the Motor City was ready. And they had their public schools to thank. "Such an important part of the story in Detroit becoming a jazz powerhouse has to do with the really first class public school education story," historian Mark Stryker said. While redlining and housing discrimination continued to divvy up the races by neighborhood and foster racial animosity, the schools themselves had been integrated by law since the early part of the century. In the classroom at least, white and Black people and other immigrant communities could mingle and play together. Their parents may have been sharecroppers and reduced to domestic help down in the Deep South, but in Detroit the next generation had the chance to pick up and study an array of orchestral instruments.

"Cass Technical was the most famous, the arts magnet school, but there was great education beyond Cass, just basic public schools were good," Stryker explained. "That meant that white and Black kids got the same opportunities. In the schools, girls and boys were treated pretty equally in the band and orchestra room. That's an important, often overlooked, part of our story."[14]

By any measure, Cass and Sidney D. Miller High School provided world-class musical educations. What Ford and Packard plants were to the world of automobile manufacturing, these Detroit schools were to the music world: veritable factories cranking out high-caliber orchestral musicians and players able to read and extrapolate on music in just about any professional setting. And chops weren't all that mattered, as all Cass students needed to maintain high academic grades and pass an audition just to study music there.

At Miller High, foundational to the musical program was mastery of classical technique as well as encyclopedic harmonic knowledge. Their touring high school big band trained the likes of Milt Jackson, Yusef Lateef, and Kenny Burrell. Berkman wrote:

> Such exceptional public high schools gave Detroit's musical youth a huge advantage, providing them with virtuoso skills and a full understanding of functional harmony. Young African American musicians brought an extremely broad musical knowledge to the many forms of popular music that were professionally available. This gave Detroit a unique reputation as a place where young jazz players "really knew their chords."[15]

There was a trickle-down effect as well. Northwestern and Northeastern High Schools wouldn't necessarily be considered prime landing spots for teenagers interested in music, but their marching bands and orchestras were high quality nevertheless. Ernie Farrow graduated from Northeastern High School with another student and close musical ally, a piano player named Barry Harris. Harris remembered Farrow fondly as "the cat I really grew up with musically all the way."[16] Harris, Farrow, and Gordy all graduated from Northeastern the same year. And while Gordy at the time was furthering his career as a boxer, Harris and Farrow jumped from the school orchestra to being part of the postwar Detroit jazz scene right away. Right out of high school, they won a battle of the bands in 1946.

Harris remembered the contest: "Ernie started out as an alto player. We were going to play an amateur show at the Paradise Theatre and he didn't play alto as good as James Thompson, so he played the bass. That's how he started on bass. All he did was say 'I'll play the bass' and he played it."[17] Farrow never looked back. Soon he was a fixture on the scene on both the East and West Sides of town, picking up gigs and holding down the rhythm duties on a nightly basis.

But beyond the schools, there was also a network of music teachers sprinkled throughout the community, willing and able to help young children learn the foundations of music. The generation of kids who had been exposed to a rich musical education in these Detroit public schools in turn began to teach a new generation of kids. And just as crucial as it was that the school desegregation made no distinction between white and Black elementary students, it also didn't differentiate between boys and girls.

"There was a network of music teachers and cultural leaders in the Black community who took an interest in youth. Women were encouraged and sometimes they were the teachers," Stryker said, adding that the two most important for the city's jazz scene were "Josephine Love and Gladys Wade Dillard. Dillard was an early teacher for Barry Harris, Tommy Flanagan, and Kirk Lightsey."

"My family lived in a big house across the boulevard from Grace Hospital," pianist Kirk Lightsey recalled. Born on February, 15, 1937, and raised on the East Side just a little north of Warren Avenue, Lightsey started piano at an early age. "I wanted lessons when I was five. There was always a piano in the house. First, I got lessons from my schoolteacher. And then she sent me to Ms. Matthews, who then sent me to Tommy Flanagan's brother, Johnson Flanagan. When he went on the road, he sent me to Tommy's teacher, Ms. Gladys Wade Dillard."[18]

Ms. Dillard knew her classical music, but she would also encourage students to broaden their listening and playing horizons as well, letting them learn popular song fare from the day, whether it be pop or jazz standards of the time. Every week, Lightsey would go to his piano lesson with Ms. Dillard:

> We were studying classical music but she would also introduce a song from *The Real Book*. A song you would hear from a famous singer, Sarah Vaughan, Billy Eckstine, one of those singers. My favorite was "Have You Met Miss Jones" and "Stella by Starlight." There's so many songs. I was ten, twelve, something like that. And Alice was studying with Gladys Wade Dillard also. We were about the same age.[19]

Alice's weekly piano lessons with Ms. Dillard gave her not only command of the liturgical canon but also a solid foundation for classical music. The McLeod home was now filled with the sound of Alice working at the piano, which her youngest sister, Marilyn, recalled: "We had a house full of music because my sister made music. I just wanted to do what my sister did. I wanted to be like her because she was a really outstanding pianist."[20]

When Alice wasn't playing for the youth choir on Sundays and during Bible class, that gospel spirit carried over to the McLeod home as well. The kids would run around the house and Alice began to wonder what it would be like if she were in the pulpit. Pulling out the drawers on her mother's dresser so as to make them into makeshift steps, she would clamber up on top of the dresser and pretend that she was leading her congregation in prayer and song. "Almost every evening, she would raise her arms heavenward and compose and sing divine songs to the Lord," Adams said.[21]

Often during services, the religious fervor at Mt. Olive would work itself into a lather. The beat of the tambourines and shakers would quicken, the piano or organ would hit harder, the chorus would sing louder, higher, so that the whole congregation began to give praise as one, the preacher guiding such energy upward. Sometimes the feeling would become so powerful that a member was likely to stand up and shout. The times when Alice would walk by other storefront churches in the neighborhood, especially the Church of God in Christ, the combustion of the Holy Spirit in there was almost palpable. It permeated the very air.

Alice could feel the Lord's presence during times at mass, but she also began to feel a constant awareness, even beyond the church walls. Out on the rough streets of her neighborhood, she could feel a sense of protection. In a recollection later recounted by Adams:

> Once she told about playing on top of an abandoned automobile, and moving dangerously close to the edge. Suddenly, she lost her balance and began to fall. Alice recalled seeing the ground coming up towards her. From out of thin air, strong Hands abruptly stopped the fall and deposited her safely on the ground.[22]

But that was nothing compared to the other things that began to transpire. Sometime after the end of the war, when Alice turned nine years old, she began to have weird things happen to her. She would be at home in her bed, when suddenly she would look around and see that she was standing across the street from her house, looking back on her building. Other times, she was in an unfamiliar room or landscape, far from home. Sometimes she would be hovering far above others, or floating through walls. And then in a rush she would be back home, shaken but safe in bed.

All she really understood was that it happened with increasing frequency and could happen without much warning. She explained it to one interviewer: "When I was young I had visions every Saturday, for some reason. And I did have out-of-body experiences from the age of nine. Every Saturday I would be sitting down, and the next thing you know I was across the street or downtown or at a family member's house."[23]

At those times, such strange events could be frightening and bewildering. It got to the point where she was reluctant to leave home on those days. She would never want to go out with the family on long outings or excursions, to picnics on Belle Isle, or any of that stuff. "On one such occasion, Alice discovered that her astral body had projected 800 miles away from her home," Adams wrote. "Alice disclosed these occurrences first to her mother, who in turn said she would speak to the Pastor. It is unknown whether her mother communicated them or not; the matter was never discussed again."[24]

Many years later, Alice would come across passages in various esoteric religious readings and books on the occult that explained such things as being "out of the body experiences" or "astral projections." But at the time, there was no ready definition for such mysteries for a young girl to uncover in Detroit's inner city. Neither her parents nor her pastor could understand it, much less explain away its meaning. What could a pastor, much less her devout Christian parents, really understand about such an unexplained act? Was it an act of God? Or a trick of the devil? Only many years of hindsight would give her clarity, as Alice explained to one interviewer:

> I think that was God's way of letting me know that there is more to life than what we see around us. And that, for me, it will be more than just astral vision or astral projection. It will be actually moving my spirit into places above this world, around this universe, beyond our universe, Divine sacred places. So that's how the Lord taught me.[25]

Much like the urge to climb up on her parents' bureau and convene a crowd of imaginary worshippers in her living room; or making up devotional songs for an unseen but clearly felt God; or the sensation of slipping off an abandoned car's rooftop yet landing without a scratch; or being overcome with God feeling while playing at the piano bench; or this new occurrence, of becoming bluish-white light and being propelled instantly through the ceiling of her tenement building, above Paradise Valley, and into the upper atmosphere overlooking Detroit and Lake St. Clair, it all seemed to be yet another example for Alice of the mysteries of her faith. There was something more for her, she imagined. Something outside the everyday, mundane world.

CHAPTER THREE

Only God Can Make a Tree

IN 1947, ANOTHER BLACK FAMILY MOVED UP FROM THE SOUTH TO Detroit. Clarence LaVaughn Walker had been sermonizing ever since he was a teenager, touring around as a circuit preacher before settling in at a parish in Memphis, Tennessee. He took the surname of his stepfather and was now known as Reverend C. L. Franklin. The reverend and his wife were raising their six children in Memphis: Vaughn, Erma, Cecil, Aretha, Carolyn, and Carol Ellan. They then briefly relocated to Buffalo for two years before finally settling in Detroit.

The Franklin family now lived in the church parish on Boston Boulevard and Oakland Avenue at the uppermost part of Arden Park. As Aretha would remember, her family home in Detroit featured a manicured lawn and lovely landscaping. All along the middle of the boulevard, shrubs and trees were planted, giving everything a green beauty that struck the young Aretha. Her father, Rev. Franklin, was the pastor of the New Bethel Baptist Church, and Sunday meant a long day at church for the family. And after four hours of service, the Sunday feast would be ready: skillet-fried chicken, baked macaroni, ham hocks, candied sweet potatoes, and homemade ice cream.

Memphis and Buffalo weren't exactly small towns, but there was something vibrant and alive about the Motor City. No matter where Aretha went, there was "music everywhere":

The street-corner doo-wop. Sarah Vaughan's bebop flowing from Cecil's attic apartment. The choirs, the organs, the brothers and sisters spreading the gospel from various churches. We felt free to walk wherever we wanted. Catching the bus and the streetcar for ten cents a ride was an adventure. Every summer I'd ride the trolley all the way to Woodward and 8 Mile for the State Fair.[1]

Passing the storefront Holiness Church near New Bethel, she could hear a service almost manic in its exaltation, "where they were shouting and praising His name strong." New Bethel and their new preacher became so popular that before long, Rev. C. L. Franklin began to broadcast his sermons over the airwaves every Sunday.

Bebop was still growing and becoming a bigger force in jazz. Two local singers in Detroit began to attract notice to touring musicians. The first was Betty Carter, who caught the ear of Dizzy and Lionel Hampton. The other was Kenny "Pancho" Hagood, who was soon scatting atop the bright horns of Dizzy Gillespie and his Orchestra, weaving in and out of the jagged lines of the Thelonious Monk Quartet. Sometime in December 1947, Dizzy and his firecracker band boarded a ship bound for Europe, the start of an extended tour that would bring bebop to the masses on the continent and last until March 1948. But the seas were rough and choppy on the way over, so that "almost everyone in the band got ferociously seasick," none more than Hagood.[2]

He wasn't the only local musician garnering notice well beyond Detroit's city limits. There were the likes of tenor saxophonist Lucky Thompson, vibraphonist Milton "Bags" Jackson, and pianist Hank Jones, all of whom had started out playing swing or rhythm and blues, before bebop emerged as the hip new sound. Soon these Detroiters would find themselves on the road most of the year or else packed up for New York City, to be closer to the real action. Thompson started in the orchestras of bandleaders like Count Basie and Lionel Hampton, before working with bebop upstarts like Clarke and Davis. Jackson got snatched up by

Gillespie and before long his shimmering vibraphone work made him in demand for the likes of Monk and Parker. Jones toured in Norman Granz's Jazz at the Philharmonic and accompanied jazz singer Ella Fitzgerald when she toured England, while also recording bebop sides with Parker.

But as these big fish moved up, there were plenty of younger musicians hungry to get on the bandstand and prove their stuff. Recent high school graduates like Bill Evans, Paul Chambers, Thad Jones, Barry Harris, Kenny Burrell, Tommy Flanagan, Curtis Fuller, and Donald Byrd were already stepping up. By 1949, Evans had already hit the road with Gillespie but returned to Detroit soon after. Around that time, he converted to Islam and changed his name to Yusef Lateef.

The Detroit jazz scene was changing and Detroit herself was about to undergo drastic change as well. In July, President Harry Truman signed the Housing Act of 1949, which loosened the government purse strings on specific construction plans, with an eye toward redeveloping blighted urban centers. Seeing as how long stretches of Black Bottom and Paradise Valley remained derelict in the wake of the Belle Isle Riots, city officials in Detroit took federal funding and began to draw up big plans for the Motor City.[3]

First and foremost, the city began to pave the way for its greatest export, the automobile itself. Much like Robert Moses was enacting his grandiose visions in New York City, razing entire minority neighborhoods to carve out space for highways and expressways, Detroit city planners envisioned an interconnected freeway system that would cut directly through downtown and the East Side.

By 1950, over 350,000 Black Americans had moved to Detroit, providing the muscle that would make it the greatest industrial center in the United States. And as more and more Black families were squeezing into the city center, more and more white families moved to the outer fringes of the city, beyond 8 Mile Road and the like in the newfangled postwar tract housing developments. The suburbs were being built as fast as possible to aid such an exodus. Even the new auto plants were being built out in suburban Detroit, some twenty in total between 1947 and 1955. And highways were needed to move folks in their cars along swiftly.

Or, in official local city government parlance, it would be the beneficial act of "urban renewal." Construction began on the Walter P. Chrysler Freeway (I-75), the John C. Lodge Freeway (M-10), and the Edsel Ford Expressway (I-94) soon after. Herb Boyd likened such construction projects to the destructive force of a tornado:

> Urban renewal meant "Negro removal" for many of the residents in Black Bottom and Paradise Valley...It took merely three years for the black community on the lower east side to be leveled; in the end more than seven hundred buildings were razed and some two thousand black families forced to relocate.[4]

A notice appeared in the *Michigan Chronicle* in April 1950: Alice McLeod was now a two-time spelling bee champion in Detroit. Her winning word? *Measurements.*

At some point during this time, the McLeods moved from their two-room tenement to a spacious home that was a bit closer to Woodward Avenue and the Wayne State University campus. The kids were older and needed more space, but the new home also meant that now music could be practiced in the home without impediment. Sometimes Ernie Farrow would have his friends and bandmates over to play the new music.

While not quite as cosmopolitan as New York and Chicago, Detroit remained a destination for musicians. For hotshot players, there were an abundance of paying gigs: in dance bands that played the ballrooms on the weekend, in smaller groups at the black-and-tans, and in new spaces that allowed for experimentation and exploration. In the bigger cities, other social ills like drug abuse, alcoholism, violence, and poverty riddled the jazz scenes. In this instance, Detroit was an exception, "a bourgeois operation in comparison to jazz networks in other urban centers," Berkman noted:

> The high percentage of black homeownership in Detroit during the 1940s and 1950s, even among working-class people, contributed to the strength of family jazz networks, as well as to the overall quality of black music. Living in a house rather than a tenement was conducive to the musical mastery needed for bebop. Space to practice and jam with peers without fear of bothering the neighbors, as well as the support of a financially stable family, was a great benefit to many young black musicians coming of age.[5]

Far more than the popular nightclubs of the day, several of these homes served as de facto incubators of the Detroit jazz scene. Four family dynasties in particular would inform jazz for decades to come, from the Burrells (brothers Billy and Kenny) and the Jones family (brothers Hank, Thad, and Elvin) to the Jacksons (brothers Milton, Alvin, and Oliver) and the McKinneys (brothers Harold, Ray, and William). That close-knit, familial dynamic allowed this music to flourish.[6]

Pianist Barry Harris likened this sort of domestic environment to late nineteenth-century salon society. "We had more what the musical greats had years ago, they had salons, that's where Chopin, Liszt, all of them would gather, play, share information and learn from each other," he said.[7] Harris recalled playing all day long at home, with the likes of Donald Byrd, Paul Chambers, and the Jones brothers all coming through. With no audience, no club owner, no hierarchy, no outside noise to interfere, no distractions of girlfriends, no pressure, players could learn and rap day in, day out, honing their craft.

Across the country, a generation of bright jazz players who looked to Bird and his heroin addiction as part of his genius found themselves strung out instead, chasing the dragon. Generational greats like Miles Davis, Sonny Rollins, and Sonny Clark were battling their addictions, and even new players just finding their way, like a young Philly saxophonist named John Coltrane, were unable to realize anything even close to their full potential.

The home environs of Detroit not only offered a safe space to play in, they also doubled as a buffer against drug addiction, alcoholism, mob influence, prostitution, and whatever other ills might interfere with the music. Playing into the wee hours at a club left you exposed to all sorts of temptations. But if you were playing at home with your mother or young sister in the next room, you could focus.

It also didn't hurt that the heroin in Detroit was trash. When Miles was kicking his heroin habit, he would hang his hat there for months on end. "The dope was so bad in Detroit...because it was cut so much. Shooting it wasn't doing nothing for me except putting more holes in my arms." And like many other jazz greats looking to put and keep a band together, the amount of talent in Detroit was staggering, as Miles soon realized: "It was a real hip city for music."[8]

The young Detroit players were listening to one another and listening closely to what was new. Lightsey remembered the hot records and players coming out at the time. "We were listening to Charlie Parker, we were listening to Miles and Chet Baker and Sonny Rollins." But he was also really into a local Detroit player: "Tommy Flanagan was my guy. I was going for his fluidity, his smoothness, his calming effect and his definite way to play the blues." His love and curiosity for the music no doubt stemmed from his study with Ms. Dillard and carried on in his education at Cass Tech.[9]

By 1951, Alice McLeod was now a freshman at Northeastern High School and also deep into her music studies. She was not only playing at Mt. Olive every Sunday but also performing at other music recitals at the parish. In the church news section of the *Michigan Chronicle*, her name crops up almost monthly during this time. She's credited as organist for one event in February, and listed as music director and chairman of the music committee for Youth Day in May (the theme: "Touch Me Lord Jesus"). Her sister Joan [sic] is also mentioned in the latter event.

One Friday evening at the end of September 1951, Miss Alice McLeod (now age fourteen) and another student, Miss Janet Hardy, gave a music recital at Mt. Olive Baptist Church. Miss Hardy began the program and played piano as well as organ. Alice's portion of the recital began as a duet with Miss Hardy of a composition by Eduard Holst from 1878 titled "Diana Grande Valse de Concert." The English composer is now most famous for his early twentieth-century orchestral suite *The Planets*, but this early work is a dynamic, intermediate-level piece scored for four hands, featuring tempo shifts, hairpin emotional turns, and a dramatic finale. Alice followed that with a more plaintive selection, the intermezzo section of Pietro Mascagni's *Cavalleria rusticana*, considered one of the classic one-act verismo operas of the late nineteenth century. Next, she performed "Ah! So Pure," an 1847 composition from the German opera *Martha* by Friedrich von Flotow.

Alice then moved into the early twentieth century with her rendition of Oscar Rasbach's "Trees." The poem was penned by Joyce Kilmer in 1913 (he was a casualty of World War I), and Rasbach set it to song in 1918. Four years after that, the art song was made famous thanks to a powerful performance of the work by Paul Robeson, the closing stanza particularly poignant: "Poems are made by fools like me / But only God can make a tree." Alice's recital concluded with a stirring piece for church organ, Postlude in E-flat, op. 113, no. 1 by Edmondstoune Duncan.

By her own estimation, Alice's study with Gladys Wade Dillard was brief, maybe six months at most, but deeply influential. As she would later recall:

> What I really carried forward was the importance of really keeping your music alive—even the classical music alive. Just take all the books, practice, keep your reading up to par. It's important to me. And from time to time I do it. I still put up the classical music. It brings the path to now. I'm kind of sorry there is no more beautiful music coming from Europe, and Russia, and places like that. Back in those days—in the

1800s—there was more incentive or motivation to write beautiful classical themes or symphonic themes and present them. Now it's still Stravinsky, Rimsky-Korsakov, Bach, Beethoven, Mendelssohn, It's still those people that get played: Grieg and Mozart.[10]

The rest of the year, Alice's services remained in high demand at Mt. Olive; her name pops up in the paper's church items nearly every week, giving a glimpse as to how actively involved she and her family were in church social events. In early November, she was hostess and also assisted at the piano, this time for the Sunday school's Annual Chocolate Sip and Fashion Revue. The next week, she and Miss Janet Hardy presented yet another piano and organ recital together, wherein "the department of religious Education sponsored them as their featured program of the year." The next week, she was the soloist during the Lord's Prayer at the Anniversary Banquet. The week after that, she gave a dramatic reading from the Bible during Women's Day at the church.

The Black church had always had a formidable presence in Detroit, but going into the new decade, the city's churches were also operating at a peak. The decade after the end of World War II is generally referred to as "the golden age of gospel" and for good reason. The likes of Thomas A. Dorsey, Mahalia Jackson, the Swan Silvertones, the Dixie Hummingbirds, and the Soul Stirrers (featuring their new nineteen-year-old frontman Sam Cooke)—to name just a few—were operating at the height of their earthly powers, drawing big crowds at church and filling auditoriums in cities like Chicago, Philadelphia, St. Louis, and Detroit.

Rev. Franklin was one of the most popular figures in the pulpit. On Sunday, Detroiters might line up around the block to get into New Bethel or else huddle around their transistors for his weekly radio show on WJLB, then Michigan's second FM radio station.[11] His early gospel songs and sermons started appearing on shellac as early as 1949, but when he recorded his most popular sermon, "The Eagle Stirreth Her Nest," his fame reached a new level. In this classic sermon, Rev. Franklin's eagle symbolized God. "The eagle has extraordinary sight," one famous passage went. "It is said that he can rise to a lofty height in the air and look in the distance and see a storm hours away... He can look behind that smile on your face and see the frown in your heart. God has extraordinary sight."[12]

In 1952, the Reverend's then ten-year-old daughter Aretha began to be highlighted as a soloist at New Bethel. Well after Aretha rose through the ranks of gospel to be crowned "Queen of Soul," those roots always came through clearly in her music. Singer Dianne Reeves said, "It's the spirit. It's what she knew about, what she learned growing up as a child in her father's church. For the people in the congregation it's a statement of faith and belief."[13] Whether you were in attendance at a gleaming parish like New Bethel, a more modest one like Mt. Olive, or any of the Church of God in Christ storefronts along Hastings, that spirit was shouting and testifying every Sunday.

As an emissary for Mt. Olive, Alice would sometimes get invited to attend other church services around the city, seeing firsthand how the spirit could move listeners. She could see it transpiring at times from the thespian bench at her own church, how the notes on the page would transform into these powerful vibrations that could make the physical bodies of the attendees begin to react to the music, but it took on added significance as she went to other churches. She was there to hear the music, but she could also bear witness to how the music became something greater, radiating outward from the heart of the church pianist as well as the hearts of the audience, until it became something far greater and more powerful. "When we were invited to other churches, I mean, I heard music that was just beyond anything I had heard before," she said. "I would hear country gospel. I would hear the down home gospel. I would hear the kind of gospel you almost wouldn't need music with. It was flowing from the heart, from the soul. After a while there was no Music."[14]

Less than two miles to the east of Mt. Olive in the McDougall-Hunt neighborhood was the Mack Avenue Church of God in Christ. And behind its plain brick façade was one of the most powerful gospel groups in the city. The Mack Avenue church featured the Lemon Gospel Chorus, helmed by their young choir pianist, Delores Ransom, just a year older than Alice. It was here at Mack Avenue that Alice had what she called "the most powerful musical and religious experiences of my youth." As she recounted:

> One day we were at this church. I was with the young people, ages fifteen to nineteen. I happened not to be at the piano at the time because there were a trio of us, and the other pianist could play anything—she was superb. The choir was singing and there was such a spiritual experience happening in that church. There was such God feeling. The people in the audience were so overcome with the spirit, they weren't singing anymore; some were just walking around the church. Half of the choir had to be carried out—even young people. The Lord just completely swept through. The pianist started playing at such a rapid pace, and everything just stopped. What could you do? All you could do was go and sit down. There were no closing remarks, there was no more singing, there were nurses attending to those who were highly overcome, and some were carried downstairs, and that was it. The service was never dismissed by the minister. Just God. God-inspired. An experience filled with the spirit of the Lord.[15]

Ransom met her future husband, David Winans, at the church and by 1953 they were married. The couple would go on to have ten children, and Mom and Pop Winans, as they were soon known, went on to be the heads of Detroit's most famous family of gospel singers, the Winans.

While the public school system of Detroit was accepting when it came to girls—both Black and white—learning music, it was still rare in that era for women to have a proper musical outlet beyond the church. Only the church was perceived as being an acceptable—not to mention ladylike—performance space for young Black women. Had Alice McLeod come of age during her mother's time, the church would have been the ceiling for her talents.

Even playing classical music professionally remained off-limits for women of color. Berkman noted:

> For a variety of reasons, classical music was not a viable professional career for most African Americans at the time, particularly for those from the East Side of Detroit. Preprofessional training requires hours of study as a young child, with master teachers who possess the proper pedigree or lineage. Alice's socioeconomic status, coupled with widespread institutional racism barring blacks from professional classical music institutions, would almost certainly have stood in the way had she wanted to pursue this path.[16]

Alice continued to perform weekly at her parish. Through the spring and summer of 1952, her name continued to appear in the paper for an array of church events: WOLVERINE STATE BAPTIST YOUTH CONDUCT CONFERENCE AT MT. OLIVE BAPTIST; YOUTH LIVING AND SERVING IN THE CHRISTIAN SOCIETY; NOTED TENOR WILLIAM PENN PERFORMS IN RECITAL BY YOUNG MATRONS OF MT. OLIVE BAPTIST CHURCH. Week in and week out, she was learning the fundamentals of the church hymnals, but also the intangibles of music, the sorts of things that teachers can't really fully transmit to their pupils.

When asked if anybody had taught her how to play for her church, Alice replied: "Nobody really, but you had some musical guidelines. But the rhythmical aspect, that came from the experience... I really think most of it just comes from the environment."[17] Even working from the church hymnals, the pages were skeletal frames of the numbers at best. It was up to the pianist, musical director, and choir to fully flesh out these songs, to get to the heart of the material and make it come alive. As Berkman wrote: "The ornamental, rhythmic, improvisatory, and timbral qualities, characteristics of black church music that clearly distinguish it from music in most white Protestant churches, are part of an aurally transmitted black musical aesthetic."[18] You couldn't teach the feeling.

Bearing witness to the "God feeling" that could overcome a roomful of attendees on any given Sunday, especially with Ransom at the organ on Mack Avenue, Alice began to understand the keyboardist's role in guiding this transformation of flesh into spirit, breath into fire, humanity into divinity, if only for brief flashes during service. The Pentecostal and sanctified services at Mack Avenue had a different feature than the more staid Baptist services. There, the keyboardist has a greater role, harmonically and melodically offering embellishments that buoy the moments in between chorus and verse, keeping the energy in the room high. As Berkman wrote: "Sanctified services were (and are) particularly noted for this manner of full congregational participation and musico-religious ecstasy. They emphasize healing, sanctification resulting in gifts of prophesy, speaking in tongues, possession, shouting, and the use of musical instruments."[19]

Alice had grown too tall to still climb up on her mother's dresser and make up church songs, but her sense of divinity was becoming more finely attuned. Nearly ten years of playing at church saw to that. Even as she worked through the likes of Beethoven, Bach, Tchaikovsky, or—for her favorite piano piece of all—Rachmaninoff's C# minor Prelude, she began to sense the impetus behind their creation, something behind mere dots on a page.

"I never really saw music as superficial," she said. "Music always had some kind of uplifting, ethereal qualities. Whether it was religious music or classical music, I always heard something that had to come from the composer's heart and spirit and soul, not just his mind."[20]

During those surges at church, with the harmonic support system for the choir and pastor, where the piano or organ needed to take the lead, the music became a conveyance that allowed a higher power to come down into the room. God, with that eagle eye, could enter any room on the East Side of Detroit and just completely sweep through. In such moments, Alice knew there was an unseen space that the music could elevate them to, where there was no music, just pure spirit.

CHAPTER FOUR

Graduation

In 1953, the McLeods' old neighbor Berry Gordy returned home from Korea. But he didn't just want to follow in his father's footsteps and run a grocery store. He envisioned big plans for himself and his hometown. He wanted to capture the sound of the street that he so adored coming up near Hastings Street. "I wanted to go into business on my own doing something I loved, and I decided to open up a Jazz record store," he said. "To me, Jazz was the only pure art form. No matter how complex the rhythms and the melodies, I loved it just because it was Jazz. All the hip young people were into it, and I was sure the people in my neighborhood would love it as much as I did."[1] It was better than trying to make a living as a boxer, which was Gordy's original career path when he graduated from Northeastern. Better to save your face and open up your ears instead.

Gordy was out almost every night, by his estimation. And why not? Every night in Detroit there was a hot jazz group cooking somewhere. Just not in Paradise Valley. The last major spot to open in that neighborhood was shuttered by 1950. The action now went down on the West Side, on Woodward Avenue and John R Street.

No matter where the young Gordy might be, he always wound up "down the street on the corner of John R and Canfield at the most popular of all, the Flame Show Bar. The top club acts performed on a stage built right into the bar. One night it might be Dinah Washington, on another Sarah Vaughan or Billie Holiday."[2] His sister worked the photo concession booth there while his brothers worked in the darkroom, developing the photos into instant souvenirs for the Flame Show Bar's fashionable clientele. One night, bar owner Al Green introduced Berry Gordy to an up-and-coming young singer named Jackie Wilson.

The biggest names in jazz from either coast—when crisscrossing the country on tour—had to make a pit stop in Detroit. The audiences were too big, too hip, and too deeply appreciative to not make it part of their tour itinerary. And bandleaders realized that the homegrown talent of Detroit was too strong to ignore. Dizzy Gillespie, Miles Davis, Charles Mingus, and more would often fill their ranks with young hungry players from the Motor City who could more than hold their own on the bandstand. On Monday nights, when just about every club was closed for one night off, there were still jam sessions to be sussed out. Out-of-town stars would jam with locals, casually auditioning for new talent.

White bebop vibraphonist Terry Gibbs came through town looking to put a new band together. Gibbs had made his name in the ranks of the biggest jazz bands of the postwar era, led by the likes of Tommy Dorsey and Woody Herman. If he was in Detroit, Dizzy suggested, he should go check out Hank Jones's younger brothers down at the Blue Bird Inn on Tireman Street.

When it opened in 1940, the neighborhood club had been at the tippy top northern end of the Black West Side. But by 1950, as the Black population crept farther north, it was in the center of all the action. By then, tenor saxophonist Billy Mitchell led the house band, with Hank's brothers—trumpeter Thad and drummer Elvin—sharing the bandstand with a buttoned-up yet stylish young Black woman seated at the piano bench, nailing frantic bebop jags with aplomb.

A gobsmacked Gibbs recalled: "I thought that maybe because I had a few drinks, this was the reason she sounded that good. There weren't many female jazz players, and the few that were around mostly played the piano: ladies like Marian McPartland and Barbara Carroll, who played good, but as the old cliche goes, they were 'good for a girl.'"[3]

Terry Pollard was more than good for a girl. "She sounded like a man," in Gibbs's high estimation, but that was also Pollard's intention, to play like a man. In the four years since gifting her old piano to Alice, she was intent on playing this music. Pollard would still drop by the McLeod house, spending time on music with her beau Ernie, or showing the eager Alice a few new ways to harmonize on a chord progression, maybe trying out a few new ideas that she was working on. She was still a student at Pershing High, using a fake ID to sneak in at the local bars and play. Pollard said years later how she had to talk tough in clubs and act even tougher to earn respect on the bandstand. She described her first gig as a seventeen-year-old in "a rough, blood and bucket type of place. When they started fightin', we'd still play."[4]

Gibbs went back to the Blue Bird straight the next night and was knocked out all over again: "Terry Pollard played piano completely different than any girl I had ever heard play. They didn't have that hard bop articulation that Terry played with. She played bebop and she could *swing*. Terry was the first female I ever heard swing that hard." He hired her that night.

A week later, Pollard was playing New York in Gibbs's new band. It was then that Pollard encountered a first: The twenty-two-year-old had never been out on the road with any band before, much less a white one. Maybe on the bandstand they could all be equals, but once Pollard and fellow Detroiter Herman Wright were offstage, it was a different story. Gibbs saw it firsthand out west:

> Stars like Harry Belafonte, Lena Horne, and Sammy Davis, Jr. couldn't stay at the hotel where they were performing. They'd have a trailer outside the hotel for them to dress in, and they would stay at a place called the Moulin Rouge, which was in the black part of town. That's where Terry Pollard and Herman Wright had to stay when we worked there. What bugged me was that after we played each set, Terry and

Herman had to go sit in the back dining room...just the two of them, sitting there. Equality for them ended the moment they stepped off the bandstand.

Gibbs was nothing if not a showman, a performer, an entertainer who could woo you with his vibraphone dexterity and his showmanship. And he knew he had a hit with Pollard. When they played at Birdland opposite Charlie Parker, Gibbs said that Bird tried to poach Pollard for his band every single night. Even Liberace fell in love with her the moment he caught their show out in Las Vegas. The smitten Liberace invited Pollard to join him at his table and have a drink, only to learn that the hotel's policy forbade such casual intermingling between races. In Gibbs's recollection, "Liberace really pitched a bitch and caused a big scene."[5] For one night at least, Pollard could be seated in the hotel lounge.

Not only was Pollard a crackling bebop pianist, she also knew how to make the vibes dance, providing a perfect foil for Gibbs's own stick work. A fast-talking Jewish guy from Brooklyn and a woman from inner-city Detroit was something else. It was that frisson between a guy and a gal, a white and a Black player, that would generate buzz. The same polite supper club segregated American society that made half of Gibbs's band hide in the back dining room in Las Vegas, that made it illegal for them to even be out on the white sands of Miami Beach, that same crowd would also be thoroughly wowed by the sight of the white and Black Terrys improvising together onstage. "When we would do the vibes duet, and people would see a black girl and a white guy battling it out on the vibes, I knew that we'd break it up everyplace we played," he said.[6]

And they did.

In the Northeastern High School yearbook for 1953, there's a photo of their A Band, a mixed group of thirty-two teens on risers who performed orchestral works for faculty and parents during special holiday programs. The boys are all buttoned up in their suits and ties, woodwinds or horns in hand. The women are in flowing dresses down to their shins. Two of the girls in band hold upright basses that are taller than them. In the back row, her features almost entirely lost against the dark back wall, stands Alice.

In her high school years, those who remembered Alice McLeod remembered her to be extremely shy and quiet. Under the heading of "Inner Life" in her book, Adams wrote:

> She did not like to talk much or socialize. Though she did well in her studies, she felt no real inner pull toward secular education. Unlike most youth, who spend their time on fun and athletic pursuits, Alice had no interest in those activities. Many of her school friends scoffed at her reasons for not participating in their popular, recreational enjoyments. Her so-called "neighborhood friends" would often joke and laugh about how she stayed in the house most of the time. They would say, "She's so old fashioned; she likes to stay inside to knit and crochet." Occasionally, they even called her hurtful names. Alice seemed not to care about their comments and name-calling. She was content with her life as it was.

Alice maintained her grades and seemed to be the kind of learner who could pick up whatever skill she put her mind to. Secretarial work was considered a most suitable career choice for a young woman who might need to seek employment outside the home. Alice became a registered Gregg shorthand secretary and when she was tested, she could type more than 120 words per minute. No doubt, she had a bright future ahead of her. As she entered her senior year at Northeastern, she was offered a scholarship in business administration to the Detroit Institute of Technology.[7]

In A Band, Alice could showcase her real talent, though. "When I went to Northeastern, there was a very good band director named Rex

Hall and when I got to high school, Alice was already there," remembered Benjamin "Bennie" Maupin, three years her junior (and one grade ahead of Alice's youngest sister, Marilyn).[8] Maupin had started out studying clarinet, but by that point in the 1950s, saxophone was the thing—thanks to the likes of Bird and Coleman "Hawk" Hawkins—so he switched. He was studying hard, but when he first saw Alice during band practice, Maupin was awestruck by how comfortable and composed she appeared, no matter the composition or instrument:

> She was playing timpani and chimes and glockenspiel and snare drum and all the percussion stuff that's found in an orchestra or symphonic band, and I was just really impressed with that, because you don't think of women or young ladies doing that. But she was there. And it was quite obvious that she really had a very good grasp of what she was doing. It was interesting to watch her going from one instrument to the other and to hear what she was actually doing with those instruments.[9]

One day Maupin and his classmates filed into a school assembly where fellow students could get up onstage and showcase their talents. Kids might "recite a poem, tap dance, whatever it was. You had a couple of moments to do your thing," he said. And then:

> I looked up on the stage, and there was Alice playing the piano! And I didn't know she played the piano, but she was playing the piano. And she actually had a trio, she had a drummer and she had a bass player, and then I found out later that she had actually been teaching them how to accompany her. I hadn't heard anyone play like that... Well she was playing some tune, I didn't know what tune it was because I didn't know that many songs, but I knew that she was improvising on whatever it was. And they played it and the kids went wild after it was over.[10]

For the young Maupin, his exposure to jazz music had been limited up until that point, so "I was just fascinated by what she was doing. Up to that point, I hadn't heard a piano trio. I was only thirteen, something like that. I didn't know what it was, but I liked it."[11]

While her musical studies continued unabated at Mt. Olive Church, at school, or on her own, Alice dreamed of continuing on with her classical music studies, maybe even enrolling at Juilliard in New York City. She also began to study jazz with greater intent. It helped that one of the prime movers on the Detroit jazz scene was her older half brother. Since graduating, he had switched to the upright bass, and Ernie Farrow was now the linchpin for any number of pickup bands thrown together to play at local parties, dances, church rec room events, and the like all around Detroit. Farrow was also down to check out "the latest thing" happening in jazz, bringing home records by Sarah Vaughan, Lester Young, and Charlie Parker.

During these formative teenage years for Alice, a young woman playing piano meant at most playing in her local church or entertaining folks gathered in her living room, since European classical music seemed to be all but a dead end for a Black woman from the inner city of Detroit. Alice credited her continued musical development to the presence of Farrow as a role model. As she told Berkman:

> My brother...played bass. That meant I got to hear everything that he was doing. And when allowed, I would go with him to the sessions and hear what the musicians were playing. And I really believed I could learn what I heard. I said, "I believe I can play this music if I put my mind to it." He showed me as much as he could...I feel that he was a big inspiration for me. Had he not been in the house, I don't know.[12]

Farrow wasn't the only inspiration, though. Pollard was a regular presence in the home as well as another important Detroit player, Barry Harris. The Harris home was already an incubator for young jazz players at the time, but Barry himself was one of the city's first great mentors. In the same way that Josephine Love and Gladys Wade Dillard were important early teachers to the likes of Harris, Tommy Flanagan,

Roland Hanna, Kirk Lightsey, and Alice McLeod, Harris in turn became that figure for new jazz musicians. The high school kids who could read music and had their concepts of harmony down still needed to translate all of that orchestral knowledge into the ever-morphing idiom of jazz. No school at the time would have been teaching this type of Black music, so that education happened elsewhere. It was closer to an oral tradition, passed down from one generation to the next. Decades before jazz was part of any school curriculum, Harris was holding forth at his home.

Mark Stryker called Harris "first among equals."[13] And just as the Detroit public schools didn't discriminate between white and Black pupils, mentors like Harris (and later on, trumpeter Marcus Belgrave) didn't look down on the young women who also wanted to play jazz. In the case of one of Harris's brightest pupils, Stryker said, "Barry championed Terry Pollard and regarded her as an equal." Man or woman, you were only at his parlor if you could play. But when Stryker asked Harris who would have been hanging out at his house during that time, Alice's name never came up.

That would be because instead of Alice studying at the Harris home, Barry Harris was instead always over at the McLeod home, courting her older sister, Margaret. He was a regular there. "The family thought Barry was going to marry her," Alice said. "He took her to the prom. We thought they were the king and queen of Detroit. Barry was like my own brother, he has shown me so much, chords, and voicings. He was at the house often."[14]

When Harris wasn't holding court in his own living room, or wooing Margaret McLeod in their family home, he could be found every Tuesday night at the intersection of Woodward Avenue and Davison Street. The World Stage, at 13525 Woodward, was what the *Michigan Chronicle* at the time described as "a dinky hard-to-find one-room building," a theater in the round located in Highland Park, just north of the Wayne State University campus. The venue specialized in theater—patrons were able to take in well-taxed productions of Shakespeare, Tennessee

Williams, or George Bernard Shaw—on most nights. But in early 1955, a student at Wayne State named Kenny Burrell teamed up with Harris (under the banner of "the New Music Society") and put forth the idea to World Stage management of an informal jam session on Tuesday nights. What had been nurtured these past few years in homes around Detroit, the aural exchange of musical ideas between one generation of jazz players and the next, was now ready to be put forth in front of a live audience.

"Tuesday was when all the clubs were closed. If you were in town, you were free to come to the World Stage," Kirk Lightsey said of the night where the music was being both played and paid forward:

> Barry would know if you were a pianist because you'd be going by his house. We were at his house almost every day until his wife put us out. If you were in town, you were free to come to the World Stage where a young person and three or four older musicians would play the first set. That's when the young guys could play with Barry, Yusef, Paul Chambers, and Kenny Burrell. If you were ready as a young person, this was the night you looked forward to.[15]

Rudy Tucich was a drummer from the white side of town who went to Cass Tech with pianist Hugh Lawson, soon finding himself over at Harris's house most days of the week. But the real lessons took place at World Stage, Tucich said. "During the first hour, the youngsters, the young cats, would play with the old musicians."[16]

The World Stage didn't really have a stage, though.[17] Tucich remembered a flat floor on the second story: "They had director chairs, those fold-up canvas chairs, about 100–150 chairs there. We just played on one side of the room, and the people kind of surrounded us. They were across from us and to our right."

Where was the bar? "Oh, no, it was just music," he said. "People paid a buck to get in and, no, there were no drinks. You just sat and listened to the music from roughly a quarter to nine till about 11–11:30."

Regulars attested to the magic of the place. For Elvin Jones, then an upcoming drummer in his twenties following in his brothers' footsteps, "the respect that the audience would show, even in that little place, it was just as if you were in Carnegie Hall. It was the same kind of reverence, the same sort of atmosphere."[18]

That first hour was foundational for the next generation of Detroit jazz players. A young guy—be it Tucich, Pepper Adams, Lonnie Hillyer, Kirk Lightsey, or Charles McPherson—might look around and see himself rubbing shoulders with older, more advanced cats like Kenny Burrell, Barry Harris, Yusef Lateef, or Paul Chambers, giving him the support and encouragement he needed to navigate the dizzying chord changes and harmonic concepts of bebop.

Having a reverent audience who would pay attention to what you were doing was integral to the success of the music during that time. Bassist Cecil McBee came to the city after the army and was struck by the synergy between musicians and listeners. Detroit's audiences demanded that if you were on that bandstand, a player had to reach deep inside, he said:

> They had to hear that—from the deepest part of your stomach. You knew if you were successful by the response of the audience and you knew and you were relieved because you know that you had connected. And you would play yourself to death until the wee hours of the morning. Here was a place that you could express or experiment on whatever you were working on and the crowd knew that that was the deal. They knew that the goal was to experiment individually and collectively and to reach out to the stars so far as your development was concerned.[19]

When he wasn't working days at the Chrysler factory, Yusef Lateef was expanding his own mind and his concept of the world, beyond Detroit city limits and the western hemisphere. In the same way that he dug into the Holy Quran as a young man and converted to Islam, Lateef turned that sense of discovery to other types of music:

I realized I had to widen my canvas of expression. I spent many hours in the library on Woodward studying the music of other cultures. At this time I was also working at Chrysler's. I met a man from Syria and he asked me if I knew about the rabat [sic]. He made me a rabat and Ernie Farrow played it on "Morning." I was looking to widen my expression and made bamboo flutes on my own.[20]

In addition to carving his own flutes, Lateef would go on to integrate the timbres and scales of instruments from around the world: the Afghani rabab, the Indian double-reed shehnai, the Egyptian arghul, and the Japanese koto, to name a few.[21] Farrow began to play with Lateef and was himself already an integral cog in the development and refinement of modern jazz in the Motor City. And back at home, he was a guiding light for his younger half sister.

"I liked the [improvisational] music he was playing—some of his friends would come over and they'd have a session and I liked it and really wanted to learn more about it, know about it," Alice said in a radio interview. "So that's how I learned about it. Just from the association with the Detroit musicians—going to sessions and what not."[22] Alice knew her church music and European classical canon, but bebop kindled a spark in her like no other.

At Mt. Olive, she still played gospel music, but her repertoire began to expand to include Stephen Foster minstrel songs of the mid-nineteenth century. An article in the *Michigan Chronicle* in late April 1955 reported on the annual fashion revue at the church: "Among selections rendered were 'Old Folks at Home,' 'My Old Kentucky Home,' 'Old Black Joe,' 'Juanita,' and 'Bring Back My Bonnie to Me.' Miss Alice McLeod was at the piano."

"Old Folks at Home"—now better known as "Swanee River" and officially recognized as the Florida state song—had originally been penned by Foster for the Christy's Minstrels in 1851. It bears more than a passing resemblance to Czech composer Antonín Dvořák's Humoresque no. 7, which Dvořák composed while he was living and taking notes on

American folk music while serving as director of the conservatory in New York in the 1890s.[23]

"My Old Kentucky Home" was another staple of minstrelsy, yet the song was endearing enough to make Frederick Douglass a fan of it, perceiving that an abolitionist intent between the lines "awakens sympathies for the slave, in which antislavery principles take root, grow, and flourish." Noted Victorian society figure and social reformer Caroline Norton composed "Juanita" in 1853; it was considered the first ballad by a female composer to achieve massive sales as sheet music. "Bring Back My Bonnie to Me" is listed in the Roud Folk Song Index as No. 1422, one of the nearly twenty-five thousand songs gathered from oral tradition in the English language and one that still lingers well into our time.[24]

But Alice was already striving beyond that repertoire. Just ten weeks later in July, a *Detroit Free Press* notice announced the United Theatres Corporation-WXYZ-TV Search-for-a-Star competition happening at the Fisher Theatre, a historic vaudeville house that at the time still featured its elaborate Mayan-themed original interior (later demolished in a 1961 redesign). Teenaged performers included a dancer, a song stylist, a tenor, an actor, and acrobat freshmen. Here, the Alice McLeod Trio made their debut, featuring Alice with fellow Northeastern graduates Bob Friday on bass and Earl Williams on drums.

How many shows that particular trio played will perhaps remain unknown, as Alice's trio doesn't often pop up in the newspaper listings. She herself said in an interview that she just picked up work here and there: "Little musical events would occur around Detroit, for example: I would play for weddings, funerals, and at the Elk's Lodge, so I had some experience."[25]

In November of that year, the *Michigan Chronicle* reported on the first big dance of the season at the Central YWCA featuring "Ira Jackson on tenor sax; Rudy Tucich, drums; William Stewart, bass; Michael Terry, trombone; Alice McLeod, piano."

Tucich didn't remember seeing Alice around all that often on the jazz scene outside from such pickup gigs. "I don't think Alice ever really played the two or three bars that had jazz: Klein's Show Bar, the Blue Bird, Levert's on Linwood Avenue. I don't think she ever played at any of those places," he said. "I don't recall her, you know, playing anywhere actually." But he did recall playing more than a few times with her. The group would play what was—in just a few short years—already canonical bebop: "Woody 'n' You," "Now's the Time," "Anthropology."[26]

How would he describe her style at the time? "She was a big Bud Powell fan," he said. "Barry Harris would imitate Bud Powell and everybody, *all* the piano players, would imitate Bud Powell. Yeah, he was the guy."

Despite not seeing her out making the scene, Tucich remembered that Alice had already worked herself into the rotation of Detroit working pianists:

> She usually got the call when Barry Harris was out or Terry Pollard wasn't available. Ira Jackson was the hustler, the alto player and he always got the gigs. And the gigs were usually Black dances that we played at in the church ballrooms, or places where the church would hold their Sunday things, wide open rooms. There were a lot of churches. On the west side there were two or three churches we played.[27]

Even when playing bebop, Alice still found herself playing it in a church.

CHAPTER FIVE

Three Guys and a Doll

AFTER A FEBRUARY 11, 1956, BRIEF ON A SUNRISE SERVICE AT MT. Olive, Alice McLeod's name vanished from the Detroit newspapers for well over a year. Soon after graduation, Alice and two friends headed to New York City,[1] where she had the dream of enrolling at the Juilliard School of Music.[2] There she could further her study of classical music. "I wanted to just go study," she said. "I wanted to go back to the books, to some technical basics. I thought if I studied for a year that would be sufficient. Then I could continue with what I was doing. But it didn't turn out that way."[3]

The concrete reality of New York City set in immediately. After plans to live with her friends fell through, she decided to move in with her aunt, Margaret Johnson, up in Harlem. At least until that aunt figured that anyone who could afford to attend Juilliard could also afford to pay the rent. As Adams said, "Because of that unexpected added expense, her plan to attend Juilliard vanished into thin air."[4]

In the Big Apple, especially in the postwar 1950s, a talented young lady who had mastered Gregg shorthand and could type 120 words a minute could always find some work. In just a few months, Alice moved from being a file clerk in an office up to secretary. And then Ernie came through town.

Her brother Ernie anchored some of the hottest bands operating on the West Side.⁵ Every night of the week, Farrow could be found at the Bohemian Club, Klein's Show Bar, or the Blue Bird Inn. A group that bandleader Hindal Butts had assembled included Farrow, pianist Hugh Lawson, trombonist Curtis Fuller, and saxophonist Pepper Adams, and the latter three soon had tickets to New York City and international jazz acclaim. Over at the Blue Bird, Farrow played in the house band under leader Yusef Lateef, featuring trumpeter Donald Byrd. But before long, Byrd had enrolled in the hard bop finishing school that was Art Blakey & the Jazz Messengers, heading to the Big Apple and decades of stardom.

Lateef and Farrow, along with pianist Hugh Lawson, bassist Doug Watkins, and drummer Louis Hayes, had what William Wood deemed "the best gig in Detroit."⁶ It was after hours at the West End Hotel and the band played six nights a week. "Ernie Farrow was one of my mentors," Wood said. "He was the house bassist. Ernie had a big sound."

At the time, it seemed everyone had a working band in Detroit. And business, like the auto industry, was booming. "We were all playing dances, school dances. Everybody was dancing to Charlie Parker's music, Dizzy's music, it was the jazz of the time," Lightsey said. "Every weekend, everybody had a gig playing a dance or at the club. At that time, Detroit was rich with people working in the auto industry. Everywhere there was an audience. We played in all the clubs. Sometimes you played for a month in the same place."⁷

"The clubs would close at two and the West End was open," Maupin recalled. "It would go till sun-up. There was food and a lot of nice musicians and a lot of nice girls, too. The music was always happening."⁸ Tucich remembered that all the guys would play their various gigs and then all pile into a car and head over in the wee hours. Touring jazz musicians would always come through. "There was exposure to great playing and great camaraderie and friendship between the musicians," Maupin recalled. "To be in the midst of that as a young musician, just to see how they interacted with each other musically and mutual respect for each other. I got to be in some amazing places." Every night a young player could learn more about the music.

But Wood remembered just how often out-of-town cats rolled in and met their match. "Gerry Mulligan, Red Mitchell, Junior Cook, got shook up a little bit," he chuckled. "Detroit has its own sound. You played *tip*, you played really on top of the beat, real crisp notes. That was our thing. So Gerry ran into Pepper Adams; Red Mitchell ran into Paul Chambers; Junior Cook ran into Joe Henderson. That gig shook a lot of people up. People could *jam*."

That much time together led to more experimentation from Lateef and his band. Lateef knew that he could take the rabab that his Chrysler co-worker had made and just hand it off to Farrow, trusting that the bassist would delve into its sound until he attained mastery of the thing. Which is just what Farrow did in methodically plucking the rabab for the ten-minute meditation that is "Morning," from Lateef's first album as a leader, 1957's *Jazz Mood*. The band made the drive from Detroit to the well-regarded recording studio that Rudy Van Gelder set up in his parents' living room in suburban Hackensack, New Jersey, and in the course of 1957 alone, they cut nine albums there.

Ernie crossed the Hudson River to find his sister in the city and set her up with a few working gigs. "It was because of Ernest I got my first gig with Johnny Griffin, who was already a fine, fine tenor player," she said. "Griffin's piano player was Barry Harris and he offered to turn his job over to me. I told him I'd take it, and before long, I'd played with a lot of major musicians."[9] She also picked up gigs with the likes of Kenny Burrell and Lucky Thompson. Her days as a secretary were numbered.

She had come to the city to study classical music, but Alice now realized the absolute freedom and liberation she felt in playing jazz and knew this was her future. "The classical pianist must recreate a composer's music, and interpret it exactly," she said. But in playing jazz, the music could dance right off the sheet and charge the air. She realized that the music "allow[s] artists to express themselves, their ideas, and perform their own interpretations or differing innovations. I just marveled at all the creativity, improvisation, total freedom, and the artistic expression of this music."[10]

It was rare indeed for a young woman in the 1950s to be allowed—much less encouraged—to pursue what she loved in the big city. In all of this, she had the undying love and support of her parents back in Detroit. "Ladies were brought up with the wonderful [principles] of children and home and families and I do strongly believe in those [principles]," Alice once said about her fellow female jazz musicians and the lack of familial structure they faced:

> Even if its only moral support, you need the support of your family. I didn't have my parents after I graduated school insisting: "You will go to school, you will not listen to this music." I had parents who encouraged me to be the best at what I wanted to try, to be the best in my work in school, however academically I wished to pursue music, to wholeheartedly engage in it. "If you succeed and want to go to New York and be in that environment, it may not be best for a young lady." But they helped me.[11]

But no matter the gig, it's a never-ending grind to make ends meet in New York. Whatever gigs she might've picked up there were short-lived. At some point, Alice returned to Detroit.

ON OCTOBER 12, 1956, TERRY POLLARD APPEARED WITH TERRY GIBBS on *Tonight with Steve Allen*, precursor to *The Tonight Show*.[12] Since joining Gibbs's band, they had recorded at a clip, Pollard appearing on four LPs, along with her own debut album.[13] Their vibraphone duets had—as Gibbs predicted—broken up the place and they performed for packed houses from Rochester to Los Angeles.

Now the Gibbs Quartet was set to break up late-night television, and footage of the performance still exists online. Gibbs is in a black jacket out front with his vibraphone as the band starts in with his tune

"Gibberish." Pollard is seated at the piano in a sleeveless dress with cowl collar, her long hair pulled back, her left leg fidgeting as it taps out the breakneck tempo. The camera zooms in close on her hands as she nimbly harmonizes with Gibbs, matching his flurry of hammering runs as the band whizzes through the tune.

Next, they tackle "Now's the Time," the iconic bluesy bebop number Charlie Parker originally wrote in 1945. Pollard joins Gibbs up front, standing to his left on the lower register of the metallophone while host Steve Allen handles piano duties. The Terrys are in sync as they render the head of the tune on mallets, and then Gibbs steps out of frame as Pollard takes the first solo, every bit as confident on the vibes as she was at the piano. As her solo concludes, Gibbs slides back in, whacking his bars in double time as Pollard clicks time on her sticks. Midway through his second measure, though, Pollard elbows Gibbs out of her way as she picks up the melody, only to have him interrupt her interruption. He's not even through the first bar before Pollard—now with both hands—shoves him completely off-camera, shrugs, then starts back into a solo on the upper bars. The two playfully nudge each other in a high-speed game of trading bars on the whirlwind Parker solo, each wordlessly singing along with the solo, backchatting, and laughing. Now it's a high-wire act as each strikes a bar on the other's side of the vibraphone like jugglers swapping pins midair, building in energy until they synchronize again on the head and draw to a show-stopping conclusion. Pollard runs up the scale then off the vibraphone entirely, thwacking her boss as they both laugh. Less than a year before, Rosa Parks refused to give up her bus seat in Alabama, and now Pollard became the first Black female musician to appear on late-night television, breaking the color barrier by being beamed into homes across the country.

Life on the road wasn't easy for Pollard, facing discrimination and insults not only as a Black musician but as a woman. Every town the Gibbs Quartet pulled into, she could expect some form of segregation, indignation, humiliation, or a combination of all three. "In addition to being a woman, there were instances where, between shows, I had to sit in the basement of the club because I was a Negro," she said. "It's hard to believe it happened, but I remember that the band always stuck with me. If I had to sit there, the band would sit there, too."[14] Pollard was passionate about the music, about playing before packed rooms and seeing the country. But she also pined for a sense of stability rather than the grind of nightlife. Within the year, Pollard returned to Detroit, quit Gibbs's band, married Robert Morris, and soon started her family.

GEORGE BOHANON THOUGHT THAT THAT GIRL LOOKED FAMILIAR. Bohanon was born August 7, 1937, and grew up on the West Side of Detroit. He met Kirk Lightsey in middle school and they got together to play back then, with Bohanon on trombone and Lightsey on piano, though Lightsey was studying at Cass while Bohanon went to Northwestern. He would stand outside the Blue Bird near his house and take in the music, and in the afternoons after school, some of the grown-ups playing jazz would encourage the teen to get his horn and sit in with them.

He knew Alice from the neighborhood and knew that she was a player. It's likely they first met through Lightsey as teenagers. Bohanon's best friend, Melvin, was going steady with Alice's youngest sister, Marilyn, and they would soon be married. They were all hanging out and before long, "me and Alice were boyfriend and girlfriend. We were real close, too. We had a relationship for quite a few years there." The details of that early relationship are vague now, but he thinks they reconnected sometime in 1956:

> We just, you know, hung out. We dated. We could go to movies and things like that. She was very, very strong in her beliefs. She came up under a strict kind of a bringing up. She wouldn't hang out all the time. You wouldn't see her hanging out on the scene, so to speak. But I'm thinking the times we were doing the music together, we were together a lot during that period. She was serious about music.[15]

Bohanon was gigging with a group called the 5 Peppers, featuring Bohanon with Joe and Jesse Carter, two slightly older musicians on drums and bass, respectively. Joe Carter was the leader of the group and for him, musical success meant making it as a smooth lounge act: "He had this concept about, you know, kind of the Four Freshmen kind of thing," Bohanon recalled. "So he was asking me if I knew any musicians. Well, what about a female piano player? And that's when Alice's name came up."

Bohanon didn't think she was going to go for the idea, "but she was probably more interested than I was at the time," he said. With a new member, they rechristened themselves the Premiers: "I thought she was too straight ahead for that. She liked Tommy Flanagan and Bud Powell, as far as jazz players. The Premiers was an *act*. We were working to be a cocktail lounge and maybe get to Las Vegas."

The Premiers was an act and a sharp one at that. "We had matching jackets and black pants, we were dressed up," Bohanon said. Motown and the concept of Black vocal pop was still a few years away, so the Premiers were—in Bohanon's estimation—"ahead of its time, really, for any Black groups to sound like that. There was no one that would play that kind of music."

All four members of the Premiers sang and harmonized, with Alice handling the vocal arrangements, a skill she picked up from her years working with all three of Mt. Olive's choirs. "Onstage, we were all standing with her Wurlitzer electric piano built up on a platform and so we could huddle close and harmonize," Bohanon said. "I did some vocal spots—King Pleasure kind of thing—like 'Little Boy, Don't Get Scared,' those kinds of tunes that were hot, pretty popular during that time, scat kind of things. And then I'd back up and play a trombone solo."

An article in the *Michigan Chronicle* mentioned the group's "smooth, layered harmonies" but credited Carter for the arrangements: "'Mood Indigo,' 'Lonesome Mood,' 'Come Dance With Me,' and 'Finis' were crowd pleasers."[16] Bohanon said the Premiers' repertoire was basically standards and the show tunes of the day, but because of Alice's classical background, the group could range to more ambitious fare. Bohanon brings up a song called "Anastasia," the opulent title track from the film of the same name that Ingrid Bergman won an Oscar for and which crooner Pat Boone had a hit with. "'Anastasia, tell me who you are / Are you someone from another star?'" He hummed a line. "I don't know where we were going to sing *that* at, but it was in our rep, you know?" Bohanon said. He mentioned other songs once in the popular imagination but long since relegated to obscurity. Recalling these old tunes, he would break into song, humming something like "Jealousy," now a forgotten tango: "Jea-lou-*SEE, da-da-da-da-da-da-dee, da-da-da-da-da-da-da*. We did all of those kinds of tunes. We had nice harmonies. And then we could always just play, too. We could just *play* as the quartet." The group began to make a name for themselves around town.

Wood was knocked out the first time he heard McLeod in that group:

> They played my neighborhood, on the East Side of Detroit—extreme East Side—and she's the same age I am. She's playing in the bar, but I couldn't get *in* the bar. Anyway, I'm in the alley listening to somebody that I'm not even looking at. But the music was incredible. They really played... some of the best music I had ever heard in my life. Alice played the organa and sang. They had these beautiful white lounge jackets... it was just a class act.[17]

By that time, Wood and about ten other friends had moved to a loft space close to Wayne State University campus. All day long, Wood and young guys like drummer Roy Brooks, saxophonist Charles McPherson, Lonnie Hillyer, and the like would jam. "We played around the clock," he said. "Musicians traveling through Detroit would come to our place and jam with us, people from Tommy Flanagan or Dizzy Gillespie's group. It was a fine forum for transient musicians to interface with local musicians."

At one point, that pianist from the Premiers also came through. "Alice used to come up and play," Wood said. "She was very, very shy.

She wasn't particularly into the bebop music. She wasn't forthcoming in terms of that music."[18]

A new student at Wayne State would also come by and sit in on saxophone. Joe Henderson (originally from Lima, Ohio) had a musical education not unlike those of the other Detroiters. "When I picked up the saxophone, I had an idea of how it could be played as far as bebop style was concerned," he told one interviewer. "After that, I started playing in high school bands, which didn't play bebop, and thus got a full appreciation of other kinds of music—classical and marches. I liked Bartok and Stravinsky and Schoenberg."[19] Henderson seemed to emerge fully formed on the scene: a tough blues player who could handle whatever complex hard bop chord changes were thrown at him, while also revealing a velvety, Lester Young–like tone on slow ballads. Henderson soon had a regular gig at Denny's Show Bar on Linwood.

At some point in 1957, the Premiers rolled over to the Fortune Records storefront on 3rd Avenue on the West Side, where shop owners Jack and Devora Brown kept an Ampex 350 tape recorder in the back. The couple had founded their label a few years before, scoring a U.S. country hit with the Davis Sisters and a regional hit in "Jail Bait" with the ribald R&B of local singer André Williams. That afternoon the Premiers cut their first—and only—45 rpm record, "When You Are in Love" b/w "The Trap of Love." Devora Brown penned the A side, which opens with Alice's organa. It might be a Hohner Organa 30, which was made in the 1950s, a four-octave electric reed organ that Alice makes shimmer like a harp on her fills, adding to the dreamy feel of the layered harmonies. Joe Carter provides an easy shuffle topped by Bohanon's trombone solo as the Premiers harmonize with him. "The Trap of Love" picks up the tempo as Joe takes the lead vocal and the break features hand-clapping and foot-stomping to accompany another trombone solo.

There's a glossy press photo of the Premiers from that time. The men are dapper in black suit and tie, and Alice is in a strapless dress seated in the middle, smiling broadly. Bohanon is broad-shouldered with a little smirk on his face, holding Alice's right hand while Jesse Carter holds her left. Joe Carter stands paternally in the back, his arms around the group. Alice had made her first record.

She wasn't the only one. Berry Gordy had encountered Jackie Wilson at the Flame Show Bar years before, which finally yielded Gordy's first songwriting credit when Wilson cut his first single "Reet Petite (The Finest Girl You Ever Want To Meet)." Later that year, Gordy would meet another enterprising young singer-songwriter who was already writing songs featuring group harmonies named William "Smokey" Robinson.

By early 1958, the Premiers were the hot item in Detroit. "Three guys and a doll!" enthused *Michigan Chronicle* nightlife columnist Ziggy Johnson in his weekly column "Zagging with Ziggy": "Finally getting their Flame Show Bar showcase. Long overdue." Two weeks on, in his "people places 'n' situwayshuns" column, another *Chronicle* writer, Bill Lane, mentioned a show at Baker's Keyboard Lounge featuring the Premiers, the Sarah Vaughan trio, and the Dorothy Ashby Trio. In a Flame Show Bar ad from April, they advertised a "Big Easter Revue" "featuring debonaire Johnny Hartman" and co-starring "3 Swinging Guys and A Gal." When the NAACP organized a show in April, the Premiers were also there. A summer tour also earned mention in both columns, as the band sent postcards from locales like New Bedford, Massachusetts, and Cape Cod. Lane's prediction? "At the rate The Premiers are now traveling they'll be in Europe or Hollywood next."

The next tour didn't get as far. A *Michigan Chronicle* article suggested that when the Premiers played down in Miami, it was a celebrity-filled coronation and augur of great things to come:

> The Premiers performed with Charles Fuqua and the Ink Spots, then Cab Calloway's Cotton Club Review in Miami Beach before opening at the New Club Calvert. This engagement featured Arthur Prysock. The opening was attended by Billy Eckstine, Sammy Davis Jr., Johnny Mathis, Dorothy Dandridge and Dave Hamilton who performed as guests.[20]

George Bohanon remembered it differently. A slick cat named Sinclair Rogers was up from Miami to buy a brand new car in Detroit and have it driven back for him. "He just heard about us and, said 'Come on, I got some work in Miami,'" Bohanon said. "We only had that Wurlitzer piano. We carried all the mics in the old setup. Joe had the cocktail drum set. Sinclair was pretty convincing, because we ended up driving his Lincoln Premier down to Florida. We played the Old Beachcomber on Miami Beach, but we were tricked into it. And then he disappeared."[21]

The Premiers found themselves stuck in Miami, broke, lugging all their gear around with no car, and with no way to get back to Detroit. "We were just out there," Bohanon said. The band found a friend in Jack Brown, who owned the lone Black motion picture theater in Liberty City. Brown took them in and helped the band scrape up a few paying gigs. Bohanon is vague on how long the group was marooned in Miami, "but I know we worked right around the Miami area and Liberty City area and made enough to buy us a Ford station wagon and drive back home."

BACK IN DETROIT, THE CITY BEGAN TO EXPERIENCE THE PAINS THAT signaled the end of the postwar boom. And the seeds of urban renewal began to emerge, a concrete shadow growing across the Black neighborhoods that furthered the racial animus and sense of injustice that had never quite been corrected—much less admitted to—by City Hall in the wake of the Belle Isle violence.

Construction began in earnest on the major highway projects, gashing neighborhoods like Black Bottom and Paradise Valley until they were but a shell of themselves. To the north, Paradise Valley was being demolished for the I-94 interstate. Black Bottom was strangled by a cement loop of 75 and Interstate 375. When the Chrysler Freeway construction started, it cut precisely through the heart of Black Detroit, replacing the entire length of Hastings Street. Save for a half-mile stretch, Hastings ceased to exist, except as a memory for its older Black residents.

By 1958, there was a downturn in automobile sales. Companies that had sold 6.5 million cars in 1950 now saw demand in 1958 slow down to just over 4 million. Plants in the center of town started to shutter and unemployment soared. Between 1950 and the early 1960s the East Side of Detroit alone lost 71,000 jobs.[22]

That loss of steady income throughout the Black community sent aftershocks throughout the fragile neighborhood ecosystems. Clubs that couldn't get enough paying patrons were shuttered. The jazz scene in Detroit began to contract around the edges, but the music was growing and maturing into fascinating new forms. Massive breakthroughs in modern jazz were just in the offing.

Ernie Farrow now led the house band at the Blue Bird Inn, which was still the place to be. Miles Davis had a hot new sextet featuring two rising stars on the saxophone, Cannonball Adderley and John Coltrane, as well as hometown hero Paul Chambers on bass. All six of them crammed onto the small stage. Detroit love for the band was so strong that Miles came through the Blue Bird in April and then again in September.

Miles's band and the music were changing fast and his sextet was on a hot streak. They had just cut *Milestones*, with an emphasis on a more modal way of approaching improvisation. Rather than navigating bebop's rushing river of chord changes, Miles stripped it all back. "What I had learned about the modal form is that when you play this way, go in this direction, you can go on forever," he wrote in his autobiography. "When you base stuff on chords, and you know at the end of thirty-two bars that the chords have run out, there's nothing to do but repeat what you've done... And in the modal way I saw all kinds of possibilities."[23]

Miles returned that fall with pianist Bill Evans and drummer Jimmy Cobb now in the fold. Emphasis on modally based improvisation and cooler tempos moved to the forefront for their leader and his sidemen. Coltrane, having kicked his heroin habit in a harrowing cold turkey withdrawal in the summer of 1957, had just released his own breakthrough album as a leader, *Blue Train*, and his solos on the bandstand revealed a startling new level of inspiration and intensity coursing through him. The bell of his horn seemed to brim with new ideas.

Taking a page from his former bandleader's penchant for worldly sounds, Farrow called his group at the Blue Bird the International Jazz Quartet, featuring altoist Sonny Red, pianist Hugh Lawson, drummer Oliver Jackson, and Joe Henderson. A *Down Beat* scene report on Detroit focused on "Farrow's outstanding group...Farrow every bit as adventurous a player as his bandleader Yusef."[24] Berry Gordy, hungry for new talent, would come through the Blue Bird often, listening intently.

Maupin's favorite place to play and hang out, though, was at Joe Brazil's house, which took on the after-hours role after Yusef left the West End. He said:

> Joe Brazil was a fine musician. He had a grand piano in his home. There was a lot of activity in his home. It was a safe place to play. I met Freddie Hubbard, Wayne Shorter, Bobby Timmons, Lee Morgan there in Detroit. I would be upstairs. I wouldn't play, I would just go to listen and observe the sounds and how guys interacted. I would hear the doorbell in the kitchen area...and got to be the doorman. I got to have the honor of opening the door to John Coltrane several times. I got to spend time with him, be encouraged by him in a different setting, away from the bandstand. He really encouraged me a lot. He and I would stay upstairs.[25]

The Premiers had finally made it back to Detroit, but Bohanon and McLeod couldn't keep up enthusiasm for the Premiers, or for their own relationship. "I lost Alice for a while after we got back from Florida," Bohanon said. "After Florida, everybody was leery about going back on the road. We put time into that group, learning tunes, rehearsing, memorizing tunes. But that trip to Florida really hit us hard."[26]

Joe Carter's big dream was to play a lounge in a big hotel in downtown Detroit, but Bohanon and McLeod had their sights set on something bigger in music, even if they didn't quite know what form it would take. For Bohanon, he picked up other gigs and a few years later, he punched his ticket out of town, joining Chico Hamilton's band, and then Bohanon found himself playing music in a different context: "Motown came in and saved me."

Meanwhile, Alice had a new love.

CHAPTER SIX

April in Paris

"Just when my career was getting started and my focus shifted to New York, Detroit was undergoing major changes," Aretha Franklin wrote in her autobiography:

> For one thing, an urban renewal program meant the end of the New Bethel of my childhood. The Chrysler Freeway was being built right through Hastings. The church—in fact, the entire neighborhood—was being torn down for the highway. (Daddy spoke of how the Catholic church, only one block away, was saved from demolition while ours was not. He couldn't explain why.) Fortunately, I would get to perform at the neighborhood's most famous nightspot, the Flame Show Bar, before the end of its golden era.[1]

The Black neighborhoods of Kirk Lightsey's youth, the buildings and street corners he knew like the back of his hand, were all quickly being uprooted and demolished:

> Urban renewal tore down so much. Black Bottom, Paradise Valley, all of that was gone. And that's what they were trying to do, renew Detroit and bring the rich white people who moved out to 9 Mile, 10 Mile Road, they were trying to bring them back into town and push

the Black people out that way. It was a massive mess. The automobile industry had a lot to do with it. And the race riots had a lot to do with it.²

But even amid this uprooting and upheaval, some new seeds were beginning to sprout. Tired of finding good recording studios and getting rejected by record labels around town that weren't hearing the music like *he* was hearing it in his own head, Berry Gordy decided to take matters in his own hands. He had tasted some success writing for Jackie Wilson and was working on new songs with Smokey Robinson. He had also encountered a promising young singer named Marv Johnson one night when he performed at a carnival. Borrowing $800 from his family, Gordy set up the Tamla label in January 1959 and got Johnson into a studio with some of the jazz cats he had been hearing over at the Blue Bird, like saxophonist Thomas "Beans" Bowles and a bassist friend of Farrow's and Wood's named James Jamerson. In less than two weeks, Gordy had recorded and cut his first record, Johnson's "Come to Me." Eight months later, Gordy would start another label, Motown.

When she drifted away from the Premiers, Alice began picking up gigs where she could and deepening her understanding of jazz. "I learned from other players like Cannonball Adderley, Sonny Stitt, who would come through our city," she said. "They wouldn't come with a piano player, so if everybody was working, they'd call me."³

Somewhere in the smoky clubs of Detroit, Alice McLeod met Kenneth "Pancho" Hagood, eleven years her senior. The Detroit native had broken through in the late 1940s as a bebop scat vocalist. That was Pancho bursting out of Dizzy's bebop classic "Oop-Bop-a-Da," with Hagood going on to record with the likes of Thelonious Monk, Dizzy Gillespie, Charlie Parker, and Miles Davis. His syrupy baritone appeared on "Darn That Dream," which closed Davis's epochal *Birth of the Cool*. But by 1959, he was scuffling and back on the scene in Detroit, where he gigged with Farrow and soon made the acquaintance of the twenty-two-year-old McLeod. How or where they met isn't clear, but soon they were a couple.

Of the handful of interviews Alice gave over the course of her lifetime, almost no interviewer ever asked her a question about her first husband, only her second. Kenny Hagood almost never gets mentioned by name. In a rare 1980 interview, he only mentioned that time in his life as being "disillusioned with the jazz scene, 'tired of bumming around,'" but Hagood didn't bring Alice up either.[4]

In talking with the players on the scene in Detroit at the time, most are only vaguely aware—if aware at all—that McLeod and Hagood even got together. The new couple realized one thing, though; the Detroit they knew was crumbling under their feet and it was time to make a clean break and go to a new city for work: Paris.

They weren't the first jazz musicians to imagine a new life there. "I loved being in Paris and loved the way I was treated," Miles Davis wrote in his autobiography, still misty-eyed at his memories of the city. As writer Adam Shatz noted: "In the dream life of black American musicians, Paris has long been the closest thing to heaven: a place where they were recognized as artists; where they wouldn't be beaten up by cops or stripped of their cabaret cards; where they could walk arm and arm with a white woman without attracting hostile stares."[5]

Hagood no doubt regaled Alice with stories of his own time there in 1948: the sights, the romantic street cafés, the arrondissements, the attentive audience who would hang on your every note, the sense of freedom that no city in the United States—no matter how urbane and open-minded—would ever give a Black person.

The couple no doubt were in love, but in Rudy Tucich's estimation, "she probably wasn't being let out the house to go to Paris."[6] Knowing their deep, conservative church values, her family wouldn't deem it proper—much less safe—for their daughter to cross the ocean out of wedlock. So at some point in 1959, Alice McLeod and Kenneth Hagood were wed. Historian Ashley Kahn wrote that "the attraction was both to Pancho...and to the city itself." As Alice's daughter Michelle would remember: "She told me about Paris, how it was so hip in that era for her, the music definitely was first, not to discount her relationship, but knowing her as I did I'm sure that it was the drive to be involved in music."[7]

At some point in 1959, the newlyweds boarded a ship bound for Paris, joining dozens of other Black artists, writers, and musicians already living abroad, including Alice's favorite pianist, Bud Powell, who had also recently arrived. Saxophonist Lucky Thompson told an interviewer that he felt frozen out in the United States, but upon arriving in Paris, he found himself flush with club gigs, concerts, and offers for television and films:

> I left this country not to run away, but in order to remain a participant in my chosen field. I realized I had to play and write, or my talent would wither and die. I could no longer buck the business end of music [in America]. Everywhere in Europe, I was accepted in the same warm, unhesitating manner. There were no social barriers.[8]

By age twenty-four, trumpeter, arranger, and bandleader Quincy Jones had toured Europe with Lionel Hampton and the Middle East with Dizzy Gillespie before returning to Paris to study composition and theory with Nadia Boulanger and Olivier Messiaen. "In France, the yoke of black and white was off my shoulders," he wrote about the country's appeal. "In France I was able to envision my past, present, and future as an artist and as a black man; I took a wider view of the human condition that extended to both art and life."[9]

Studying with the famous Boulanger opened Jones's eyes even wider. Even as he familiarized himself with the Eurocentric classical canon, she would tell him to forget about composing great American symphonies, because they were already within him as a Black man in America. "'You already have something unique and important. Go mine the ore you already have,'" he recalled. "This was years before most universities in my own country, including many black universities, even thought of teaching jazz. In America they taught Beethoven and Bach as if they had a direct line to God. Stravinsky himself admired jazz."

Not that France was free from its own racial turmoil. Jones and his bandmates realized that the Paris streets could get just as fraught as any in the United States, and they could still be stopped because of the color of their skin:

> We opened at the Alhambra Theater in Paris just as the Algerian crisis hit. We could hear machine-gun fire in the street during our rehearsal. Police and soldiers roamed the streets around the clock every day. There was a boxed notice on the front page of the *Herald Tribune* that said, "Any swarthy-complexioned person is advised to stay off the street after six o'clock in the evening." It was 1959 and several of us, going to and from the theater, were stopped by police with cocked machine guns. People were afraid to leave their homes at night to get a carton of milk, let alone to see a show.[10]

For Bud Powell, that was still a marked improvement over life as a jazz musician and Black man in America. One night after a gig in Philadelphia, Bud Powell was drunk and wandering near Broad Street Station when he encountered the Philadelphia police. The cops promptly arrested Powell, but not before they clubbed him on the head until he blacked out. Back in New York, still reeling from the police brutality, his wounds, and agonizing headaches, Powell made the mistake of checking himself into Bellevue Hospital. The aftereffects of such cruelty haunted Powell the rest of his short life, with him being sent to psych wards and undergoing electroshock therapy.

Paris was about where Powell found the most peace. He moved there with his common-law wife, Altevia "Buttercup" Edwards, and her young son in 1959, living at the Hotel La Louisiane in the sixth arrondissement. From there, it was a short stroll along the banks of the Seine River to the eighth arrondissement for his long-standing gig at Le Blue Note. A *Down Beat* feature on Powell described his routine:

He'd sit there in the churchyard beneath the towering spires of St. Germaine de Pres. Not a muscle would he move nor sound make and his fingers laced in the fashion of men grown old. It was then he seemed most at peace. He'd watch the passer-by at peace with himself... In the early hours of morning, after his gig at the Bluenote Club was finished, Bud walking back to the right bank so that he could buy red wine with the money that was his taxi fare.[11]

Le Blue Note opened in the fall of 1958 and quickly became a hub for the Black American expats living in Paris. It was originally a milliner's shop, and Kenny "Klook" Clarke, himself an expat, remembered the venue well:

The Blue Note was a long, narrow room with chairs and tables on either side, and a small stage at the far end with a miniature dancefloor immediately in front of it. The bar occupied half of the right-hand side of the room... To gain access to the Blue Note on most evenings it was necessary to circumnavigate the 240-pound bulk of its manager, Ben Benjamin, who spent much of his time standing in the entrance, welcoming guests and chain-smoking furiously.[12]

Tenor saxophonist Lester "Prez" Young made a series of guest appearances there in early 1959, including his last-ever performance in March 1959. Many jazz greats habitually appeared: Chet Baker, Stan Getz, Sonny Rollins, Donald Byrd, Lucky Thompson, and more. But it was the regular appearances of Powell at the piano bench that cemented the club's reputation as the premier jazz club in Europe.[13] As Powell's friend and guardian angel of sorts, Francis Paudras, remembered about that time: "Those evenings revealed to me even more about the soul of this man I thought I knew so well."[14]

Upon the Hagoods' arrival in Paris, Alice was struck by the welcoming atmosphere of the city and marveled at the way the city was "culturally minded, culturally oriented, so appreciative of American music." Perhaps the City of Lights dazzled her in such a manner that she wasn't able to notice that upon disembarking from the ship, Pancho had gone out to score. Hagood's heroin addiction had derailed his early career and while he had cleaned up his act in Detroit (thanks in part to the stepped-on product that Miles Davis described so well), his habit roared back with a vengeance here, unbeknownst to his new wife.

Alice Hagood was instead intent on furthering her musical study in Paris. In the exile community she already had connections and soon found herself landing gigs with Thompson, double bassist Oscar Pettiford, or Clarke. In these Parisian nightclubs, Alice might look out and see the likes of Prince Aly Khan, Rita Hayworth, or Elvis and Priscilla Presley taking in the set.

She also sought out Bud Powell so as to study with the master. "When I went to Europe and met Bud Powell, I think I just became more determined in my resolve to continue," she said.[15] However, "study" might be too formal for the conveyance of bebop's unwritten codex. "It's hard to imagine Bud teaching anything formally," Detroit historian Mark Stryker said. "'Taking lessons with Bud Powell,' [meant] she hung out at Bud Powell's house and watched him practice and play…mostly it would be to soak up and be in Bud's aura."[16]

In Paudras's book, he mentioned that at the start of the new year in 1960, "Bud was back at the Blue Note, playing with Jimmy Gourley and Lucky Thompson. They shared the bill with a young pianist named Alice McCloud [sic]."[17]

Miraculously, deep in the French television archives, there's a three-minute video of Alice Hagood playing "Woody 'n' You"[18] at Le Blue Note with Gourley, Klook, Thompson, and bassist Pierre Michelot. Her posture is bolt upright, hair piled high, sleeves pulled up on her knit dress, pearls around her neck. Her right hand dances through the changes, and when the French camera catches her straight-on, her smile radiates with joy.

In March 1960, Miles Davis brought his band to Europe for a run of dates in France, Sweden, and Denmark. It was part of a package tour put together by jazz impresario Norman Granz, which also featured artists like Stan Getz and Oscar Peterson. By that point in time, his saxophonist John Coltrane had already left the band to lead his own quartet, but Davis cajoled him into going on one last tour in Europe. As Davis wrote: "[Coltrane] grumbled and complained and sat by himself all the time we were over there."[19] The quintet played the Olympia Theatre in Paris on March 21, 1960, and Alice Hagood was at the show.

It was there she caught her first glimpse of John Coltrane. It would have been hard not to notice him, though. By this tour, Coltrane was well beyond the modal cool of *Kind of Blue*, as well as the standard songbook that he and Miles had mastered over the years. He had just released his own seismic new jazz statement, *Giant Steps*, a month before, but it's unlikely anyone would have been familiar with the "sheets of sound" that Coltrane was now exploring with his horn.[20]

While Coltrane himself had a front row seat to the sound of new developments happening in New York City, like the debut of Ornette Coleman at the Five Spot, Parisians hadn't heard this "new thing" yet. His solos now drew on dissonance and overblowing and at times the crowd would hoot and whistle. Whether or not Alice took part in the whistling, something deep down in her soul was stirred by Coltrane's mountainous vibrato and his unceasing cascade of ideas and pure sound. It lingered with her long after she left the Olympia. She began to feel that there was another force moving behind that music, pushing it into a higher realm. She knew well the standards that Davis and his band played, knew well the changes, but in Coltrane, she could feel that he was moving beyond the boundaries into something unknown. She knew there was a change coming in the music, and she wanted to be ready for it.

Just close proximity to Powell proved to be a stabilizing force in the twenty-two-year-old's life. "He was still physically able to work and to just function like an ordinary man," Alice said. "He really took an interest in me. He liked that I was interested in his music. He helped me to really develop technique when it came to the keyboard. His type of playing was the root beginning of the music I'm into now."[21] She described Powell's lowkey mentorship to Berkman as "a guiding light" for her being so far away from home. "His sound, his knowledge of chord changes, dexterity. I felt that he was the best inspiration for me," she said, then adding that the informal sessions with Powell gave her familial and spiritual sustenance in addition to musical knowledge:

> Sometimes we would have...at home reunions. We would sit down and talk about Detroit and New York. Talk about the family. Talk about the children, the music. Talk about church! We would do that and they were very heartfelt times. We would reminisce about roots, family, and friends. Those who were not with you now, and some only God knows when or if you would see them again. So those were very special moments. Almost like sacred moments. Sometimes we would even sing a hymn or two, or a gospel song. It was just beautiful...I have always stayed close to the church, wherever I was.[22]

That Alice Hagood could feel stability in the Powell home is no small miracle. Powell still struggled with his precarious mental health. Sometimes he might wander lost in Paris for days, coming home disheveled. Other eyewitnesses to that time period point to Powell's tumultuous life with Buttercup. Paudras witnessed Powell suffering physical as well as mental abuse at her hands: "Tender was the last word one would use for Buttercup. She was ponderous, violent, extremely loud, and quite vulgar...Every day she found new ways to hurt Bud...Every day it became more chaotic...The atmosphere bordered on hysteria."[23]

Powell himself was self-medicating in the form of vin rouge, bountiful at every café at any hour of the day or night. To Paudras's horror, he soon noticed a zombielike pall fall over his friend that was far beyond mere drunkenness. It took months before he realized that

Buttercup, in an effort to wean Powell off wine, began medicating him with a powerful, dangerous antipsychotic medication, Largactil. For a highly sensitized artist like Powell, the effect of the drug was devastating on his playing and demeanor: "He would fall into a sort of lethargy, his movements became slower, and he lost interest in everything around him."

Alice Hagood was working steadily, but she no doubt felt a lingering sense of estrangement. Her husband would vanish for hours on end, leaving her to navigate this foreign country on her own. She missed home. She was determined to make it here and knew if she just put her mind and thought to it, she would have a breakthrough. Not long after that appearance at Le Blue Note, Alice realized she was pregnant. And she knew what she had to do.

Michelle Hagood was born on October 22, 1960, in Paris. A tourist ship originating from the French port of Le Havre, France, left Southampton, England, on November 8 and crossed the Atlantic Ocean. On November 14, 1960, it docked and was stamped upon its arrival in New York City. The passenger and crew list includes Kenneth, Alice, and Michelle A. Hagood. By the time they were on land, Pancho and Alice were already legally divorced, and Alice and her newborn daughter were on a train back to Detroit.

In the span of less than a year, Alice had gone from a newlywed living and playing jazz in Paris to being a single mother living back at home. She had just turned twenty-three. She was shell-shocked, yet her faith remained unshaken. There had to be a reason she was back in Detroit again and she was determined to make the most of it, whether or not she had a man in her life.

Less than two weeks after her return home, John Coltrane and his new band played at the Minor Key on the West Side of Detroit. It featured a young pianist from Philly named McCoy Tyner, bassist Steve Davis, and Detroit's homegrown thunder god, Elvin Jones, on the drums. It had been a watermark year for Coltrane. He was a major signing for Atlantic Records and his first album on the label did not disappoint. Coltrane released *Giant Steps* at the beginning of the year. The title track featured a daunting set of chord changes (subsequently called the "Coltrane changes") that even flummoxed seasoned pianist Tommy Flanagan at the session, yet it nevertheless quickly became a standard and a way for players to flex their chops. Three other albums were cut in quick succession.

The month before, Coltrane, Tyner, Davis, and Jones had gone into the studio, and this time Coltrane brandished the soprano saxophone that Miles Davis had bought for him on their final tour together in Europe. Since then, Coltrane had been diligently studying to master it, and he knew the perfect song to showcase it. The American musical tandem of composer Richard Rodgers and lyricist Oscar Hammerstein II had a new hit show on Broadway, *The Sound of Music*, and one number, titled "My Favorite Things," had piqued Coltrane's interest. The song was a sunny, happy jaunt that was already a crowd pleaser. But in its E minor opening Coltrane heard something worth exploring at length. With Tyner, they dug beneath its cheerful chord changes to find something deeper. Davis and Jones played the rhythm as a waltz, while Tyner toggled between E minor and E major, never fully resolving to the original's G major.[24] Meanwhile, Coltrane's new horn worked like a snake charmer's horn, making something wholly familiar foreign and mesmerizing. He had recently taken to listening to folk and classical music from India, and some of those Eastern scales emerge here. In a few months' time, *My Favorite Things* would become a startling commercial success and the title track would even become a hit single for Coltrane. Fresh on their minds, it's highly probable that the band played it that late autumn night in Detroit, as it would become a constant in Coltrane's concerts for the rest of his life.

Alice had to see this saxophonist again and make sure she hadn't imagined what she had heard back in springtime in Paris. This time, rather than being in the back of the Olympia, Alice made sure she was on the side of the stage at the Minor Key in Detroit, so that she could really hear and feel what Coltrane was playing.

The power was instantaneous and undeniable. "My God this man! Where does this sound come from?" she said, the memory still lodged in her body after all those decades, as if just the thought of that encounter could make her feel the music reverberating through every cell down into her very soul all over again:

> It was something I recognized, like this is something that is coming from him or going through him—an energy, a power that I could identify with. And then I think, at some point, I thought it was a part of me, a part of my being that he's now allowing me to reawaken to, to hear this still, pure energy. This pure light and sound vibration that's streaming forth, flowing into your being.[25]

It was the sound of the preacher at the pulpit on Sunday morning, shouting and testifying and the whole congregation standing and shaking with the spirit, channeled through a saxophone on the bandstand. It was the feeling of those storefront Church of God in Christ services transferred to the confines of a small nightclub, the listeners not in their Sunday best but in their Saturday night finery, working up a fever from the music. That feeling was there for Alice. The Lord just completely swept through when Coltrane was playing.

Alice and some friends tried to go backstage after the concert. As Adams recounted:

> They saw John sitting in a rather pensive posture with eyes downcast. As Alice was about to speak to him, an acquaintance greeted her and...due to circumstances, Alice and her friends had to leave soon after, and she did not meet John that evening.[26]

When the baby was down for the night, Alice would go to see friends in the clubs, like her longtime friend and mentor, Terry Pollard. Pollard, busy raising her own family now, still had a little trio on a weekly engagement at the Hobby Bar. Will Austin, who was a bassist for the trio, recalled Alice sitting in with them more than a few times: "She was something! She played almost exactly like Bud [Powell]. When Terry and Alice got up there, very few horn players wanted to get up there with them. They played up tempos constantly...that was something to hear! Alice on piano and Terry on vibes."[27] Alice and Michelle were back home, wondering what would come next.

CHAPTER SEVEN

Soulsphere

Alice McLeod was back at home with her parents, who helped with the baby. Her brother Ernie Farrow—after having a go in New York—was also back in Detroit. There was still pickup work to be had around the West Side, and Alice found gigs at various show bars, like the Hobby Bar on Linwood Avenue. In playing these gigs, she reconnected with an old high school acquaintance three years her junior, Bennie Maupin. They didn't really know each other all that well at Northeastern, though Maupin's memory of Alice playing drums in the orchestra—and then returning with a piano trio—lingered in his mind years later.

"I got to meet her when she came back to Detroit after living in Paris. That's when she had Michelle. Michelle's like my baby sister. I used to hold her," Maupin said. "I was always at Alice's house, at the family house, because the piano was there. I went there often. She'd say: 'Yeah, come on over, I'm here at the house taking care of Michelle.'"[1]

It had been a whirlwind few months for McLeod: becoming a mother, leaving Paris and seeing her dreams come crashing down, returning home, and having no idea what would come next. It was a challenging time for her as she picked up the pieces and tried to figure out what she would do now to support herself and her young daughter. She never discussed her life with Hagood with Maupin and never talked about Paris either, though she did mention one time that she had met John Coltrane in Paris. "It was like a casual meeting, it wasn't anything other than that, but they did connect," Maupin said.[2]

Now McLeod and Maupin were hanging out and exploring new ideas in music together. The past few years had brought about revolutionary changes in jazz.[3] New players were tired of being boxed in any pre-ordained chord changes and were figuring out how to free their music from such harmonic constraints. Sometimes McLeod and Maupin would just hang out in her parents' home, listening to the latest releases and talking through their concepts while Michelle crawled around on the floor, putting whatever she could find into her mouth to gnaw on. As they listened, a phrase would come up on a record and McLeod would play it back on the piano. Maupin remembered:

> Alice and I would be in the living room listening to whatever we were listening to, or she's playing something for me on the piano, or helping me to interpret some of her stuff, you know, working on a lot of different things with her. In retrospect, I realize I was working on my ear training. She was teaching me things about, you know, voice leading—she was teaching me about how to interpret her music, specifically. And about phrasing and about all kinds of different stuff. You don't think about it when you're young like that, you're just kind of grabbing ahold of it. That was a period that was maybe a two-year period or something like that, but you know all of that I consider very significant. And I don't think that she realizes to this day how much she taught me.[4]

One aspect of Alice's musical talent that most impressed Maupin was her ear. She could transcribe almost anything she heard on a record directly to staff paper. And by this point, she was paying close attention to what John Coltrane was doing in his music.

After the breakout successes of *Giant Steps* and then the commercial success of *My Favorite Things*, record producer Creed Taylor scored a major coup when he scooped John Coltrane from Atlantic and signed him to his newly established jazz imprint under the ABC-Paramount Records umbrella, Impulse Records. Already a force in the pop world thanks to artists like Paul Anka and Frankie Avalon, ABC-Paramount had recently expanded into jazz, handing Taylor the reins. One of Taylor's first major acts was signing R&B star Ray Charles, pairing him with hotshot arranger Quincy Jones (since returned from Paris) for the breakout smash of *Genius + Soul = Jazz*. Taylor soon followed that up with Coltrane's ambitious debut album for the label, *Africa/Brass*.

For Coltrane, it was a chance to experiment with what historian Ashley Kahn called "an unusual extravagance." His record label not only footed the bill for studio time at Rudy Van Gelder's (now moved from his parents' home out to a new redwood-lined room in Englewood Cliffs, New Jersey), which allowed him time to rehearse in the studio, but it also allowed him to expand his working quartet to a big band of sorts, some nineteen players all told. Credits would list tuba, piccolo flute, two trumpets, two bassists, three euphonium players, and five French horns. The piece would be built from a field recording of African music he had at home. As Coltrane told Ralph J. Gleason: "I have an African record—they're singing these rhythms, some of the native rhythm, so I took part of it and gave it to the bass and Elvin...McCoy managed to find some kind of chords...I had to make the melody as I went along."[5]

An orchestral French horn player named Robert Northern remembered his phone ringing one day in late spring 1961:

> John Coltrane literally called me and I could hardly believe it. I said, "Who is this?" "This is John, man." The date was called for two in the afternoon I believe...almost everybody was there, we couldn't wait to get there. I mean all these cats in there: Bill Barber, Booker Little, I just couldn't wait to get there. Dolphy was the key man, he conducted everything and Cal Massey, the trumpet player, he did some work. I said to Trane: "What you want me to do, Trane?" He said, "Play like an elephant." I'm saying "What??" I had never seen an elephant outside of the Central Park Zoo, so I never heard an elephant. There were no windows.

We started around midnight and we didn't stop until dawn. We were totally transformed to another reality. It was a magical session and it's so vivid. It's like it happened like yesterday. Trane just took us to another level.[6]

For a player who had already made great leaps between *Giant Steps* and *My Favorite Things*, *Africa/Brass* was another bold move forward, auguring what was to come in the years ahead on the Impulse label. At the time, jazz critics sniffed at it, though: "If one looks for melodic development or even for some sort of technical order or logic, he may find none here," said *Down Beat*.[7]

But younger listeners were keenly attuned to what was going on in the music, even if they weren't really the jazz audience. A young California musician, Phil Lesh, told Kahn he was struck by the quality of Trane's playing on that album, which would become foundational for Lesh's band, the Grateful Dead. Folk guitarists Roger McGuinn and David Crosby (in the years before they formed the Byrds) checked out *Africa*. As McGuinn told Kahn:

I was just blown away. I'd heard the more Dave Brubeck-y kind of stuff, but never anything that kind of pushed the envelope. I felt an actual pain in my chest. It wasn't a heart attack or gas pain, it was like some emotional pain, like it was opening up a new emotional area. It hurt at first, and then I liked it.[8]

In Detroit, it had a similar effect. Alice McLeod had already tuned into the emotional power radiating from Coltrane's saxophone, but now she could see how the deep musical wisdom and openness to other cultures was also in play. She had watched her brother learn to master the buzzing sound of the rabab, so the idea of drawing on what the cognoscenti might have deemed "primitive" non-Western instrumentation and ideas (in this case African rhythms on a record) could further such jazz exploration. European classical music didn't corner the marketplace on serious composition. The likes of Yusef Lateef and Ornette Coleman were looking for a way out from under the hierarchy of Eurocentric thought (and its microcosm of American racial repression that elevated Western culture and denigrated African, Latin, and Eastern culture), a way to expand the world of potentiality rather than flatten and constrict it. Coltrane was looking intently to India and Africa to find a deeper resonance and bring it to bear on his own sound.

For Steve Reich, a young student fresh out of Juilliard studying in San Francisco, *Africa/Brass* has a paradigm shift:

> That was by far the most influential on me. Because you have an entire side of an LP in [the key of] E. "What's the changes, man?" "E." "Then what?" "E!" E, for half an hour! That was enormously impressive. What it showed is that you could maintain a harmony for a very long time… At that same time, I was listening to recordings of West African drumming, which doesn't move harmonically but has tremendous rhythmic complexity… All this pointed out the possibility of harmonic stasis.[9]

Coltrane's meditation in E was like the titular subject in Jorge Luis Borges's fantastical short story "The Aleph," a point in space "probably little more than an inch, but all space was there, actual and undiminished. Each thing… was infinite things, since I distinctly saw it from every angle of the universe." Through Trane's horn, you could hover in one place, over a single note, and hear the entire universe. The enthusiasm and sense of unlocking of new vistas that Reich heard was also there in the McLeod living room.

"We were already daily listening to *Africa/Brass* and just marveling at what had happened there," Maupin said. "No one had made a recording like that. You know, with that kind of intensity, with the sounds of animals, and you know, it was just, it was just very different."[10] He added that "some of the things on there, Alice transcribed them on paper and I actually got to play them with her. Yeah, she was that well put together, musically. She was awesome."[11]

But beyond the harmonic innovations, the sense that there was a way that the drone of Indian classical music and West African drumming might fuse with the concepts of jazz improvisation, Alice could discern something else. As she put it in the 1990 documentary *The World According to John Coltrane*:

> I remember upon listening that I felt something beyond the music realm... it was like an inner experience that I had listening to his music. And it was very memorable, very notable... I just seemed to identify with that person, like I was hearing his heart speak or his soul speak, and I related to that.[12]

By 1961, she must have known deep down that bebop—while still a thrill to play—was quickly becoming passé. Bebop's primary characteristics: its challenging chord changes, its swinging drums and walking basslines, its reliance on twelve-bar blues or the standards songbook, its clever quoting of other songs in improvisations—while still popular at bars and nightclubs—had a clear shelf life. Hard bop furthered some of those ideas, but there were still other ideas and areas to explore and embody in jazz. Alice had already been dabbling in writing original music for her piano trio, but under the influence of her brother and the example of Coltrane, she began to think in terms of bigger concepts. Working with Maupin, as well as her former Premiers bandmate George Bohanon, she began writing original compositions for sextet, taking concepts she heard in Coltrane as well as other artists exploring modal approaches to improvisation like Miles Davis and Bill Evans.

Maupin told Franya Berkman that Alice's compositional and improvisational technique, as they were working out these new concepts in her parents' living room, were highly adventurous affairs:

> We had these forms that she had created. And so they would be, like, basically points of departure, but the improvisation that took place inside them was very adventurous. It wasn't like the standard, the AABA

kind of tune like most bebop forms, or a twelve-bar blues, or something like that. I mean, we might have some of those too, but some of the forms were sort of extended, and the structures, just harmonically, were quite different.[13]

According to bassist Cecil McBee, Kirk Lightsey encouraged him to come down to Detroit after college, "because it promised to be a playground of development for both of us. That's where I met Alice McLeod. Every convenient Sunday, she had jam sessions at her house for any musicians who were willing to come over and play for a bit, including those who were more well-known. I met Roy Brooks at one of those jam sessions."[14] McBee remembered the home as "a big Victorian house with a large living room and a lot of space and a grand piano in the center of that room. It was sort of common for folks who were local and those who were passing through to join everybody there at about one in the afternoon on Sundays and play until about 7 or 8."[15] Barry Harris or Elvin Jones might drop in, but the convening was all about the music, not idle chitchat. "Alice was a very personal, serene, tender, gentle person that presented herself to you in very serious fashion pertaining to the music," he said. "But after that she was gone."

In addition to hosting these Sunday sessions, Alice had a trio and also formed a sextet to play this new music she was ideating. The sextet included drummer George Goldsmith; bassist Ray McKinney; Bernard McKinney on euphonium; and Frank Morelli, Maupin, and sometimes Bohanon on sax and trombone. Maupin remembered Morelli as an Italian guy who was a beautician who cut hair and also played with Lateef: "Morelli only has one credit to his name, a hard-blowing baritone sax number called 'Defunk Brothers,' which some suggest may have inspired the legendary Motown backing band to adopt that sobriquet."

George Goldsmith told writer Lewis Porter that the sextet was a cooperatively led group and sometimes Farrow would play bass: "Alice was kind of a fixture around the city. She was a great piano player, she was playing a lot of bebop. And she could play vibes, too."[16] She even wrote a song for Michelle that became the group's set-closing theme song at the classy 20 Grand Lounge on the West Side at 14th Street and Warren Avenue, where they sometimes worked.

According to Maupin, they also played at the Mr. Kelley Lounge on Chene Street on the East Side. Lightsey recalled catching them one night: "It was forward motion. It was with that thought in mind. It wasn't the usual Bud Powell and Charlie Parker Dizzy's, Miles's music, and all of that. It wasn't just that. It was a little bit more freeform. They were stepping out a little further."[17]

Not only were they stepping out a little further than was usual for the astute ears of the Detroit audience, but Alice could even nudge things further into the unknown for her own bandmates. "Some people play it safe. They'll play things pretty much the same each time. Alice never did," Maupin said:

> I mean, when she played, the lines would be uniquely different. And I listened to her enough to know they were different. I knew the lines were different, and it wasn't... she didn't repeat herself just because she knew the particular figure would work in a particular place or something. It was never about that—she was always reaching for something, you know?"[18]

When asked, Bohanon doesn't remember many concrete details about the sextet.[19] He does remember her sensitivity as a player and recalled a tune that wound up being recorded for Roy Brooks's 1964 debut, *Beat*, one of only eight full-length LPs that Gordy's Motown offshoot, Workshop Jazz, released during its brief lifespan. Jazz may have been the only pure art form in Gordy's eyes, but it wasn't moving units like his nascent Tamla/Motown empire was.

Curiously titled "Soulsphere," it's Alice McLeod's first writing credit. It's an uptempo number with three horns that keep the melody aloft— like a puff of air to keep a feather from falling—so that the line keeps rising upward. It's a jaunty, airy bop number of the time. "We used to play that tune," Bohanon said. "I played it with her somewhere, but it's just not ringing a bell."[20] Maupin remembered that they would play "Soulsphere" every time they got together, but when I ask about the sound of the sextet, what the other compositions were, words fail him:

> I can't describe it in words. It was hers. It was unique. As far as I was concerned, it was heaven she was writing every day. We never recorded, but we played a lot of those pieces. For me, the only thing I can equate it to is going to heaven. [*laughs*] It was that good. I learned so much from her. She was so patient and sensitive, to be able to listen to things and to remember them and put them on paper. All I remember is the way it felt. It felt great.[21]

In a newspaper search, the sextet doesn't turn up in any show listings or club ads. There's no mention of them in any weekly columns. Unless some sheet music from 1961 turns up in the family archives, it's unlikely that Alice's first compositional forays will ever be heard. It plays on only in the memories of Maupin and Bohanon.

LIKE ONE OF ALICE MCLEOD'S EARLY CHILDHOOD ASTRAL PROJECTIONS, we now zoom skyward until we are high above 1961 Detroit, fly 650 miles due east, and travel a hundred years or so into the past. That's where, in 1853, the first few bricks of a nondescript five-floor loft walkup were laid down, the beginnings of a building erected at the corner of West 28th Street and Sixth Avenue in New York City. It was registered for commercial purposes by one George E. Hencken.

Even in a cramped city like New York, the brick building felt especially narrow by nineteenth-century standards. Just over a hundred years later—its commercial usage long since forgotten by generations of other owners—this dilapidated spot suddenly became a nexus for the city's local jazz musicians. Pick any night in 1954 and you were liable to see a headlining jazz star or three—as well as dozens of hungry unknown young players looking to make their mark—lug their drum cases and horns up flights of the building's creaky, mildewed stairs to the loft spaces and play until dawn, reverse-commuting amid the squares heading to work in Midtown.

The spot didn't really have a name; most cats would just refer to it as the "jazz loft." It was owned by a war photographer correspondent-turned-photojournalist-turned-obsessive named W. Eugene Smith. Smith, along with trumpeter Dick Cary and Hall Overton, a classical teacher at Juilliard by day, jazz piano teacher and arranger by night. Overton and Smith lived on the third floor of the building and there always seemed to be something cooking in those rooms, whether creative or destructive. Author/historian Sam Stephenson lists just some of the people who came through: Bill Evans, Zoot Sims, Jimmy Giuffre, Roy Haynes, Sonny Clark, Stan Getz, Jim Hall. Miles Davis and Charles Mingus workshopped their one-off collaboration *Blue Moods* there, with Elvin Jones on drums and Teddy Charles on vibraphone. As Charles told one interviewer: "We were just going and having these really free-wheeling, swinging jam sessions. Really cookin'. Nobody's around and you're just among yourself—that's when the best jams happen. You take chances on things."[22] A billionairess and a young composer alike (like Steve Reich) could study with Overton there.

But physical and spiritual decay was also part of life in the jazz loft, as Stephenson described: "The door facing the sidewalk could be unlocked or completely missing—a cave or mine shaft in the dead center of Manhattan—and junkies snuck in, climbed the stairs, and stole things to pawn. Roaches and mice and rats and stray cats loved the place, too."[23]

For newcomers to New York City, it offered the equal forces of allure and repulsion of Gotham in microcosm: brilliant art and music arising out of the minds of speed freaks and junkies; geniuses having to duck the skittering rats in the hallways. And amid the exhaust of the diesel trucks lumbering by and the reek of piled-up garbage, the scent of fresh flowers. Growers out on Long Island would truck their wares into the city and along 28th Street to flower shops that still exist to this day. The center of the jazz universe at the time also served as the center of the fresh flower market in New York City. Like some sort of concrete garden ecosystem, the metal gates would come down over the flower storefronts as jazz players slowly emerged like crepuscular animals. And then come daylight, the cycle would reverse.

As onetime resident Steve Swallow recalled:

> Here were the dregs of the 1950s jazz scene, on their way home at dawn, mixing with the flower-shop owners who were unloading fresh flowers off of flatbed trucks. Dawn was always the best time to smell those flowers. The streets were quiet. The light and the air seemed new. I loved coming out of that loft and smelling those flowers.[24]

While Smith had garnered acclaim for his photorealist style of reportage—from the front lines of the Pacific theater during World War II to the daily life of a country doctor practicing in small-town Colorado—unbeknownst to the musicians who dropped in, Smith had surreptitiously wired the practice spaces, stairwells, and hallways with microphones. In addition to taking some forty thousand photos over that time, Smith also recorded over four thousand hours of audio: not just music but neighborly chitchat as well as street patter from passersby.

It was a speed-fueled quest to try to document the totality and abundance of daily life. Maybe Smith thought he could endeavor his own version of "Akashic records," that theory put forth by nineteenth-century theosophists like Madame Blavatsky, Rudolf Steiner, and Edgar Cayce—and embraced by freethinkers decades on—that on a higher plane than we can comprehend here on Earth, there are these indestructible tablets of astral light that record the life experiences of every human being since time began. Or maybe he was just a documentarian at heart and wanted to capture that spark of creativity, that first thought that kindled the greatest music of his visitors.[25]

By 1961, jazz was changing and that meant that the players stopping in at the loft were also changing. Now you could hear the likes of new arrivals like Ornette Coleman, Don Cherry, Charlie Haden, Roswell Rudd, Joe Henderson, Chick Corea, Joe Farrell, Henry Grimes, Roland Kirk, Albert Ayler, and Steve Swallow on Smith's tapes. In a few years' time, some of them would become generational icons, but here their voices are disarmingly young and fresh; they're just hoping to be heard at all.

In September 1961, a new voice was heard. A new tenant had moved to the fifth floor with her friend Joe Henderson. You can hear the voice of Alice McLeod as she bumped into Gene Smith in the hallway:

> I was coming this way tonight; I was coming from the store. And I saw this man coming down the street. I didn't pay any attention to him. Jimmy went to work and left the door unlocked. So I was coming from the store, and so I turned around and just like, he turned around... I didn't even look at him, but he passed me and... I don't... These people see you like it just looks like you're going into a side place or something, you know, with all these stores and things, you know. But he had seen me coming from the corner, you know. And he walked past the building. And I walked; I was on my way up the stairs, and the... he's... you see this house... or something, so I turned around and he just stood there.[26]

Just what led Alice to come back to New York in 1961 isn't quite clear. But she and Henderson were determined to make it this time. They weren't alone. Fellow Detroiters like Bohanon, McBee, and Wood had also split for New York. Alice's friends Jimmy and Sandy Stevenson had also left Detroit and wound up living on the fifth floor. By September, they had their newborn baby, Jimmy Jr. On another tape from September, you can hear street noise coming in through the open windows as Stevenson and Smith chatted with her:

> When I first moved in here it was nothing but a dope fiend pack of rats up here, all kinds of weird people who were up here when I first came up

here. I mean it was just like, it was open havoc. I mean, it was ridiculous. And I myself changed the lock on it and ordered all those people away from this place. You know, because there wasn't any door downstairs.[27]

Another conversation between Smith, Stevenson, and McLeod also dated from that month, discussing the ethics of amateur tape recording in the loft. Critic Don Heckman, years later, would recall seeing her:

I remember hearing and jamming with her in the early '60s at photographer W. Eugene Smith's loft in Manhattan. At that time she played with a brisk rhythmic style immediately reminiscent of Bud Powell. Like a few other people who'd heard her either at the loft or during her early '60s gigs... I kept hoping she'd take at least one more foray into the bebop style she played so well.[28]

How long Alice might have lived in the jazz loft, in a building where any junkie could walk in day or night unimpeded, isn't clear. Alice didn't bring Michelle with her to New York, leaving her with Ann back in Detroit. Was she trying the Juilliard route one last time? Or trying to situate herself back on the New York scene? The city must have still held something for her. What was she thinking as she traversed the city this time around? How was she going to manage? One wonders what she was feeling as she stepped over winos passed out on the sidewalk, or piles of flowers crushed under truck tires. She would breathe deep, the air an uncanny mixture of car exhaust and sweet, sweet flowers. Her voice doesn't crop up on Smith's tapes after that month.[29]

The next month, Alice's name instead appears back in the Detroit paper. The *Michigan Chronicle*'s "Theatre Notes" column mentioned Monday night sessions going down at the Gold Room at the 20 Grand on the West Side: "Nat Adderley, Ramsey Lewis, Les McCann, Stan Getz, and John Coltrane all in a mellow jamming mood. Locals like George Bohanon, Frank Morelli, two piano girls, Terrie Pallard [sic] and Alice McCloud [sic]."[30]

While tantalizing to think that John and Alice would have interacted on the Gold Room's small stage, it's never hinted at in any other interviews. Maybe they didn't jam that night, but it's a distinct possibility that—after the times that she had gone to his concerts—John Coltrane heard Alice McLeod play that night.

Alice and Bennie Maupin would go see Coltrane again when he next came through Detroit, a weeklong residency in January 1962 at the Minor Key,[31] which used to be an old furniture store. Maupin remembered the night:

> They had an area that you could kind of sit in upstairs, so we were able to get upstairs and sit right in front of the bandstand, so we could look right down at the band. And we sat there all night, you know, and just listened to that music, you know? That was a very special night for us that I'll never forget, because we sat there and we listened to the music. The music just overwhelmed us.[32]

CHAPTER EIGHT

Always

Terry Gibbs had a sixteen-week U.S. tour all booked, but he needed a new band. Just who introduced Alice McLeod to Terry Gibbs, however, is open to interpretation. Franya Berkman said it was Alice's mentor Terry Pollard who told her about the opening with Gibbs's band. Gibbs said it was bassist Herman Wright who suggested Alice. She said it was Ernie who told her about the gig.

Gibbs had a thing for lady pianists, first hiring Terry Pollard for four years and then Pat Moran when Pollard retired from the road. "There was a novelty about having a girl in the band," Gibbs admitted. "But it was *good*! When I wasn't playing, I wanted to listen to somebody play good. That's why I hired them!"[1]

Gibbs also had a penchant for Detroit players, knowing that they had the education, dexterity, and chops to keep up with him and his brand of crowd-pleasing bebop. "When I moved from California to New York, I called Herman because I was going to put a quartet together," he said. "He said there was a girl from Detroit that you may like. It didn't take me more than four bars to know if it was what I'm looking for. I'm a bebop player and anybody who plays with me has to be a bebopper." So he called an audition and booked a room for a few hours at the old Nola Studios on West 54th and Broadway, within view of the original Birdland, with himself, Wright, and drummer

Bobby Pike. At this point in 1962, Alice was back in New York City, as Gibbs clarified: "I didn't see her in Detroit, I saw her in New York. She lived in NYC at that time."[2]

Four bars in, Gibbs knew he had found his new pianist: "Right from the introduction Alice played on the first song, I knew that she was something else. She sounded just like Bud Powell. She played chorus after chorus, and every note was a gem." Terry remembered Alice as "very shy and quiet. In person, she could be funny. Subtle kind of humor but it was funny. She was the most ladylike person I had in my band. Not that the others weren't, but she was really ladylike."[3]

The Terry Gibbs Quartet's first gig was with Gene Krupa at the Metropole Café[4] some ten blocks south of where they rehearsed, and then they hit the road. "The normal tours we did would be going from New York to Syracuse, Rochester, Buffalo, to Toronto to Detroit, out to Ohio or maybe St. Louis, up to Philadelphia," Gibbs said. "That was the circuit."[5]

At some point along the way, William Wood also joined the group. "That was an interesting group," Wood said. "We traveled to the Midwest: Chicago, Ohio, Canada. Terry was popular. He wasn't just a jazz player, he was a showman. He put on a show. A show band is gonna work more than a jazz band. A show in Detroit, you'd have a house band, a shake dancer, and an MC...it was a package."[6] As Alice recalled: "It was a nice time of my life. Some of the music was very serious."[7]

A notice from October 12 had Johnny Mathis in the main room at the Latin Casino in Philadelphia, while the quartet is in the casino's popular Turf Lounge. Three days later, listings in the *Philadelphia Daily News* show the quartet still in residence at the lounge. A ten-minute stroll south down Broad Street would put you at the Douglass Hotel, where John Coltrane and his quintet (he had just brought fellow saxophonist Eric Dolphy into the band) had just started their residency at the Showboat.

The Gibbs Quartet played to full houses and the set always climaxed with Gibbs and McLeod dueting on vibraphone for "Now's the Time."

Gibbs said it went down just like when he did it with Pollard seven years earlier:

> We played that same scene you saw me play with Terry Pollard, but we played it twice as slow. It didn't have to be fast. I showed her all the hand techniques and all the stick. I wasn't looking to wipe her out. I let her play and do her thing, she played a few choruses, then I'd play a few choruses.[8]

Wood remembered that she would get up from the piano midsong and double on the vibes: "They would have a contest, see who could get the most applause. It was a lot of fun."[9]

The Gibbs Quartet had a homecoming in February 1963, pulling in to play at the Grand Bar. "By this time, I taught Alice to play the vibes and she was a natural… Every week she was better than the week before," Gibbs said. "Terry came to the club to see us and I got her to play vibes with Alice and me. The people went nuts."[10] The band headed out west for six weeks of club dates on the West Coast.

Life on the road inherently was a grind, even if you were top billing and packing 'em in at the clubs on both coasts. Gibbs said that in those days:

> Sometimes we would finish the job at a club on a Sunday, three to six p.m., then work till nine till three in the morning. Pack our clothes, then drive to the next job. Get to the job maybe just in time and go right to the job. Go into the bathroom and change our clothes into the suits we wore. I swear to you, it was like somebody doing up eighteen pounds of cocaine. All of a sudden we were up! Our brains were up! It was all about the music; we just wanted to play it.[11]

A teetotaler like Alice had to put up with a lot, not only abstaining as her entire nights were spent inside smoky bars but out on the road as well. Her daughter Michelle said: "She tolerated all kinds of behavior.

There's a story about her standing outside the car freezing because the rest of the band were inside the car smoking a joint."[12]

Still, Alice enjoyed living the jazz musician life. She was living this music and had enough pay to send something home every few weeks. And she loved the challenge of playing bebop, as she told one interviewer:

> You see, Terry was strictly from the bebop era. He knew that in Detroit we were all highly bebop orientated. There was nothing modal or freeform in my background. We came out of Charlie Parker and Dizzy Gillespie, and the musicians we'd formed our styles around were the key local players, Milt and the Jackson brothers, plus Elvin Jones and his family. And I think even today it'd be hard to improve on that bop background. Learning to play that music gives you a strong focus. I learned all the standards, the ballads, everything from the semi-classics to Broadway shows, and it was, if I look back on it, a pretty strategic kind of study. It's paying your dues. All that work goes into forming your own style.[13]

Gibbs had a hot act. But jazz was changing all around him, the landscape growing topsy-turvy out on the road. "We felt we had to be contemporary, we didn't want to be stuck back in the swing era," Wood said. "So it was very natural for us to have discussions around the music because we were serious musicians and we had to figure out how we were going to—yes play in his band—but also have our own expression."[14]

For serious players like Alice and Wood, they began to bristle at the confines of straight playing and silly gimmicks onstage. "Terry Gibbs had a more traditional approach to music. He played more traditional changes and had a more traditional approach to the rhythm," Wood said. "Alice and I were more innovative."[15] Other jazz artists out there were releasing records like *Africa/Brass*, or Eric Dolphy's *Far Cry*, or Sonny Rollins's *The Bridge* and there was a risk of becoming old hat or just left behind. Because of Wood's and Alice's advanced concept of harmony, they would sometimes pull sly moves on the bandstand:

When Terry would finish his solo, she would go into this modal thing. You can take the foundation harmonies and alter it to give it a different sound. Miles did that with Bill Evans. Trane had a song based off the same modality as "So What," called "Impressions." Very fast, but it was just one chord change. It went up a half-step, then back down. So Alice was doing that before some of the other musicians. She had a very innovative concept of harmony. She would change the harmony when she played her solos and she and I would improvise. She taught me what she was doing in private. She would teach me what she was doing in altering the harmony. And Terry knew we were doing *something*, but he couldn't figure it out. It was a funny thing going on.[16]

In late 1962, Gibbs went into the studio with Alice McLeod and some studio players to cut *Hootenanny My Way* for Bob Shad's Time Records imprint. From the title on down, it's a conceptual album that imagines an urbane jazz band doing a residency in a rustic red barn. The song selection is—well—corny, from "John Henry" to Burl Ives's kid-friendly "Polly Wolly Doodle." Yet while the themes of most numbers here suggested someone in a beret playing jazz flute atop a bale of hay, the solos tucked within are intriguingly advanced. Like a kindergarten teacher in a sparkling evening gown, Alice's solo on "Polly Wolly Doodle" feels far more sophisticated than its surroundings. Her intricate right-hand work showcases all she would have gleaned from those afternoons in Bud Powell's living quarters at the Hotel La Louisiane. Same goes for her bars on a conga-laced version of "When Johnny Comes Marching Home." It lasts barely half a minute but sounds beamed in from an obscure Blue Note bop session.

Most fascinating is their version of "Greensleeves," the famous English broadside ballad, first registered in September 1580. Author Eric Nisenson noted that in the 1950s "there was a movement to put greater emphasis on European elements"[17] in jazz, citing the decidedly Eurocentric program music of the era's two most popular jazz groups, the Dave Brubeck Quartet and the Modern Jazz Quartet. An old

English ballad like "Greensleeves" was again becoming part of the folk repertoire in coffeehouses and hootenannies around the country.

But at the start of the 1960s, artists like Harry Belafonte and Miriam Makeba were infusing the American popular music scene with strains of Caribbean and South African fare.[18] Their vision of folk didn't have to just be songs culled from the British Isles. John Coltrane had cut "Greensleeves" for *Africa/Brass*, alighting on that famous air but strapping it to a more powerful engine, suggesting a fusion between Europe and Africa. Alice had deeply studied his ideas on how to approach the old ballad and while Gibbs gives it a mild, swinging midtempo read, Alice's solo is a blur of ideas, as if she's hurrying to fit it all in before the chorus.

Early in 1963, Terry Gibbs and his quartet were doing a residency at Birdland. On that Friday, January 11, they popped over to A & R Studios in New York City, this time with fellow Detroiter Herman Wright joining on double bass. In the spirit of Belafonte and Makeba making folk music that reflected their own heritage, Gibbs drew on his childhood, growing up Jewish way out in Brooklyn. "Everybody was incorporating Latin rhythms in music and growing up in an authentic Jewish neighborhood...that music always fascinated me," he told one interviewer. "Old Jewish musicians never brought music to a job. They always play what they have from the old country that they know. So I wanted to do a date playing authentic things that have never been written out."[19]

The result was *Terry Gibbs Plays Jewish Melodies in Jazztime*, and the songs selected drew on both the traditional Jewish/Eastern European songs and popular Yiddish fare of his childhood, like "Bei Mir Bist Du Schön" and Herman Yablokoff's "Papirossen." It was a festive atmosphere in the studio. Gibbs remembered that Quincy Jones—who did A&R for the date—"showed up wearing a yarmulke and a tallis that Jews wear when they pray in synagogues. What made it even more fun and authentic was that in the middle of the date, Lalo Schifrin, another friend of mine, brought me a box of matzoh."[20] The yarmulke and box of matzoh added to the authentic and relaxed feel in the control room, but in the studio Alice McLeod (erroneously credited as Alice Hagood on the album) was serious about putting her recent musical studies to use and the Phrygian dominant scales underpinning these compositions gave Alice plenty to work with.

Gibbs already noticed how Alice's playing had started to change in the band, detecting John Coltrane's influence: "She was starting to incorporate some of John's harmonic structure in her playing, but she was still playing bebop." Already obsessing over Coltrane's exploration of Eastern modalities, Berkman notes the trancelike intensity of Alice's solos amid the klezmer tunes:

> The bebop idiom clearly pervades Alice's work here. One is immediately aware of the influence of her jazz mentors Barry Harris and Bud Powell, and the dominance of the bebop vocabulary popular among her Detroit peers... She regularly disrupted the formal and metrical aspects of Gibbs's compositions with extended modal passages and rhythmic and melodic motifs played over the bar line. Subdividing and expanding each beat, she achieved enormous feats of virtuosity.[21]

She goes on to contend that while it was only Alice's second full recording date, her solos are "not the work of a young novice, but that of a seasoned musician already disposed toward the emotional, technical, and spiritual intensity [of Coltrane and]...also up to date on the latest rhythmic and harmonic innovations occurring among her peers."[22] In Leonard Feather's review of the album, he also picked up on Alice as being "harmonically advanced and technically an accomplished musician."[23] Even Gibbs had to admit: "Alice actually stole that date from me. She was making those Eastern-style runs on the minor songs and they sounded very authentic. All the Jewish musicians flipped out about how she weaved in and out of those kind of chord changes, those minor chord changes."[24]

The week after the recording, the Gibbs Quartet played at Penn State, and then Alice was back in Detroit for a stand at Grand Bar. On

February 19, Gibbs recorded *The Family Album* with Alice's half brother Ernie on bass. Farrow appeared with them at the University of Notre Dame's Collegiate Jazz Festival at the end of March. Two weeks later, they cut *El Nutto*.

Sometime that summer, William Wood took over bass duties in the band and the Gibbs Quartet was back in New York City in mid-July. They had a weeklong engagement at Birdland with the John Coltrane Quartet.[25] Not that Gibbs was a fan of Coltrane's musical evolution by that point:

> His playing was very extroverted. It seemed like when he played, everything he was hearing in his head came right out of his saxophone...I must admit that I didn't like his playing at that period in his life...this sounded like he was just screeching. It sounded like he couldn't get to the highest note that he was looking for. It seemed like the melodic part of his playing was missing.[26]

In that perception, Gibbs wasn't alone. The critical gatekeeper consensus was that Coltrane had gone so far beyond the pale so as to no longer be playing jazz but rather some abject, indulgent, inchoate noise. *Coltrane "Live" at the Village Vanguard* (recorded in November 1961), with Eric Dolphy, drew such heavy fire from critics that the two reedsmen took to the pages of *Down Beat* to explain their musical philosophies and answer the heretical charge being leveled at them that their playing was now "anti-jazz."

The Impulse albums that Coltrane and his Quartet—pianist McCoy Tyner, bassist Jimmy Garrison, and drummer Elvin Jones—recorded in late 1962 and early 1963 might be seen as a corrective. They recorded with Duke Ellington and singer Johnny Hartman (the same singer the Premiers had once opened for five years earlier), and cut an album of ballads, perhaps as a way to push back on such ridiculous charges: "See, Coltrane isn't a fire-breathing jazz *radical*, just a misunderstood mainstream star upholding the tradition."

By his own account, 1962 had been a rough year for John Coltrane, a time to reassess and recalibrate. As he told writer Frank Kofsky: "That was a funny period in my life, because I went through quite a few changes you know, like home life—everything, man."[27] In 1955, Coltrane had married Juanita "Naima" Grubbs in Philadelphia, with the other members of the Miles Davis band serving as his best men. Grubbs had seen him through the brutal weeks of his heroin withdrawal. She's the subject of one of the most poignant ballads in the history of jazz. But as Coltrane biographer Lewis Porter notes, "As far back as 1958, there were stresses on the marriage." Naima had had two miscarriages and Porter wondered if Coltrane subconsciously "yearned to be a father, and that the absence of new children made for a gap in his married life." As Coltrane's career trajectory was ascendant, his love of music obsessive and all-consuming, Porter also wondered if—as a nonmusician—Grubbs found herself simply having less and less in common with her husband.[28]

Whatever the professional and personal strains weighing on Coltrane, he was as diligent with his music as ever. That first week in July, the John Coltrane Quartet played the Newport Jazz Festival, followed by a week residency at the Showboat in Philadelphia. Now they were back at Birdland, then the center of the jazz world.

Alice had seen John from many rows back at the Olympia Theatre in Paris; then from the wings of the stage and balcony at the Minor Key on the West Side of Detroit; and she had heard him on record and transcribed just what she heard. And now she was about to have a front row seat in the center of the jazz universe to witness its greatest star. "We went on first and afterward I would get a nice seat where I could see and hear him good,"[29] Alice said:

> When I heard his recordings I would hear not only what goes into your intelligence or your senses, your mentality—but also something else, like another message. I connected with this other message. It was like he had to be saying that to me. Of course, that could be just the imagination.

But I was connecting with another message that I perceived as coming though his music.[30]

At Birdland, the table facing the back of the band doubled as the musicians' table. Gibbs would look over and already see that "Alice was really fully in love with what John was playing. She was getting into it, that style of playing."[31] Gibbs likes to take credit and say that after realizing how shy and quiet both Alice McLeod and John Coltrane were as people, he introduced them to one another.

As Wood tells it: "Alice and I would sit together because we were the two Detroiters in Gibbs's band and I knew her from Detroit. John came over and said 'You two make such a nice couple.' [*laughs*] And I went, 'Please sit down, Mr. Coltrane.' And I left. That's where it started. I sorta introduced them."[32]

Who did the introduction? Whoever it was, they would have been the only one speaking. When John Coltrane finally met Alice McLeod, they spoke through their music and knew at once. Who even needed words? How many notes would it have taken for her to know this truth down deep in her soul? She had heard the "other message" in his music and just knew: "I had an inner feeling about him."[33] She knew that his music was in communion with a higher power. And she knew that he knew.

Being at that back table put her in direct communion with his music and vice versa: "When you open for somebody, they checking you out your whole set," Wood said. "He was able to see her level of musicianship. And then, when they follow you, you check them out. I'm sure he checked her out and thought he would put his money on *that*!"[34]

Ask anyone who knew Alice, and the words they most often use are "quiet" and "shy." In that, she had met her equal. Nights passed at Birdland and the two still hadn't really spoken. But every night, the same uncanny feelings Alice had in listening to *Africa/Brass*, in seeing him concertize, surged back stronger than before:

When we were there at Birdland, and he was in performance, that same feeling would come back, like some kind of inner knowing, or recognizing something that I'm hearing, something that I comprehend was associated with my soul or spirit. I would think the first two days it wasn't more than you speak. That's it, "hello." And you just go sit down and don't have anything to say. He was the most quiet person! Quiet as quiet. His silence was loud because it was so pervasive—like he didn't hear anything. This little waiting room that the musicians would sit in before their performance, I don't believe it took up more space than around twelve by five or something. But he would sit there and the quiet was strong. It didn't make you feel isolated, but part of. I identified with it right away. And it was a kind of silence that you don't want to disturb. You don't interrupt with, "Oh, would you like some tea?" You respect it.[35]

Little more than "hello" was exchanged in the cramped confines of Birdland, but the spark was kindled. Alice remembered that it was only "after about three days, we did speak, and I was highly impressed by his calm mannerisms, his beautiful hands, his serene face, eyes and smile, and his soft, gentle voice. I felt wonderful. It was a joy to converse with him. He talked about music, art, architecture, science in terms of Einstein's theory of relativity, yoga, vegetarianism and so much more."[36] But even more than the topics discussed was the music itself. There was the mighty quartet on the bandstand, roaring through material like Cuban percussionist Mongo Santamaría's "Afro Blue" and the modal firestorm "Impressions," as well as Billy Eckstine's swooning, awestruck ballad "I Want to Talk About You."

And then there was this melody Alice heard one day. "I will never forget one particular moment backstage," she said. "I was walking down the corridor and totally unbeknownst to me John was following me with his horn, and he began playing 'Always.' That was John's tender and charismatic way of expressing his thoughts through song." No doubt Irving Berlin's lyrics resonated within her:

For the longest while / I'd forget to smile / Then I met you
Now that my blue days have passed / Now that I've found you at last
I'll be loving you always / With a love that's true always.

She turned around to compliment him, their eyes locking, dancing in that held gaze. "He said, 'It's for you!' I said, 'Thank you very much. It is so beautiful!'" Alice said. "From that moment on, from the moment that words were shared and exchanged by the end of the week, well...it was the termination of my time with Terry Gibbs."[37]

Not *quite* yet. Terry Gibbs's quartet was back on the road, this time for a week's residency at the Crawford Grill in Pittsburgh. Then on to the next city. But Coltrane would travel to wherever they were playing. "John would come to visit us on the road when he was off," Gibbs remembered. "John came on the road a few times and got his own room. There was no hanky-panky between the both of them! Without a doubt, I saw two people falling in love. He was awful shy, so both of them talked to each other, it took a half hour for each one to say the next word."[38] Out on the road, John and Alice read about the March on Washington, looked at the photos of the 250,000 people gathered peacefully. He read Dr. Martin Luther King Jr.'s speech and marveled at its message of hope and unity in such uncertain times.

In early September, John Coltrane moved out of Naima's house and—bags not quite unpacked—the John Coltrane Quartet was back on the road, pulling into Buffalo and Cleveland. The first two weeks of October, the quartet returned to Birdland. Recordings made on the 8th wound up being issued as *Live at Birdland*. When John couldn't be in the same city as the Terry Gibbs Quartet, he was on the phone with Alice. "I Want to Talk About You" indeed. "When we really actually met, it was really like two friends that had known each other many, many years, like meeting again," Alice said of those whirlwind weeks after Birdland:

It was so beautiful. And so everything on my agenda stopped. He said, "You are concertizing with this group, but I would like you to get permission from your mother to travel with me wherever I'm going around the world." So I told him that if I got my mother's permission and blessings that I would leave that group and I would travel with him. So I called her and she gave her permission.[39]

Meanwhile, the Terry Gibbs Quartet had just landed their most plum gig yet, at Chicago's famous London House. The likes of George Shearing, Errol Garner, Oscar Peterson, and Nat King Cole often held residencies there, Gibbs said. "And she came to me about a week before and said, 'Terry, John wants me to go to Sweden with him.' *Noooo!*"[40]

On October 22, Alice McLeod boarded a flight with John Coltrane and the rest of the band. A whirlwind two-week European tour of Sweden, Finland, Denmark, and Amsterdam began, as did their whirlwind romance.

"Alice was one of the nicest people who ever worked for me," Gibbs said, and then asked a rhetorical question as if knowing the formidable power he was up against. "How do you stop a woman in love from doing anything?"[41]

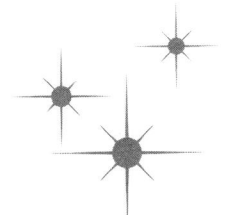

PART 2

Alice Coltrane

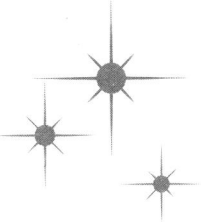

CHAPTER NINE

Your Lady

HATE TRIGGERED CHURCH BLAST KILLS 4 LITTLE GIRLS
The headlines horrified. On September 15, 1963, Ku Klux Klan operatives planted nineteen sticks of dynamite under the stairs at the eastern entrance of the 16th Street Baptist Church in Birmingham, Alabama. The explosion injured dozens of parishioners and killed four young girls: Addie Mae Collins, Denise McNair, Carole Robertson, and Cynthia Wesley. But when was Alabama and the Deep South not in the news? There was the ghastly beating of Freedom Riders in Birmingham in 1961, then the jailing of Martin Luther King Jr. in April 1963 when he organized protests and marches aimed at addressing that city's severe segregation. And then on the nightly news, every American household could tune in and see Birmingham's commissioner of public safety, Bull Connor, giving the order to blast young Black people with firehoses.

Horrifying as it was to read in newsprint and to witness it in vivid black and white on television, such violence would have come as little surprise to Alice, who knew from the stories of her mother and father the brutal segregation they experienced as children in Alabama. And she had her own young memories of the Belle Isle Riots, where even the holy sanctuary of the church was no bulwark against the hatred that lay in some men's hearts. John was in turn stirred by King's speech, given in the church sanctuary barely three days after the tragedy, and began to compose a new song, working on it in the weeks after hearing the news.

On November 18, Coltrane took his band to Van Gelder's to record two songs, "Your Lady" and "Alabama." The former was written especially for Alice—based on the phrase that Naima used to refer to her—and the latter was based on King's speech. Writer Ben Ratliff noted that Coltrane used the rhythmic inflections of King's delivery as the melodic basis for "Alabama," the resultant ballad both a high point of his entire catalog and a true snapshot of the nation's psyche: "If anyone wants to begin to understand how Coltrane could inspire so much awe so quickly, the reason is probably inside 'Alabama'... [which] is also an accurate psychological portrait of a time, a complicated mood that nobody else could render so well."[1] Its recording came four days before President John F. Kennedy was assassinated in Dallas, Texas. The country, grieving, teetered on the brink.

"Alabama" *is* a political statement, but not in the manner one expects. The moment you hear Coltrane, it outstrips the confines and connotations of that word. Coltrane was no doubt inspired by King's example, but not in terms of writing a song to serve as a rallying cry or anthem. It's as honest an expression of grief, empathy, anger, and sympathy as anything that the minister and activist himself could deliver. And like King, Coltrane also perceived a redemptive force at work beyond such tragedy. In a radio interview, Alice was asked if she saw John as being a political force or using his music platform to convey a political message:

> Never was. Never. And I think that's really the makings of a true musician, when he can—even though he's in sympathy with what the movements be, you know—not to react. He could have easily done it. There's so many people, even artists who left their own profession who were really talented and gotten involved in these politics. Not that... We all sympathize—everyone is in sympathy with the movement—but see the only thing is there are real leaders, like King and Malcolm X, qualified leaders to lead in a political movement. But not some of these musicians

and other artists who God has concentrated the energies in a more artistic way. And they laid it aside to attempt to direct and lead people. But John was never guilty of this. The song "Alabama" is *sympathy*. That's all it is. You can even detect it, if you listen carefully. You can't even *feel* that it's a political motive, it's all sympathy, it's all that. He expressed his *own* sorrow behind the death of these children.[2]

The bombing would serve as catalyst for grassroots groups as they increased their push for civil rights in the years ahead. Sides would be drawn and powerful—sometimes deadly—forces would be set into motion. Already, jazz artists saw themselves as being spokespeople as well. Charles Mingus, Max Roach, and the like would turn increasingly vocal about their demands for equality. Mingus's "Fables of Faubus" cussed out Arkansas's bigoted governor Orval Faubus, who had called in the National Guard to prevent the racial integration of the public schools in his state. Max Roach's *We Insist* featured on its cover a group of Black men at a sit-in at a white lunch counter, and the powerful music within was just as unapologetic.

The next generation of jazz artists coming up on the scene were increasingly militant about Black Power, and the sounds they could elicit from their horns broke free of the perceived rules of jazz. If Coleman, Taylor, and the like could get rid of those polite swinging rhythms, the underlying ABA structures, and tricky chord changes, then notes and melody were next for the chopping block. The revolution was coming.

Coltrane was in alignment with such feelings of seething anger and anguish, but he understood that his role as a musician was to provide succor and uplift, to find a way to convey that tumult of conflicted feelings, that "complicated mood," in a way that didn't have actual words, but spoke to people nevertheless. Alice went on to explain:

Some musicians will tell you "Yes, I'm angry" and "I use my instrument to get these feelings off of me." They will tell you this. I'm in sympathy with that, too. If that's the way you feel and this is the only way you can feel you're doing your part, then okay. John never ever used his instrument to incite or to make people to get up and get together and do our thing. It was always out of his own love and own sympathy for what had happened.[3]

In December 1963, Alice accompanied John and his band out to the West Coast. They played live on KQED-TV in San Francisco and then did a two-week residency at Shelly's Manne-Hole in Los Angeles, before flying back to New York City for Christmas and a New Year's Eve concert at the barely two-year-old Philharmonic Hall at Lincoln Center with the likes of Cecil Taylor, Albert Ayler, Art Blakey's Jazz Messengers with Wayne Shorter, Freddie Hubbard, Curtis Fuller, Cedar Walton, Reggie Workman, and Eric Dolphy. It was a time of great merriment.

Sometime that month, John and Alice conceived their first child. Did they know that good news as they rang in the New Year uptown? Or know that the Philharmonic stage would be the last time John Coltrane would ever see his close friend and collaborator Eric Dolphy alive?

JOHN COLTRANE WAS IN LOVE. DEEPLY, BLISSFULLY, GRATEFULLY. His first child was on the way and he brimmed with unadulterated joy: for his lady, for his family-to-be, for God. To look outside was to see the world teetering at the edge of chaos. But in his heart, he felt a sense of stability and fulfillment in himself he hadn't known these past few years. His prayers had been answered.

And Alice was just as deeply in love: "When I met John, I was more interested in knowing what married life would be like; I wanted to experience that. It was very easy. I didn't walk in the shadow."[4] After years as a working musician scraping to get by, doing her best to provide for her daughter while on the road, doing what she could to erase the memory of her disastrous first marriage, now she knew the kind of love and devotion that her own parents had for each other.

In the same way that he provided for Naima's daughter from a previous marriage, John opened his heart immediately to young Michelle (or Miki, as was her nickname), now three years old. He couldn't contain his gratitude toward Alice, toward God. A handwritten note he left for her dated January 6, 1964, reads:

> good morning my dear-another new day. Another new chance to share in gods great story. {to be to give} don't forget to be kind to be forgiving to be helpful—to be strong & just & to be fair. Pray & give thanks. You are born again. Work & love. You are born anew.[5]

It seemed like every morning, Alice would wake up to a note or poem left by John. Another one read: *How kind you are to me-to give-the universe revealed I see / Yes now I'll go to sleep it's right, sweet—I rest in peace / At night-*

The inspiration that poured through him on the bandstand could also flow through his pen at home. Ashley Kahn described these little notes: "They read sincerely and simply, and could be interpreted equally as declarations of personal adoration or as expressions of spiritual love."[6] Much in the same way that he could hear the music when MLK spoke at the lectern, Coltrane began to hear a melody wind through his attempts at poetry.

They wouldn't officially marry for another three years, but in their hearts and in the eyes of God they were already husband and wife, and the couple were already home-shopping for their imminent family. They liked a house out on Long Island. Without traffic, John could be in the city or in Englewood Cliffs, New Jersey, in an hour. Yet from the house, situated on three acres, you couldn't hear the Long Island Expressway at all. You could wander the yard and imagine you were way out in the country. When they finally closed on that house at 247 Candlewood Path in Dix Hills, Alice set to work on making it into a home.

Alice was everything John could have hoped for in a partner. She was as knowledgeable and obsessed with the music as he was, as rooted in her faith as he was, ready and willing to start a family with him. They could pass hours in the living room without saying a word yet also feel like a long, inspired dialogue—all unspoken—had transpired between them. At times, she could feel what he was thinking and vice versa. But in matters of God or a book he was reading or how to approach a particular scale, they could also converse for hours on end. She understood his quest to realize the divine in this music. Their preternatural calm was amplified in the other's presence. As John basked in this new love, it all seemed foreordained somehow for him: Alice was also the name of his mother and of his maternal grandmother. "Alice seems to be a calm personality who created a kind of maternal, protective world for John," Lewis Porter said. "Surely, at some level, conscious or not, this added to the appeal that she held for him. And with Alice he satisfied his desire for children. Equally important, she was a fine musician who could fully participate in his career."[7]

Alice couldn't have been happier. She knew that being a wife and homemaker would mean not performing, but she was all too ready to accept that mantle, to keep home for John. "There was no more question about direction," she said about when they got together. "Yes, it is a very positive, high energy that manifested itself. He, I felt brought out the best in me musically: as a woman, his wife, mother of his children."[8]

But in the back of her mind, Alice was worried about news from back home. "The Stained Glass Window," a church column in the *Michigan Chronicle*, ran a notice on January 18: "Annie McLeod is back home after being confined to the hospital the past few weeks." Her mother had long been ill and her health was failing.

After a month off the road, John Coltrane played a two-week stand at McKie's in Chicago, followed by a week in Montreal, then a week in Toronto, before coming home for an extended stand at the Half Note. In April, he would also play with Sonny Rollins and vocalist Sheila Jordan at the Five Spot as part of a benefit for the Congress of Racial Equality (CORE).[9] The next day, Coltrane took his group across the

Hudson River to commence work on a new album based around a new composition, *Crescent*.

Home was their sanctuary and the couple were very private. John Coltrane would practice at all hours of the day and night. Stories abound about the saxophone being in bed with him when he finally turned in for the night. Their music room in their new home was expansive, their collection of instruments burgeoning. "He would pick up the closest thing and play it, like a flute early in the morning," Alice remembered. "He would practice drums, playing his horn while doing the bass pedal of the drums."[10]

John's weight constantly fluctuated and at home, he tried his best to adhere to a healthy diet. Alice recalled that John "liked grains, cereal, raw juices. He used to get this blender and grind all his stuff."[11] But in addition to a sweet tooth and love of sweet potato pie, he also had a tendency toward fad diets and the like. During the *Africa/Brass* sessions, trumpeter Freddie Hubbard recalled seeing Coltrane and Dolphy "drink honey out of the jars. They would eat those sunflower seeds and raisins. They were on an energy kick. I said, 'Man, you're going to get diabetes or something, man! You drinking raw honey?'"[12]

It was unfortunately a tragic foretelling. In Dolphy, Coltrane found a peer whose curiosity, passion, intelligence, and questing nature to understand all he could about his muse mirrored his own. Dolphy was a musical polymath who not only mastered alto sax, bass clarinet, and flute but also intently studied twentieth-century composition, familiar with the works of Charles Ives, Olivier Messiaen, Anton Webern, and Alban Berg. Critic Richard Brody once wrote: "For all its cerebral majesty, Dolphy's playing was also noise music, a visceral blast of musical energy."[13] That quality led to the scathing responses to the music that Coltrane and Dolphy made together in 1961, affecting the latter professionally and personally for many years. And while their collaboration was sadly truncated, it freed up Coltrane's own playing.[14]

On June 27, Dolphy traveled to West Berlin to play but fell seriously ill upon his arrival and collapsed onstage. He was rushed to the hospital, but his condition worsened. Much like Coltrane did after kicking heroin in 1957, Dolphy also embodied a clean lifestyle, and he didn't drink, smoke, or use drugs. But to the attending staff at the German hospital, the jazz stereotype preceded him; an American Black jazz musician who had fallen ill was surely a heroin addict who had overdosed, in the eyes of the nurses. They left him in his bed to let the drugs run their course, never thinking there was another possibility: Dolphy had fallen into a diabetic coma. Left untreated, he died in the hospital two days later.

Coltrane and the rest of the jazz community were grief-stricken. "I can only say my life was made much better by knowing him," he said. "He was one of the greatest people I've ever known, as a man, a friend, and a musician." Later, Dolphy's mother would gift Coltrane his flute and bass clarinet, which would be set in the family music room. On the road, Coltrane always carried a photo of his dearly departed friend, hanging it in every hotel room.[15]

Much like Dolphy, Coltrane was a wide and avid listener. If you had ducked into the Village Vanguard during that residency back in November 1961, you might have found yourself ensorcelled by a buzzing, mesmerizing, seemingly endless piece of music that never moved off the G pedal point. Coltrane performed on soprano sax while Eric Dolphy played bass clarinet, their two reeds weaving like double helixes in the upper registers of their horns in a manner that mirrored the double bass work of Jimmy Garrison and Reggie Workman (utilizing his bow to make more of a drone) rumbling in the low end. (A similar sort of pedal point also powers lengthy explorations like "Africa" and "Olé.") On any given night, they would take flight and that piece could last between ten and fifteen minutes as Coltrane's short, repeated, yet evolving phrases would resemble the runs of Indian sitar. The piece was titled "India," and one of those Vanguard performances opened Coltrane's 1963 album *Impressions*, making clear the impact of North Indian music on his sound.

The purpose of music in African and Indian cultures also differed from its role as a form of entertainment in the West. John Coltrane was performing in nightclubs where the liquor and good times were flowing, but he increasingly saw his music as being the means to a far greater end, and the very dynamic between performer and audience began to change. Coltrane's saxophone wasn't just there to give you a familiar tune to only nod along to; he was now imploring you to make this inner voyage, to plumb the unknown with him, wherever that might lead. In a setting suited to casually sipping a highball or martini while being entertained, Coltrane offered a waterfall instead. You could no longer be a passive listener in your seat. You were now bidden to also take the trip.

Those longer solos that defined Coltrane's last tour with Miles Davis now became something beyond a surfeit of ideas: "His solos became even longer, as he began reaching still deeper inside his soul and psyche for his inspiration. His audiences felt either mesmerized or assaulted, but were never apathetic [witnessing] the experience of watching a man create, at a fierce tempo, an hour or hour-and-a-half solo."[16] Elvin Jones remembered that during one matinee performance they played one piece for over three hours, giving the audience far more than they bargained for.

"There were so many cultures of music that he listened to," Alice said. "I cannot say which one that he would state 'This is my favorite,' 'This is my highest inspiration.' He listened to so much music. I mean music from Buddhist temples, like the bells from their temple worship. Japanese music he listened to, the shakuhachi and koto and some of their beautiful instruments. He listened to their spiritual music and music for worship. Again, music of Africa and the classical music of Brazil. He researched, he investigated all the musics of the world, because he knew that everyone had something."[17]

Albums on the Folkways and Lyrichord labels held particular interest for him. The scholarly liner notes included in the albums would situate the music and tradition of these far-flung field recordings and provide references that a thoughtful seeker such as Coltrane could use to dig deeper into a distant culture, all from the comfort of home. Composer and jazz scholar Bill Bauer believed that the inspiration for this particular Coltrane composition stemmed from a recording of a Vedic chant that was issued on a Folkways album.[18] And if Coltrane dug into the notes, he would learn that these Vedic chants originated from the Vedas, the religious books of India that began to circulate on the subcontinent around 1500 BCE. No doubt Coltrane would have next gone in search of such texts himself to understand better where this music originated.

"I've already been looking into those approaches to music—as in India—in which particular sounds and scales are intended to produce specific emotional meanings," he told Nat Hentoff:

> I would like to bring to people something like happiness. I would like to discover a method so that if I want it to rain, it will start right away to rain. If one of my friends is ill, I'd like to play a certain song and he will be cured; when he'd be broke, I'd bring out a different song and immediately he'd receive all the money he needed. But what are these pieces and what is the road to travel to attain a knowledge of them, that I don't know. The true powers of music are still unknown. To be able to control them must be, I believe, the goal of every musician.[19]

That curiosity soon led him to explore and better understand the religious thought behind the incidental or ceremonial music he was hearing on these albums. And that led Coltrane away from the hierarchal mindset that European classical music was the pinnacle of human musical expression, and therefore everything else in the world was primitive and pagan. Nisenson wrote:

> The most profound concept of non-Western music for Coltrane was its cyclic, rather than linear, nature. Viewing the flow of music, as well as human life itself, in terms of cycles seems incompatible with a linear, Aristotelian worldview. These cycles, like the rounds of an infinite spring or a Möbius strip, have no beginning or end, no outside or inside... By looking toward Africa and India for his inspiration and using the most

profound aspects of their aesthetic outlook in the creation of his own music, he made a tremendous contribution toward black pride. He demonstrated that a serious musician did not have to look for inspiration only in the European musical tradition.[20]

Leading by example, Coltrane began to turn the trend away from the popular model of the Modern Jazz Quartet, which conceptualized jazz as a high art form that could emulate Western classical music. In doing so, Coltrane subtly reinforced the concept of Black pride in his own effective, nondemonstrative manner: "His involvement in the music of non-Western countries was clearly a statement about the value of non-European cultures, particularly those of Africa and India... he simply made clear the equal value of non-Western art."[21] And as he questioned the Western perception of the world surrounding him, it inevitably led him to look closer at his own religious upbringing.

"He had such a beautiful appreciation of all cultures," Alice said. "It was mainly in a musical and artistic way, but even though he was looking at the contributions musically, he also looked at their spirituality."[22] There's speculation as to who introduced John Coltrane to the Holy Quran, whether it was Yusef Lateef or Naima, herself a devout Muslim. Coltrane himself never converted, but the Quran kindled an interest in looking at the religions from India and Africa, so as to better understand the greater concepts just beneath the surface of—yet wholly informing—the music.

His maternal grandfather, the Reverend William Blair, was a minister at the African Methodist Episcopal Zion Church in High Point, North Carolina, and he grew up in the church there and in Philadelphia. And with increased exposure to other cultures and other concepts about God, he began to read and study more. Was there a right religion, a right God? The more he read, the less sense it made. "I was disappointed when I found how many religions there were," Coltrane said. "When I saw there were so many religions... it screwed up my head. And, I don't know. I was kinda confused... and I just couldn't believe that just one guy could be right. Because if he's right somebody else got to be wrong, you know?"[23] Coltrane had more questions.

Asking questions is foundational to Western thought, from the catechism of Christianity to Socratic dialogues, but by the 1960s, the long-rooted religious identities of generations prior began to change in the wake of two world wars and greater social mobility. How to come to grips with a God who would allow the death of millions in his name? What God would allow such atrocities and cruelty to occur? Generations prior, your local church would have bound you in terms of class, locality, and ethnicity, but as more people moved for better economic opportunities, the fabric of the faith began to stretch and fray. Berkman noted that religious practice in the 1960s became more inwardly focused, as the search for meaning meant exploring an inner world. Christianity seemed to be running out of answers during an era that theologian Gayraud Wilmore called "an unprecedented era of black theological reflection."[24]

Just as Coltrane kept his public life as a jazz star and his personal family life distinctly separate, he also kept his political and religious beliefs close to the vest. Even though he played with Coltrane for many years, McCoy Tyner mentioned he went to their new Dix Hills home on Long Island on only one occasion. Once John and Alice were settled in, there's no instance of a writer being invited out to profile John in his home, no glossy magazine spreads of him lounging around the house.

Even without such insight, a jazz critic might look at the relationship between an established jazz luminary and a younger pianist and presume an unequal power dynamic between mentor and disciple, or worse still, star and hanger-on. That distorted perception would crop up in reviews in the years ahead. In most Coltrane biographies, the index reveals multiple entries for Coltrane's first wife, Naima, yet very little mention of Alice.

According to Berkman, "it was an intimate and complex marital partnership, in which family life and religious exploration provided a foundation for their mutual development. In fact, I believe that John

Coltrane's biographers have significantly underestimated Alice's deep influence on him as a partner."[25]

To look at the recorded history of John Coltrane is to bear witness to the transformation that meeting Alice immediately manifested on his own music. Whether or not John Coltrane recorded mellow, classicist, enchanting though middle-of-the-road albums to serve as a course correction after the "anti-jazz" controversy surrounding his work with Dolphy or to further explore his "gentle side," he was emboldened the instant Alice entered his life. From that life-changing meeting at Birdland, he would intently, fearlessly, resolutely move forward without ever looking back.

There's an incandescence to this version of "Afro Blue" that's captured on *Live at Birdland*, the Impulse album he recorded mere months after that fateful July residency at the club, Coltrane downright ebullient when he soars off in solo. It's balanced by the profound pathos of "Alabama." Whatever tentativeness or doubt about being misunderstood he might have held was eradicated. The strength and solace he found at home with Alice emboldened him to go higher, deeper, further than he or any other jazz musician of the time could imagine. "I feel that it was always in him being born with this gift, this God-given gift of music; that it was there," Alice said. "And of course, [with our] association, it fully manifested; there was no more question about direction. Somehow he was also inspired to bring out the avant-garde music."[26]

The latent spiritual force behind Coltrane's music rose to the fore now. "I know that his grandfather was a preacher, and he came from that experience," fellow saxophonist Wayne Shorter said.[27] On the bandstand, those lengthy solos became more like sermons, incantations, sounds that could transcend chord changes and instead penetrate the heart of the audience. Impressionable young listeners who picked up on the vibrations of *"Live" at the Village Vanguard*'s "Spiritual" began to think of Trane as less a jazz superstar and more like a jazz guru.

"When I first met Trane, it was three years before he met Alice, in 1961, he was still with Juanita," remembered saxophonist Archie

Shepp. "When he was with Nita, it was more a family arrangement. When he was with Alice, his life and their lives became centered around music. With Alice, he became even more spiritually engaged with the music. Within that quartet, he created what became for me a new music. Like Bach and Mozart, Coltrane actually raised this music from the secular to an area of serious, religious world music. It was like being in church."[28]

John Coltrane became a vegetarian, and jazz photographer Valerie Wilmer remembered that "it was the first time I had ever met anyone who talked about health concerns, and a far cry from the popular image of the wild, drug-crazed jazz musician beloved of the press... [through Coltrane] I began to discover a new way of looking at the world as well as the music."[29]

Alice witnessed firsthand John's deepening search for meaning:

> It took him into science and math and checking out people like Einstein. The science thing just took him to a point. Even scientists when they get to the atom, that's it. That's the bottom, the basic reality, that atom. There's no point beyond that. *Something* had to create that first atom. *Something* had to give it all of its structure. So science comes to that point and that's it. This is when his thinking turned to "Well, what created that? What is the cause of this?" It took him out of science and into religion.[30]

He read widely and could discuss different theological ideas with others, be it Egyptology with Sun Ra or the Rosicrucians with Sonny Rollins. John picked up Paramahansa Yogananda's *Autobiography of a Yogi* as well as the writings of Mahatma Gandhi and J. Krishnamurti. Sun Ra turned him on to Sufi teacher Hazrat Inayat Khan's *The Mysticism of Sound and Music*. A new jazz player on the scene, Lonnie Liston Smith, recalled finding that particular book in the basement of the East Village's occult bookstore Weiser Books, where he also saw Ra and

Coltrane browsing the shelves.[31] Coltrane was known to carry around a book by British occultist Mabel Collins titled *Light on the Path: A Treatise Written for the Personal Use of Those Who Are Ignorant of the Eastern Wisdom, and Who Desire to Enter Within Its Influence* as well as the work of another British female philosopher, L. C. Beckett's *Neti Neti (Not This, Not That)*, a slim book that sought connections between quantum physics and Eastern mystic thought.

For a seeker like Coltrane, this search for spiritual meaning might also entail doing away with the Christianity forced on Black people dating back to their arrival in the New World as enslaved people. As historian Melani McAlister noted, there was a political dimension to Black Americans' interest in non-Western religions, a means to find "alternatives to official policy, framing transnational affiliations and claims to racial or religious authority that challenged the cultural logic of American power," adding:

> The attempt to construct a new black culture was deeply intertwined with the search for religious alternatives to mainstream Christianity, a search that included not only Islam, but also a renewed interest in the signs and symbols of pre-Islamic and traditional African religions (such as the Yoruban religion) and the study of ancient Egypt. These influences were often mixed together... in an eclectic, sometimes deliberately mystical, mix.[32]

John Coltrane didn't stop believing in the concept of God that he grew up with in the African Methodist Episcopal church, but he expanded his concept of what God was, seeing not the vindictive, restrictive God of the Old Testament, but a far greater, more benevolent universal force instead. He checked out Zen, Zoroastrianism, Sufism, Egyptology, and other things beyond the Judeo-Christian monotheism of his youth. He could see these other paths, other religions, and perceive that they all led up to the same thing. There were many paths to get to the top of the mountain.

With John's help, Alice began to explore these other ways of thought as well. Alice perceived her way of thinking about her faith and herself "like an ordinary person," adding:

> In this country, you just have Western teachers, you have Western thinking, you have the Bible and whatever books come out of Western culture. So I really wasn't into anything before he started saying: "Well, Alice, why don't you check out this book?" Why don't you read this book by this Swami? Read this book by this teacher, read this book on Egypt." This got my thinking from out of such a one-way kind of thinking. It was such a local thinking; it got me into a more universal concept.[33]

John had already adopted a daily meditation practice and shared it with Alice. He taught Alice how to meditate as well. In that practice, Alice began to realize a greater profundity about God. "He liked to meditate and we used to meditate together," she said. "I think it started with him, because I was born into a Christian family; I spent many years in the church. And it wasn't so much a turning away from that, as it was a direction that I was given to follow."[34]

Even with her steadfast, rigorous religious upbringing at Mt. Olive Baptist Church, Alice began to realize that God existed well beyond the church walls, that the rituals and ceremonies of the church paled in the light of the truly divine:

> Even people into religion, they can't realize some kind of an Absolute. They can't form it. They can't imagine it. But they're into religion. People with teachers cannot get themselves to realize an absolute cause. I know there's something motivating me, there's something that motivates the universe. I know that there's some order that makes the sun revolve with the planets. There's something in that man preventing him from realizing there's an absolute cause for the whole thing.[35]

As the couple began to meditate together, John's inward enlightenment began to emanate outward with greater clarity and purpose in concert. Asked by an interviewer if John's music was an expression of the absolute, Alice replied:

> I think so. It came out of his own experience. All of his music is relating—through music—his own experience. This is why you saw the change. You saw an ordinary man gifted, but he played from his environment, from what was happening in an outward way. When he got into religion, he saw things from a more universal, a more transcendental level that was beyond his own environment.[36]

The spark that he had long felt in his heart when concertizing on the bandstand became increasingly clear as he and Alice meditated together, studied, played, prayed, and read some more. Berkman noted that Coltrane's personal philosophy rested on three basic tenets:

> First, music making is based on personal spiritual expression, and the artist should be fully committed to expressing an authentic self as a musician. Second, music making should be universal, erasing aesthetic boundaries and proscriptions about style. And third, such musical universal—it requires branching out: it is inclusive, pluralistic, and multicultural.[37]

Music was the means to celebrate God and give thanks. Now the challenge for John Coltrane was how to put all of these concepts into his music in a way the world would understand.

CHAPTER TEN

Song of Praise

IN THE WANING DAYS OF WORLD WAR II, WHILE HE WAS STILL enlisted in the navy, a little melodic fragment would come to John Coltrane. He would forget about it, then happen upon it again every few years, a little spark of an idea not yet fully formed. He might be on the bandstand and that four-note phrase would pass by in a cascade of notes, but then he would lose sight of it again. John struggled to grab hold of this kernel. "When he was in the navy, he had a vision that he couldn't interpret at that time," Alice told author Ashley Kahn. "It was just beyond him, and he didn't know who to turn to who could provide any clarity to it."[1]

Saxophonist John Slate, then a busboy at a jazz club in Boston, recalled the first time he heard this four-note melody:

> When Coltrane came in it was really unique: Jimmy Garrison fell down the steps with his bass and they had to get another bass. And Elvin was there with the two Dobermans, and McCoy was playing piano. Before the gig even started, Trane was in the bathroom, just woodshedding. He was practicing these chromatic patterns and [sings theme to "Acknowledgement"]. And they got up and played what ended up being parts of *A Love Supreme* for almost an hour set.[2]

It had been a hectic summer for John Coltrane. John and Alice closed on the Dix Hills house on July 6, and they promptly began moving. The quartet also had a two-week stand in Chicago. They would combust onstage each night, then go back to the hotel to see news of the riots happening in Harlem. An off-duty white police officer shot and killed fifteen-year-old James Powell and the streets erupted in protests with increasing violence. The animus in Harlem spread to Bedford-Stuyvesant and Brownsville in Brooklyn and then to South Jamaica, Queens, then up to Rochester, and later to Jersey City, Elizabeth, and Paterson, New Jersey, the kindling of these inner city ghettos catching fire. Alice was at home with Michelle, unpacking boxes, setting up their home, and getting through the heat of summer in the final weeks of her pregnancy as best she could. The expectant mother worried about the kind of world she was bringing her child into, wondering if there might ever be peace.

Everywhere the John Coltrane Quartet went in their Chrysler station wagon, the cities seemed to be sweltering, from the summer heat and the festering resentment of inner-city neglect. The civil rights March on Washington had drawn a huge crowd the year prior, yet the government had done little other than ignore it. Malcolm X continued to speak out on the harsh inequality of the country. Vietnam was barely mentioned on the nightly news and the peacetime economy flourished everywhere, except in these ghettos. Coltrane returned to New York City for a week at Birdland (with Les McCann and singer Irene Reid on the bill), then headed out to San Francisco for two weeks at the Jazz Workshop. Three days of driving later, they were back on the East Coast at the Half Note.

The penultimate night there, Alice went into labor. On August 26, 1964, she bore John Coltrane a son, John William Coltrane Jr. The next day, Alice turned twenty-seven and celebrated her birthday in bed, nursing her newborn. "One of my warmest memories is of [John] holding our first son," Alice recalled. "I do not think any mother could have held a child more gently."[3] Even as he heard about the rioting and police brutality going down less than a mile away from where he grew up on N. 33rd Street in Philly, John knew firsthand the supreme joy of fatherhood.

Coltrane felt true contentment. He had all he could have ever asked for from God, as both a jazz musician and a man. He was madly in love with Alice, the loving wife who just bore him a son. He had a new home with a huge yard and a German shepherd and plenty of space for expanding their new family. For a man who grew up in rural North Carolina and was often called "country" by his friends and family, he had accomplished that American Dream often closed off to people of color: he had attained the comforts of the middle class, both for himself and for his wife, who grew up in the ghettos of Detroit. He had attained a level of jazz stardom and financial stability that few others could have ever imagined. "He was a sort of reflective person, a kind of meditative individual. I can understand him being at peace," McCoy Tyner said. "He was very happy there."[4] The home, the family, the love of Alice, it was all due to God, and Coltrane was deeply humbled and grateful for it all.

In the early weeks of September, while Alice tended to both John Jr. and four-year-old Michelle, John felt inspiration move him like never before. He gathered up his saxophone, pen, and paper and gently ascended up the red carpet stairs to an unoccupied room in the attic, next to the walk-in cedar closet. The wide windows faced to the east, filled with the vibrant crimson and gold foliage of the huge oaks in their backyard. Alice remembered:

> It was late summer, or early fall, because the weather was nice at the time in New York. There was an unoccupied area up there where we hardly ever went, sometimes a family member would visit [and] would stay there. John would go up there, take little portions of food every now and then, spending his time pondering over the music he heard within himself.

Every day, Alice would prepare food for him and set it at the bottom of the stairs. "He had meditated that week I almost didn't see him downstairs," she said. "And it was so quiet! There was no sound, no practice!"⁵ She didn't know what to think, but she knew John was deep in thought on something unlike anything else he had ever attempted before. And then she heard his footsteps finally descend. At once, Alice detected that John, his face usually serious in thought, now appeared wholly at peace:

> It was like Moses coming down from the mountain, it was so beautiful. He walked down and there was that joy, that peace in his face, tranquility. So I said, "Tell me everything, we didn't see you really for four or five days." He said, "This is the first time that I have received all of the music for what I want to record, in a suite. This is the first time I have everything, everything ready."⁶

At the heart of it all was that four-note melody that had first come to him in the war. Now he had finally heard the whole thing and captured it on staff paper. Not long after, Coltrane and his band had an eleven-day stand at Pep's in Philadelphia. It was the first time the audience heard the melody line from a part of this new composition, which would be titled "Resolution."⁷ And then they were out on the West Coast again while Alice tended to the new family. In November, the Coltrane Quartet split time between Birdland and the Half Note. That same month, she became pregnant again.

That first week in December, Tyner, Garrison, and Jones—along with two Latin percussionists—drove out to Van Gelder's studio and cut *McCoy Tyner Plays Ellington*. After that Monday and Tuesday session, they drove back out the next day, this time with their boss en route. It had been the longest John Coltrane had been away from the recording studio. With John Jr. on her hip and Miki running in the yard, Alice watched John load up the Chrysler and head west to Van Gelder's.⁸ On December 9, John revealed his new composition to the band and in one night, they laid down *A Love Supreme*. The next night, they tried it again, this time with a second bassist, Art Davis, and a second horn, Archie Shepp, though those versions were not used.

When Alice finally heard the resultant music from his extended mediation upstairs, she couldn't believe her ears as the new piece started:

> If you say "A Love Supreme," that's what I hear first, every time. It's like a beautiful city, but we don't enter, because we have to go through the portals, the corridor, and then we reach the entranceway. When that chord hits, that E major, the doors start to open. That's what it's like for me—the very first invitation to this beautiful place that's here, that's in our heart and spirit.[9]

Their shared spiritual study, the deep meditations they had explored together, their growing understanding of a truly benevolent higher power, that personal feeling of God that both she and John felt, all of it was conveyed in the opening moments of the music. But rather than set the table for an extended flight, Coltrane takes that four-note phrase and sets it in every key. For biographer Lewis Porter, he saw it as a means to express the ineffable: "He's telling us God is everywhere in every register, in every key."[10]

It evoked an ancient Gnostic text dating back to 250 CE, yet something that had only been unearthed in 1945 near Nag Hammadi, Egypt. Around the same time that Coltrane first heard those four notes of *A Love Supreme* flutter in his head, archaeologists thousands of miles away unearthed *The Gnostic Gospels*, its many apocryphal, noncanonical writings—the Gospel of Thomas in particular—with sayings credited to Jesus. One entry quotes Jesus: "It is I who am the light which is above them all. It is I who am the all. From me did the all come forth, and unto me did the all extend. Split a piece of wood, and I am there. Lift up the stone, and you will find me there."[11]

At one point, that repeating phrase becomes an incantation from John: "A love supreme," over and over and again. Wayne Shorter noticed that rather than bring in a vocalist, Coltrane instead relied on himself: "I think he was going back to square one where the voice is the first announcement of your humanity—your humanity is your instrument."

Alice agreed: "It's as if he's saying, It doesn't matter what we think we play that's man-made. God, you gave all of us an instrument. We can also offer you praise with the use of the voice that you created in us."[12]

Producer Bob Thiele must have known they had something special as the album was pressed up and prepared for release just a month after the recording was completed. The cover photo, an informal photograph of John standing in the parking lot outside Van Gelder's studio, captured the import of the music within: "The one they did use is a great, great photo," Alice said. "I see everything in it. Ev-er-y-thing. The seeker. The devotee. The musician, father, son. The man."[13]

Their new album completed, the band got back to work. In the waning last weeks of 1964, the John Coltrane Quartet returned to the Half Note and then played a benefit with Max Roach, Abbey Lincoln, and others at the Village Gate for the civil rights periodical *Freedomways*. Right after New Year's, they were in Montreal for a week.

Upon the album's release in January 1965, *A Love Supreme* cemented John Coltrane's legacy at the forefront of jazz and resonated well beyond jazz into other forms of music. He was no longer just the greatest saxophonist in jazz but someone signifying something greater, spiritually and politically, across the culture. That spiritual message conceived in his home now radiated outward, cutting through genre, boundaries, divisions, going straight to the heart of its listeners.

A young saxophonist out in San Francisco, Frank Lowe, heard it and realized in an instant that Coltrane had "urbanized the spirituals... instead of compositions being 'Old Rugged Cross,' they became 'A Love Supreme.'"[14] Singer Patti Smith remembered hearing it while still in community college in New Jersey. She was already a fan of folk and rock artists like Bob Dylan and the Rolling Stones, but Coltrane landed different for her: "I listened to it alone [and] my love of Coltrane developed at that time into a deeply personal experience."[15] An incoming freshman at Bard College named Donald Fagen chatted up a piano player he knew on campus and asked if he had heard *A Love Supreme* yet. "He said, 'Heard it? That's the Bible, man.'"[16] Rick James remembered that all the musicians he knew up in Toronto—Joni Mitchell, Gordon Lightfoot, Neil Young—"were down with Coltrane."[17] Freed from the confines that had ghettoized jazz in America, Coltrane's music now reverberated far and wide. Nearly seventy years on, *A Love Supreme* remains totemic, the greatest jazz album as rendered by its last great innovator. And it raises the question: Could it have been conceived without the presence of Alice?

In looking back at history, a woman's presence isn't always represented in the final work. In the album liner notes that he himself penned, Coltrane gave all the glory to God. But one wonders what role Alice—barely a year after they met—could have played in such divine inspiration. Shankari Adams wrote: "It was no coincidence that Alice found herself in the presence of a musical genius. His values, like her own, reflected deep commitment to God" and goes on to quote Alice: "I think music provided a special means of communication between us, but it was John's and my love for God that was our real connection."[18]

As their son Ravi Coltrane recalled: "My mom would often tell stories about my father working on a piece of music, and my mother would play something from the classical canon or turn him onto some different music that he hadn't heard before. She'd often make suggestions about certain things harmonically."[19] Alice did not write or perform any of the music, but her inspiration and light, her deep devotional love for John, is fully reciprocated by him in this profound work.

It is an offering to God and divine love, but through another lens, it's an expression of Coltrane's earthly love for his spouse as well. It's unfathomable to think that John would have had the space and mental clarity to compose such a work while out on the road, living out of a suitcase, dealing with the tumult of his disintegrating marriage to Naima. Being with Alice, having her presence in the home, tending to their children, with her also keeping the house, allowing him the time and space required to practice without ceasing, so as to receive such a divine inspiration from above, all proved to be crucial factors in the manifestation of *A Love Supreme*.

Alice naturally deflected such statements, but also affirmed that such spirituality in the music was a goal the couple shared:

> I think all of it is a part of it because he was always inspired. He was very much a family man, always at home, if he was not traveling and concertizing. I do believe that all of those factors contributed to his higher involvement, his higher innovation in music... As a result of our association, I saw him more one-pointed, focused in the direction he was going without question. I think there were questionings from others around him, associates, musicians. But he seemed to focus on his goals with a conviction. What we did was really to begin to reach out and look toward higher experiences in spiritual life and higher knowledge to be obtained in spiritual life. This is what we did. And our basic root was, of course reading and hearing discourse, talk by spiritual leaders and teachers, as well as our own engagement in meditation.[20]

The popularity and profundity of the album drastically altered John Coltrane's art ever after. Every composition that followed was in some way or form a benediction given to God. Not that it was always clear to writers. "At that time his critics were saying, 'He's nihilistic. He's taking standards and recasting them. He's anti-jazz,'" Alice said. "From *A Love Supreme* onward, the titles of his records and his songs did have a spiritual word in them."[21]

The mixture of nihilism and divinity was increasingly reflected in the world around Coltrane. The continual fight for equal rights from Black people was increasingly met with violent pushback from the white establishment. Beacons of hope were snuffed out with overwhelming darkness. On February 21, Malcolm X was executed before his family's eyes while giving a speech at the Audubon Ballroom in Harlem. The next month, Martin Luther King Jr.'s March on Alabama was met with unfettered police violence on a bridge outside Selma. "I think that's what you hear in that music," poet/writer Amiri Baraka said of

Coltrane. "You hear the struggle against opposite forces, but you hear a kind of transcendental embrace of what is, and what is going to be, in his music."[22]

Coltrane played a Village Gate benefit for the Black Arts Repertory Theater/School with Cecil Taylor, Archie Shepp, Albert Ayler, Sun Ra, and Betty Carter. Coltrane had already brought the young Shepp in the studio and had also allowed a young drummer from Philly named Rashied Ali to double up on drums, which didn't sit so well with Elvin Jones.[23]

Alice, pregnant and chasing around a crawling John Jr. while also keeping track of Miki out in the yard, remembered that John's sense of purpose was unwavering. After he drove off to record or play in the city, Alice would walk back into the house and "discover a note that he had left stating his love and adoration for me. On any given day, he would bring me flowers. When holding hands in silent moments, I could feel a warm and tender magnetic energy flow from his palms. It was truly very comforting."[24]

The doting husband and thoughtful partner would be all business when he arrived at the club. The shows that Coltrane played that spring at the Half Note continued to echo in the memories of all who caught them at the time. Jazz historian Dan Morgenstern, admittedly never the biggest enthusiast of this era of Coltrane's work, recalled one night:

> The intensity that was generated was absolutely unbelievable. I can still *feel* it, and it was unlike any other feeling within the music we call jazz... It carried you away. If you let yourself be carried by it, it was an absolutely ecstatic feeling. And I think that kind of ecstasy was something that Coltrane was looking for in his music.[25]

A young trumpeter from Poughkeepsie, New York, named Joe McPhee felt wholly overwhelmed by what he heard emanating from Coltrane there: "I thought I was going to die from the emotion...I'd never experienced anything like that in my life. I thought I was just going to explode right in the place. The energy level kept building up, and I thought, God almighty, I can't take it."[26] A few years later, McPhee would be inspired by Coltrane's example to switch from trumpet to saxophone.

Off the bandstand, though, Coltrane the inexhaustible flamethrower inspiring spontaneous combustion in his audiences transformed back to being a quiet, contemplative father and husband living in a quiet suburb in Long Island. His contract with Impulse provided a level of stability rare for all but the most elite jazz musicians like Miles Davis, Louis Armstrong, and Duke Ellington. And none of them were pushing themselves to such physical, mental, and sonic extremes like Coltrane was. "He created a stable, even bourgeois, environment, a safe haven where he could pursue his quest through music and his avid study of esoterica," Eric Nisenson said. "Reading increasingly took up his free time, and many of the books he read were directly related to his music. With his holistic, relativistic perspective, he was always open to all sorts of connections to his music."[27]

John had freedom to practice his horn at any given hour of the day, read at his leisure, then go back and explore on any number of the instruments in the house: his horns, the horns gifted to him by Eric Dolphy's mother, bagpipes, piano, a drum kit, the rented harp, even an acoustic guitar. "Our father would be sitting with the instrument cases open on the floor and the reeds and mouthpieces all around," Michelle recalled. "I remember the smell of the saxophone case, and I loved putting my feet in it and never being scolded."[28] His extracurricular readings, which ranged from spiritual doctrine to architecture to mathematics to astrology, would lead him to experiment in forms of composition that drew on star maps and graphs. In one interview, Alice said that there was one Coltrane composition that was derived from the shape of a cathedral.[29]

In Alice's recollection of that time, home life couldn't have been more nurturing and supportive:

He loved to be at home. He was an excellent husband, father and obedient son to his mother, Mrs. Alice Coltrane, Sr., who lived in Philadelphia. We always had dinner together whenever possible. I could not cook as well as his mother, but I loved to cook good vegetarian meals for the family, and occasionally bake his favorite apple pie. We spent a lot of time outdoors taking pictures of our children, watching them play and grow. We were so close; he was so very gentle with us. John never once raised his voice at me or the children. He was at peace with himself and didn't feel he had to use anger to express his feelings. He was fulfilled in his mission in life.[30]

John and Alice's musical and spiritual connections were wholly in alignment, though Alice once said: "I think John could have just as easily married another woman... Not myself and not because I was a musician, but any woman who had the particular attributes or qualities to help him fulfill his life mission as God wanted him to."[31] Which is humble to the point of near denial.

Whether or not Alice was an apt pupil helping John "fulfill his life mission," her roots in the church and her musicality had to have been enticing and encouraging in equal measure. If you were a tad more superstitious about God's intentions, you wouldn't have to look further for a sign from above than to have your significant other share the same name as your mother *and* grandmother.

In a story told about his time with Naima, John was fascinated by Harpo Marx (aka the silent Marx Brother) and his harp playing in films and would often playfully rib Naima about taking some harp lessons. At one point, Coltrane even kept a harp in his place in Queens, telling writer Joe Goldberg that "it helps me with harmony."[32]

From the start, Alice pivoted away from being a working jazz musician to being a full-time housewife and caregiver, and she was fine with these new maternal demands that fully occupied her time. Though she might not have been your typical suburban housewife, in that her idea of kicking back and relaxing would have meant studying Paramahansa Yogananda's *Autobiography of a Yogi* rather than idly flipping through ladies' magazines. And when he was at home, the couple would play together. "John and I did have a wonderful time making music together," she said. "We'd sit at the piano and go through Stravinsky and Schoenberg and Copland, and the children would be around us running and playing."[33] Alice was well familiar with the Romantic composers from her own study, but it was through John's own deep admiration for Igor Stravinsky that Alice became thoroughly engrossed with the Russian composer's compositions, a fascination that would last throughout her life.

Coltrane had rented a harp for their new home, as he thought it might help him with a new composition.[34] And perhaps unlike Nita, John could convince Alice to try it out herself. Not that it would be much of a challenge. Getting Alice to explore a new instrument was second nature to her. She had watched Ernie figure out the rabab at home. She had mastered classical piano and then pivoted to bebop. She played percussion in the school orchestra and had figured out a daunting Charlie Parker tune on vibraphone while on the road with Terry Gibbs. Every once in a while, Alice would go into the music room, tilt the shoulder of the harp against her and try to figure out some chords on it. Nothing much came the first few times she dabbled, but almost every strum of its strings elicited a warm, resonant tone that made her body quiver like a string traveled through her body.

Chapter Eleven

Expression

BLACK ANGER AND RESENTMENT CONTINUED TO FOMENT IN THE ghettos, on the streets, and on campuses nationwide, as well as on the nightclub bandstand. Players pushing against polite, cocktail jazz could find themselves blocked from club gigs or unable to present their new musical ideas in a way that could jibe with bar sales. In October 1964—between the time when John came down from the upstairs of the family home with a full composition in hand to when he laid *A Love Supreme* to tape—trumpeter/composer Bill Dixon happened upon a small spot in the basement of a café on West 91st Street and conceived the October Revolution in Jazz, a four-day festival in new music that showcased the likes of himself, Archie Shepp, Paul Bley, Jimmy Giuffre, Giuseppi Logan, Sun Ra, and many other acts. Within a year, more than a few of the performers would cut a record for ESP-Disk', the Esperanto-themed label from a local lawyer named Bernard Stollman. In the wake of that success, Dixon and a few others soon formed the Jazz Composers Guild as a way to support one another in the creation and presentation of new works. To paraphrase Karl Marx, the artists were seizing the means of production and presentation.

"The New Thing" began to make its presence felt all around New York City, but not everyone dug it. That clash of equal and opposite forces soon manifested within John's own quartet. By 1965, Coltrane began to push further and further out, and his accompanists weren't always willing to follow him into the stratosphere. Younger cats arriving in New York City began to push the music into terra incognita, and Coltrane, himself an elder statesman on the scene, was turning an ear to who was coming up from behind.

Coltrane wasn't one to hang out in clubs by this time. He would much rather be back home with Alice and the kids. But he was picking up records to play at home and no doubt heard something that stirred him in early "New Thing" documents like *The Archie Shepp–Bill Dixon Quartet*, Pharoah Sanders's first album on ESP-Disk', and above all else, the first recordings of Albert Ayler. In much the same way that he was left gobsmacked by seeing John Gilmore with Sun Ra and Ornette Coleman's Five Spot debut in 1959, Coltrane heard in Ayler what he himself had been looking for in his own music: a way to connect directly with his own tumult of emotions, beyond structure, beyond notation, beyond notes.

This newfound fire in Coltrane didn't always slot into the group dynamics of the quartet. They had gone out to New Jersey to record their first album after *A Love Supreme*, titled *Plays*. It featured another famous movie theme transformed into something turbulent and transcendent, this time "Chim Chim Cher-ee" from *Mary Poppins*. But rather than a nanny merrily floating with an umbrella in hand, Coltrane (with Tyner's clanging, dissonant chording in accompaniment) transformed the song into something akin to a white-knuckled flight in the night sky, bewildering at times. A second bassist, Art Davis, bowed his strings to lay a foundational drone to a version of "Nature Boy." From that point on, no studio album released in Coltrane's lifetime featured the unadulterated quartet again. Every other release would feature a second drummer, bassist, horn, or more.

A week later, the quartet returned again for a session that sat unreleased for five years, later released as *Transition*. Saxophonist Joshua Redman described how this particular recording date affected him:

At certain times in my life this music has kind of swept me up and transported me to a place where I can sense that there is something greater than the material existence of things. And a fabric that binds the material world together and offers an escape from that world. This is definitely one of the last for this band where everything is still happening around a tonic center, a mode... And they're still operating in these even-numbered bar phrases... You can hear the band pushing the limits of its style. You can hear Trane's desire to escape. Part of Elvin is pushing in that direction too, but part of him wants to stay, wants to keep those cycles in place. McCoy probably even more so than Elvin. You can hear that McCoy is a little bit closer to the ground. And so you can hear a little tension in the group.[1]

That tension would become not just audible, but deafening less than a month later when they convened at Van Gelder's once again. The quartet was there, augmented by Davis on double bass again. That came as no surprise, as Coltrane had long been enamored with the possibilities of two bassists since *Africa/Brass* and *Olé*, giving a solid foundation for whatever might be built atop it. Alice argued it wasn't just a matter of being bigger for the sake of it: "He was always looking and listening for that special sound, special blend. How would it sound with one bass on this side, one bass on the other? What is the interplay?"[2]

But the presence of six other horn players suggested that Coltrane was now looking for something far bigger and more profound than just another Impulse recording date. Now the live room at Van Gelder's was filled with alto saxophonists John Tchicai and Marion Brown; tenor saxophonists Archie Shepp and Pharoah Sanders; trumpeters Dewey Johnston and Freddie Hubbard.[3] Outside of Hubbard, everyone else had blown on fewer than ten recording dates up to that point. Aside from prior recordings with Shepp and Hubbard, it's doubtful these other reedmen had ever played with the quartet before that day.

The inverse of *A Love Supreme*, Coltrane drove to the session with no written music in hand, no preconceived notion of what would happen once everyone had convened. There had been earlier excursions into this free playing: Ornette Coleman's *Free Jazz* album (featuring two quartets playing simultaneously) imparted the name to this new wave in jazz. And Albert Ayler had assembled a sextet for his *New York Eye and Ear Control* soundtrack for a Michael Snow film that similarly reveled in its unbound sense of freedom. But these were the works of outsiders pushing their way past the gatekeepers; Coltrane himself represented the mainstream of jazz and he went even bigger, with eleven players in total. Coltrane would call it "a big-band thing."[4] According to Marion Brown: "Trane had obviously thought a lot about what he wanted to do, but he wrote most of it out in the studio. We ran thru some things…until we were together, and then we got into it."[5]

"It" being *Ascension*, a line in the sand between jazz's storied legacy and its always uncertain future, between John's status as torchbearer and an uncontrolled fire. It spoke to jazz's raucous ensemble sound of its roots in the turn-of-the-century jubilee of New Orleans bands while blasting away all the rules of the form. Or, as Shepp put it: "This is like a New Orleans concept, but with 1965 people."[6] Anything extraneous or old hat was chucked overboard: swing, harmony, chord changes, the head-improvisation-head pipeline. Brown said the date was "wildly exciting. We did two takes and they both had that kind of thing in them that makes people scream. The people who were in the studio *were* screaming. I don't know how the engineers kept the screams out of the record."[7] More exhausted and decidedly less moved was Jones. After one run-through of the piece, Jones was shirtless, sweating, gassed, but Coltrane wanted to take another pass at the amorphous, shrieking, centerless piece. When the second take drew down, Jones smashed his snare at the studio wall to make sure they wouldn't play it again.

Ascension commenced what writer Ben Ratliff called the final years of Coltrane's life playing what "amounts to one interconnected song. It is music of meditation and chant, the sound of his interior cosmos… melody lines were now a matter of intervals and cells, musical vitamins to keep the drone healthy."[8] Such a descriptor makes the mind drift to the image of sourdough starter or kombucha mother, of a music perhaps not recognizably human-concerned, but now a living culture and entity. An ecosystem, a forest, an unseen mycelium network. It reflected democracy at its most balanced and messiest. If in an ideal democracy everyone had an equal voice, you now had to hear everyone shout at top volume.

It might have even reflected how John understood fatherhood, in that he was now tuned in to what the younger generation was saying. The patriarchy of the 1950s generation began to cede ground to who was coming up from behind. And rather than simply dismiss this new sound as jive and noise (like many of his peers did), Coltrane embraced the change. The "New Thing" had landed and Coltrane's benediction and blessing conferred a newfound status on these young, hungry players. Thanks in part to such proximity to Coltrane, the likes of Shepp, Brown, and Sanders would all go on to release multiple albums on Impulse and have long careers.

For Alice, *Ascension* was a natural evolution and a manifestation of how John had begun to think about the music he was hearing in his head:

> Someone might say, "Well, it's only a quartet," [but] see, his thoughts were more lofty, his vision more broad, he was seeing higher dimensions in sound. Who knows, maybe the man was hearing fifty instruments at a time, or a hundred, like many of the great classical composers. They have to be able to hear it to be able to conduct it. He was slowly going toward that—two basses, two tenors, he was thinking about it in bigger terms.[9]

Coltrane was expanding his mind in many ways. He dedicated even more time to meditation with Alice in their shag-carpeted meditation room built out over the garage, to studying Eastern philosophy and its concepts and applying it to his music. "A higher principle is involved here," Alice explained. "Some of his last works aren't musical compositions. I mean they weren't based entirely on music. A lot of it has to do with mathematics, some on rhythmic structure and the power of repetition, some on elementals. He always felt that sound was the first manifestation in creation before music."[10]

And at some point in 1965, Coltrane turned on to the paradigm-shifting effects of lysergic acid diethylamide (LSD). He had struggled to overcome his heroin addiction and had maintained a healthy lifestyle; at that point, he saw LSD as being therapeutic medicine rather than an addictive substance, some three years before the U.S. government classified it as a dangerous Schedule I drug, akin to heroin and heavy barbiturates. In this exploration, Coltrane was not alone, as the likes of Allen Ginsberg, Thelonious Monk, Bob Dylan, and the Beatles had all tuned in to the profound possibilities of this chemical compound. For a new generation already seeking beyond established religions to expand the parameters of the possible, the drug was a gateway to get a glimpse at something beyond the everyday perceptions of the mind and its senses. Eric Nisenson wrote:

> Although it has been stated by some that he took it only when he recorded *Om* later that year, he actually took it far more often during the last few years of his life, according to a number of people, including a member of the quartet who would prefer, like others, not to be quoted directly on this subject. One friend of his remembers that Coltrane would get so disoriented from acid during some gigs that after intermission he had to be guided back to stage... For Coltrane and his quest, LSD was a remarkable tool to dig deeper into his own being so he could discover the essential and absolute truth at the center of his being.[11]

Whether it came from her husband's influence, reading books on spirituality, or some other means of exploration, Alice began to perceive her Baptist upbringing and the restraints and prohibitions of mainstream Christianity in a decidedly different light.[12] She said:

The Eastern philosophy gives the aspirant the opportunity to develop himself. In other words, I found a kind of situation in the Christian Church—you're instructed, like a mother instructs, guides, directs, tells you to believe in the Father. They introduce you to Christ and you're supposed to revere, respect, and love Him—it never [mentions] that you can become more Christ-like, achieve Christ consciousness. There are certain wonderful statements made by Christ—"Greater works shall ye also do." He's telling you that you have a higher and greater potentiality; "I fed five thousand, I want you to feed five million."[13]

The dovetailing of Eastern philosophy with LSD-induced visions, the way that acid could dissolve the narrow confines of ego to let the entire universe pour into the individual mind, took hold in Western counterculture. College students, bands, artists, and the like all began to incant the mantra that Dr. Timothy Leary—himself an early proselytizer of LSD—helped slip into the mainstream: "Tune in, turn on, drop out."

But Coltrane knew that the peace-and-love trappings that would come to define the hippie generation weren't true enlightenment, weren't the *real* reality. The only constant is change, whether that idea came from pre-Socratic Greek philosopher Heraclitus or Krishnamurti, whose books Coltrane read with great interest. Krishnamurti knew that meditation wasn't just sitting still in silence, but a reckoning with the underlying nature of reality itself: "Meditation is never-ending movement... [it] is emptying the mind of the known... [it] is always new... It has not the touch of the past. To meditate is to transcend time... [it] is the awakening of bliss; [it] is the summation of all energy."[14] Which could double as a way to describe Coltrane's late period, its never-ending movement, its disregard for the past, its energy. Nisenson described Coltrane's personal religion as a reckoning with God's true nature:

> His vision of God and his universe is not one of angels peacefully plunking harps amid billowy clouds in a static, calm sky. To Coltrane,

the universe is a place of explosive dynamism, of stars bursting apart and reuniting, of atoms and molecules in a constant state of wild flux, with a God who is not peacefully sitting on his throne under shade trees but constantly in motion, changing the universe and being changed by it.[15]

His music began to reflect the unceasing change that is the underlying nature of our reality. John and Alice could look all around them and grasp this tenet of life on Earth. On July 29, 1965, after a long illness, Alice's mother, Annie C. Johnson McLeod, passed away. Nine months pregnant, could Alice have even been able to travel to Detroit for the funeral services? A week later, grieving the death of her mother, she welcomed her second son, Ravi, born on August 6.

Less than a week later, the Watts Riots combusted in Los Angeles and violence convulsed the city for nearly a week. It took nearly fourteen thousand National Guardsmen to finally tamp down the fires and looting, but the destruction was nevertheless shocking: thirty-four deaths, thousands of injuries, and millions of dollars of damage wrought by the violence.

John Jr. celebrated his first birthday with his new baby brother. After the birthday festivities, John Coltrane crossed the George Washington Bridge to cut a ferocious session in a single evening, later released as *Sun Ship*. But the Classic Quartet, who on a nightly basis could conjure the intensity of the infinite, who could convey in musical terms what was happening in the gaseous cauldrons of the cosmos, was quickly reaching a breaking point.

They headed out west, first to San Francisco and then up to Seattle. There, Coltrane played one night (a set later released as the paint-peeling *Live in Seattle*) and then two days later performed *A Love Supreme* in its entirety. It's one of only three known live performances of the piece; the band expanded to include West Coast reedmen Carlos Ward, Donald Garrett, and Sanders, the latter a standout on *Ascension*. The night before that, Coltrane brought this expanded group out to a home studio in Lynnwood, along with an old friend from when he used to frequent jam sessions in Detroit, Joe Brazil. Coltrane and the others chanted a passage from the Bhagavad Gita, before erupting into wails of "I am Om!" A holy terror broke out and chaos reigned for nearly a half hour.

Whether or not John Coltrane was on acid (as was often rumored), the group played in a chaotic, disjointed, free-form manner for over six hours. There was shouting, shrieking, discord, and more, equivocal to the elevated din of *Ascension*. *Om* as a Hindu concept held deep significance for Coltrane: "The first vibration—that sound, that spirit, which set everything else into being. It is The Word from which all men and everything else comes, including all possible sounds that man can make vocally. It is the first syllable, the primal word, the word of power."[16] But he was also embarrassed by the end result, begging Bob Thiele to not release the album.

Two weeks in Los Angeles yielded another intriguing, expanded band sound, *Kulu Se Mama*. Garrett and Sanders were still onboard, and there was a second drummer to augment Jones as well as poet Juno Lewis reciting verse and playing hand percussion. In the wake of a massive blackout in New York City that November, the band returned to the Village Gate. "When John left for work, he'd often take five instruments with him," Alice recalled. "He wanted to be ready for whatever came. That was characteristic of John. His music was never resigned, never complacent. How could it be? He never stopped surprising himself."[17] At the Village Gate, Coltrane whipped out the bagpipes and bass clarinet and young guns continued to sit in.

Terry Riley, a young composer from California living in New York City at the time, remembered seeing Coltrane at the club. At the time, Riley was well aware of Coltrane's use of modes and drones and had even incorporated it into a composition of his own at the time that reveled in all the glorious possibilities of staying in one key, "In C." Riley also had been interested in Indian music and philosophy and was struck by what he heard onstage:

Coltrane was with this really large group: two drummers, two bassists, all his saxophone comrades: Pharoah Sanders, Albert Ayler, Don Cherry was in that group. Coltrane came out and started reading from the Bhagavad Gita. He would read a few pages and when he came to the word *om*—not for the first time—he started *om*-ing, very powerfully with all of his voice, almost shouting. And the band started taking that pulse and it just grew into this mountainous drone, this fabric that was hard to distinguish any individual sound out of it. It was just this big sound fabric, with everyone playing as hard and fast as they could. It seemed like it went on for an hour. That was it, that was the concert.[18]

An eloquent sense of order flowed right below the surface of all that molten lava on a November date. Coltrane had already made a first pass at a piece he titled *Meditations* but wasn't satisfied with the result. For the second pass, he added Sanders to the frontline and brought Rashied Ali back to be second drummer. This date captured that sense of constant change in the group. It's the sound of the Classic Quartet but with the influx of a new energy in the form of these two younger players. By this point, Pharoah Sanders and his caustic, overblown primal screams on the horn had found a home as second tenor in the group. In the album liner notes, Coltrane laid out his philosophy for the world, quoting the Platform Sutra in the process:

> There is never any end. There are always new sounds to imagine, new feelings to get at. And always, there is the need to keep purifying these feelings and sounds so that we can really see what we've discovered in its pure state. So that we can see more and more clearly what we are. In that way, we can give to those who listen to the essence, the best of what we are. But to do that at each stage, we have to keep on cleaning the mirror.[19]

Coltrane could envision a new sound on the horizon, but his band couldn't. Amid the sonic spumes of Coltrane-Sanders and Jones-Ali,

McCoy Tyner quit the band at the end of 1965. Tyner had been at the piano bench since recording "My Favorite Things" and was the cornerstone of the Classic Quartet.[20] Coltrane had befriended him as a teenager and watched him grow. Yet even Coltrane was mystified by Tyner's style, telling one interviewer: "Tyner plays some things on the piano, but I don't know what they are."[21] Coltrane's style had dramatically evolved since being with Alice, at once more forceful and more philosophical. "It wasn't even about the tenor sax anymore, it was about exploration," saxophonist Frank Foster said. "It was more about finding oneself spiritually than trying to turn the tenor saxophone into something."[22] At times, Coltrane could be so overcome by the spirit on the bandstand that he would take the reed out of his mouth and pound his chest. He sought a sound beyond what could sometimes be articulated through an instrument. And now John Coltrane needed a new pianist.[23]

Alice remembered John coming home with the enthusiasm of adding Sanders and Ali to the group, but she was startled when he suggested a new pianist for the band, her:

> We had talked about me coming into the band, but it would have been on vibes. At the time, I was into it and I was practicing vibes. This was the first idea for me, to come in on vibes and maybe even harp. Before I could really even have the chance to begin to play with the quartet, they broke up. So I came in on piano instead. With Pharoah and Rashied, they came in before me and then I came into the group.[24]

Alice wasn't sure she was up to the task. She hadn't played piano outside the home since she and John had gotten together in 1963 and had prioritized homemaking and child-rearing over keeping up her chops. Last time she had been onstage, bop was still the thing and now it was this "fire music"—as Shepp had once called it—that swept through the scene. She wasn't sure what to say to John. "I didn't know whether to accept...because I'm considering there are so many other people who'd be more qualified," she said. "I really was quite conventional. I wasn't innovative or exploratory. I saw music as conforming to the basic chord progressions that were being played by so many musicians around the country."[25]

But it would also make a dream come true to finally play music with John, to fully be with him and further their musical explorations, to support him not just at home but also onstage, to wed their spiritual practice with music study and realize this vision together. Alice recalled how John encouraged her: "He said, 'You know you can do it, and I want you to!' His confidence in me was so strong. One day he said to me, 'This music is like a second nature to you. It's just like it's a part of you, a part of your life.'"[26]

What could John Coltrane hear in his wife's piano playing at home that redoubled this belief in her? What was it that made him know that this new music would come as second nature to her when even she had only really ever played bebop in bands and had her own doubts and reservations? Hearing her at home, John must have realized, much like Terry Gibbs did when she "stole" his *Plays Jewish Melodies in Jazztime* date from him, that Alice possessed a preternatural ability for the music. He said that she "continually senses the right colors, the right textures, of the sounds of the chords."[27]

Much like he was at home with the children, John Coltrane was gentle, insistent, and encouraging in assuring his wife that she could do this. "He never said, 'Don't play like this,'" she recalled. "I was encouraged to play the instrument fully, to give myself totally."[28] When she struggled with the music in the beginning, "he saw that I was playing with only a few octaves. He told me to play the whole piano, utilize the range so I wouldn't be locked in. It freed me."[29]

There was something about this new iteration of jazz that beckoned to her and her sensibilities, a newfound sense of freedom that allowed her to transcend the demands of bebop piano with its intricate chord changes and dense harmonies. In much the same way that John's example allowed her to accept a more universal religious philosophy beyond the restrictive tenets of the Baptist Church, so could she now perceive a way forward in the "New Thing." She said yes.

Once she jumped in, the sense of liberation and total freedom thrilled her with its unlimited possibilities and potential:

> I do not dislike it [the old style] but I prefer avant-garde music because it isn't as restrictive... If you're set in this 12-bar pattern, you don't change from that; you stay within that confinement. For people with limited ability, maybe it's a safety measure to play in that context. But for innovative people, that's quite limiting... Avant-garde music to me is like journeying across the country until you come to a beautiful park. You say, "We'll stop here for just a moment." After a while you decide to go onward because you know of a nice area ahead, but before you leave, you see a lake that you didn't notice before, and you decide to stay and experience that for a while. Sometimes your moment is there like an eternity. This type of thing is quite prevalent in my music.[30]

Alice traveled with the band out to San Francisco, and one night into their residency, Elvin Jones split unceremoniously, flying all the way back to Paris to join Duke Ellington's band. But a new quartet was already in place, with Pharoah Sanders, Rashied Ali, Jimmy Garrison, and Alice Coltrane supporting Coltrane now.

The sound of the Classic Quartet was undeniable, the force of Elvin Jones and McCoy Tyner irreplaceable on the bandstand. But as deep, hypnotic, and overpowering as such relentless forward drive could be, of Trane steaming down the tracks that Jones-Tyner laid down for him, Coltrane was moving on. He was no longer a train heading in one direction but an interplanetary craft given to moving higher into the atmosphere. In the way that the industrial revolution gave way to the space age, Coltrane needed the freedom to rove however high or far afield the spirit took him, regardless of meter or harmony or any of the other trappings. Ali's drumming style did away with landing on the "one" that Jones always favored, and the steadying, structural support of Tyner gave way to Alice's more lithe, gentle style. "Rashied...was very sensitive, very responsive," Alice said:

> He developed a rhythmical kind of vibrational approach to the music, which was like a component of what John was hearing...He creates a kind of freedom by not defining the steps a soloist must take, where you don't always need to know where "one" is, but where he gives you a route to the upper causeway, and I thought that was so beautiful.[31]

To Pharoah Sanders, Alice's presence on the bandstand was the correct choice. "To me, she fits in," he said. "She is with everybody else in whatever goes on. She spiritually fits and she is able to feel where the music is going...she's being inside of what's going on. She is being herself, she couldn't do it any other way."[32] While in San Francisco, Coltrane took the new quartet to Coast Recorders and paid for studio time himself. He recorded a new composition, "Peace on Earth." It was an early glimpse of this new quintet, what writer Ekkehard Jost called a "rubato ballad," the defined tempo disregarded so that the piece moves more like a human heartbeat, quickening and slowing as emotions are stirred and resettled. It was gentle but volatile, intense and lyrical. It could soar to the stratosphere and then glide back down to Earth within a measure. Wherever Coltrane wanted to go, the group was instantly with him.[33] On the drive back, they were booked to play Detroit's Cobo Hall but got snowed in, along with Thelonious Monk's group. For one night, John Coltrane sat in with his old bandleader, and later John and Alice played duets together into the wee hours.

In mid-February, the new group was booked at Lincoln Center's Philharmonic Hall for a concert billed as "Titans of the Tenor." Its original January date had been pushed back due to the New York City transit strike, and it featured the likes of Coleman Hawkins, Zoot Sims, Yusef Lateef, Sonny Rollins, and John Coltrane. Rollins, Coltrane's longtime peer, played briefly but said that he would come back later to join Coltrane onstage.

Ascension had only arrived in stores that month, so the total transformation of Coltrane's band baffled the audience and some of the other artists, especially as more and more outlandishly attired young horn players strolled out onto the Philharmonic stage. And when the music started, they were shocked by the roars and cries that came forth:

> Most fans expected the Classic Quartet plus one. Instead he came out with Rashied Ali and J.C. Moses on drums, Alice Coltrane on piano, Jimmy Garrison on bass, and on the front line Pharoah Sanders, who brought a paper bag of auxiliary percussion; Albert Ayler and his trumpeter brother, Don; and alto saxophonist Carlos Ward. They played 40 minutes. Coltrane started with "My Favorite Things," but this was just a point of departure...Coltrane began to move like a whirling dervish, then, toward the end of the set, chanted the Buddhist mantra *"om mani padme hum."*[34]

Despite five other horn players on the stage, Rollins declined to join the din. Most of the Upper West Side audience fled, while a teenager named Gary Giddins left the show "in a state of confused elation...I soon realized it had unscrewed something in my mind in regard to musical indeterminacy."[35] *Down Beat's* breathless review of the show ran months later: "John Coltrane's current playing—and this program included a healthy sample of it—is little short of astonishing...The resulting personal esthetic odyssey makes almost every exposure to his work a memorable experience...they seemed literally on the verge of blowing their instruments to pieces." Eight paragraphs of individual player analysis followed, with one exception: Alice didn't warrant a single mention.[36] But in a Leonard Feather column from early 1966, he noted that Alice deserved to be on the bandstand with John: "Nepotism played no role...a gifted musician with a moody, modal style not unlike Tyner's. She now has to make a decision, to go on the road with the combo or stay at home and take care of the two very small Coltranes."[37]

After nearly three years of being at home in Dix Hills, being back onstage and concertizing with her husband was liberating for Alice.

Despite John's status as jazz royalty, he eschewed that sense of patriarchal hierarchy in his band. He never overtly voiced the chords to be played but rather gave his bandmates the freedom to express themselves in the music. As she explained:

> It was such a concept where a person was allowed to cultivate his own music, he wasn't confined to just play someone else's ideas or someone else's notes. He had a chance to really bring out himself and really find his own place in the music. This is why you saw so much development in the quartet. They were given the freedom to really express their own ideas and create their own music along with John's. He couldn't just have musicians play one way. The best way for a person to develop is to let them have the freedom to do it, otherwise, how can they grow?[38]

In another interview, Alice talked about working in this new realm of jazz:

> When I began working with John, and started playing freeform, it gave me another plateau entirely on which to work...He saw higher vistas, higher echelons to reach...He had a concept of how you would sound, but he never told you how to play or stated what would take place—you developed your own way through his music, and you heard innovation happening.[39]

What might have sounded like freeform noise to the uninitiated, to Alice sounded like the next logical step after the innovations of Bird and Diz, the new freedoms that had been introduced by the upstarts like Ornette Coleman and Albert Ayler. "I don't think I ever left anything behind from my earlier way of playing," she said. "It gave me a foundation to build on, but soon I was making music a different way. I remember one day John saying to me that it sounded as if I'd been playing this way all my life. I felt that was a great compliment, coming from him."[40] As Franya Berkman noted: "Even though the music she played with

Coltrane was 'avant-garde,' she found herself in an extremely familiar musical situation. Given the spiritual intent of her husband's music... Ms. Coltrane stepped onto the bandstand in the familiar role of church pianist. She was also performing with a close family member, as she had been throughout her earlier professional life."[41]

Freedom in this sense didn't just mean noise and tumult. In a way, the music of Coltrane's last band evoked the Eleanor Roosevelt statement: "With freedom comes responsibility." Alice said that playing free didn't mean nihilism or selfishness to scream as loud as you wished to without regard to anyone else: "You have to be disciplined, you have to be concentrated. You can't just say, 'Oh, I'm playing for me and I'll do as I please.' Otherwise it would break down, like chaos."[42] And being onstage with John every night furthered that sense of freedom: "Being with him in such a professional association was wonderful. There was no limit to how much one could glean from John's very essence. He inspired so much freedom. He encouraged one to expand—to play their instrument to the fullest extent, and to express one's self completely."[43]

In making emotionally honest music that came from the heart during the mid-1960s, how could it not reflect the turmoil and bedlam of the times? There was discord in the United States as the struggle for civil rights intensified and the conflict in Vietnam drew more and more young Americans to their jungles to die. But for Alice, this music was ego-abnegating, allowing for a greater good. It could serve as a beacon and new possibility: "It felt as if you were to just walk out of this door and see a new world, a new universe with so many opportunities in it. You know, so many things to discover and so many vistas to look upon. It was so perfect for me."[44]

After the rigors of bebop, Alice's creativity dilated as she no longer found herself hemmed in by the demands of meters, bar lines, or needing to constantly provide harmonic support for the saxophones. With John's encouragement, she ranged widely over the seven full octaves of her instrument, always seeking out new tonalities. She could reexamine the pentatonic sounds from her church playing, the shifting harmonies from her time with Gibbs, and now explore the dissonance made possible in John's playing. She was a quick study in this free music and credited her husband:

> Of course, John Coltrane is the one who inspires everybody, if you were fortunate enough to be in his presence in those days. He would always encourage you to fully express what you had. Not half of it, because it's not made that way, or three quarters—the entire experience of the expressive self. Truth on your instrument. That just opens so many doors, so many avenues, so many vistas, so many plateaus. You could hear your sound, music, light, coming from the ethereal, heavenly realms. When you played in octaves that you would never go—your bass area, and your contrabass area, or your tenor area. You heard all kinds of things that would have just been left alone, never a part of your discovery or appreciation.[45]

In March, Coltrane's new band played a week at the Plugged Nickel in Chicago. A young local drummer named Jack DeJohnette, at the time a member of Charles Lloyd's group, got a call from John to join them: "It was quite an experience because it was very, very free, very, very so-called out. It was very powerful and the audience really didn't know what to make of it, although the place was packed every night. It was very raw." At one point, Coltrane explained his headspace to him: "He said, 'Jack, I know it sounds maybe not together and rough but there's something in the sound, something I like.'"[46]

Having seen the Classic Quartet so often in Chicago, DeJohnette knew that group was more straight-ahead. But onstage with them now, "everybody was more or less on their own." He said that they would still play something familiar like "My Favorite Things," but after the stated melody, they entered into an entirely new realm:

> It was total improvisation, not general timekeeping but just more sound. More sound and rhythmic phrases. It just sounded like a wild jungle. I

wish I had tapes of it to listen to, because at the time it wasn't clear to me exactly what it was. I knew what he wanted. I knew he liked the sound, to play off all the energies. The more sound, the more he got off on it. A lot of people were confused, to them it sounded like noise. Of course I played very loud. The music lent itself to that kind of energy, but you couldn't play that way with anybody else. It would be too overpowering. They called Coltrane's music angry, or "new wave" or "new thing," and you know, I call it multi-directional, because it's diverse. I just play music.[47]

DeJohnette recalled driving John and Alice home after one show and Alice confided that "sometimes she would wake up and John'd still be sitting on the bed with his flute. He would play on the intermissions. He was just obsessed—no, not obsessed but *possessed* with music all the time. I know I played so hard on that gig when I finished I would go home and sleep till about 2 or 3 the next afternoon. I mean I was just wasted."[48]

Nisenson pointed out Coltrane's "forthright decency in using his wife" in his band at this point. "Sexism was a major force in jazz," he wrote. "Musicians who angrily and repeatedly decried racism and injustice thought nothing of their own often dreadful treatment of women. Miles Davis...complained loudly about racial intolerance and mistreatment, [but] nevertheless regularly beat the women in his life."[49]

To DeJohnette, not only was Alice more than capable of keeping with the demands of playing at that high physical and mental level, she was also the catalyst for her husband's change. "She understood what John was reaching for and I think her role in that group was more to help with the expansion of where John was going," he said. "They changed each other. They moved into this vast sort of sound spectrum, soundscapes I would call them, of different rhythms, energy, harmony, sounds. And that was John's nature, anyway, to constantly change."[50]

After Chicago, the group drove on to California to play at Stanford. Juno Lewis and Donald Garrett again joined them onstage and Elvin Jones sat in on a second kit. He also accompanied them up to San

Francisco's Jazz Workshop before the Coltranes crossed the country again for a week stand at Pep's in Philadelphia. The show was reviewed by Ron Welburn for a short-lived zine called *Change*, which only printed two issues. Jones and Ali are both present, the former described as "cannon fodder enveloped all of Broad Street" while Ali is "like a hovering catastrophe, the youth coming into the mind like an army." Next, he described "Mrs. Alice McLeod Coltrane, a tall black woman—you can't imagine—something like McCoy, or maybe Sun Ra; her work with a similar kinetic energy, when you hear it (and you could, if you heard all these things at once)." When Pharoah and John let loose, he described the maelstrom of sound: "My mind could envision murders, slaughters, hangings...and hear Harlem, Sharpville, the Congo, Kenya, Watts, Vietnam even...All of these singular forces speaking together as one massive energy of strength; hoping, moving through the heavy air/giving birth."[51]

In April, John Coltrane made a rare swing through the south, with a date in Atlanta and in Austin, Texas, at the first Longhorn Jazz Festival. The band ultimately didn't perform at the festival, but John and Alice did cross the Rio Grande, finalized John's divorce, and got remarried down in Mexico. Later that same month, the Coltranes decamped to Englewood Cliffs to record new compositions.[52] They were then invited to play a benefit in Brooklyn at St. Gregory's Rectory at the behest of John Coltrane's longtime friend Calvin Massey.

Massey was one of Coltrane's oldest friends; they had met as teens back in Philly. Massey strolled past the Coltrane home on N. 33rd Street one day and heard the most immense sound of the saxophone coming out of the basement and had to see who it was. The two became fast friends, though they couldn't have been more different. Coltrane was tall, while Massey topped out at five feet, seven inches with a waistline to match. Massey called Trane "country" because he was so quiet, while Massey rapped a mile a minute, loudly called women "bitches," and cussed every other word or so. While Coltrane abstained from drugs and alcohol, Massey drank heavily and chain-smoked, losing a kidney due to tuberculosis and ballooning up to three hundred pounds. But when it came to music, they were in close alignment.

Cal Massey was a heavy in the Black Brooklyn community, putting together self-produced concerts across Park Slope, Bed-Stuy, and Crown Heights. As themes of artistic self-reliance and self-determination became key for artists, Massey was already doing it for himself and for his community. He organized shows to benefit the Black Panther Party and had local Black entrepreneurs and shop owners invest in his visions. He knew this new music could raise the consciousness in the community.[53]

St. Gregory's Roman Catholic Church in Crown Heights had recently torn down an old convent, leaving an empty lot behind. Massey envisioned it as a playground and set to work planning a benefit concert, tapping his old friend John Coltrane to play. It was a sunny April Sunday morning and Massey and his kids helped set up the event, collect the $2.50 fee at the door, and hand out food and drinks to attendees. Saxophonist Cecil Payne lived in the hood and described the scene: "They were just regular people from the neighborhood that came—they weren't like jazz fans going out to hear jazz. And they really enjoyed it, because it was something they would never think of going to see or to hear." The Coltranes drove in from Long Island and the kids ran around while John and Alice got ready to play. "John made his own decision to perform 'Acknowledgement' from *A Love Supreme*...and to recite the poem during the program," Alice said.[54]

French jazz fan Daniel Berger was one of the lone white faces in attendance. "It was mostly families in a non-show business, non-jazz concert atmosphere—quite casual," he said:

> Toward the end of the afternoon, Trane, his wife, and their little kid arrived on the scene, calmly, followed by Elvin [who was there to perform with saxophonist Roland Kirk as well] and Jimmy Garrison. Instead of playing, he began to recite his poem "A Love Supreme." I don't know if he cried, I don't know if he smiled. I know that he was infinitely calm,

that his voice came out timid, fearful...He read his page without haste and looking in the air, staying in the same place. Nobody said anything. Then he began to play at the limit, yet again, of the possible and the perceptible...He never played without giving all.[55]

Alice played a spinet provided by the church. And while most Coltrane sets were cataclysmic, that afternoon was a decidedly more subdued performance. Cal's young son Zane recalled:

It was so intense. I was very young, but I was very touched by that music. It was a very long performance—Trane played for over an hour. They played for so long that there were puddles of sweat. Where they were standing John, Jimmy, Elvin—there was literally water there on the floor...The band was playing, and he was reading the prayer. And I remember in the back of the room it was all musicians and they were chanting his name, "John, John, John." Rahsaan [Roland Kirk] was actually crying, and I couldn't understand. I was in shock, because I hadn't ever seen anything like that before.[56]

For Alice, the communal effect of the music drew her back to her Detroit days, when parishioners would be overcome with the Holy Spirit:

It's very kinetic, this music, very powerful. I've seen listeners do all kinds of things. Someone in the audience would stand up, their arms reaching, and they would be like that for an hour or more. Their clothing would be soaked with perspiration, and when they finally sat down, they practically fell down. The music just took people out of the whole material world; it lifted them up.[57]

It was the final time that Coltrane would perform that piece live. "To speculate on why *A Love Supreme* was rarely performed opens up many variables," Alice replied when asked. "Why that evening in a Brooklyn church? I believe the sacredness of the event may be a reason."[58]

The next month, John and Alice Coltrane were back at the Village Vanguard for a span of ten days, one set recorded for release as *Live at the Village Vanguard Again*. Such shows could often find the audience in conflict with the direction Coltrane was taking. "You can get almost as avant-garde as you want to be, as long as you keep that steady pulse," saxophonist David S. Ware said. "But Coltrane lost a lot of people when he broke that time, and went into that other world and started messing with that multidirectional time."[59] Two long, transformed versions of "Naima" and "My Favorite Things" showed just how far out the band could take such tunes. But even the familiar had mutated into something beyond recognition.

"They wanted to live in the past, and that's something you couldn't get John Coltrane to do," Alice said:

They'd say, "We want to hear 'Equinox,'" or "We want to hear 'Mr. PC.'" He always played "My Favorite Things" and they liked that, but a lot of the other older pieces he wouldn't play.[60]

In another interview, Alice said:

When he became avant-garde, as they termed it, he lost many people, many followers. They didn't like it, they didn't approve of it, they didn't appreciate it. And there was no way he could go back, there was no road to return to. It was his commitment, it was his decision.[61]

They played Newport[62] that summer, then flew to Japan for Coltrane's first tour of the country. When they finally landed after nearly a day of travel, they were tired and jet-lagged. Looking out the window, they realized that there must be a movie star or celebrity on their flight, as they could see a crowd gathered on the tarmac.

Only when they had descended the stairs did they realize that *they* were the celebrities. "They had life-size posters and bigger cutouts of each one of us at the airport," Rashied Ali recalled. "Then they took a red carpet and rolled a red carpet from the plane into the terminal for Coltrane. That's the way they did it in Japan."63

In the photographs taken upon the band's arrival, you can see the bewildered look in Alice Coltrane's eyes, tired yet bedazzled by the love and adoration—barely meted out to them in America—yet ebulliently bestowed upon them in a foreign land. Dozens of flowers were handed to her. Once they arrived in the Magnolia Room at the Prince Hotel, the air was sweet with their gentle fragrance. Alice's thoughts might have drifted back to those fraught early days in New York City at the jazz loft, how—no matter what the trials of the day had been—in the wee hours of the morning the air would suddenly fill with the smell of fresh flowers being delivered to the florists on her old street. At some point on this trip, Alice also knew that she was pregnant once again.

The group barely had time to sleep or adjust to their new surroundings before a whirlwind tour began. They played Tokyo, Osaka, Hiroshima, Nagasaki, Fukuoka, Kyoto, Kobe, and then Osaka and Tokyo again, some fifteen shows in fifteen days. There's a famous photo of John Coltrane bowing his head in prayer at the war memorial in Nagasaki.

Two of these nights were released years later as *Live in Japan* and the music within is breathtaking, bewildering, almost beyond what the conscious mind can grasp. If there is a jazz equivalent to Beethoven's late string quartets, to James Joyce's *Finnegans Wake*, to Einstein's attempts at a unified field theory, it's in here. There's a similar quest for unification: where theme and improvisation flow into each other without divide, where any key or tonal center is in harmony with everything else, where the expression of the music and expression of faith are one exhalation. What can sound like chaos in his long soloing is, in Porter's words, "improvisations [that] were devoted relentlessly to the exploration of abstract motivic ideas."64

It's also the first time that Alice's early piano forays into the unknown can clearly be heard. Nisenson highlighted her solo that emerged after both horns dropped out on "Peace on Earth," now a twenty-five-minute meditation: "Her playing is fascinating, quite idiosyncratic and filled with feeling. Like her husband, she too was influenced by Stravinsky, and her rolling lines have a polytonal melodicism not unlike that of the great Russian composer."[65]

In a four-hour interview given to the Japanese media, John Coltrane explained his pragmatic religious belief as best he could: "As I look upon the world, I feel all men know the truth. If a man was a Christian, he could know the truth and he could not. The truth itself does not have any name on it. And each man has to find it for himself, I think...I believe that man is here to grow into the fullest, the best that he can be. At least this is what I want to do." To the question of what did he plan to do in the next ten years, he quipped: "Become a saint."[66] There was little time for John and Alice to shop for souvenirs, but they bought a koto and some wooden reed instruments, as well as some gifts for the kids.

The band returned to the United States resolute. *This* was the way forward with this music and they would see it through. They landed in San Francisco and played two weeks at the Jazz Workshop. A young guitarist named Robert Quine considered himself a Coltrane fan, but late albums like *Ascension* and *Meditations* had flummoxed him. "I'm in the front row and all of a sudden, these two horns are right in my face," he recalled decades later. "I said 'Yes, I understand this.' I understood it emotionally. I had been trying to analyze it too much."[67] Saxophonist Burt Wilson joined Coltrane and Sanders—as well as another bassist and drummer—onstage, and he recalled the power radiating off Coltrane: "At his most intense [John] would glow. You could see a gold and red aura 6 or 8 inches off his body."[68]

After that tour of Japan and the West Coast, Coltrane needed a breather. He told writer Frank Kofsky that Sanders helped "because physically, man, the pace I've been leading has been so hard and I've gained so much weight, that sometimes it's been a little hard physically. I feel that I like to have somebody there in case I can't get that strength. I like to have that strength in the band, somewhere."[69]

Two weeks before Alice's twenty-ninth birthday, the John Coltrane Quintet played at the Village Theatre in NYC as part of a summer-long series titled "The Avant-Garde: A Perspective in Revolution."[70] A review in *Jazz* deemed John Coltrane "the Buddha in the temple, giving forth the music of his journey towards the heaven or hell he has reached." It went on to praise the masculine traits of the group to the detriment of Alice's own contributions:

> There was so much virility and sheer rippling muscle in this music, I had a difficult time placing Mrs. Coltrane's solo in the overall mass of what I had just heard explode. Many of her progressions seemed innocently off-key and made too much of air to penetrate beyond the stage area.[71]

In late October, Coltrane played a Village Gate benefit for Cal Massey with the likes of Max Roach, Betty Carter, Archie Shepp, and many others. Alice's old friend from Detroit and onetime roommate at the Jazz Loft, Joe Henderson, was also performing, a tenor star in his own right. The group was supposed to travel to England, the Netherlands, and elsewhere in Europe in November, but the tour was canceled. On Veterans Day, the band drove down to Philly to play at Temple University.[72] On November 20, 1966, Alice's father Solon McLeod passed away at age sixty-six. Both of her parents were gone.

After he developed some rolls of film from Japan, Rashied Ali realized that in many of the photos, John was holding his side, as if in pain.

CHAPTER TWELVE

Seraphic Light

THERE WERE LOTS OF PLANS TO BE MADE FOR THE NEW YEAR AHEAD, and John Coltrane teemed with ideas. After his travels through Japan, he now dreamed of traveling to India and Africa so as to examine the music that had so enamored him over the years. One night at the Jazz Gallery, Indian sitarist Ravi Shankar came to see John play, and the two became fast friends.[1] His admiration for the spiritual nuances within Shankar's music was such that he named his second son after him. Shankar implored John to come to India to experience the country firsthand, to better understand the Hindu philosophy behind the music. Coltrane had also befriended African percussionist Michael Babatunde Olatunji.

Olatunji arrived from Nigeria in 1958 to study at Morehouse College in Atlanta before furthering his education at New York University. When he wasn't studying, he formed a small percussion group, which led to performances at Birdland and Radio City Music Hall by the end of the 1950s. While their influences were clearly felt across his most iconic albums, Coltrane still held out hope to one day record with both Shankar and Olatunji. "I intend to make a trip to Africa to gather whatever I can find, particularly the musical sources," Coltrane said, telling Olatunji that he wanted to transfer Yoruba chants to sax.

One day late in 1966 or early 1967, John and Alice Coltrane found themselves in Midtown and strolled over to the Lyon & Healy harp showroom on 57th Street. Smitten with the harp and its beautiful liquid glissandos, he placed an order on the spot for a top-end, hand-gilded concert harp for Alice. It would be handcrafted and delivered out to their Dix Hills home.

Live at the Village Vanguard Again saw release at the end of 1966, the first John Coltrane album to feature his wife on it. *Down Beat*'s review is fifteen paragraphs long, but Alice warranted only one line: "Mrs. Coltrane's piano support is always firm and appropriate, never overbusy or obtrusive."[2] *Kulu Se Mama* followed soon after.

Oran Coltrane arrived on March 19, 1967, the third son of John and Alice in less than four years. "I loved to see him outside with the little ones, while they played ball and rode tricycles," Alice recalled.[3] Miki was nearly seven, John Jr. was three, and Ravi was teetering around, not yet two. John would walk the property with them, pointing out the trees and wildlife. He had recently purchased a film camera, and many home movies of John and Alice with their expanding family were captured on film. John also had big plans for their Dix Hills home. Construction had begun on converting the basement space into a full recording studio complete with control room and live room. Soon he wouldn't have to trek all the way to New Jersey. John could just descend the stairs to the garage to put his music down to tape.

Coltrane had always been diligent in going out to Englewood Cliffs to record new ideas. But in early 1967, he began to book time as often as he could. A long day of recording by the band in mid-February, with a *very* pregnant Alice, yielded nine new compositions.[4] The next week, John was back to record a series of duets with Rashied Ali.[5] Less than a week later, they recorded again, with Marion Brown on alto instead of Sanders, recording two pieces: "E Minor" and "Half Steps." The first week in March, with Alice due any minute, they recorded "Number One" and "Ogunde." Alice also recorded her first solo piano piece, "Altruvista." Ten days after giving birth, Alice and her husband went back out with Garrison and Ali to record six cryptic pieces that were given numbers rather than titles.[6]

He had recently renewed his contract with Impulse and his advance was now $40,000 a year. But this was still more music than any jazz label could release in a timely fashion. At the same time, John and Alice had conceptualized a new endeavor, Coltrane Records. "John would speak about taking control over your own destiny in terms of recording," Alice said:

> A lot of musicians do not want to be bothered. They don't want to handle statements, they don't want to be concerned about audits or payments that go out to others, you know, the whole buying and selling process. He said, "Young people should think twice about how they regard their musical career—they should take more control over it. If you can go over to someone else's studio to record and give your tape to that company over there, do it yourself!"[7]

That ethos carried over into other endeavors as well. Inspired by what he saw his friend Cal Massey doing for the Black community in deep Brooklyn, Coltrane wanted to set up a space that let more people hear the music. Rather than be dependent on bar sales and nightclub owners, he imagined a space without age limits or ticket prices to hinder young people from checking it out. "His goal...was to get a loft in the Village," Coltrane's producer Bob Thiele said. "He wanted to set up a place where people could come in, listen to his music...just the price of a Coca-Cola, ten cents if you wanted anything to drink, but this was definitely an ambition of his."[8]

John deeply wanted a space to practice and perform in that wasn't tied to alcohol, to sales, but to listening and understanding. In Japan, the quintet had concertized at grand halls and centers for culture and arts. But in the States, it was back to the dingy, cramped, smoke-filled clubs where drunken chatter and the clanging cash register vied with the music for attention, not to mention the violence of the underworld element that lay just beneath the surface of such spots, undercutting the spiritual import of the music. "He was disturbed because the type of music he played was confined to nightclubs. It was music for listening, not for drinking in all the places where there is so much buying and selling," Alice said:

> We had thought of setting up a center that would be like a church, we wouldn't call it a church, because it might frighten people away and they might wonder what kind of church it was, but it would be a church in that it would be a place for music and meditation, and maybe someone would feel like praying. It would bring others a kind of fellowship based on music, because he thought music was a single universal force and that there could be no dividing lines or categories.[9]

Olatunji envisioned opening a Center for African Culture on 125th Street in Harlem, and Coltrane helped out financially whenever he could. With Yusef Lateef, the two planned a date at Lincoln Center's Philharmonic Hall that they would self-produce, cutting out concert promoters. When Olatunji's dream became a reality on April 23, 1967, John Coltrane was booked for two sets on the center's opening night. That night, Rashied Ali saw something he had never seen before: "[Coltrane] sat down on the bandstand. I still didn't think he was sick, because when he put his horn to his mouth, there was no faltering; the fire was up full blast."[10]

But Coltrane was sick. Concerts for the spring and summer were canceled, including at Newport. Coltrane's cousin Mary Alexander remembered that "some Saturdays, he would come over... By that time he couldn't eat a lot of food and all that sort of thing, and I would always have something he might be able to eat."[11] Alice herself, having always given her husband such leeway at home, didn't quite recognize what was going on. "Maybe I didn't know how bad he felt," Alice said. "He wouldn't tell me. I used to leave him alone when I thought he wanted to be alone. I was busy with the kids and I didn't want to bother him, to get in his way or to bug him."[12]

Once, when the stomach pain got overwhelming, Alice drove him to the hospital:

I had to practically take him to the doctor for an examination. He tried to avoid it by saying, "Everything is okay, it's alright." Following that initial examination, the gravity of his condition was discovered, yet not fully defined. The doctors said that they needed one more test to fully evaluate the situation. He was in pain, very tired, debilitated. Then he told me, "I cannot play my horn anymore." I was shocked. I was speechless.[13]

The doctors took a biopsy that revealed cancer of the liver, but the chance of success on the operating table was too slim to risk it. Coltrane preferred to be at home. He lay on the couch for hours at a time, listening closely to the recent tapes made in the studio and planning out what to include on his next album.

In her meditations earlier that summer, Alice said, "I began to see different things about him. I was seeing that we would have less time to spend together. In this visionary state, I saw him walk up to me and say, 'I have something to tell you of great importance, and it is that I am going.' I asked, 'Where are you going?' And he said, 'I'm going on to enlightenment.'"[14]

But such discussions never made it into the couple's real-world conversations. Coltrane would tell family members and close friends that he was going to get better. And for all his plans for creating a new record label, a new recording studio, a new community center, and a new album, he didn't draft a will. He met with Bob Thiele on Friday, July 14, to discuss a new album with four recent pieces on it. It would be titled *Expression*.[15] By then, he couldn't take on soup and could no longer eat.

In the wee hours of Sunday, July 16, the pain was too much for him. Alice and the kids climbed into the car to drive him to Huntington Hospital. "He was such a strong man that he walked out the door himself," she said. "He was walking slow, but he made it. And then he went down so fast."[16] At the hospital, Alice stayed by his side. "Are you ready for this?" he asked, his hand growing cold in hers. By four a.m. on Monday, July 17, 1967, John Coltrane left his body.

PART 3

Turiya

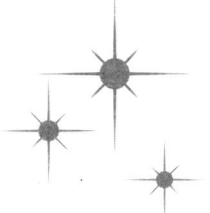

CHAPTER THIRTEEN

Manifestation of Cosmic Energy

3 DEAD IN CITY RIOTS: MOBS LOOT, START FIRES[1]
The riots in Newark fulminated for nearly a week that July; plumes of smoke from burning cars and vandalized storefronts rose in the white-hot summer sky. The Black people ghettoized in other U.S. cities—oppressed by their police and municipalities—combusted like kindling, the riots spreading all through New Jersey. The glowing embers of Newark scattered to burn anew in cities like Irvington, Orange, Montclair, Elizabeth, Paterson, and Jersey City, on down to Asbury Park. Some nine thousand miles away in Vietnam, American soldiers faced intensified fighting. War raged between Israel and Egypt, dogfighting planes over the Suez Canal less than a month after the furious Six-Day War ended in the region. The world was burning. And John was gone.

The funeral for John Coltrane was held four days after his death. Over a thousand people convened at St. Peter's Lutheran Church in Midtown. Pews swelled with over six hundred mourners coming to pay their last respects. Hundreds of others stood outside the church. Upstairs in the balcony, Albert Ayler and his quartet played "Truth Is Marching In," and the primal cry of Ayler sounded the grief of the gathered.

"Rarely have so many musicians congregated in one place," the Rev. John G. Gensel sermonized. Coltrane's casket could barely be seen under the profusion of yellow roses and white lilies. Bouquets sent by the likes of Duke Ellington, Nina Simone, Stan Getz, Max Roach, and others crowded the altar. Next to the casket were two images forever linked to Coltrane: Bob Thiele's off-the-cuff photo at Van Gelder's and a Victor Kalin portrait. Both images appeared on *A Love Supreme*.[2]

In lieu of a eulogy, Calvin Massey recited "A Love Supreme." Alice and the children wore black. Rev. Gensel also read from that album's liner notes, ending with the refrain: "It is all with God. All praise to God. With Love to all, I thank you." Ornette Coleman's quartet rendered the sorrow of the room into bittersweet sound with "Holiday for a Graveyard." The pews slowly emptied and the family drove out to Pinelawn Memorial Park on Long Island, where John Coltrane's body was interred.[3]

The silence inside 247 Candlewood Path was deafening. Alice had woken up countless mornings to the sound of her husband playing flute or his horn, the kids roused by the breath of their father, gently nudging them awake in melody. Their days had always been surrounded by music, and now Alice sat in stunned silence on the royal purple carpet of their bedroom. "In terms of the children, it was very difficult for me," she said years later. "The youngest was only four months old. The older ones couldn't understand why their dad did not come home from the studio. I had to wait until they were older before I could fully explain his absence."[4]

Her hand was still in his in the hospital bed, the palm skin growing cold; the body no longer resembled that of her husband. His spirit had flown to be with the ancestors, and Alice was left behind in her body. Her own skin felt like a shell. "I felt his real seeking. He was a man who believed in his heart that he could realize God and reveal God through his instrument. He was looking for God," she said. "That is why we heard music that we hadn't ever heard before, because I believe it wasn't all from this world. He played from another realm, a spiritual realm."[5]

Alice would sit in silence, overcome in her meditations. One wave, then another, then another more devastating than the last. The waves kept coming. They hadn't even known one another for more than four years, yet their marriage felt like two spirits in recognition from eons before. Rama and Sita. Their time together felt multidimensional, on the bandstand or at home with the kids as they ran wild through the yard. Their spirits had always been as one, together on the piano bench or with John standing nearby as they duetted together. But now? Alice was a bereaved widow with four young children to raise all by herself in this big empty house.

"His passing left a huge void in our hearts," Alice said. "We think of him always and know that he is with us in spirit."[6]

But in the day-to-day reality, such loss felt insurmountable, impossible. The kids, confused by the grief of their mother and the absence of their father, didn't quite grasp what was happening. Every thump they heard made them hope anew that it was the sound of their dad's footsteps coming down the hall or descending the stairs. As Shankari Adams described it: "His loving arms which welcomed them warmly were no longer a place of comfort… All they knew was that he no longer returned from concerts, and they were sad."[7]

There was no will, but John had provided for his family. His estate was valued at $318,500, and Alice and their children were provided for with trusts and life insurance.[8] Royalties from his records continued to come in every quarter. Even Naima, his cousin Mary, and Naima's daughter—who Coltrane had adopted—were provided for. Cards and telegrams from around the world poured in all summer long. Alice was struck by such kindness shown to her and her family in their time of grief.

The days became a blur. There was no need to look at the newspapers, to turn on the news, but it seemed everywhere that the world was descending into chaos, despite the stories that also proclaimed this to be the Summer of Love. Riots in Spanish Harlem roiled the city for a week.

And Detroit was burning again. There had been a police raid of a Black club on the West Side, where Black friends and families had convened to celebrate the return of two GIs from Vietnam. A crowd gathered, a bottle was thrown, and bedlam ensued. Angry mobs looted gun stores and both firefighters and police faced sniper fire. It was all-out urban warfare. Five days later, when the rioting was finally extinguished, the devastation to Detroit looked grim. The Belle Isle Riots wounds had been left to fester for decades, and the damage to Detroit now was far worse: forty-three deaths, over a thousand injuries, over seven thousand arrests, and nearly five hundred buildings destroyed. The Motor City continued its downward spiral.

Just before her thirtieth birthday, Alice sat deep in meditation in their bedroom. The door opened and John walked in. "He had an instrument that looked like the soprano sax he used to play," she said. "He was playing it. Sometimes he looked better than when he was alive."[9] In this liminal state, she could see her late husband, hear his music again, feel his spirit fill the room around her.

Meditation is the most profound, slippery, and subtle of spiritual disciplines. It is the utmost expression of "being," even if it appears to look like someone just sitting silently with their eyes closed. "Meditation is the action of silence," Krishnamurti said.[10] What transpires in the mind of a meditator is wholly unknown to the outside observer. What occurred deep within Alice Coltrane's meditations would be impossible to notice externally.

The devastation of the world reflected the inner devastation she felt. What happened in Alice's internal world broke from the external world. John wasn't there, but she could see and hear him. The disconnect was severe.

Outside that vision, Alice suffered. "Luckily we had these neighbors with an older daughter and she would babysit us," Michelle said. "They would pitch in." Alice's sister Marilyn came out to help and neighbors looked in on the children. But as Franya Berkman described it: "From a psychiatric perspective, it might appear that Alice was experiencing extreme depression or psychosis...burdened with the responsibility of raising four small children she would have had ample cause."[11]

Alice wasn't sure what would come next for her. She hadn't touched a piano in months and couldn't imagine playing music without him. She certainly was over going down into smoky, lurid nightclubs in the late hours of the night to make spiritual music that couldn't be heard over the din. And Alice had four kids at home to mind; there was no way she could go out on tour for any extended amount of time. "I didn't feel I should go into music after his death," she said, adding:

> I felt that I needed a period just to be quiet and realize what has happened and adjust to what happened and just more or less go into meditation and to see what it is I had to do. Where was my life going? Since the one who had been the main directive person, the real directive energy, wasn't directing at that time...I felt that some soul work had to be done, I mean spiritual-wise, to give me more of an understanding what's really going on with myself, my environment, my community. How am I to live?[12]

If she thought that was a question posed to the Supreme Lord, to the universe, to the Father, to Ohnedaruth,[13] we can never know. But she soon had her answer. An immense wooden crate showed up on her doorstep early one morning. As the kids danced around in wonder, she pried it open, and the crate revealed that Lyon & Healy Style 11 double-action, hand-gilded, concert grand crowned pedal harp with a resplendent gold finish. John had special-ordered it for Alice as a gift. It had taken over a year to be constructed traditionally by hand at the harp factory on Lake Street in Chicago.

When John Coltrane was still with them in Dix Hills, when he still had the rented harp in the music room, sometimes a gentle breeze would move through the house. Suddenly, every room sparked to life with a beautiful sonority. "If it was by an open window, the breeze coming in would cause the strings to sound and he could hear the wind playing through the strings," Alice said with a sigh. "The harp has to be played with the fingers plucking the strings, but it also uses air, and that's what I liked so much about it. It's such a wonderful instrument. Maybe that's why we think of heavenly and divine things when we hear the harp, because we get that rush of the wind."[14]

Alice had become curious about the harp when it was in the house previously (and from her husband's appreciation of French harpist Carlos Salzedo), but it was still seen as primarily a classical instrument and one used more for embellishment rather than as the lead instrument. But she also had intimate knowledge of its possibilities dating back to her time in Detroit on the club circuit. The Premiers often shared the stage with fellow Detroiter Dorothy Ashby, who pioneered the use of the harp in a jazz setting, managing its forty-seven strings and making it coherent in a bebop setting. In Alice's mind, Ashby was "a most beautiful harpist, the very best."

Ashby also came up in Detroit, graduating from Cass Technical, and faced what she once characterized as "a triple burden... The audiences I was trying to reach were not interested in the harp, period—classical or otherwise—and they were certainly not interested in seeing a black woman playing the harp."[15] Nevertheless, Ashby recorded a dozen albums as leader, ambitious in presenting the harp in an array of settings, from postbop and cool jazz to ambitious orchestral soul.

John was no longer of this world, but he appeared to manifest in the form of this magnificent harp. Alice would carry on his mission of realizing a universal sound, a cosmic music. It was a challenge for her to master a new instrument. The hand positions were vertical instead of horizontal and the ergonomics of the instrument were totally new to her, but she diligently began to practice daily, knowing that in a way she was carrying on John's wish. "For that reason, when I began to play the harp, it was something particularly close to me," she said.[16] Like the breeze before, she could feel his presence whenever she sat down to practice.

The recording studio in the basement was also completed during this time, with both a live room and control booth. The Coltranes' Dix Hills neighbor, Roy Musgnug, who worked as a recording engineer for Decca Records, helped Alice design and build the studio and get it up to spec.

Unlike her husband, Alice would no longer need to make the commute to Englewood Cliffs to record. Once the kids were all tucked into bed, she could just walk downstairs and get to work.

Which is what she did at the end of January 1968. Former bandmates Jimmy Garrison and Pharoah Sanders came out to the house, joined by her Long Island neighbor and Thelonious Monk drummer Ben Riley. With Alice guiding the group from the piano, they played a few of her recent compositions: "Lord, Help Me to Be," "The Sun," and "Ohnedaruth."

As executor of John's estate, Alice also started on the formidable task of going through all of her late husband's trove of recordings and deciding what would posthumously be released. *Expression* had been overseen and titled by John in his very last days, but there was so much more tape to comb through. Five days after her first session as a bandleader, *Om* saw release. While at the time John had been displeased with the recording, in the wake of the Summer of Love, *Om*—with that Sanskrit symbol for *om* on the cover—spoke directly to a younger generation of listeners, the flower children who were looking for something *way out*. In that, *Om* hit like a comet. For those amid the catharsis of an acid trip, this disjointed, seething whorl of sound and moans that arose out of a passage from the Bhagavad Gita made a certain kind of sense at this point in the 1960s.

Om was given to Impulse Records, but Alice also went back to the recordings she had made with her husband two years before in San Francisco. Those sessions he made—and paid for—himself, so technically they didn't fall under the auspices of the label. She could do with them as she saw fit. And Alice began to also prepare these tapes for release. There's no credited producer, but as she put it: "This was one of the ones we produced. I say 'we' as if he was right there with me."[17]

With John as her guiding spirit, Alice took "Manifestation" and "Reverend King" and paired them with the two pieces she had just recorded, "The Sun" and "Lord, Help Me to Be." "Reverend King" was inspired by a speech of Dr. Martin Luther King's that had resonated with John, much like it had years before when he had written "Alabama." It featured John taking a solo on his late friend Eric Dolphy's bass clarinet, and the improvisation opened with John and Pharoah chanting "Om mani padme hum," the Tibetan Buddhist mantra most closely associated with Avalokiteshvara, the bodhisattva of compassion. The notes say the chant "symbolizes the seven breaths of man and the truth that humanity is Divinity enshrouded in flesh." But after that quiet opening, the piece builds in intensity with trembling rhythms that seem to shake the piece to the point of disintegration.

While the pieces featuring her husband were intense and searing, hers were more subdued, contemplative. "The Sun" took a snippet of an invocation that John and Pharoah recited in the studio back in 1966: "May there be peace and love and perfection throughout all creation, oh God" and grafted it onto her new composition, a pentatonic piano ballad that rode the gentle waves of shaken bells and Riley's struck cymbals. You can just make out a voice humming along and as the piece draws down, there's also a spliced-in second of tape. John utters, "Alice?" and it abruptly ends. Alternating between his work and hers, Alice assembled these four pieces in such a manner that struck a balance akin to the taijitu symbol in Chinese philosophy, or the Hindu trimurti between Brahma the Creator and Shiva the Destroyer.

King would have been at the forefront of her mind. On April 4, 1968, the Rev. Martin Luther King Jr. was shot and killed on a hotel balcony in Memphis, Tennessee. As the news emanated over the radio and news, over a hundred U.S. cities combusted in anguish and rage over his death. A week of mourning appeared as flickering flames in white and black across the nightly news.

Thinking back to the many discussions she had with John over their years together, as he turned to look at star maps, the arches of cathedrals, the crescent shape of Islam, the many religious symbols that so fascinated her husband, she kept coming back to the concept of "Cosmic Music." In the light of the cosmos, humanity is all united. The riots in all these cities, the burning flames, how different could these be from the exploding stars thousands of light-years away? There was fire everywhere. God created and destroyed with equal measure.

Look to the galaxies and you see the resplendent trace of God, not as something still and static, but something always roiling, always all-powerful, a fire so brilliant it can be seen from eternities away in the night sky. There had been many names for this kind of music that John and Alice ideated: It was the "New Thing," it was "Fire Music," it was "Avant Garde Music," it was "Free Jazz," it was "Spiritual Jazz." But they had been breaking free of that loaded word *jazz*, knowing that what they were pursuing flared far above the trappings of that slang word, a word that could trace back to the whorehouses of New Orleans, to the Jim Crow South. This wasn't jazz. John and Alice envisioned it as "Cosmic Music," a sound that could hearken up to the stars and back:

> The use of the term (jazz) I feel, is inadequate in its description of the music created through John. A higher principle is involved here. Some of his latest works aren't musical compositions. I mean they aren't based entirely on music. A lot of it has to do with mathematics, some on rhythmic structure and the power of repetition, some on elementals. He always felt that sound was the first manifestation in creation before music. I would like to play music according to the ideals set forth by John and continue to let a cosmic principle, or the aspect of spirituality be the underlying reality behind the music as he had.[18]

On Easter Sunday, April 14, Alice Coltrane made her solo debut and staged a concert at Carnegie Hall.[19] She billed it as "Cosmic Music" and dedicated it to the "Cosmic Beloved Lord." Her group consisted of her old Detroit friend Joe Henderson and Pharoah Sanders on tenor saxophones, Jimmy Garrison on bass, Rashied Ali and Jack DeJohnette on drums, and Alice on piano and harp, premiering the instrument she taught herself how to play mere months after it arrived at her doorstep.

Two days before the concert, the first feature story on Alice Coltrane appeared and she spoke about carrying on her husband's legacy:

> My husband had a love for all music. He believed music was a universal art. He respected the contributions of all cultures, and he was always interested in whatever each race could offer. If he had lived, I wonder what he'd be doing now... or five years from now. He was just something as a musician. Just something.[20]

The piece detailed the home studio and how John encouraged her to learn the technical aspects of the studio:

> He said to me just a few days before he died that I should go ahead and do this myself. At night, after I put the kids to bed, I come down here and play and write. This is my practice room, too. We're rehearsing here for the concert. I've done all the arrangements, but I've followed patterns my husband set. It's really his music.[21]

The sextet premiered five original pieces that Sunday. First was "Mantra," credited to John Coltrane; it was followed by "Infinity," a piece credited to Jimmy Garrison; third was "Lord, Help Me to Be"; next was a harp solo by Alice titled "Oceanic Beloved"; and the concert concluded with another John Coltrane composition, "Manifestation of Cosmic Energy."[22] Alice Coltrane delineated what the concert meant for her going forward:

> I don't want to start traveling on the road with a group. I don't want to work in clubs. There's nothing I like better than being with my kids in my home. This is it for me. I'm not interested in the financial aspects of it, either. It's not a matter of necessity. I just want the music to be presented in the right way.

The mind thrills at what a frontline of Henderson and Sanders would have sounded like in early 1968, how the mercurial drumming styles of Ali and newcomer DeJohnette would have meshed, how it would all be helmed and held together by Garrison and Alice. But there was no review of the concert reported in the *New York Times* or in any jazz periodical. To date, there are no surviving tapes of that performance either. Coltrane, Henderson, Sanders, Garrison, and Ali have all joined the ancestors.[23] Sanders talked about actualizing the music of Coltrane in those final years:

> Always, it was like a communication through music, like he knew some things that I wanted to know that he could express musically, and that maybe I had some things to contribute, too. It's hard to talk about it, except in spiritual or religious terms, actually. Whatever he did, he wanted it to come from inside himself, and he did not want to hold anything back, or hide anything he found there. Good or bad, it had to be expressed.[24]

That urgency of expression carried forward with Alice now. "I'm going to try to do my best to do the things John wanted done—to reach the people," she said. When asked what type of message she wished to communicate, she replied: "Well, I don't know exactly how to put it. But everything I do is an offering to God—that's the truth. The work I am trying to do is a sort of sharing with my sisters and brothers of the world, my all; the results I leave to God."[25]

Alice began to put together an album that would be the first release on Coltrane Records. There was a gatefold with a collage she conceived and arranged: the Great Sphinx of Giza, Siddhartha Gautama, Krishna, Jesus of Nazareth, and John in deep concentration; the Sanskrit Om, the Islamic star and crescent, and the Star of David, all dancing against a star field. The back cover had a photo of John praying before the Peace memorial in Nagasaki, Japan. For the cover, Alice took one of the many sketches he kept in a notebook—a pattern of swirls like pinwheeling distant stars—and enlarged it for the cover art. Alice Coltrane called the album *Cosmic Music*.

Cosmic Music appeared that summer and caught Impulse completely off-guard. Neither Impulse producer Bob Thiele nor Impulse's parent company, ABC Records, had any idea that the project was in the works, and now there was another label vying with them on the very popular and lucrative John Coltrane album market. Label bosses realized there would be problems if Alice held all of the master tapes and started putting out the music herself. But how it would look to have John Coltrane's record label sue his widow within the first year of his passing? Not two weeks after *Cosmic Music* hit the shelves, there was a notice that Impulse had signed Alice to the label as a solo artist.

"They were very courteous and not in any way forceful or unkind," Alice recalled. "They simply said, 'Why don't you let us do it? We can take this album you've done, put our Impulse! stamp on it and let's start from there.' So for that short time I think I learned something, but I was not inspired to have a record company. It was a good experience, though."[26]

Now her attention could turn wholly on her own music, itself an expression of what Ohnedaruth had been working toward at the time of his transition to the spiritual world:

> A few years ago...I asked him what it was that he was doing in music. These are his exact words: He said "I am looking for a universal sound." At the time, I didn't quite understand him fully, but I think what he was trying to do in music was the same thing he was trying to do in his life... to universalize his music, his life, even his religion.[27]

A spread in *Jazz and Pop* featured not just a photo of Alice but also individual portraits of her four kids, conveying the maternal role she also had to manage. Whereas John had the ability to give his music his full and undivided attention, Alice had to tend to the house and kids, and only after a woman's work was done could she then turn her attention to the music. At one point she admitted that she didn't have the talent or genius of her husband, "but I will try to elevate the music as much as I possibly can."

Which can read like the free jazz equivalent of Ginger Rogers doing everything Fred Astaire did, but backward and in high heels, in that she composed new music, mastered a new instrument, did bedtime reading, washed and folded all the linens, mopped the kitchen, and *then* got to work. She said, "I usually practice at night because during the day I'm busy with the children and can't really concentrate. But at night, at 11 or 12 o'clock, I practice the piano, listen to tapes, practice the harp. I practice a good hour on harp."[28] Alice had to carry that all forward, while at the same time being a loving, devoted mother. But the burden and strain weighed heavy on her.

CHAPTER FOURTEEN

IHS

SOON AFTER *COSMIC MUSIC*, ALICE SET ABOUT MANIFESTING HER own vision of this universal sound. Working into the wee hours of the night, she would not fall back on the musical modes she had previously mastered, she would forge ahead. This "cosmic music" would remain free-metered and loose in structure, with an open modality that allowed every collaborator to bring themself forth in the music.

Yet the first pieces she composed and recorded at Dix Hills that summer hearkened back to the gospel feel of her earliest memories of playing at Mt. Olive Baptist Church. That summer Alice stripped back the sextet and called for a classic piano trio session featuring Garrison and Riley. A song like "Gospel Trane"—with its shaken sleigh bells and Alice's left-handed comping—evokes the feel of a Sunday service call-and-response, but the music feels slippery. Her piano moves like an initiate mind in meditation: sometimes intensely focused, other times drifting into new realms high up in the piano register, expanding and contracting with every breath.

"I Want to See You" resonates with that sense of loss and ache. It also features her newfound harp style.[1] As heard on "Lovely Sky Boat" and "Oceanic Beloved," discernible chords and melodies give way to the overwhelming waves of sound on the harp. "Lovely Sky Boat" is liquid and ever-changing. These new Alice Coltrane compositions exemplify that rubato template as established on John's late piece "Peace on Earth." Six ruminative pieces comprised *A Monastic Trio*, its title suggestive of a Zen Buddhist koan.

Back in Detroit, Ernie Farrow received a glowing rave in *Down Beat*, confirming his presence in their hometown.[2] And at the end of 1968, Impulse brought forth their own version of *Cosmic Music* (now with cover art of John's face juxtaposed onto the surface of the moon) and released Alice's debut, *A Monastic Trio*. For some, the void left behind by John could never be filled. A double review in *Coda* rhapsodized John's music on *Cosmic Music*: "This is music of energy, love and universal dedication to existence. There is little else to say." It then went on to say: "With his absence, the completeness of the music and the energy and direction disappear, leaving just an empty shell...For the rest of the music on these two albums, Pharoah Sanders and Alice Coltrane amount to little. The sound result [of the harp] seems like she is accompanying someone who is not there."[3]

Another review praised Alice's *Cosmic Music* half over John's "mad in thought" music, calling her "a composer of many colors" and stating that "The Sun" is "a masterpiece, period. The piano expounds, demands, cries and berates like the essence of everyday humanity."[4] The same reviewer heard strains of European composers like Carl Nielsen and Jean Sibelius, but "very little of the original black element of jazz in the album...a possible mutation of the classical and jazz veins."[5] Archie Shepp himself noted that Alice was "classically trained and her music had an impressionistic bias...It always had a spiritual element. One had the feeling of the gospels, traditional African American music." He added: "It was the kind of music I grew up listening to when I went to church with my grandmother, the Baptist church down in Ft. Lauderdale and in Philadelphia."[6]

Much like John did on albums like *A Love Supreme*, Alice used the liner notes of her first album to communicate directly with listeners: "I would like to take this opportunity to say thank you, sincerely, in behalf of my family and myself, for your kindness." Another review of *A Monastic Trio* detected "a heavy sadness" and "many moments of expressive grandeur here, times of peace and sadness and long and love," but also said that the harp pieces weren't completely together, summarizing that "while total greatness escapes her here, the future holds certain glory."[7] But first she had to persevere through this heavy sadness.

To the outside observer—to her friends, neighbors, family members, and others—the perception was that Alice Coltrane experienced a total nervous breakdown around that time in 1968. She refused to eat for days at a time and her weight plunged 40 pounds in just a few weeks, down to 105 pounds. Soon she wasted away even further, dipping to 95 pounds. Jackie came from Detroit to stay with them and wept openly at the sight of his baby sister in this near-skeletal state. Even with family members in the house, Alice would stay isolated in her bedroom, not talking to anyone, not seen for days at a time. Or worse still, she said, she would find herself performing "humiliating and self-effacing austere sacrifices" before her family.

Alice couldn't sleep but only for a few hours a week; she would wander the house in the middle of the night in such a zombified state that she startled the family dogs. She might stand at the doorjamb and stare at her children as they slept. She would meditate for hours upon hours. She would collapse without warning. In dealing with such overwhelming grief and loss, she stated that she had the "inability to shed even a single teardrop."

Alice was racked with visual as well as aural hallucinations. She described having encounters with interdimensional beings and "a malefic, demoniacal entity, or just a plain mischievous spirit."[8] She would hear explosions, piercing sirens, and deep rumbling bellows that seemed to shake the house, sounds and sensations that no one else heard or felt. She would feel her heartbeat stop entirely for extended periods, or else shift to the other side of her chest. More troubling were the voices that commanded her to do things to harm her body. Once, she attempted to throw herself out of a second-story window.

She described falling into a patch of broken glass, but not realizing that the glass was embedded deep into her flesh until three days later. She would look down and hallucinate that her body was on fire or else realize that she was bleeding, not knowing why or how. Alice at one point described metal entering her body: nails, needles, razors: "Marked from head to toe, the greater part of my body resembled the stigmata of a crucified person—blood issued from almost every part of it."[9]

One night, the self-harm was so horrific that Alice burned her right hand to the point that the nails blackened and fell off. As she stared at the gruesome burn in a catatonic state, her family rushed her to the hospital for treatment. Once there, though, she refused any sort of medication from the attending physicians to alleviate the pain of her third-degree burns.

As her family begged and pleaded with her to get help, to take care of herself, she was thoroughly disengaged and detached from reality. She would stare mutely, unable to have such mundane conversations. She had "experiences which were somewhat like rehearsing for one's own funeral."[10] Alice could see herself dead, her body lying in state. And the people around her no doubt feared that this would soon be the case.

Slowly, Alice Coltrane emerged from the abyss. For many years, Alice Coltrane didn't openly discuss those lost months in the wake of John's death. When she finally did, it was as a small fifty-three-page book that she self-published a decade later titled *Monument Eternal*. She depicted this time through her own lens, reframing the past few months of her life in a new light.

Instead of a nervous breakdown, she depicted a drastically different internal experience than what could be perceived externally:

> Following a long period of elementary meditating and reading of some of the diverse books on spirituality and world religions, I felt the deepest transcendental longing to realize the Supreme Lord. This longing was soon acknowledged, for within a short period of time I experienced the first rays of Illumination and spiritual re-awakening… Upon inception of

the Supreme light, the force of the Lord's energy acting upon the human psyche...delivers the spiritual Illumination simultaneously with the profound ordeal of *tapas*. The procedures of *tapas*, which encompass every aspect of spiritual and physical suffering, have to be endured. And they are sometimes *endured beyond human comprehension* [emphasis added].[11]

There's no exact English translation for the Sanskrit word *tapasya*, which generally translates to "generation of heat and energy," or an "internal spiritual fire," though the most readily associated Christian word for it is *penance*, a self-mortification of the body and senses so as to attain higher spiritual goals. Radha Botofasina explained it as a "reawakening, meaning the reawakening of what was already there. To be an instrument of the Lord, you have been finely tuned."[12] Shankari Adams described this time period with a gentle understatement: "From a human perspective, [her] stark experience of *tapas* could be described as extremely rigorous and severe."

One night during her evening meditation:

Alice clearly heard the Lord's Voice ask a question that astounded her... "Do you want Me?" From the depths of her innermost Self, without one moment of hesitation, she answered, "Yes!"... On that unforgettable day, when Alice said "Yes" to the sacred contract, the Lord responded, "Then I Will Arrange It."[13]

Adams likened it to Mary of Nazareth hearing God or when a young Albanian woman born Anjezë Gonxhe Bojaxhiu devoted her life to God, joined a convent, and rose to the title of Mother Teresa.

In Alice's telling, this deep longing was recognized by the Supreme Lord, who then proceeded to guide her through the various forms of tapasya. Even more startling is that she then added that "for more than 600 million years of human life, the Supreme Lord has gently instructed me in the way of *tapas*."[14] Meaning that she understood this severe ascetic practice from eons of such practice across many previous lifetimes, each instance more an act of a "reawakening" to her true higher self. She had been here before and knew well the rigors ahead. Not only that, she trusted what the outcome of such extreme self-mortification would ultimately be.

"My *tapas* in this lifetime initially began with increased waking hours and extended meditations," Alice wrote. "Long fasts were maintained and sleepless vigils endured...My heart was stopped several times a day, and sometimes the heartbeat shifted to the right side of the body. All the hair on my head sometimes stood on end as if it were being electrically charged." In this view, what appeared to be self-starvation was instead a test of will. The separation from her sense of self was acute: "My physical frame grew increasingly thin and emaciated; my facial features changed slightly, and to some people my face was beyond recognition."[15]

The astral projections that had occurred when she was a young child returned in force, affecting her nearly every day. At any moment, Alice might find herself projected out of her body. She now understood this childhood sensation in a greater context, a spiritual act that she had long known and mastered in another lifetime. For Alice, it was like riding a bike and she discussed the act of astral projection as if it were a quotidian experience: "In an astral body, you can fly through glass, through the brick wall of a building, or through any material obstruction, without pain or impact. And you can move on air, smoothly and swiftly, without stepping or foot-pedaling like a human being."[16]

She noted the nuances between these astral planes of being, discerning the subtle differences between these planes of existence that she could now ascend to. The second stage she described as still having a "twin" astral body—while when she ascended to the more refined third stage, she described it as more "etheric...which is a bluish-white or silvery ectoplasmic apparition." At the fourth stage, you become transparent and circular in form, a clear round globe[17] devoid of all human parts, while the fifth stage is "Absolute, Manifested Formlessness...It is irrefutably Unrefutable."[18]

Rather than sleeping, she spent long hours in meditation:

The night revealed many of its secrets to me. For instance; the ectoplasm of the spirit bodies of my sister and her son—during their sleep—floated several feet away from their physical bodies. Their spirits vibrated like flags in the wind. One evening, I was sitting down on the children's bed; their dog was asleep in the room. I became projected from my physical body, and as my spirit arose, I called the dog's name out loud. When the dog saw my spirit, he cowered and fled, frightened.[19]

Next came mental tests:

The mental tests began with radiations upon the mind: Such things as electronic elementals, cosmic sounds, astral explosions, intrafractory rays, oceanic and abyssal waves, astral earthquakes, subterranean shocks, and etheric sirens were brought to bear upon it. There were meetings and confrontations with both disembodied souls and phantasmagoric entities with astral deformations.[20]

The fantastical things encountered here (intrafractory rays, abyssal waves, astral earthquakes) strain the limits of the earthbound English language to adequately capture. One can only wonder at the sonic phenomena that Alice Coltrane could hear inside her mind during such extended meditations and astral projections. She delineated one sound as "the sound of planetary ether," a sensation so disorienting that it knocked her to the ground and into "shattered glass... I did not discover the glass in my skin until three days later."[21]

That sense of disorientation continued as she wrote about burning her right hand: "After watching the flesh fall away and the nails turn black, it was all I could do to wrap the remaining flesh in a linen cloth."[22] Matter-of-factly, she added: "Immediate medical attention became necessary. The physician who treated the hand actually recoiled at the first sight of it. If a doctor would administer a pill to me, I would never ingest it. The healing life-breath of the Lord... would daily exercise the injured hand."[23]

Adams recounted some of the other tests Alice Coltrane was subjected to during this time of extreme tapasya: "During one test, I was told to take two steps into the abyss. When I moved to take the steps, there was no abyss." Another time, Alice was told to throw herself out of a second-floor window in their house: "Without a second thought, she approached the window to follow the Lord's instructions. The window was sealed shut, yet the test had been presented to measure the extent of her obedience."

Beyond the acts depicted in *Monument Eternal*, Adams goes into more detail about Alice's trials during this period: "My entire time was spent in one room. Time, as we relate to it, was suspended. I knew sunrise and sunset. I listened, watched, and followed the Lord's instruction... One day the Lord instructed [her] to empty the closet of all her belongings. She complied without hesitation or question."[24] She also wrote about how daily life transpired for Alice's kids:

> In addition to non-communication with relatives, all external activities were suspended. There was no driving, playing musical instruments, or even activity for the care of her children. Yet Michelle, John, Ravi, and Oran were well taken care of. The Lord's perfect plan inwardly directed two women neighbors to arrive each day to prepare the children's meals, and get them off to school. In the evenings, the same women returned after their work to again prepare the children's meals, bathe them, and help them get ready for bed. She recalled that, although she did not converse with the two ladies, she knew that the children received excellent care. They were never neglected. Sometimes during her early morning meditations, astral nurses, provided by the Lord, would arrive to care for the children, who occasionally awakened early or became restless in their sleep. At other times, her younger sister tended to the children.

The disconnect she felt from her family and children is nevertheless shocking. As a result of these spiritual realms she was inhabiting, she wrote that it was "almost impossible for me to bring the mind down to mundane thoughts and general conversations."[25] Shown her own name, Alice could scarcely recognize the letters that composed it.

Like a transatlantic flight that can reduce people to microscopic dots, cars to mere colored specks, and giant cities to undistinguished gray blocks from the perspective of being tens of thousands of feet in the clouds, Alice's time in deepest meditation put her in an uppermost echelon of consciousness that transcended all human scale. In this rarefied plane, the constructs of humankind and human history became mere abstractions.

Yet these trials of tapasya slowly drew down. Adams wrote that after several months, the austerities ended and the Lord "manifested before her in the sunlight, in a visible form." Slowly the door of this God-like consciousness began to close, and Alice began to drift back to the surface of the Earth. The astral nurses and the two women neighbors receded so that she could resume her daily activities. She could converse with people again, calibrated back to the ordinary daily consciousness that we generally inhabit. Looking back on this time, Alice Coltrane said:

> That time of *tapasya* was a profound time in my life. What I most cherish were the twenty-four hour manifestations of God in the house. At such moments, one does not have to go to the meditation seat to communicate with the Lord. The One meditated on is always, fully present... When I think about those days of austerities, I do not dwell upon the pain. When one suffers for God, it is for righteousness sake.[26]

Alice Coltrane emerged from the brink of the abyss, back to being the mother of her four children, back to being the caretaker of her late husband's musical legacy, back to playing music. While *A Monastic*

Trio failed to sell many copies or garner many positive reviews, to those who did tune in, this new cosmic music arising from Alice's heart began to reach the people. Blues guitarist Taj Mahal enthused about Alice's first album: "Have you heard her play piano? And harp? Man, she has a monstrous talent. It's hard for a chick who plays to keep her identity. But she KNOWS. She really knows."[27] UCLA basketball phenomenon Lew Alcindor was profiled in the local newspaper and the reporter noted that Alcindor put on *A Monastic Trio* first thing in the morning and let its placid, rippling harp figures mitigate the migraine headache he was dealing with.[28] Her bandmate and close musical collaborator Pharoah Sanders released *Karma* in May. Despite the fact that its main composition, "The Creator Has a Master Plan," stretched over both sides of the album and clocked in at a whopping thirty-two minutes, it became a hit on college radio and was a dorm room staple that year.

As her *tapasya* receded, Alice Coltrane convened her old bandmate Rashied Ali and fellow Detroiter Ron Carter for another trio session at her Dix Hills home. They cut six songs on May 14, 1969, which became *Huntington Ashram Monastery*, a bit of a joke on the Coltrane home and the royal-purple-carpeted bedroom where Alice was cloistered most of her days. Her liner notes referenced the likes of Paramahansa Yogananda, Swami Chidananda, and Sri Swami Sivananda.[29] Alice explained that *ashram* means "hermitage" and added: "I feel that the real 'ashram' is in your heart."[30]

Whether due to her arduous *tapasya* or some other unknown factor, *Huntington Ashram Monastery* remains the most contemplative album in Alice Coltrane's discography, a fresh re-imagining of what the jazz harp/piano trio could sound like.[31] The music has an intimacy redolent of being made at home, of Alice heading down to the basement as was her wont to capture a moment. As Ben Ratliff noted: "Her music carries a drift not of commerce or entertainment but of daily practice."[32] Rashied Ali witnessed Alice "sometimes getting frustrated trying to learn [the harp],"[33] but whatever growing pains she was experiencing didn't affect the music on the first side. And where someone like Ashby used that sort of setting to render smooth standards, Alice's harp work here is redolent of dabbed watercolors, light and impressionistic. The title track, its foundation a pliant ostinato pattern from Carter, moves like hands roving across the surface of a stream. "Turiya," a word that Alice said signified "the high state of Nirvana, the goal of human life," utilizes her harp's dreamlike timbre to let the listener lilt up toward such a sublime state.

Her bluesy piano style takes up the second half of the album. "Jaya Jaya Rama," the first instance of Alice drawing directly on an Indian chant for a composition, is curiously the one piece on the album that sounds most like a blues gospel standard.[34] "IHS," she explained, stands for "I have suffered," her gospel playing opening up to reveal negative space and engage in some hushed interplay with Carter's bowed bass and Ali's shimmering sleigh bells. This heart-rending ballad revealed the profound depths of grief she was still processing in her own life.

The album showcased her on both the instrument she grew up playing in the church as well as on an instrument she was self-taught on in the span of just a few months. Alice was attracted to the timbral possibilities of both:

> The piano is the sunrise and the harp is the sunset... All that energy, light, brilliance, and clarity that's in the rising sun—or what we call rising; it's actually us moving over toward the light—you can hear in the piano. Then listen to the sonorities of the harp, the subtleties, the quietness, the peacefulness; that's like our sunsets. But the sun is always the sun and a person is always who he or she will be.[35]

The most stunning composition on the album is "Paramahansa Lake," the harp like a garden magically blooming to life. Inspiration for the four-minute musical meditation came from a recording of a monk who was part of Paramahansa Yogananda's Self-Realization Fellowship, the church that Yogananda had established at the crest of Mt. Washington in Los Angeles back in 1925. Paramahansa Yogananda was one of the first Indian gurus to come to the United States, invited to the White House by then-president Calvin Coolidge in 1927 and traveling around the country on speaking engagements. The fellowship church Yogananda established welcomed all faiths and denominations. No doubt this concept of universal faith spoke directly to Coltrane. In her liner notes, she wrote about meeting Swami Chidananda (whose name translates as "one who is consciousness and bliss") when he lectured in New York. In the midst of her spiritual quest, Alice was still seeking a guru, someone who might cast light and provide some understanding, someone who might guide her and alleviate the anguish she still felt in the wake of John's death.

CHAPTER FIFTEEN

Mantra

WILLIAM WOOD HAD SPLIT DETROIT FOR NEW YORK CITY around the same time as Alice did in 1961, and after leaving Terry Gibbs's band, he picked up gigs wherever he could. Much like he had in Detroit, he lived in a loft space down on the Lower East Side where he and his roommates could play music all day and night. As fascinated by Eastern music and thought as his early mentor Yusef Lateef, Wood was already an avowed vegetarian when he first got to New York. He hit spots like Weiser Books, looking for more spiritual insight.

He also went in search of a yoga teacher and learned about a space way up on the Upper West Side with an Indian teacher who taught yoga out of his apartment. The space was called the Integral Yoga Institute, where instruction on various yoga practices was led by Swami Satchidananda, an Indian yoga master with voluminous locks and beard who was becoming known for his wisdom and spiritual teachings.

Born C. K. Ramaswamy Gounder in a small village in the southernmost Indian state of Tamil Nadu, "Ramu" was a precocious youth. At age seven, he impressed attendees at a 1921 conference by speaking lucidly about the concept of ahimsa (nonviolence). As a young man, Ramu went into his uncle's automobile import business, married, and started a family. In his biography, he spoke about having visions of his young wife dying tragically and one day received a phone call that "his wife had suddenly passed away. He was surprised by his own sense of calm...His interest in business and family had come to an end."[1] His lifelong interest in matters of the spirit moved to the forefront as Ramu dedicated himself to his spiritual practice, wandering throughout India.

At one point he reached the town of Rishikesh, pilgrimage center for many seekers nestled at the foothills of the Himalayas where the Ganges River emerges from the mountain range. His guru, Sri Swami Sivananda, was the founder and spiritual head of one of the largest ashrams in Rishikesh, and he initiated Ramaswamy into the sacred order of Sannyas, bestowing upon him the name Swami Satchidananda Saraswati.[2] He would study with his teacher for the next seventeen years. In 1955, Swami Satchidananda returned to the south, teaching at an ashram situated in the country of Ceylon.[3] Eschewing the renunciation and withdrawal of most spiritual teachers, Swami Satchidananda was considered a modernizer in the sense that he demonstrated how yoga could be integrated into daily life and reached people from all walks of society.[4]

After a decade of teaching in the region, Swamiji was visited by a young American named Conrad Rooks. An heir to the Avon fortune, the restless young Rooks was a recovering addict who wished to study yoga, which led him to Ceylon. Rooks was smitten by the wisdom and sheer presence of Satchidananda. An afternoon lesson stretched to two weeks and then Rooks decided to stay on longer. When business matters in Paris forced him to leave Ceylon, he promised to return to Swami.

Instead, Rooks purchased a ticket for Satchidananda to instead meet him in Paris. While he was there, visual artist Peter Max came to visit with Rooks and there encountered the guru in the flesh. "The Swami leaned over the table and shook my hand and I was completely relaxed within two minutes," Max said. "He offered me some hot cocoa that looked just like his beautiful eyes did."[5] The peace that Satchidananda imparted on his young Western artist friends was paradigm-shifting for them and they insisted that en route back to Ceylon, Swami Satchidananda must come to the United States. Little did he realize that this brief visit would mark the beginning of a lifelong connection with the United States, even as his teachings took him around the world.

His hosts—Peter Max and several of his artist friends—arranged for Swami Satchidananda to stay at the Oliver Cromwell Hotel, in a sprawling nine-room apartment with bilious green walls, bare floors, and peeling wallpaper.[6] Swami Satchidananda taught yoga and philosophy in the living room. His message of divine love, universal harmony, and inner freedom resonated deeply with the New Yorkers who visited.

Wood encountered Swamiji there at 500 West End Avenue: "He was teaching some of the classes. I was initiated. He gave me a mantra and he gave me the name 'Vishnu.' It was about fifty people and I was the last one. He had this funny persona. He and I were like, two guys, which was nice. He could be that flexible."[7] Now christened Vishnu Wood, he soon had the opportunity to tour through the Middle East and Africa with jazz composer Randy Weston on state-sponsored tours of the region in the mid-60s. For a few years, Vishnu Wood was based in Morocco, immersed in his study of Eastern instrumentation and philosophy.

By 1969, he returned to the United States and was back on the scene, which had changed drastically since he split. Where his playing of instruments like the oud had once been like an exotic spice, now the mindset of jazz had shifted to wholly embrace the modes and timbres of Africa and the Middle East. "I had been playing with Pharoah and his group. It all worked out pretty well," Wood said. "After John died, Alice called me up. She had been using Pharoah and Pharoah told her I was playing the oud. She knew I had been over in Morocco." And he knew that his old friend was suffering:

> She was having some *psychological* issues after she played with John. I can understand that. When you play with a genius on that level, that's a challenge, that's a huge mountain to climb, night after night playing music at *that* level. I never played with Trane, but I listened to him every night, six days a week. To play at that emotional level every night, I think... it was

very hard. She had to go deep to get that. And I think that had an effect on her outcome. Something happened.[8]

Something did happen. Ernie Farrow drowned in a backyard swimming pool in Detroit on July 14, in what was ruled an accident. In the span of less than three years, Alice Coltrane suffered the profound loss of her mother, her father, her husband, and her half brother, the four people who had most closely influenced and determined her outlook on life, spirituality, and music. She was adrift.

Wood also fell back into attending yoga classes at IYI as well as the lectures that Swami Satchidananda gave nearby at the Universalist Church on Central Park West and 76th Street. Satchidananda's talks were edifying and Wood thought that there might be some wisdom in there that could help his friend.

Thanks to the Immigration and Nationality Act of 1965, Swami Satchidananda could now stay in the United States on a permanent visa, which was approved in August 1968. Per the description on the visa, Swami Satchidananda was "A Minister of Divine Words." He was interviewed by *Life* in their Year of the Guru issue. On January 31, 1969, Satchidananda gave a talk at Carnegie Hall and sold out the entire hall. His message of a divine, universal love and nonattachment began to reach the people.

Toby "Tulsi" Reynolds was in her late twenties when she first encountered Satchidananda. "Did you ever see a picture of him? He was *sooo* beautiful," she said:

> If you want an image of what God looked like, he looked like Satchidananda. I was *stunned* by him. My teacher once told me that you could learn more about the spiritual life from watching Satchidananda enter and leave a room than you can by reading for ten years. He was so beautiful, he just glowed. He had an emanation, it was just extraordinary. Satchidananda was like the father of the world, so I was very close to him for a long time.

Reynolds was born in 1937 and grew up in New York City, a child of Russian Jewish parents. She became disenchanted with her Orthodox upbringing and her mother "deciding whether to wear the mink to synagogue on high holy days and I thought '*ohh gawwd*.'" Her father died when she was eight and Reynolds watched her mother fall apart before her young eyes: "It was like living with a corpse in the living room. It was a very difficult situation. From that point on, nothing made sense to me."[9] Like many flower children of the era, she was searching for answers to the meaningful questions about life and death that her organized religion failed to prepare her for. Tulsi Reynolds began performing as a singer on the West Village folk scene and also got into Indian music.

Satchidananda's apartment on West End Avenue attracted all sorts of artists and creative types. Soon his entourage included not only Rooks and Max but actors like Raul Julia and Sally Kirkland as well as popular artists like Felix Cavaliere of the Rascals and Laura Nyro. For many of these people, their popularity and material successes did little to alleviate the feelings they were having. Starring roles, hit records, sold-out concerts, the world was at their feet, yet they still didn't feel happy. When Nyro first met Satchidananda, she "burst into tears," said Cavaliere. "She told me later she had never seen anything so clean, so pure, in her life, and it just kind of hit her."[10]

While Satchidananda attracted a wide range of followers, Vishnu Wood would have been one of the rare Black devotees during that time period. Eastern religions like Buddhism and Islam had large working-class and minority converts, while Hinduism tended to attract middle- and upper-class types.[11] But Wood felt that the lessons imparted by Swami would provide succor to his dear friend. "I knew that she was really struggling and that's the reason that I introduced her to Satchidananda," Wood said. "I didn't know what else to do. I felt that the woman had been through something that she probably didn't want to talk about or whatever she didn't talk about, so it was apparent. I could feel the suffering that she was going through. Suffering is suffering, it doesn't matter the source of it."[12]

That Satchidananda could provide healing for Alice seemed evident, as he had helped so many others. Reynolds remembered yoga classes at the apartment that Swami would conduct and informal talks given in the living room. But soon the crowds outstripped the rooms at the Oliver Cromwell and so everything moved to the Universalist Church. "Just his presence was very healing," she recalled. "He really was a saint. I really believe that Satchidananda was a saint, because his presence was completely healing. Something about him was so sane and so peaceful. It just radiated." She continued: "A few teachers, it didn't matter what they said, it was their presence that just changed the energy in the room. It was so developed, they were so evolved, that they just vibrated differently. So I got very involved with Satchidananda and that's where I met Alice."[13]

Just when Alice first attended one of Swamiji's lectures at the church isn't clear, but it appeared to have been in the months after Satchidananda was brought upstate to speak to a large gathering of young people. In the middle of August 1969, concert promoters planned a large outdoor music festival situated on a dairy farm in Bethel, New York, called "Aquarian Exposition: 3 Days of Peace & Music," also referred to as Woodstock. The promoters worried that more hippies were caravanning upstate than the pastures could properly accommodate. While the organizers had sold about 186,000 advance tickets, nearly 500,000 people showed up. Alice recalled that the Woodstock promoters had "called and said that they were so fearful that those young people were going to tear the place apart, that [Satchidananda]'d have to come out and do something. So he went and talked to them of peace, and he said there was not one incident in the whole three days."[14] Satchidananda delivered the opening benediction at Woodstock, for many the defining pinnacle of 1960s rock music and youth culture: "Music is the celestial sound and it is sound that controls the whole universe, not atomic vibrations. Sound energy, sound power, is much greater than any other power in this world."[15]

Alice Coltrane wasn't at Woodstock,[16] but she no doubt knew that truth about sound energy and its effect on the universe. She wrote about those summer months of 1969, as her tapasya stretched on and her astral projections continued:

> When visiting the astral worlds, I encountered a number of highly intelligent astral entities and discarnate beings; also many newly-deceased persons who were not accustomed to being without a body. In certain realms, the most beautiful landscapes, mountains, and seascapes were seen. On other planes of existence, I met many beings who had lived on earth thousands of years ago, several of whom were exalted souls who were serving specifically as guides to prepare souls for their return to earth. In the nether regions, one can see exactly how souls who were guilty of similar sins are grouped together to suffer the same punishment. A "lake of fire" does exist here.[17]

One Friday night, Vishnu Wood brought Alice Coltrane with him to Satchidananda's weekly talks at the Universalist Church. "I thought it was excellent," she remembered. "He had a number of young people down there who thought he was a very interesting person. They felt like he had become like a father to them and they all felt like a family. He had got a lot of them away from drugs that steal their sweet life."[18]

By this point in her esoteric studies, Alice Coltrane believed in a universality to all music and religion and consciousness, "and if we put in one fourth of the time into trying to understand our spirituality that we put into wanting to grow more wealthy, we would find some of the incredible things occurring in our universe that we need to be aware of."[19]

Swamiji spoke directly to her heart. "I learned that in life we make appointments," she said. "And when we make an appointment there's desire connected with it, which creates the possibility of disappointment, frustration and all kinds of negative responses when they're not fulfilled. So he says, 'Go back to the root of the whole situation, don't attach yourself to an idea so strongly that you make an appointment.'"[20] Swami Satchidananda taught the principle of nonattachment, a teaching from the Bhagavad Gita, wherein actions are performed with sincerity and dedication while not being attached to the results. He taught that a mind free from clinging to specific outcomes remains peaceful and open. By working without attachment, one cultivates inner freedom, flexibility, and true fulfillment.

Out at Dix Hills, Alice had found herself being overwhelmed by the demands of running her own company, combing through and curating the voluminous tapes left behind by her late husband, concertizing, and raising her family. "I had a small staff of people working with me," she said. "But they were incompetent and I had to do all of the work. So when [Impulse] offered me a contract that would allow them to produce John's private sessions that I edited, I accepted and closed the company."[21] Making every executive decision for her work as well as John's had begun to wear on her. John's longtime producer and confidant Bob Thiele had left the company almost as soon as she arrived, so she felt fully invested in each and every decision made. It weighed on her mind. Already, she was being ravaged in the jazz press for decisions she had made regarding John's music, had read the bad reviews for records released under her own name. Those outside thoughts might obscure her own.

Swami Satchidananda's words eased her anxiety. Rather than shouldering the emotional burdens she had been carrying the past two years, he helped her realize that their weight was no more substantial than air. She could perform her duties as a mother, musician, executor, archivist, and more without the binding ties of attachment. "Say you want to build a ship, build it in a detached manner," she said about Satchidananda's example of nonattachment:

> Don't build it subjectively, don't build it by putting your full faith into a technical, temporary, mundane, or materialistic thing. Go about it in a detached way. Detached doesn't mean disliked, it just means that I don't want this project to consume me. It will if I allow it. If I subject myself it ends up binding and controlling me. I can't sleep at night because that's

all I'm concerned about. So I will go and do my work objectively. That's one of the best lessons I've learned that he taught us.[22]

Much like the others before her who convened weekly at the Integral Yoga Institute, Alice felt fully at peace in the presence of Swami Satchidananda, and freed to do her own creative endeavors and the archival work of her late husband without being buried underneath the weight of expectations. She began going to meetings and events as often as she could.

For all intents and purposes, Swami Satchidananda became Alice's guru. As she explained, a guru is "the one who removes discrepancies, he removes doubt, he removes disbelief. He's the one clearing the area, purifying in your life, removing obstacles and impediments in the way. But he cannot do your work."[23] Her own sense of self-determination was already there, but in Satchidananda, she had finally found the teacher who could help her to clear away those doubts, that disbelief.

"The thing I remember most about Alice was that she was very quiet," Reynolds recalled. "But she was very present. And we became very friendly." At the informal get-togethers at IYI, they would sometimes play music together. And Vishnu Wood soon found himself also playing with his old bandmate again. "She was very quiet and you could tell that she was spiritual. A lot of respect for herself and other people," he said. "But she liked to have fun." In the span of their time together with Terry Gibbs at the start of the 1960s to the end of the decade, he was shocked at her musical transformation. "Her playing was very different after she played with John," he said:

Because she came from the church—as Aretha came from the church—and musicians who come out of the Black church, they have the spirit in their music. Alice always had that spirit. And the spirit was very high in her music. I'll give you another example. I practiced Buddhism. And the tenets of Buddhism are very... hard to understand. But if you apply yourself and you follow the principles that lead to the practice and lead to enlightenment, then it's available. So when she played with Trane, she had to play it on a different level. So after she played with Trane, her music, her playing changed tremendously. It was just like almost celestial.[24]

By the end of the year, Alice's spiritual trials began to wind down. "I have fasted for three months on water and protein drinks, and similarly for 10 months at a time," she said:

> I have stayed awake from three to four days in an effortless, meditative state, with little or no communication with others. In terms of austerities known as mortification of the body, I have experienced them. Foremost, I do not recommend that anyone engage in them, they can be dangerous to the unadept, also to those who are misguided by something or someone.[25]

Alice had gone through the spiritual fire, sometimes literal fire, to reach the other side. As she put it in a short documentary made for a segment of National Education Television's *Black Journal* television program:

> There were days that I know I spent more than 20 hours in meditation and there were periods of time that lasted beyond two or three weeks that I know was well beyond what the human endurance is when it comes to meditation. I found out so much about myself and the people around me and about my husband and family. Also, I found out that whatever questions that I might have had in my mind concerning whatever events in the future or past were answered. From my personal experience, meditation brought me face-to-face with God, hand-in-hand, heart-to-heart, and almost to the point He was me and I was Him. Or we were just us. I don't know how to phrase it. It was just a closeness that it's just impossible to be that close with a human.[26]

The interviewer asks: "What kind of effect has it had on your life since then?" To which Alice replies: "It gave me freedom, it gave me my true independence... There were demands made, *definite* demands, which took me away from the world." Her brow furrows and her voice cracks. She swallows hard as she continues:

> At one point, almost away from everything: music, family, and all. Because the sacrifice had to be within an inch of my life. Almost literally, and I feel that because it was such a high price paid—now I can't say it wasn't the highest price as Buddha or Christ—because that was life. Or Martin Luther King, that was *life*. But I've been very close to the end of my life and I feel that I've been given my freedom now. I can act, I can be, I can live as I want to and nothing can... there's no claim. No one can buy me. There's no action I have to pay. I have no karmas to pay. All of it has been given back to me. That I'm free.[27]

Her years of searching for answers were finally resolved with her introduction to Swami Satchidananda. Through these teachings on nonattachment, she learned to let go of concern for the results of her work. As her anxiety lessened, her creativity expanded, allowing her to envision her music with a broader, more liberated perspective.

CHAPTER SIXTEEN

Journey on the Ship of Satchidananda

IN THE FIRST WINTRY WEEKS OF 1970, AN INDIAN MUSICIAN IN HIS fifties named Pandit Pran Nath landed in New York City. Born in Lahore in 1918 (then still part of British India before becoming Pakistan), Pran Nath was an avid music enthusiast who studied the Kirana Gharana, a Hindustani vocal tradition. Pran Nath was especially taken with its austere singing style, with an intense focus on the slow-moving alap that emphasized close intonation. If you lived in India, you could have heard Pran Nath's singing, as it was broadcast regularly on All India Radio. At some point in the 1960s, a few tapes drifted over to listeners in the United States and to producer Alan Douglas, who had worked with the likes of Duke Ellington and the Last Poets. Douglas released some of this music on a 1968 album titled *Earth Groove*.

An Indian therapist, teacher, and musician named Shyam Bhatnagar began to play these tapes for New York friends like Fluxus artists La Monte Young and Marian Zazeela as well as Terry Riley, and soon Pran Nath was brought over to teach this idiosyncratic vocal raga style in the United States. Tulsi Reynolds recalled going to author/editor Barbara Stacy's apartment down on 14th Street on Monday nights, where sometimes Bhatnagar also taught meditation classes. She also began studying with Pandit Pran Nath and recalled some crossover between the crowds for Satchidananda and Pran Nath, seeing Young, Zazeela, pianist Pat Rebbilot, and others at the Universalist Church. She also began to study vocal raga and tamboura with Pran Nath. Reynolds recalled:

> The way that you learn to sing is you lock eyes with your teacher and you play the tamboura. At first, Panditji would tune it, because he didn't trust me to tune it. And he was very rough. So he would, like, throw me the tamboura. He would sing and he would look at me, and I would look at him, and we would sing. And you have to do what he's doing. But in that school, every note has three degrees of sharp and three degrees of flat and the tambura also has three degrees of sharp and three degrees of flat, so the tuning and the singing is so difficult. So I remember we were doing one phrase and I could never get it right. Finally, I got so frustrated, and I said, "Panditji, I don't know what you want. I don't know what you want me to do." So he said, "In Western music, somebody sings, somebody listens. In this music, nobody sings, nobody listens."[1]

Reynolds began to apply her downtown studies of raga uptown at the Integral Yoga Institute. "I remember getting ready for some celebration we were having and rehearsing there," she said. "It was Alice, me, Raul Julia, Felix from the Rascals. It developed very quickly."[2]

Outside of jamming at IYI, Alice started work on a new album with help from a new producer at Impulse. Ed Michel got his start producing jazz and blues albums at World Pacific and Riverside Records before moving over to Impulse in 1969. Up until that time, he had only conducted business over the phone with Alice, but on January 26, Michel rented a station wagon in Manhattan, picked up saxophonists Pharoah Sanders and Joe Henderson and bassist Ron Carter, before driving everyone out to Dix Hills. "That was the oddest part of the day, waiting in the station wagon...for everybody to get their stuff together, get down to the car, and drive out there," he said. After two hushed trio albums, it would mark the first time Alice had recorded with horns since John.

Upon arriving at 247 Candlewood Path, Ed Michel finally met Alice Coltrane face-to-face. "It was a normal home filled with instruments," he recalled:

> From the garage, you walked downstairs to the basement to get into the studio. It was a professionally built home studio. There was an isolated control room with capability of talk between the recording side and the musicians-in-studio side. It was set up for four-track recording; There were two Ampex ½-inch 4-track machines and at least one Ampex 2-track, and a nice selection of professional microphones. I'm sorry to say that I don't have a sense of my impressions or her presence—the usual hustle and bustle of setting up a recording in a new studio took precedence.[3]

While the Coltrane kids were in school that Monday, Alice convened Sanders, Henderson, Carter, and her neighbor Ben Riley for the date, while another neighbor, Wally Barneke, helped to engineer the recording. Michel recalled the way it played out that day:

> It wasn't all that unusual to do a quintet album in a single-day session, especially one without involved arrangements. I don't remember how much music was written out; Certainly it was not a lot. I can't recall a lot of rehearsal—perhaps running down the head of a tune and discussion of the form. What I principally remember is the ongoing conversation between Pharoah and Joe, which was about extended-range saxophone technique, since both of them were masters. I recall thinking it went down like a "blowing date" and I was surprised that it was less 'out' than I had anticipated. I actually believed that there were a couple of cuts that would get airplay on 'free form' and college radio.[4]

Four pieces were laid down that winter's day, more focused yet more ambitious than what Alice Coltrane had previously attempted. The epic title track "Ptah, the El Daoud" remains unlike anything in her discography, a sprawling fourteen-minute march that goes through a vast topography of emotional peaks and valleys. It's also one of the rare times Alice Coltrane drew on her nascent study of Egyptology and books like *The Teachings Of Ptahhotep*, referencing Ptah, the ancient Egyptian god of creation, with the epithet in the title translating as "the beloved." In the liner notes, she explained:

> My meaning here was to express and bring out a feeling of purification. Sometimes on earth we don't have to wait for death to go through a sort of purging, or purification. That march you hear is a march on to purgatory, rather than a series of changes a person might go through.[5]

After all she had endured over the last year, her words cast the piece in a more autobiographical light, reflective of her own period of spiritual purification and something likened to death. (Or, if you're on a march to purgatory, one can read that as a progression away from hell.)

The two saxophonists here offer a thrilling study in contrasts, a frisson that Alice had already tapped into with her *Cosmic Music* concert. "Joe Henderson is more on the intellectual side, while Pharoah is more abstract, more transcendental," she said.[6] "Between [Pharoah and Joe], they knew more about the mechanics of the saxophone than anybody I'd ever met," Michel remembered. "It was astonishing. I was curious before the date about how they would play together and it was as though they'd been rehearsing for months. They had very different approaches to things but could blend beautifully and deal with it."[7]

Both tenor players had been on a tear by that point, operating near the peak of their powers. Sanders—fresh from the commercial success of *Karma*—was pushing further afield with *Jewels of Thought* and avant dates with Gary Bartz and Don Cherry. After leaving Blue Note, Henderson cut the early fusion Black Power statement *Power to the People* with Herbie Hancock, Carter, and DeJohnette. (The day after *Ptah*, he and Carter would head out west over to Van Gelder's studios to cut

Freddie Hubbard's soul-fusion landmark *Red Clay*.) All of that profundity and earthly power comes to bear on this session. Michelle Coltrane remembered: "I got to be on the other side of the glass a few times. As the only daughter, the oldest, I was of service for her, mother's helper. I just liked the sound. I never recovered from hearing that music in the studio. The sound was *sooo* good."[8]

"Blue Nile" highlighted the gains made thanks to Alice's diligent practice on harp. Both Sanders and Henderson switch to alto flute, giving the subdued piece a decidedly Eastern feel. It also anticipates the ambient, unhurried breath of her next phase of composition with its emphasis on mood and vibe, "more a feeling than a melody." That subliminal pulse beacons ahead to future generations. "Mantra" stands as the most through-composed and avant-garde of the pieces, Alice's piano prominent in its support of the two dynamic saxes. "She was very clear about what she wanted and how she wanted it done," Michel said. "She was very clear in letting everyone know what she expected. This was also true about mixing and editing." For Michel, the hardest part about the session was properly recording the harp. "The harp has a wider tonal range than the piano, and those damn noisy pedals! She was very clear and specific about corrections in the mix and where she wanted edits."[9]

The most evocative, heart-quaking performance occurs on "Turiya & Ramakrishna." Again, Alice evokes that Sanskrit word and the hushed, contemplative ballad finds her return to her piano trio roots. She explained that the name Ramakrishna also referenced a monastic order in India that was dedicated to spiritual cultivation and philanthropic work. Carter's empathetic bass work supports her while retaining all the delicacy of her gossamer melodic line. Alice said it was built around three notes:

> You'll notice near the end where I modulate from D Flat up to D and back to the D Flat before going out, there's a suggestion of "Parker's Mood," the part to which the words went "Come with me…" It's like God asking us if we want to go home—that kind of feeling.[10]

In early February, Alice loaded up the kids and the Lyon & Healy harp in the Chrysler station wagon and drove out to Van Gelder's. There she met up with her late husband's former bandmates Elvin Jones and McCoy Tyner for the latter's *Extensions* recording session. With Gary Bartz and Wayne Shorter[11] in the frontline, it made for a formidable sextet. In a certain light, it might have been a glimpse at what the John Coltrane Quartet would have sounded like had Alice joined the group (though on harp instead of vibes as originally bandied about). Alice's connection with Carter, so soon after the *Ptah* date, is immediate, her harp like blossoms on the bough of his bass. Her harp solo some eight minutes in positively shimmers in iridescence. It's a remarkable spiritual jazz session, recorded at the cusp of fusion taking over the sound of jazz. Unfortunately, it sat unreleased by Blue Note for over two years.

Later that month, Cal Massey staged a benefit concert for the Black Panthers to help fund their legal defense in court. As was Massey's wont, he assembled a fifteen-person group to perform an ambitious eight-part suite, titled "The Black Liberation Movement Suite," with Alice prominently featured on harp. As to how the finished suite sounded, we may never know. Of the eight movements performed, only three were ever recorded, two by Archie Shepp, one by John Coltrane dating back to 1961, but left unissued from the *Africa/Brass* sessions. One can only wonder what "Reminiscing About Dear John (for John Coltrane)" with his widow on harp might have sounded like that day in downtown Brooklyn. Later that summer, Alice would also participate in another Massey concert, this one held on a boat in New York Harbor.

In April, she headlined Saturday night at the Black Arts Festival at Stony Brook on Long Island. Michelle Coltrane remembered the drive out:

> Before seat belts, we'd pile into the station wagon and the harp would be in the car with us. We'd be going to Stony Brook for a spiritual retreat, and we'd be playing a tent or fort game under the harp. The car would stop and me and my brothers would slide everywhere. On the car radio,

she would shush us and make a reference to something in a classical piece, or point out John Coltrane licks on a jazz tune.[12]

A glimpse of this performance was captured on 16mm color film, with Sanders on sax, Ali on drums, and Vishnu Wood on bass and oud alongside bassist Reggie Workman and Alice on upright piano. A smile breaks across Alice's face as a version of "Africa" starts to stampede. You can just glimpse the kids goofing in the wings, their Afros bobbing behind their mother at the piano bench. The dynamic performance ends with a standing ovation for her.

One week after that show, the Ohio National Guard opened fire on an anti-war demonstration at Kent State University. Four students were killed and nine others wounded or paralyzed from the bullets. Eleven days after that, another confrontation between highway patrolmen and student protesters happened at Jackson State College in Mississippi, with police firing over four hundred times into a gathered crowd, killing two students and wounding a dozen more. The search for peace continued amid such needless violence.

On a sweltering afternoon day in spring, Alice sat at 500 West End Avenue and received mantra initiation from Satchidananda. Another initiate recalled:

We waited there for about three hours to get our mantra initiation. I think Gurudev (Swami Satchidananda) was late on purpose—to really test our sincerity—because about half the people left before he arrived. [Alice] and I were seated opposite each other and even though she was a big celebrity, she sat cross-legged on the floor with the rest of us. She never asked for special treatment and delicately wiped the sweat from above her lips.[13]

Alice became more involved with events happening at the institute. She played on fellow devotee Laura Nyro's album *Christmas and the Beads of Sweat*, adding sweeping harp glissades as Nyro's piano runs build toward a sexual climax within the song. It's perhaps the lone instance of hearing Alice in a carnal setting. Otherwise, her musical intention was always oriented toward something higher.

A *Newsday* feature on Alice that spring found her hard at work mixing and engineering a recording made at home.[14] The reporter noted the plush blue carpet and the burning incense in the room, as well as a high stack of boxed tapes behind the studio door of unreleased John Coltrane sessions. "I just had to find out where the fuses were instead of calling my neighbor or an electrician every time the lights went out," she said:

> But other than that, I have tried to carry on my life as if John were still here. I learned to edit and work the control board by watching the engineers that recorded me. Now I have about 17 privately recorded albums my husband did, in addition to having two albums of my own to do so I have to put the children to bed and come down late at night to practice and work.[15]

Sometime in May, a young reporter named Angela Dews went out to visit the home and spend the day with Alice as the kids ran around. "She was very open with me," Dews recalled. "I was at her house, she was barefoot, the kids were running around. They played, they'd run up and down the stairs, and she did, too. I felt a real, real connection with her." Dews spent most of the day out on Long Island:

> She'd walk around, she'd see something, she'd sit down and play, or she'd do something, you know. She was very much a person who made music all the time. It was very natural, moving from their instruments to her kids, to a conversation with an interviewer. They had a meditation space... off to the side of the music room. I do remember that the feeling of it was everywhere, there were the images that showed that they were meditating and they had a spiritual life... When she talked about John, she would look away, you know, she was still connected in some way.[16]

About a week after their interview, Coltrane mailed Dews a typewritten letter, laying out her worldview: "My music and life are both based upon a simple, integral principle; i.e. spirituality and truth. I believe that spiritual growth is just as important as the physical and mental development of an individual." In the last paragraph, she discussed her life with John:

> Being married to John was an out of sight experience. It was really together. There was such a similarity between us in thought and aspirations. We almost always agreed upon the same things... I was very fortunate to be married to a genius. A woman may be the sustaining power in the home, but the man, I feel, is the energy and soul force behind the whole structure.[17]

Later that month, Alice took her group down to Philadelphia to take part in a festival presented by the Philadelphia Jazz Society with the St. Joseph's College Black Awareness Society on Friday celebrating John Coltrane, with Archie Shepp now performing with her group. Sometime that summer, Alice performed on the new PBS show called *Soul!* Hosted by Ellis Haizlip, a pioneering Black television producer, the episode also featured singers Kim Weston and Bobby Hebb. TV listings of the time blurbed: "Mrs. Coltrane chatted with host Ellis Haizlip and performed harp with her quintet for 'Blue Nile' and 'Leo' with Archie Shepp." Shepp's memory failed when the show was mentioned. Worse still, the early years of *Soul!* were not deemed worth preserving or archiving and this performance is now considered lost.[18]

On a sticky eighty-eight-degree Fourth of July day, Alice Coltrane performed at the Village Gate. Wood had performed with the group since earlier in the year and he brought his oud with him and switched between instruments during the concert. "Rashied Ali was on drums, Pharoah or Archie played horn sometimes, Jimmy Garrison made some gigs on bass," he recalled. "Sometimes I would play the oud, but I was also playing an Indian instrument called the dilruba, tamboura, and all that. She had a pretty large ensemble when she played."[19] For that particular performance, former Ornette Coleman bassist Charlie Haden was in the group and they performed a long, unmetered improvisation titled "Isis and Osiris."[20] Alice's audacious blending of oud (an instrument that wasn't played in ancient Egypt), harp, bass, drums, and soprano sax created a fusion that transcended its willfully eclectic "world music" trappings to invoke these ancient Egyptian deities to sublime effect. When *Ptah, the el Daoud* was released that autumn, critics mostly remained indifferent or hostile to the music.[21]

Sri Swami Satchidananda and his Integral Yoga Institute family quickly outgrew their housing at West End Avenue and went in search of a larger, more settled space. Hari Zupan, one of IYI's administrators, found a six-story building on West 13th Street in Greenwich Village and quickly moved to negotiate a deal for the building. But as it came time to make a down payment to take the building off the market, Zupan learned that they were just short of funds. He called uptown to Satchidananda—then in conversation with Coltrane—who seemed unbothered by the predicament, offering no real solution and hanging up quickly. Time was running out and Zupan's next call again yielded no decision from the guru. As recounted in his biography, Alice then asked unprompted:

"I have been coming here and benefiting so much from your teachings. Is there anything I could do to help the center? Is there anything you need?"

He simply said, "Whatever you feel moved to do, you can do."

"Well, do you need anything urgently?"

"In my life there is no urgency."

"Okay, fine, Swamiji. Thank you. I don't want to take up any more of your time; I should go now." As Alice walked away from West End, she realized she had left her purse behind and doubled back. Again she sensed that there was something the center needed:

You know I'm really embarrassed about this. I came with the idea of giving some contribution. Then when you said that there was no urgency, I thought I would wait and give something later. But it seems that God wanted me to make a donation immediately. That must be why I forgot my purse and had to come back for it. I'm going to write a check right away.[22]

Swamiji extended an invitation to her to accompany him when he returned to India that winter to attend the World Scientific Yoga Conference. Alice was now part of Satchidananda's inner sanctum of devotees, contributing not just financially but musically as well. "[Sally] Satya Kirkland put on a program on the life of Buddha and I had a chamber orchestra at the time so I played the music," Alice recalled. "Gurudev liked it very much and so my proximity to him developed from the programs and the music which was what I felt I could offer to Him."[23] Tulsi Reynolds was also part of this program, playing tamboura in this intimate ensemble at the center. "And I guess she was impressed with the way I was playing it," Reynolds said:

I became a really good tamboura player, mostly because Panditji scared me into it. So Alice invited me to join her and we would just play together there. She played piano and I played tamboura and there were people playing flutes. It was really free form. And then one day she said, "I'm going to be recording and I'd like you to play some tamboura." So I said, sure, you know. And we started working on the album. We had very little rehearsal.[24]

As Reynolds recalled, she came out to Dix Hills in the middle of the day. The kids weren't around, but the rest of the group was. "The studio was sort of like a wing of the house and then you came in and there was a door and these steps and the studio was a whole wing by itself," she said. "So we were in the studio and I remember it was daylight. And like, there was not music to prepare." The group included Pharoah Sanders, Rashied Ali, and Cecil McBee, who Reynolds had gigged with a few times at Café Au Go Go in the West Village:

> Cecil and I had become very good friends, but Pharoah had no idea who I was. When Pharoah walked in and he saw a white lady playing tamboura, I thought he was going to faint. Alice just looked at him and said, *"Pharoah."* And he calmed down. Cecil was laughing hysterically because he knew me. I didn't say anything. I just picked up the tamboura. And of course, once we started and he saw that I could really play, then he was fine.[25]

There may not have been much prepared in the way of written music, but Alice knew what she wanted and imparted that to the group. The music would be an expression of gratitude at her newfound relationship with Satchidananda and the hope that it kindled in her heart as well as an expression of her two and a half years of tapasic mortification and self-effacement, which—as she wrote in a September 30 entry in *Divine Revelations*—finally drew to an end. The music would contain all the grief and suffering of that journey, as well as the hope and healing that now emerged on the other side of her trials.

She also began to envision what her trip to India might be like. It had long been a goal of John's to one day visit the country, to experience its music and spiritualism firsthand. Now, through God's divine grace, it was coming to pass. As McBee recalled of the session:

> It was very, very spiritual. The lights were low and she had incense and there was not much conversation, dictation, or verbalization about what was to be. Her desire of your essence was all very, very tangible. The spiritual, emotional, physical statement of the environment, it was just there. You felt it and you just played it. It was very subtle but powerful. I can remember it to this day. It was all novel to me, but I knew that it was something very spiritual and very special. No doubt about it.[26]

Alice's first recording, a 45 cut with the Premiers in 1957. *Courtesy of Yale Evelev*

Left to right: John and Alice Coltrane, Pharoah Sanders, Jimmy Garrison, and Rashied Ali onstage at Sankei Hall on July 10, 1966, in Tokyo, Japan. *Photo by The Asahi Shimbun/Getty Images*

In Mussorie en route to Rishikesh, December 1970. Left to right: unknown, a swami from Sivananda Ashram, Amma DeBayle Kidd, Inga Fairweather, Alice Coltrane, Swami Satchidananda. *Courtesy of Integral Yoga Institute*

At the Ceylon home of Inga Fairweather, who hosted the meditation retreat, January 1971. *Courtesy of Integral Yoga Institute*

Fisk University, Nashville, Tennessee, 1971. *Photo by Robert Abbott Sengstacke/ Getty Images*

On the beach with Swami Satchidananda, Long Island, 1972. *Courtesy of Integral Yoga Institute*

Alice Coltrane, Swami Satchidananda, and Ishwara Cowan (a devotee of Sri Swamiji) in Woodland Hills, California, early winter 1974. *Courtesy of Integral Yoga Institute*

Richie Havens and Alice Coltrane performing at an anti-apartheid protest in Oakland, late March 1986. *Courtesy of Radha Botofasina-Reyes*

Holy day event at ashram, mid-1990s. Left to right: Uma Everett Pierson, Ramah Elynda Hickson, Swamini, Sudarshana Malhotra, Dhaneswar Wesley. *Courtesy of Radha Botofasina-Reyes*

Alice Coltrane at home, 2002. *Courtesy of Jake Walters*

Alice Coltrane at home, 2002. *Courtesy of Jake Walters*

Alice Coltrane at home, 2002. *Courtesy of Jake Walters*

Pharoah had been Alice's closest musical collaborator for close to five years, but even he felt a bit of apprehension when approaching this ineffable music. "You know, her playing was amazing. I loved what she was doing. But I always felt like what I was doing wasn't good enough," he said. "At one point, I had told her, 'I don't know if you like the way I'm playing or not. I don't know whether this fits, or what.' She said, 'You're doing O.K. Just keep on playing. Keep on blowing.'"[27]

Foundational to the music recorded that day in Dix Hills was Reynolds's unhurried thrum of the tamboura. Her teacher Pandit Pran Nath is crucial to understanding the rise of American minimalism in the 1970s, thanks to his famous students: La Monte Young, Marian Zazeela, Terry Riley, Jon Hassell, Rhys Chatham, Catherine Christer Hennix, and Charlemagne Palestine. Yet his lesser-known pupil's presence at Alice's home meant that Pran Nath also informed a shift in spiritual jazz as well. "What the tamboura does is it sets down a sonic field in which all the other instruments can float," Reynolds said:

> If the tamboura is tuned correctly, you hear all the other little intervals that are resounding within that. So you can play almost any note and it will work, *if* you touch it exactly right. It sets out a field that everything else floats in and the trick is to sustain it. That can never break, because you cannot miss a note. Any break in that sound field and the whole thing falls apart.[28]

That moment of magic is evident from the first buzz of "Journey in Satchidananda." Tulsi's tamboura appears to radiate and widen as it makes its way across an infinite ocean. McBee's steadfast ostinato roots into Reynolds's drone and spires high above it. And when Alice arrives, it's like the gates of Eden swinging wide, her harp glissandos beckoning you into paradise. Sanders takes a rare turn on soprano. His solo conveys both a deep gorge of grief and a yearning for transcendence. Alice soars to the uppermost register of her harp, punctuating her phrases with steep descents into the lower octaves and back. No matter how high each musician's searching solo takes them, Tulsi's tamboura offers a soft landing.

This new composition announced Alice Coltrane as an artist in her own right, actualizing that "universal sound" that her husband strove toward with his later music. "Journey" is cosmic music, a vessel that transports you to the highest stratospheres of inner space. While it was not the first instance of Western jazz engaging with Eastern instrumentation,[29] there was still little like it in jazz music up to that point in time. It's an audacious fusion of tamboura with harp, two instruments whose histories on two separate continents reach back to 2500 BCE yet rarely if ever meet. As Alice explained:

> The harp sound is flowing, oceanic, and ethereal. It has a celestial sound that people often associate with heaven. For me, the older instruments have more of a mystical sound, and tambouras, hand cymbals, and mridanga drums were made for worship. In fact, if played devotionally, all instruments could be used to honor the Lord.[30]

Both remain rarities in modern jazz. But *Journey* is also a profound reimagining of what spiritual jazz could be. The peers, legends, and label mates of Alice—Pharoah Sanders, Sun Ra, Archie Shepp, Albert Ayler—constituted the masculine faces of the form. Yet the number of women who participated in this music was lamentably low. The negatives that critics saddled Alice's music with—"delicate," "lacking muscle," "wispy," "subdued," "content," "pretty," "going nowhere"—all became strengths in this new environment she created. "Journey in Satchidananda" inverted all of that.

Lao Tzu once wrote: "Shape clay into a vessel / It is the space within that makes it useful."[31] So did Alice amplify "the space within" of this music. King Kong might scale the side of the Empire State Building, but could such power climb up a trellis of flowers or dance on a spiderweb? What male critics bemoaned as "feminine" traits (using every coded word imaginable to not say it out loud), Alice elevated into a receptive, nurturing music. At the height of the Vietnam War's daily violence and that entire cataclysmic era of the late 1960s and early 1970s, such gentleness and empathy *was* radical.

The Impulse sales team knew they had something very different on their hands, and a promotional sleeve was designed to look like a doctor's pharmaceutical script pad. *Instead of taking a red or blue pill to relax- Tonight take ALICE COLTRANE and JOURNEY TO SATCHIDANANDA. It's smooth but contains recommended amounts of pure energy*, it read, signed by a Dr. I. M. Peaceful.

It's silly—especially for an artist who never medicated herself in such a manner—but even if they couldn't quite pinpoint what "Journey in Satchidananda" *was*, they knew it was something unheard before, a hybrid of contrasts. It was avant-garde free jazz, but calm and centered. It drew on classical Indian music, but you would never mistake it for Ravi Shankar. There was fire flaring up from Sanders's horn, but it was tempered and soothing. It sounded profound loss and longing—of a widow pining for her soul mate, of a soul longing to be united with the Supreme Lord once more—yet imparted a distinct sensation of uplift and affirmation.

In the preceding copy, there also appears to be an error: instead of reading "Journey *in* Satchidananda," it instead used the prepositional *to*. Which does make more sense, in that you travel *to* a destination. Michel's session notes bear slightly longer titles.[32] "Shiva-Loka" was instead "Almighty Shiva-Loka" and the original title of "Journey in Satchidananda" was "Journey on the Ship of Satchidananda," her guru like a great, benevolent vessel. But at some point in the album process, Alice realized that for all her imminent intercontinental travel, this particular journey was more intimate and immediate than that. She wasn't going "to" a place, nor was she "on" something either. She shifted to the prepositional "in" to signify a more profound truth: Satchidananda was not an external destination to be journeyed to, but rather something (or someone) to be discovered within your own self.

Studying with Satchidananda,[33] Alice embraced Hinduism and the tenets of Advaita Vedanta (nonduality), in which the Self (the Atman) is a reflection of and identical to the Absolute (the Brahman). God wasn't someone far off in the heavens. It was as Jesus said in Luke 17:21, "The Kingdom of God is within you." The title of the piece makes that truth evident. "To get Self-realization, fulfillment, that's the point," Alice said. "And it isn't selfish—that term—it just means that you go to your fullest and highest potential, and not be limited by some tenets of some doctrine that says that we come here, here's the minister, and that we pay our tithes and go home and go back to your job or business or whatever and do everything you want."[34]

"Shiva Loka"—the exquisite complement to "Journey" yet forever in its shadow—rearranges those same acoustic elements into a breathtaking new configuration. McBee's bow work dovetails with tamboura to create a powerful drone. Sanders looses a heartrending cry on his horn, while Alice's harp gushes forth like a fresh spring.

"Something About John Coltrane" uses the complementary low frequencies of Tulsi and McBee again to meditative effect, accentuated by overdubbed sleigh bells from Majid Shabazz. The piece is evocative of John's great modal explorations, and the solos from Alice and Pharoah are especially poignant, redolent of the Classic Quartet era, rather than the more challenging explorations of the late quintet. But both were aspects of the titular man himself, all part of his spectrum, his quest, whether it was articulated as a scream or serenade.

While there was a serenity about it, Alice's music remained every bit as political and radical as the more vociferous shrieks to be heard elsewhere in "free jazz." Much like her husband did with "Alabama," Alice's sympathy is present in every note. As McBee explained:

> We were critical of the limits that were being placed on us. And we felt that our musical words could penetrate steel walls, so long as we said them with honesty, and perseverance, and creativity from the deepest [part] of ourselves. So we were political in that way. But things were rather novel, as far as civil rights were concerned. There were those who were much more eloquent than we were with words, like the Malcolm

Xs and the Martin Luther Kings, the Angela Davises. We let them have that verbally, but we said it in music. And we were able to say it in music. We got across equally as well as they did with what we expressed. So Alice Coltrane, when she arrived, was more subtle in her statements, from a very spiritual point of view. She was very quiet, expressing the various sounds and waves of spirits and essences of the gods and the earth. Where we were trying to come from, with the loudness and bombast of our music, she made these statements in a more delicate, graceful, articulate, and uniform way than we did.[35]

Every bit as radical as the unspoken politics in the music, Alice decidedly broke from the Baptist faith. At this point in her life, Alice Coltrane could no longer accept the restrictions of her upbringing, especially when the question came to death and reincarnation. It's a shift reflective of what was happening across the young culture, as more and more kids of the new generation began to interrogate Christianity and find it lacking. As she put it:

The Western Church has failed, especially with young people. It was set up to serve needs it's not meeting. Ask a Swami Hindu monk or someone else from the East about life after death and you'll get answers that are real about direct experience, about looking to God. It has helped me to go on.[36]

With these new pieces recorded, Alice fully intended to go on. But not everyone did. Such bleak times fomented despair. The day before Thanksgiving, Albert Ayler—less than three years after he performed at John's funeral—was dredged out of the Congress Street Pier on the Brooklyn side of the East River. He was only thirty-four years old.

CHAPTER SEVENTEEN

Universal Consciousness

AFTER MORE THAN HALF A DAY UP IN THE HEAVENS, ALICE COLtrane's plane touched down in Delhi on December 17, 1970, where she joined Swami Satchidananda for part of his World Peace Tour. She accompanied him through northern India, visiting Delhi, Mussoorie, and Rishikesh, before continuing to Sri Lanka for an Integral Yoga retreat. This was not simply a physical journey following Swami Satchidananda; it became a deeply transformative experience spiritually—just as she had sensed it would be.

For new arrivals, India overwhelms the senses from the first intake of breath. The air is by turns fragrant and repugnant. One breath can be flavored by curry, the next by diesel exhaust. One inhale brings in frangipani, the next dung. The eye espies a blue statue of Krishna and a beggar with mangled limbs in a blink. Cows, hand-drawn carts, bicycle-drawn taxis, and rumbling trucks all vie for space on the roads. There are gleaming golden spires, vibrant flowers, and children reduced to living skeletons in alleyways. The sacred Ganges River is crystal clear up in North India, an opaque brown by the time it reaches the holy city of Benares, where the bodies of hundreds of shrouded dead pilgrims are submerged into its depths around the clock (or burned on funeral pyres along its banks). For Alice, she could witness a thousand Indias and know there were millions more left unseen, riven yet somehow unified, all jostling and attaining a cosmic balance.

Swami Satchidananda had already been traveling on the subcontinent for a few weeks before Alice's arrival. According to his personal assistant at the time: "That particular trip was not a group trip. This was Swamiji traveling with one or two assistants. Those were the days when it was really informal and it was very wonderful. And though it was informal, the nature of their relationship was certainly teacher and student."[1] Alice's luggage was simple, save for the slightly smaller harp that she traveled with, even purchasing a ticket for it to ensure safe passage. Amid the throngs of people everywhere in India, sometimes people would be struck by the sight of a tall Black woman from the West carrying a magnificent harp with her. "It was stunning to people there, that somebody came from the West to play. She made quite an impression—but she was always very modest," a student said.[2]

Soon after her arrival, Alice Coltrane performed at the World Scientific Yoga Conference. It was a meeting of gurus and students, as well as scientists and scholars. There's a quick glimpse of Alice onstage at the conference, resplendent in white; the light comes from a low angle on the stage so that the shadows of her and her harp loom large in the background. There's no sound, but the focused look on her face conveys the devotion of her performance. On a frigid, hazy morning soon after, you can also see Alice bundled in a black trench coat with Swamiji, himself clad in a dark gray robe, as they visited the tomb of Mahatma Gandhi.

Next stop was Rishikesh, nestled at the foothills of the Himalayas, where the holy Ganges River emerges from the mountains, cold and pure from the runoff of deep Himalayan snow. Alice Coltrane was not the first Western musician to make this trek to Rishikesh. Most famously, the Beatles had traveled there to study at the ashram of Transcendental Meditation founder Maharishi Mahesh Yogi in early 1968, along with the likes of Beach Boy Mike Love, singer Donovan Leitch, and actress Mia Farrow. (Saxophonist Paul Horn had made the pilgrimage the year prior, sneaking inside the Taj Mahal with his flute to make what's considered the first New Age album, *Inside*.)

When they arrived at Sivananda's ashram, it was "filled with an intense vibration of deep peace," per the voiceover. The next scene showed the group on the banks of the Ganges. Swamiji performed yogic arm balances on a rock, other devotees did handstands, while Alice sat perched on a rock in the back. Cut to Alice watching her guru as he offered up puja and then plunged into the icy Ganges, still crystal clear this far up in the mountains. He vigorously rubbed his face and beard in the holy river. As she watched the radiant flower petals as they swirled and danced on the surface of the river, her thoughts might have traveled back to those nights at the loft in New York City, when the earliest dawn was breaking and fresh petals from the florist shops dotted the sidewalk.

They drove fifteen miles up the Ganges where Swamiji showed his guests the cave where his guru, Swami Purushottamananda, would meditate. Some six minutes into the clip, Alice stands in a sleeveless white flower print outfit. She's led knee-deep into the river by Swamiji, holding her left hand as her feet wobble uncertainly on the cold, slippery rocks. Steadied by him, she slowly sinks down into the Ganges and splashes water all over her body, shivering in the winter sun. The holy dip in the Ganges complete, the narrator notes that "this river carries with it a positive, purifying vibration. It is considered as a blessing to even touch its holy waters. We felt an undeserved and unfathomable blessing to enter her in Swamiji's presence."[3]

Music was often featured during the many lectures, temple visits, and public celebrations leading up to Swami's Satchidananda's birthday celebration on December 22. Alice performed on harp whenever she could. After years of listening to Indian music on record with John, she experienced the music of India up close and personal. Whether it was at an ashram in the Himalayan foothills near Rishikesh or in Madras (the capital city of Tamil Nadu in southernmost India), she heard these fascinating chants being performed on harmonium, tabla, and tamboura.

Even though she didn't speak Hindi, something about the words beckoned to her.

Bhajans in their most general definition are a type of South Asian religious antiphonal music that serves as a song of praise to God or a deity. Bhajans stretch back as far as the eye and ear can perceive in terms of human history. Anyone's best guess is they arose within a thousand-year span between 1500 and 500 BCE. Such songs were rarely written out or ascribed to a single composer. They echo all the way back to the Vedic era in ancient India, to the first spark of humankind realizing there was a higher power. In a manner of speaking, they seem to have always existed, forever the sound of people giving praise to God. Like her beloved church hymns, the bhajans were seemingly simple structures featuring a call-and-response between devotees. Yet they were sturdy, flexible improvisational structures that could build higher and higher, attaining ecstatic heights. Long fascinated by those century-old church hymns she grew up on, Alice was instantly fascinated by these Indian songs of praise.

While visiting the home of an Indian family, Alice experienced another intriguing phenomenon. She saw a photograph of Sri Sathya Sai Baba, a revered holy man from outside Bangalore, and wrote: "It appeared somewhat alive. The smile was very beautiful, and his hand was raised. I observed astrally that it moved."[4]

On Christmas Day, Alice and eight other of Swami's devotees arrived in Ceylon to stay at Swami's old ashram. Many natives and ashram dwellers gleefully greeted their guru upon his return. Many gathered to see Swamiji and offer their respects, following traditional customs such as washing the feet of a holy person and adorning him with garlands. Celebrations included musical performances, singing, the traditional Bharata Natyam dance between Lord Shiva and Goddess Parvathi, and Alice's iridescent harp. At the start of the new year, more students arrived in the mountains for a ten-day retreat with Swami. Footage featured the gleaming emerald hillsides of tea plants and of devotees performing traditional yogic kriyas (drinking enough salted water to easily induce vomiting to clean out their stomachs) as well as Swami gamely playing Frisbee like a senior on the quad.

At the end of the retreat, the camera caught Alice and a few others saying good-bye to Swami, as they began to make the long trip back to the United States. India had been a blessing, even amid the hardships of the country. "The only thing she couldn't get together was the poverty in India," Archie Shepp recalled. Alice hoped that she could only return again and deepen her spiritual practice. "Before leaving India, he gave me the name Aparna which is a name of Parvati," Alice said. *Aparna* is a Sanskrit name meaning "leafless," a reference to deep asceticism.[5] Swamiji may have chosen this name in recognition of the spiritual intensity and challenges Alice had already endured on her path. "I asked Gurudev, 'Would you ever consider initiating me into *brahmacharya?*' He told me, 'That is possible. When you are ready and it's the right time.'"[6] Alice pondered what a nunlike celibacy would do to help her to go further in her spiritual journey.

Later, Alice would explain to Radha Botofasina what sort of sacrifices one must undergo in order to properly hear and be attuned to the Lord. "If you see a glass and you pour oil in the glass, and you empty it out, then there's just like a sheath, just like a thin layer. That's as much ego as you possibly should have," Botofasina recalled. "Because you have to be this empty vessel so that the Lord can use you. It's never a situation, she would explain to us, where you're going to impose your will. It's always whatever the Lord's will, as we learn in tapasya: 'Thy will be done.' And that's the reality of it."[7]

Journey in Satchidananda was released on February 20, 1971, less than a month after Alice returned home. "I hope this album will be a form of meditation and a spiritual awakening for those who listen with their inner ear," Alice wrote in the liner notes. *Down Beat*, downright parsimonious regarding her previous albums, gave it a rapturous review, announcing her as an artist in her own right: "Like John Coltrane's *A Love Supreme, Journey In Satchidananda* is more than a musical composition—it is a profession of faith... This is sacred jazz of the highest order."[8]

Reynolds believed the tamboura's presence imparted something missing from Western instrumentation. "It's very powerful and it touches something so deep in people, it touches that place where you can finally be still," she said. "That's the genius of the tamboura, it allows this space around it, so that all of those feelings, all of those sounds, everything can manifest. It's not just the sound itself, it's the space around it. And what's happened is that the impact of that music just keeps growing."[9] Alice tuned into its uncanny drone and used it in a startling new context. The tamboura provided grounding so that all the emotions of this music, the deep depression, the sorrow, the catharsis, the heart-swelling power, the ultimate redemption, could all rise.

The week of the album's release, Alice played a string of shows, starting at the Ben Light Gymnasium at Ithaca College, followed by a headlining Saturday night slot at Blackextravaganza, a festival presented by the Black Student League at the Community College of Philadelphia.[10] The next night she returned to perform again at Carnegie Hall, as part of a benefit for the Integral Yoga Institute. The bill featured her many friends and colleagues from the institute, like Laura Nyro and the Rascals. And the band Alice assembled for the performance was a formidable one, a modified double quartet: Pharoah Sanders and Archie Shepp on saxophone and flute; Jimmy Garrison and Cecil McBee on bass; Clifford Jarvis and Ed Blackwell drumming; Kumar Kramer playing harmonium; and Reynolds on tamboura.

For Tulsi Reynolds, it was a heady occasion:

> It's overwhelming to step out on that stage and say, "This is Carnegie Hall," especially because I'm a singer. But you're so focused, the demands of that instrument is such that you're so focused that you have no time or room to relate to anything else that's going on. You have to be so completely concentrated. The tamboura is a very difficult instrument to use in those kinds of situations, because it requires quiet and it's very hard unless you're in a meditative environment. You can't have that going on when people are having drinks and talking, it would just shatter the

sound. Thankfully, the audience was very enthusiastic and respectful. As always, when the things from the album were playing, they were very quiet.[11]

The original plan was just to perform the title track, but the fervent response to "Journey" was so rapturous that show promoter Sid Bernstein urged the band to keep playing. Next was "Shiva-Loka," which benefited from its dilated duration. Ed Michel tapped engineer David Jones (famous for capturing the Bill Evans Trio *Live at the Village Vanguard*) to record the concert. The plan was for Impulse to release a live album featuring three of its most popular and prominent jazz artists, only to have the executives balk at the idea. The tapes sat unreleased for decades and were ultimately lost, save for a two-track reference copy Michel dubbed as he was leaving the label in 1976. (It finally saw release in 2024.)

Aside from the microphones not picking up Kramer and Reynolds at all (the aural equivalent of only looking at the top hundred feet of a California redwood), the concert remains nothing short of astonishing. Just hearing Shepp and Sanders together is downright revelatory, a meeting between the two spiritual jazz titans who outside of John Coltrane's *Ascension* date never recorded together. A *Down Beat* live review depicted that what might "have been a cutting contest developed into a mutual respect and admiration society, as Sanders and Shepp grooved on each other and were inspired to their best playing."[12] Both men paid their respects to the Coltrane matriarch. "We were approaching the music from different sides," Shepp said. "Pharoah was playing more like John, mine was more influenced by my meetings with John, things that he told me and taught me." But concertizing with Alice was unlike any other experience he had had:

> I hadn't had much experience playing with harp. She could convey beautiful elements. It was a very rich experience when she played harp. There was an impressionistic Debussy element. As far as I was concerned, I

had great respect for her. She might not have been accepted by the jazz critics of the time, but they didn't understand Coltrane's music. I'm sure a number of the critics had absolutely no idea what was going on. There wasn't much precedent for her. There was Mary Lou Williams, Hazel Scott, Terry Pollard, but they were more inside the idiom, they were strictly swing players.[13]

Still riding high, Alice moved over to piano and the group went into "Africa," the John Coltrane composition that she had transcribed off the record a decade ago in her family's living room. Now she led a ferocious rendition of it on the Carnegie stage. They capped off the hour-long performance with one of her husband's last compositions, "Leo." On piano, Shepp gleaned a another facet of Alice's music:

I heard a lot of gospel music and the blues. I always thought Alice's music was closer to spiritual and gospel music than jazz. I approached it that way. It's more about going into yourself. She was a very original pianist. Because she didn't follow the traditional methods of jazz, as it were, some of the critics missed her brilliance. I never heard her play more traditional jazz music. She took me right away into a more spiritual groove, more structure-oriented, the music of the Baptist, but it wasn't strictly Baptist. She had a serious classical background, so the music was frequently a combination of African American spiritual music and what I would interpret as Western classical music.[14]

Despite the hippie trappings of the audience and the docile sounds of Nyro and the recently reconstituted Rascals, the response to Alice's cathartic music was immediate, the crowd roaring with applause.[15]

A few days later, she performed upstate at Buffalo State University's Black Arts Festival, with Pharoah's own formidable group opening. Alice emerged onstage with Garrison and McBee on bass, Freddie Waits on drums, and Shepp and Sanders back on the frontline. Incense burned onstage in long thin plumes. A review in *Coda* described the opening moments:

> As she plucked the first string, a beautiful soft shower of notes floated down to the audience. This was echoed in Pharoah's melodic soprano and vibrant string temperament of the bassists. The sound experience exuding from Alice's harp is difficult to describe, difficult to do justice to; one is wholly engulfed in the mystical depth of her rich playing.[16]

The review concluded with the kicker: "I am sure the Creator was well pleased with their musical offering." In her meditations, Alice was told by said Creator: "The suffering tapasya that you have undergone in this lifetime would have resulted in the death of numerous persons had they attempted it. Yet, you survived tapas of the severest kind, and your spirit could not be broken."[17]

Alice had survived and arrived. Yet she was already outward bound again, newly rekindled by her experiences in India and a new sound she heard within. As she explained later that year in a radio interview as her young children played in the studio underfoot[18]:

> So the past four years have really been involved in that aspect of really trying to see what's going on and finding my place in the spiritual world. So now I feel that I've gotten some answers; I've gotten *quite* a few answers. There isn't such an urgency as it was before to really go into meditation and spend so many hours in-drawn. Now I feel that I've been given an opportunity to come out, to be with you tonight, to play, and get into music. This is really what I felt from the meditation. Now is the time to really look at music.[19]

She began to envision a sound that wouldn't be reliant on breath or strummed strings. Piano keys attack but they also decay, thrummed harp strings fade away, and reed instruments need an inhale to sound the next note. "If the father [John Coltrane] had remained on this earthly plane...I'm sure I would have stayed with the piano, because it was very complementary to what he was doing," she said. "He had the power, intelligence, the skill, the knowledge to carry on. He didn't need anyone else so the piano served as a nice quiet complement."[20]

She wanted something that could sustain and replicate the feel of the infinite, something that could also exemplify her newfound strength and self-determination. "When we talk, we break, we breathe, we go through all of our human tendencies," she said. "Things heard from an astral or spiritual place—coming from a spiritual place—does not contain unbrokenness. No breathing, agitation. It's like a perfection, it's pure and unbroken."[21]

Thinking back to the bhajans she heard on her travels through India—the pneumatic wheeze of the harmonium, the shruti box, the tamboura—all lingered in her thoughts. "I listened to a lot of beautiful sitar and vina music and I'm going to use some of the chants heard... some of the essence of the East," she said.[22]

"An organ has a peaceful, meditative sound," she said. "A smaller, hand-pumped organ, called a harmonium, is played in many temples in India and around the world. The sustained, vibrating sound of *Aum* that it makes is adulation to the Supreme Lord."[23] The closest thing she could find to such instrumentation here was the Baldwin portable organ. She bought one and began to experiment on it at home, but that wasn't quite it either.

"In one meditation it was told to me that the organ had reached an age where it wouldn't serve properly, and the precise instrument I should get was revealed to me," Alice said. "I could even read the insignia right there on the wood. So I went out to find the Wurlitzer I now have. I didn't need to do any research; it was just conveyed to me."[24] In the Wurlitzer 805 Centura, fitted with two full-size keyboards and an Orbit III analog synth on top, she discovered a liquid electricity that could evoke the church organ of her youth, the droning waves of Indian music, as well as the strafing fury of her late husband's horn. It could all be contained within her self, those multitudes blasting out like magma from the center of the Earth.

> As I continued in my music after the Father left, I found other keyboard instruments a necessity, because I did not want to have to depend on anyone either. When I started playing organ and it's the truth; I hope I'm not misunderstood—I found that I didn't need anyone! When you have two or three manuals and complete bass in the pedals, if you play it the right way, you don't need any percussion. Not that drums and bass aren't welcome. I appreciate the skills of people like Reggie Workman and Roy Haynes, those kind of people. They are very great musicians and contributors to music. But I tell you, when I began to play the organ, there came the freedom and understanding that I would never have to depend on anyone else musically.[25]

Vishnu Wood recalled a Satchidananda talk at the Universalist Church with Alice offering support on organ. "I hadn't really heard her play the organ ever, didn't even know that she was playing that instrument," he said. "It was a very profound experience because she was able to play a music I hadn't heard before. It was obviously from another sphere. The deepest expression I heard from Alice was on the organ. Because it has whatever it takes to express the deep expressions she has as a human being."[26] On the organ, Alice felt an immediate connection to the infinite, the godlike, the ever-present Ohnedaruth, able to channel all of that intensity and transcendence to her keys. A stunning, intensive iteration of cosmic music emerged in the wake of her return from India.

In April, she began work on new music with an expansive, radiating sound that would more than earn its title. "*Journey in Satchidananda* was a much more meditative, internal kind of focus," Reynolds said. "I think that the *Universal Consciousness* music was much more connected to John...to that train of thought."[27] Shepp recalled going out to the house to record with Alice and drummer Clifford Jarvis during that period of their collaboration.[28] "Alice was quite a sound engineer," he said. "I remember her working between the piano, her instruments, and the recording booth. She was an extraordinarily talented woman."[29]

Later that April, Alice flew out to California with Shepp, Garrison, and Jarvis for a performance at the fifth annual UC Jazz Festival, sharing a bill with the Last Poets and Sun Ra and His Astro-Infinity Arkestra. It was a bone-chilling night onstage, and reviews of the concert noted that the conditions affected the tuning and performance. At one point, Alice told the shivering crowd: "We're sorry we can't communicate with you tonight because it's so cold we can't play our instruments properly."[30] The show did introduce young flamethrower Frank Lowe into the fold, as he was the second horn and would soon take over saxophone duties entirely. But not before he got hazed by Shepp: "They would make me learn different changes by teasing me," Lowe recalled. "Ask me if I know certain tunes, I say 'No, I didn't know them.' They say, 'Damn, man, I thought you were some young genius or something and you don't know *this* blues tune?'"[31]

Back at Dix Hills preparing her fifth studio album, Alice did away with the breath of the horns so as to augment these radical new compositions with the near-infinite sustain of the violin.[32] Much like *Journey*, her palette seemed to snatch at many disparate timbres all at once: her harp and piano, as well as the jazz trio foundation of bass and drums. Tulsi's tamboura[33] was present again, but now it was amplified in larger waves by additional strings. Rather than just use one violin, or assemble a classic string quartet, Alice instead massed four violins together into a giant ball of shrieking, wailing sound.

Ornette Coleman is credited with transcribing the string charts, but producer Ed Michel said that Alice soon "realized that she could do what she wanted herself, and from that point further on she did all the string writing."[34] Alice used classically trained players like John Blair and Joan Kalisch, session musician Julius Brand, and free jazz violinist Leroy Jenkins to create an ecstatic frisson. There are unison strings and modal melodies between the four that create a monolithic mass of sound not unlike the drone encountered in Indian music. But there's also a freedom given to the players, allowing them to add trills, aleatoric improvisation, and a tactile messiness that imparts a visceral, live wire energy coursing through it all. You would never mistake the strings on *Universal Consciousness* as an attempt at Western classical, a buttoned-up third stream experiment, or an easy-listening move toward the mainstream akin to *Charlie Parker with Strings*. Instead, it's a white-knuckle ride through the upper stratosphere.

If the gentle, soothing opening moments of *Journey in Satchidananda* are like easing into a warm bath, *Universal Consciousness* is a plunge in the bracing holiness of the Ganges. Little can prepare one for the vivid, spiky string quartet that lurches to life in the opening seconds of "Universal Consciousness." If Alice wished to convey the terror and discombobulation of an astral projection, it's right here, a sheer ascent taken at an impossible speed. Violins slash and flutter around her harp, before a quick tape splice plunges us into Alice's lavalike organ work and the spilled mercury of Jack DeJohnette's drum fills, a bewildering mix of chaos and breath-catching beauty. Alice's quick study of the mixing board and her engineering prowess allowed her to punch in her harp or organ as she saw fit for each piece, making bold studio choices that most jazz players still disregarded.

Roving over, under, and all around like an interplanetary vessel able to defy the laws of gravity at whim is Alice's Wurlitzer. Her June 19 duets recorded with Rashied Ali on "Battle at Armageddon" and "The Ankh of Amen-Ra" are dizzying marvels, hinting at the same energy whorls that Ali had once recorded as a duo with John Coltrane in early 1967 (which would not be heard by the general public for another three years until they were finally released as *Interstellar Space*). Of the former, Alice wrote that the piece depicted not an external conflict of good and evil, but rather "this great spiritual battle [that] takes place within the nethermost regions of the human soul, literally, every day."[35]

"Oh Allah" weds her organ to the violins, conveying a preternatural sense of drift. Rather than the four violinists entering en masse, there's a natural fraying to this otherwise elegant sound, "ragged entrances and exits and a bombastic vibe—you hear each player's *intent*," as violist/conductor Nadia Sirota once explained it. "It's not a commonly-used device in classical music and I personally love it."[36]

Alice's most ambitious fusions transpire on the second side of the album. Alice saw the potential of bhajans as a transcendent, avant-garde vehicle for rhythm section and orchestra, something strikingly unique in jazz, Western classical, or Indian classic music. "Hare Krishna," the first of two traditional chants she heard while in Swamiji's entourage in India and subsequently set to music, established a precedent that would in a few years become de rigueur on her later albums. One could overlay that now-famous Hare Krishna chant atop the slow-moving melody, but when Alice's organ enters, the piece soars into uncharted territory. The violins convey a disembodied sensation of cresting over a bank of cumulus clouds, with Reynolds's tamboura hum, Garrison's bowed bass, and Alice's organ supporting such flight, making for a sublime eight minutes of gravity-free sound. Experienced in the right frame of mind, it's downright transformative.

"Sita Ram," the second composition based on a bhajan chant, foregrounds Tulsi's tamboura, with Alice layering little plucked upper-register harp filigrees and her incantatory organ atop it. The music seems to breathe, rising and falling in unmetered fashion, an approximation of the amoebic alap section in Indian classical music, with Clifford Jarvis's intermittent snares, bells, and shakers approximating the supple rhythms of the tabla.

While Alice's meditations, mantras, and travels with her guru situated her firmly in Hindu thought (the gatefold featured a photograph of her on the banks of the Ganges River with him), the liner notes for *Universal Consciousness* suggested that her own personal philosophy was still a grab bag of different modes of religious thought in the notes, which she signed as Turiya Aparna.[37] It's the lone instance where she used the name bequeathed to her by Satchidananda and an early public instance of her new spiritual name, the name that she heard Lord Rama call her by: Turiya.[38]

Conceived over the course of eight days, "Cry" was a birthday present for Alvin Ailey's mother, Lula Cooper, who had raised him as a single parent amid the horrors and indignities of Jim Crow–era Texas. Danced by the company's principal female dancer, Judith Jameson, the sixteen-minute piece featured Laura Nyro's "Been on a Train" and the Voices of East Harlem's rendition of Chuck Griffin's "Right On, Be Free." According to Jameson:

> Alvin had difficulty finding music for the first section, but finally decided on a piece by Alice Coltrane. When I first heard it, I felt that the music was all over the place. I did not know Alice Coltrane; I knew John Coltrane and the shapes that he used musically. Her music was very foreign to me. I didn't know what to expect... Even though the first part is gentle, your energy is so keyed and pointed to convey that kind of stillness, it takes as much energy to do that as it takes to do the last section.[39]

Ailey selected "Something About John Coltrane" and it set the tone for the entire piece. Jameson—statuesque in a flowing white dress with a long white shawl that's a veil, a funeral shroud, a shackle, a washrag, a head wrap—expressed a tumult of conflicting feelings in the opening section: deep maternal love, sacrifice, the remnants of slavery, beauty, the burden of the world, hope and sorrow. Ailey never explained the meaning, but Jameson did:

> In my interpretation, she represented those women before her who came from the hardships of slavery, through the pain of losing loved ones, through overcoming extraordinary depressions and tribulations. Coming out of a world of pain and trouble, she has found her way—and triumphed... She walks across the stage defiantly as if to say, "Look at me. I'm a gorgeous being. I have something to say. I'm here." If I had been told that I was to represent every Black woman in the world, I would have dropped the cloth and left the stage immediately.[40]

The response was ecstatic. The *New York Times* raved: "There is pain here as well as power, and the music, so oddly modern as a contrast to Ailey's atavistic and archaic images, murmurs its special grating message as a counterpoint to the measured and flamboyant choreography."[41] It became one of the most iconic dances in the company's repertoire, a tour de force and yardstick for every principal female dancer to measure herself against. Alice's music reflected and amplified all of it.

In July, the Alice Coltrane Quartet performed a rare set at a jazz club, Slugs' Saloon in the East Village, and then did a quick Northeast tour through Chicago, Pittsburgh, and Philadelphia. Tulsi also remembered Alice and the kids coming out to visit her later that summer on Fire Island:

> John's death was very hard on her. But I understood that, because of what I went through. So I said to her, "Come, come out and spend the day." I said, "We don't have to talk," which she liked, so they came out for the day. The kids were just running around. She came out and just being there, being on the beach, looking at the ocean, walking on the streets, it was just *that* that she needed, not my conversation. It reminded me of that line in the Dylan song: "When you want someone you don't have to speak to / won't you come see me, Queen Jane."[42]

Almost everyone who spoke about the memory of Alice Coltrane mentioned her natural shyness, her quiet temperament, but Reynolds also remembered Alice's gentle sense of humor. The two would be driving somewhere and no matter how crowded the parking lot, they would always find an open space in the front. "And she'd say to me, 'I don't know. This happens all the time.' It was like a blessing she had," she said. "She could *always* find a parking space." As her friend at the time, Tulsi also understood that sometimes it was important to just be there for Alice:

> It always felt more appropriate to me to just be there. To not like drag out of her the details of what she was going through. She would tell me

what she wanted to tell me—or not—and what was more healing for her was just the presence of a friend who didn't make any demands. Who didn't ask any questions. Who didn't want to be told "when one door shuts a window opens" cuz I know if anybody had told me that I would have told them to shut up! She needed to work everything out herself.[43]

Universal Consciousness was released to strong reviews. One raved: "Alice makes cosmic music. To the uninitiated, her non-western, atonal orientation can be a rude shock. It often sounds noisily anarchic. Rather, its very heady, spacey music... *Universal Consciousness* makes very powerful, cleansing meditational magic."[44]

Over fifty years later, *Universal Consciousness* remains an audacious album statement, whether you are experiencing it for the first time or the hundredth. There's nothing like it in jazz or classical music, an assured amalgam of the two that is indebted to neither musical genre. Alice never settles or falls back into a previous pattern or musical concept. She's restless as a seasoned mountain climber, fully allowing for gorgeous new sonic vistas to be experienced yet looking ahead to the next peak. With regards to her peers, Alice's music stands apart. Pharoah Sanders was in the midst of a run of transcendent Impulse releases that used African polyrhythms as their bedrock, allowing his horn to reach skyscraper highs. Archie Shepp fused free jazz with an array of other strains: R&B, soul, spoken word, classic Duke Ellington. Ornette Coleman scored *Skies of America* for the London Symphony Orchestra and explored an eclectic tumult of acoustic and electric instrumentation on *Science Fiction*. But no one sounded as fearless as Alice Coltrane at the time.

She also assembled the John Coltrane Memorial Concert at Town Hall in New York. Former bandmates like Elvin Jones, McCoy Tyner, Archie Shepp, and Pharoah Sanders all brought their groups out, with Alice headlining a new group with Lowe, Tulsi, Reggie Workman on bass, and Ed Blackwell on drums, featuring fifteen string players and her on organ and harp. A *Down Beat* live review noted sound problems, but said: "Pictures on album covers cannot fully convey Mrs. Coltrane's beauty. Her smiling presence radiated a spiritual glow throughout the hall...adding what sounded like Sun Ra's space organ to the ever-expanding musical explosions. At this point, the entire string ensemble joined in some uninhibited free playing that built to a joyous climax."[45] The next month, Alice Coltrane returned home to Detroit to perform for two nights. Of the concerts for *Universal Consciousness*, the levity of the music was offset by the feeling it imparted. "I think the music sounded exploratory," she said. "[The reaction] wasn't, 'Oh my, we have to go into some mystical experience.' The people just heard a joyfulness, a light-heartedness about it."[46]

Chapter Eighteen

Galaxy in Turiya

Angela Dews's feature on Alice Coltrane ran in the December issue of *Essence*, the most intimate glimpse of life inside her Dix Hills home up to that point. The boys ran wild in the woods without their coats on, Mom barefoot watching them through the wide kitchen window. Then they were inside sliding down the carpeted stairs on their tummies. When Oran fell and cut his lip, Alice comforted him and soon he was running wild again. Miki Coltrane, now eleven, stopped just long enough for a photograph and then disappeared into the house. Throughout, Alice was a calm, comforting presence, level whether she was watching the kids, talking to a stranger in her living room, or dabbling on the piano in the music room. "She wasn't reprimanding or anything; she was sort of watching them be themselves. It was very cool," Dews said. "And she did it easily. It was very natural, moving from their instruments to her kids, to a conversation with an interviewer and all of that was very, very natural for her."[1]

For Dews, she felt like a fan more than a music critic, and perhaps that allowed Alice to lower her guard a bit. "My music isn't jazz, not really," she said. "It is closer to spiritual music. It's universal and it's freedom." She also spoke candidly about life as a Black woman in the United States:

I'm free. John did this. I got an offer to go to Japan but I won't go 10,000 miles on someone else's terms. I've been taking orders, in some form, all of my life, being a woman I've always been subservient—servant, nurse, cook. The man is number one. He must assume the position of leadership or where is he? In this country, the Black man is not leading. The only hope is through enough money to pay his way to privacy, freedom, independence… I'm glad I'm not a man. My true expression is in my art and my kids.[2]

Music once again flowed through the Coltrane home. The kids would sometimes wake to the sound of their mother at the harp or at the piano, crawling under the piano to feel the strings and wood vibrate. "We got a hi-fi stereo with a record player inside it and lid on top,"[3] Michelle Coltrane recalled. Even though her aunt Marilyn had graduated to being a songwriter at Motown in Detroit, Michelle doesn't recall much soul or pop music being played in the house, though Alice did tell Dews that she could discern the spirit coursing through the music of Ray Charles and her fellow Detroit church alum, Aretha Franklin.

"I don't remember her playing a lot of jazz, but I heard it being recorded in the basement studio," Michelle said. "Obviously where we lived was on top of the basement. Our rooms were there. I don't know how good the sound-proofing was, but I could hear the tape in reverse: *rrrVvrr, rrrrhgbgbg, jjjjjgh*, I kept hearing *that* all the time." Michelle also fondly remembered lots of classical music. "My mother was a big Stravinsky fan. We would turn the stereo up with the Stravinsky on and dance around the couch and we would just go nuts."[4]

Ravi Coltrane recalled that Swami Satchidananda was a frequent visitor. "He made many trips to our home," he said. "My memory is aided by home movies of him playing with our dog."[5] He also remembered his mother's love for Stravinsky during that time:

> Her favorite pieces were *The Rite of Spring* and, more so, *The Firebird Suite*. We heard music constantly, but there was something about *The Firebird* that really spoke to us… The very end of the piece begins in this

very tranquil way and builds into this overture, this very simple theme. We used to dance around to it like we were on the stage. It is a ballet, *The Firebird*, so I guess we were channeling that idea.[6]

A profile in *Soul Illustrated*[7] a few months later featured Alice talking about her role as a mother for her four kids:

I try to let them live by my example. I believe in giving them basic home training—cleanliness and kindness towards each other. They are all eating fish only once in a while. Most of all, I do not want to take away that part of being children that they enjoy. They watch television, play games and records... Parents must not let the children know every problem or worry that exists. Children don't need this, they need their freedom from all parental worries so they can grow up healthy and free from unnecessary stress.[8]

Much in the same manner that she mastered the harp and the electric organ, now Alice turned her attention to writing and arranging for strings. Ornette Coleman had helped out a few months prior, but now Alice intuited just what she needed to do to score the music she heard in meditation—and on the family hi-fi—and applied it to sheet music. In this way, she also began to move toward a dream that John had always had, to have his music realized in bigger ensembles, not just the Classic Quartet but entire orchestras. He had always wanted the music to expand beyond jazz.

That November, Alice commenced work with a bigger ensemble and sound palette. She had outgrown the home studio in Dix Hills and booked two days at the Record Plant. Frank Lowe played saxophone, with Reggie Workman and Ben Riley comprising the rhythm section. She also booked a concertmaster and a fifteen-piece string orchestra for the session. She said:

Recently, I have been feeling that there's a part of music that—had [John] been alive—we would have really went into this area. So, I'm starting to do it myself this year. That is getting involved in most of the instruments which can produce a more spiritual sound. Like the instruments which require breathing, to me I'm more in line with what's happening on an earthly level. The instruments that can produce a sound that is continuous, to me express the eternal, the infinite. The organ, right. And strings also. The strings can continuously produce without a break. This is the extension as far as I see. The piano is very percussive and it is not harmonic. The organ isn't percussive, but it is definitely a harmonic instrument. That thing I mentioned about the strings is there. You can sustain a tone indefinitely. From my research into meditation, the sounds that could be heard during meditation periods were sounds that were unbroken.[9]

It was Frank Lowe's first studio date. "I really enjoyed playing with Alice. I was encouraged to play as loose and original as possible, so really got a chance to stretch out," Lowe said. "Of course, I couldn't play bebop things in that context, but that was okay. The purpose of music is to blend. You do what is necessary to present the music as well as your own ego as much as possible."[10] His fierce tone was a thrilling juxtaposition with the more lush string arrangements that Alice had created.

For *World Galaxy*, Alice tapped her IYI colleague Peter Max to design the cover art. It featured a windswept portrait of her gazing off to a distant horizon, with eye-popping explosions of vivid colors all around her. "When I think about Alice, I always see her in my mind with a very faraway look in her eye," Tulsi Reynolds said. "She was always working something through internally."[11] A fifteen-piece string ensemble suggested greater vistas and bolder visions. Tellingly, three of her compositions featured the word *galaxy* in the title. If that weren't bold enough, she also took two of her late husband's most iconic pieces and added careening Wurlitzer runs and colors as bright, gaudy, and funky as the cover art: "My Favorite Things" and "A Love Supreme."

On the former, the Wurlitzer replicates all the shrieks and flames of her late husband's soprano sax runs, leaning into the electrified timbre of her keys in such a manner that it also brings to mind the searing guitar solos of the likes of Jimi Hendrix or Carlos Santana. It soon tussles with high-frequency whooshes of backmasked tape (which brings to mind the sounds Miki remembered hearing in her bedroom at night as the tapes were rewound in the basement studio). It gives the piece a vertiginous feel, of Rodgers and Hammerstein getting dizzy on a nightmarish carousel.

"Galaxy Around Olodumare" is named for the Yoruban deity, a supreme but remote spirit above that religion's four hundred or so lesser gods and goddesses. Olodumare serves as the lord of heaven. Lowe's horn offers a frenetic and fierce counterpoint to the heavy and dramatic strings, which seem to submerge the piece down to an unplumbable depth, while timpanist Elayne Jones makes the orchestral drum rumble like thunder.

Baker Bigsby engineered the session, the first of many he would do over the course of Coltrane's recording career, and recalled: "I kind of stumbled on what she was looking for by chance. There was always this bass-heavy stuff. She liked her low tones a lot, so sometimes her compositions sonically were kind of dark, but there was more bass than you would normally hear on a record. She liked that."[12]

The piece dissolves into "Galaxy in Turiya," Coltrane's most opulent work to date, a nine-minute fantasia for harp and orchestra, which evokes comparison to the rare harp and orchestra pairing of something like the Adagietto section from Gustav Mahler's Fifth Symphony. The scored trills of the string section—rapidly moving between the primary pitch and the note just above it—gives the sound a sense of freneticism and unfettered energy. As composer Nadia Sirota noted, this sort of notation in Coltrane's score allows the strings to swirl in a manner similar to her harp glissandos, the added tremolos on the violins making everything quiver in vibration with even more energy.[13] One gets the sense that the same hand gestures moving across Alice's harp strings are now amplified across several instruments, a flick of the hand creating these outsized waves of energy.

"The amazing thing was her teaching the strings how to play free," Ed Michel recalled. "I mean, these were studio string players and the last thing on their minds was free music, but she managed to convey it very quickly and they soon got into the idea. It was liberation."[14] It also allowed for an aleatory effect in the strings in juxtaposition to the monolithic string textures elsewhere. Allowing each string player the freedom to improvise glissandos and tremolos at different times can recall the skin-prickling effects of Hungarian-Austrian composer György Ligeti.[15]

Her version of "A Love Supreme" featured the deep intonations of Swami Satchidananda. "Turiya was not a Swami at the time, she was a student of Satchidananda," Bigsby said. Ed Michel remembered Swami coming out to the Village Recorder studio in Los Angeles to record a benediction for the album: "He chanted in Sanskrit for about 15 minutes, which not only let us adjust the mic levels, but allowed us to fool around with quadraphonic echo." On playback, Swami said the echo was "what it sounds like when you chant way up in the Himalayas." The spoken-word part for Alice's rendition of "A Love Supreme" was done in one take. "[Swami] was loose, he was funny, and he had that smile going that people who are past worrying about stuff have," Michel said. "He couldn't have been easier to work with. He gave his narration and was gone."[16] Swamiji speaks of love with a booming, echoing voice like God on the mountaintop, and Leroy Jenkins turns his violin into a buzz saw, while Alice roots down for a very funky turn on the organ.

Despite the avant-garde deployment of orchestrations, the presentation of John Coltrane in a manner that moved the music into another world of sound, *World Galaxy* was met with conflicting reviews. The *San Francisco Examiner* noted it as "more classical than jazz," with "eerie, amorphous pieces...and beautiful versions of two of her late husband's classics," but *Down Beat* passed: "Super-saccharine, often corny and terribly repetitive."[17] Future avant-garde guitarist Eugene Chadbourne also reviewed the album: "The music itself gives the illusion of complexity, but is really simple to the point of nausea...Alice herself plays with no apparent interest or concern."[18] If the reception to Alice's setting John

Coltrane's iconic works in a more avant-garde orchestral setting was dismissed out of hand, her next recording project would be even more controversial in the jazz press.

On March 15, 1972, Alice Coltrane wrote an entry in *Divine Revelations* that at Lord Rama's bidding, she was astrally projected "through space to the Egyptian temples at Giza and the Sphinx with two tall angels, a scroll in one, a scale in other. 'The Lord told me to solve the riddle of the Sphinx.'" Her response: "Sphinx is humanity that has the face of an angel with the body and brain of an animal possessing a god-like soul."[19]

That same weekend, she was back home in Detroit and performed with a local assemblage of string players in Ann Arbor on Friday and then on Saturday evening in Detroit: "The diva of soul, as Alice Coltrane is called, was disappointing... Her solos are ethereal, flighty masterpieces. But Friday night, she couldn't surmount the embarrassing failure of the fiddles to sound even passable."[20] That Sunday, she returned to Mt. Olive Baptist Church, performing for a fundraiser she had recently established, the Annie McLeod Scholarship Fund, named in honor of her late mother. She swung through Boston for a triple bill with Pharoah Sanders and violinist Michael White (broadcast live on WBCN-FM)[21] and then performed in Rhode Island for the first time since her days in the Premiers.

Since John's passing, Alice had been diligent in combing through the many recordings her husband had made toward the end of his life, assembling them with due care and thought. Five full albums had come out posthumously, each adding new angles to the public's understanding of the man: *Om* and *Cosmic Music* in 1968, *Selflessness* in 1969, *Transition* in 1970, and the kinetic *Sun Ship* in 1971.

In April 1972, Alice pulled out some tapes that John had made across a five-month span at Coast Recorders in San Francisco, paying for the studio time out of his own pocket. The Classic Quartet could be heard on two titles, while his last group was on the other two pieces. A session was called at the Village Recorder in Los Angeles, what Ed Michel always referred to as "my home studio." She stated her intention for these tapes a few months prior on Columbia University's WKCR:

> I'm going to work on one album of John's, a quartet or something from the last group. Most of the stuff is on two-track. I want to see if there's a way that I can get some better sounds, even if it means some overdubbing or going to 4- or 16-track to bring up the sound. Not that the music needs it. There's some tracks I'm on myself that I feel I might add to some of the sound to get away from that two-track stereo sound from five years ago.[22]

"All the John Coltrane recordings were made before I arrived at Impulse," Michel said. He deemed himself a John Coltrane fanatic and admitted that "I was always struck by the Coltrane masters, and by the players he influenced directly that I was privileged to work with." He had a hand in producing the run of reissues but for these sessions, he would be actively involved. For these unreleased two-track recordings, "Turiya wanted to add the strings after we had done string albums together. I was not happy with the idea of 'tampering,' but she was in control of the Coltrane estate and had final say."[23]

In the wake of Bird recording with strings, it kindled in every major saxophonist the desire to blend their horn with violins and cellos. But even then, Michel said that "strings on jazz dates were still rare. Turiya was the only artist I recorded who wrote her own string arrangements. Everybody else used arrangers."[24] And in her estimate, the pieces were unfinished. She and John had devoted countless hours to absorbing the likes of Stravinsky and imagining what their own music would sound like with the manifold possibilities of these different timbres and colors, and now she had the skill set to actualize yet another dream of her late husband: she would add orchestrations to his music for a new album, *Infinity*.[25]

Despite his initial misgivings, Michel by this point knew to trust his artist's instincts. And he also knew that Turiya's "will of tungsten" would not be denied: "I didn't know what to expect from the strings, other than a mature artist was making a choice about direction in sound and concept."[26]

In the early 1970s, Juilliard-schooled Murray Adler was a busy violinist hustling around Los Angeles, working as a session player for movie soundtrack work. With only a few recording dates under his belt, he was called for this session with Coltrane. "She absolutely knew exactly what she was doing," Adler said. "Her music was not accidental. She was very bright and I had great respect for her musicianship."[27] Adler served as concertmaster on the *Infinity* dates and was surprised to learn that she had taught herself how to score for strings with no formal education.

In creating the lead sheets for the session, Michelle Coltrane remembered how her mother "would write them out by hand for each instrument: viola, the violin, bass or cello. She did that work. She was one of the most disciplined and self-taught people that I knew. She did that with language too, learning Indian Sanskrit." And then Turiya would hand them off to the only copyists she had on hand: "She would get us kids to very carefully do the notes. We would duplicate them by hand. We would do the balls and then she—in her beautiful handwriting—she would do the sticks. All the kids would be transcribing the lead sheets."[28]

"Peace on Earth" was one of her husband's last major compositions, never quite realized in a studio setting (though it's especially poignant on the *Live in Japan* recordings). On *Infinity*, it opens with nearly one and a half minutes of orchestral fanfare before John's iconic tenor emerges. As his horn moves into a span of dissonant overblowing, the strings scrabble and scrape, adding turbulence that only smooths out when he reaches another plateau in his solo. To hear John's horn meld with Turiya's elegant arrangements and her strafing dives across the harp strings feels bittersweet in hindsight, a glimpse at what might have come to pass had John lived.

"Living Space" featured the original Coltrane Quartet. In the studio, Coltrane had already augmented the session with an overdubbed horn melody, adding another pattern to the mix, but now it featured an array of strings and hand percussion. At times, the strings overwhelm the sound of the quartet, but it remains a fascinating hybrid between dynamic group improvisation and thought-out arrangements. Listen closely and you can even make out John's youngest, Oran, just five years old at the time of the original recording, shaking sleigh bells.

Maybe it's a half century of hindsight, but *Infinity* remains unfairly ignored in both John's and Alice's catalogs of work. It is the lone album to offer a tantalizing glimpse at what a truly equal John and Alice Coltrane album might have sounded like; the tenor titan's powerful horn matched with his wife's eloquent harp and string charts, each operating at a peak. It's a match that is made in heaven, so to speak, the tireless, ever-questing sound of Coltrane's horn weaving through a kaleidoscopic tapestry of strings, something unlike anything else in his oeuvre. It's beautiful, opulent, overwhelming at times, two forces of nature together at last.

The week after recording these new overdubs, Turiya set out on a quick tour: Skidmore College in Saratoga Springs, New York; Lake Forest College in Chicago; Portland State University in Oregon; then down to San Jose State College and Berkeley[29] with a triple bill featuring herself, Archie Shepp, and newcomer John Klemmer.

At some point in her meditations for that year, Turiya Coltrane was told directly by the Supreme Lord that she would move to California and establish a Vedantic Center. "Otherwise, there was no reason to leave that house [in Dix Hills]," she later explained to Leonard Feather. "I really didn't care about California too much. It's sunny and nice, but it didn't have the character of New York."[30]

The Dix Hills house was put up for sale and the family boxed up all their belongings so as to move out west. But she still wasn't sure it was the right move: "Even after a year I even questioned the children 'Do you want to go back to New York?' And they said 'no, we don't want to go back. It's too cold.'"[31] The Coltranes initially rented a little house with a small pool in the neighborhood of Encino, before moving ten miles farther west to a house in Woodland Hills. It was here that the seeds of the Vedantic Center were planted.

She explained the underlying concepts behind her embrace of this ancient Eastern philosophy:

> Mine is a Vedic, Eastern path. The name comes from the Vedas, the world's oldest known scriptures proclaimed as emanations from God and compiled during meditation into Four Testaments by the saints and *rishis*, or holy men. The *rishis* would write on stone or palm leaves to keep a record of the spiritual renderings and transmissions, and then impart them to the people. Vedas and other scriptural literature always come through meditation by holy men and women of God. The Vedas are teachings for life, family, government, military warfare, arts, sciences, marriage and, moreover, spiritual guidance for liberation and self-realization.[32]

By this point, Ed Michel had worked with Turiya on four studio albums and a slate of John Coltrane reissues, and now they were finally located on the same coast. "It's never 'strictly business'—at least for me," he said about their working relationship. "I met the family when they'd moved out to California. There was one occasion when Turiya's youngsters and my two daughters were playing in the control room while the grownups were involved in mixing/editing."[33]

In July, the Coltranes were finally settled in California and Turiya began work on her new album. This time around, she booked nine days of studio time at the Village Recorder. Built by Freemasons in 1922 on Santa Monica Boulevard—almost smack-dab in the middle between Beverly Hills and the Pacific Ocean—The Village Recorder had served as a Masonic temple for decades, before it was taken over by successive spiritual owners with a penchant for prime real estate: first a Bible institute, and then later by Maharishi Mahesh Yogi. The Maharishi transformed it into his West Coast nerve center for his brand of Transcendental Meditation. It's said that the Beatles used to meditate in the large auditorium on the first floor, but by the early 1970s, it was a proper recording studio, the birthplace for everything from Steely Dan's *Aja* to Fleetwood Mac's *Tusk* to Alice Coltrane's seventh studio album, *Lord of Lords*. The album would summarize her entire professional musical life to date, spanning from her early days playing piano at Mt. Olive to her days in the high school band playing percussion, from her most assured orchestral arrangements to the inner space contained within her meditations.

"While I was there, Steely Dan was also using it as home base, and the Stones passed through during their stay in LA, and later Fleetwood Mac spent a lot of time there," Ed Michel said. And while he doesn't remember Turiya bumping into these rock stars in the hallways, he remembered one particular day of the session, even though there's no tape documentation of it. "She was warming up before a date started, Charlie Haden was the bassist and Ben Riley was on drums and the rhythm trio was *burning* in straight-ahead bebop," he recalled. "And she absolutely *forbade* me from running the tape machine. And with Turiya, one did what one was told!"[34] Turiya might have been beholden to the expression of cosmic music, but she still knew all the licks that she learned in Detroit.

Murray Adler again served as first violin and concertmaster for the sessions. He now commanded a platoon of strings: twelve violinists, six violists, and seven cellists in total. Despite the rigors of Adler's classical training, he admitted that at times he felt intimidated by Turiya's improvisational prowess: "I always prided myself that I could play anything that was written down. But I didn't feel free enough to improvise something on my own with her. I didn't feel comfortable, especially in her presence. I have to tell you her music was beyond me. I didn't really know what she was doing." He added: "She was extremely spiritual, it just emanated from her, her goodness and her godliness." Even though Turiya was self-trained, "I had the deepest feeling that she knew exactly what she was doing. There would be parts of the music where she would improvise and I would just watch her and then she would nod when it was time for the strings to come back and I'd bring everybody in."[35]

On *Lord of Lords*, Turiya used the massed swells of violins, violas, and cellos both to augment her own harp, organ, and timpani playing and to elicit a tonality that hovered beyond the realms of jazz or classical. Coltrane's string arrangements resonated with new possibilities like a portal to higher realms, where she served as a conductor—not in the classical sense—but as a channeler of energies.

That tactile sense of cosmic energy courses through opener "Andromeda's Suffering," a musical composition that seeks to convey the supergalaxy "whose rays extend two billion times brighter and deeper than the light from the sun of our solar system. Inside this magnificent superstructure of spiraling stars, the suffering and sorrows of humanity burn brightly."[36] Recalling her time in the Northeastern High School band, Turiya played timpani, deepening the bewildering, dramatic effect of the piece. On the breathtaking coda, Turiya said she could still hear the Lord's voice, and added: "I feel the Lord's suffering within my being everyday."[37]

The title track finds Turiya pushing herself to new compositional limits, the longest studio composition she had ever laid to tape. It's an eleven-minute opus that begins with her crashing cymbals and slowly opens up into the infinity of deepest space. Her harp emulates the whorl of distant galaxies, and the shivering strings convey a profound sense of weightlessness. The extreme bass growls via her left hand on the Wurlitzer are counterbalanced by gentle chimes. It all amalgamates to impart an astonishing sense of inner and outer space. It's a direct dedication from Turiya to the Supreme Lord, the one whose bliss is "so extreme, the human body can hardly bear it; the One who Death shrinks away from at the sight of... the One who never sleeps, who follows me where I go."[38]

While one can detect her overt admiration for the likes of Stravinsky and Rachmaninoff in her grand sweeping themes, when she turns toward the atonal scraping of strings, it can elicit comparison to the likes of Ligeti's *Atmosphères* (as used to visionary effect in Stanley Kubrick's *2001: A Space Odyssey*) or Krzysztof Penderecki's *Threnody to the Victims of Hiroshima*. Coltrane's arrangements are big, grand, and tumultuous, reflective of life itself. Even on Earth, it conveys the physical sensation of traveling to the farthest reaches of our solar system. That pull between the extremes of heaven and earth is reflected here, toggling between jaw-clenching dissonance and relaxed, open fifths.

Ed Michel remembered that more often than not, the family's Jaguar would be in the shop, awaiting some expensive part from overseas, so he would give Turiya a ride back to Woodland Hills after a day in the studio, about a forty-five-minute drive up the 101. "I was playing a cassette of a live performance of John's 'Classic Quartet' and they were absolutely flying," he recalled. "I 'whew'-ed and said that was amazing. And she replied, 'That's what broke up the band...because it was too easy for them.'"[39] Michel might at times be confounded by Turiya's creative decisions, but her musicianship still left him gobsmacked:

> She'd be playing harp swirls and she'd say, "Oh, there's an F sharp in there that shouldn't be." I would say, "It's like a 128th note, it's going by so fast there's no way I can take it out." She'd reply, "Oh you can, we'll do it right here." She was right. She would stop sessions and tune the strings: "Third viola player, would you bring your D up just a little bit?" in the middle of this oceanic stuff. She had an astonishing ear.[40]

As the *Lord of Lords* sessions continued, she encountered some difficulty. In her mind's eye, Turiya knew just how the music should sound: a blend of incandescent jazz and whirling strings that—when their timbres came together—would suggest the divine. But she couldn't figure out just where to make the cut on the studio tape. Neither could Michel.

They had just recorded Turiya's version of Russian composer Igor Stravinsky's *The Firebird*, the ballet he had first written in 1910 that had become a staple in the Coltrane home, a lifelong favorite of John's, later of hers, and now beloved by the whole clan. She now envisioned it as a compact six-minute dervish of sound and vertiginous strings. Franya Berkman wrote: "Given Stravinsky's appropriative tendencies as a composer, there is a wonderful irony in the manner in which Alice has molded portions of *Firebird* into a free-jazz improvisation...an act of daring requiring an enormous sense of creative license."[41]

In the album liner notes, Turiya wrote at length about an encounter with Stravinsky that had occurred on March 20, five days after she was astrally projected to the Sphinx in Egypt. At that point, Stravinsky had been dead eleven months: "He had the appearance of an elderly man, but none of the weariness or age lines shown on his face." The composer who her late husband had astutely called a "universal musician" presented her with a glass vial containing a clear liquid and bid her drink down this elixir:

> To my surprise, it was difficult to swallow... Since that time, it has been incumbent on me to proceed forthrightly into the great master Stravinsky's works. Divine instruction has been given to me throughout the entire arranging of this music, even down to the smallest detail.[42]

Rather than a direct rendition of *The Firebird*, Turiya's "Excerpts from the Firebird" feels more personal. Sirota noted: "It's sort of all the notes you'd sing if you were trying to remember how *The Firebird* went, but when Stravinsky gets super weird, she gets weird in her own way, employing her aleatoric vibe."[43]

And yet the marriage between jazz trio and orchestral strings still sounded off. "There was an edit that needed to be made, and I regarded myself as the Charlie Parker of the razor blade; I could do impossible edits," Ed Michel said. "But I just broke my back on that one and couldn't make it work."[44]

"I'll go home and meditate on it," Turiya told her longtime producer, and left for the day. When she arrived at the studio the next morning, she had her answer: "I got some help from Bach and The Father [which is how she always referred to John after his passing] and Mr. Stravinsky. Mr. Stravinsky said, 'Cut it here.'" Even after years of working together, Michel was incredulous at the suggestion. "She would always talk about her meditations and the people in her meditations," he said:

> She showed me where to make the edit and I told her, "I'll make it, but I'm going to have to put it back together again, because there's no way that

edit is going to work." I made the edit as instructed...and it was seamless, it was *perfect*. And she just said, "Yes, Mr Stravinsky did it, I didn't make that up." I thought, "OK, just shut up and do as you're told."[45]

Despite proximity to outer-realm recording sessions by the wooliest purveyors of spiritual jazz during his career at Impulse, from Sun Ra to Michael White to Pharoah Sanders, Ed Michel admitted that he didn't consider himself to be a spiritual person. When he finally told Turiya as much, he got her to belly laugh at the notion. "I mentioned to her that I had tried meditating, but that it didn't seem to work for me," he said. "She guffawed, and said, 'When you're mixing, you meditate like a Yogi.' 'But that's just concentrating...' More laughter. 'How can I be meditating if I don't think I'm meditating??' And she laughed so hard that she literally fell out of the chair."[46]

For the final composition on the album, Turiya again evoked another iconic classical composer and a piece of music that hearkened back to her childhood. Czech composer Antonín Leopold Dvořák began composing symphonies at age twenty-four and by 1892, he was invited to the United States to serve as the director of the National Conservatory of Music of America. It was here that he would compose many of his greatest works: the highly regarded Cello Concerto, his String Quartet no. 12 in F major, op. 96, and his ninth symphony, often called the *New World Symphony*.

Throughout his composing career, Dvořák gleaned ideas from folk music and other indigenous music forms in his native Bohemia. In the United States, he again looked to the native flora for inspiration. His Black composition student Harry Burleigh had sung spirituals for him and may have also provided the composer with a compendium titled *Negro Music*. Dvořák himself was vocal in praising the music arising from the New World's decidedly second-class citizenry: "In the Negro melodies of America I discover all that is needed for a great and noble school of music."[47]

The "Largo" section of the *New World Symphony* bore striking resemblance to the spirituals of the day, but the source of origin is further obscured in that—roughly thirty years after the debut of Dvořák's Ninth—his former pupil William Arms Fisher paired it to lyrics he wrote in dialect that "should take the form of a negro spiritual accords with the genesis of the symphony."[48] Despite provenance of a white composer who published *Seventy Negro Spirituals*, "Goin' Home" soon became a popular gospel hymn in the early twentieth century. In Turiya's eyes, it was a Black spiritual first and foremost, and she credited "Goin' Home" as a traditional spiritual, though her arrangement and adaptation hews to the symphonic aspects of "Largo." You can hear almost every iteration of music she had embodied over the course of her thirty-four years on Earth. You can hear the blues inflections in her organ solo, the down-home feel of the hymn, the imitation of the church choir in how she voices the chords, the eloquence of her own harp at the introduction, and the grandeur of Dvořák, as well as her own journey through the upper echelons of this cosmic music.

It's as autobiographical as Turiya's music could get. "It was one of my parents' favorite songs," she wrote. "Gospel and Spiritual music are some of the greatest Attributes of the Creator to have been bestowed abundantly upon the children of the Nile, i.e. African Americans."[49] For Michelle Coltrane, this hymnal still evoked a bittersweet feeling: "It's happy and sad, whatever that emotion is. I'm still deeply moved by it."[50]

Decades later, *Lord of Lords* remained close to Turiya's own heart:

> That record was so special to me because practically every aspect of it is like a meditation and the [cover] photograph was so unlike anyone ever taken. When I looked at it I could see it was more like identifying with my soul than it was with my external features. Then the music became a meditation, where each selection told its own story. Although it's one that you can write down, I sometimes think things are better left in that realm of mystery or the unknown.[51]

CHAPTER NINETEEN

Angel of Sunlight

Two months after Alice finished *Lord of Lords*, *Infinity* hit the record shelves. The jazz press hated it. They were absolutely mortified to have such precious, unreleased, near sacrosanct John Coltrane recordings adulterated by Alice Coltrane's harp and organ (not to mention having Charlie Haden's rerecorded bass parts), as well as full string arrangements. Writer Bob Blumenthal said it wasn't *quite* like drawing a mustache on the *Mona Lisa* but close enough, bemoaning that the interplay between Coltrane and quartet was "clipped and filled with Alice and the (string) Intruders," then went on to excoriate her further:

> This kind of after-the-fact production can be expected in popular music, but you wouldn't think John Coltrane would get this kind of treatment from his wife. Alice may have the legal right to Trane's musical estate, but her treatment of that gift in this instance is highly questionable. She can feel free to call John Ohnedaruth and continue to build a wall of mysticism around his memory, but she shouldn't mess with the music.[1]

To Michelle, the music felt deeply personal, a glimpse into the communal musical exchange between her parents: "It was just a real touching way for someone that knew John, not only musically but personally, to pay tribute to him." Turiya heard such complaints, but knew in her heart that it was the right choice with regard to her late husband's wishes. "Some people didn't like the addition of strings," she told a writer decades later:

> They said, "We know that the original recording didn't have any strings, so why didn't you leave it as it was?" I replied, "Were you there? Did you hear his commentary and what he had to say?" So it became something that I consider didn't require an answer. We had a conversation about every detail; [John] was showing me how the piece could include other sounds, blends, tonalities and resonances such as strings. He talked about cosmic sounds, higher dimensions, astral levels and other worlds, and realms of music and sound that I could feel.[2]

Lord of Lords, on the other hand, garnered more positive reviews. "The album is a euphoric mind excursion in which organ, piano and harp progressions intermingle with translucent tones of 16-piece string orchestra," read one.[3] Another: *"Lord of Lords* is immediately recognized as her personal synthesis of the universalness of man and his music... with each new release the meaning of her music will become defined to those who listen."[4] One columnist called it "accompaniment when you are soul-searching, meditating or just being quiet."[5] Another expressed skepticism for the mystical claims, but compared the strings to Northern Lights and found "an electric presence to it...each cut is a trip, a magical mystery tour of the cosmos."[6]

Released the same day as *The Best of John Coltrane: His Greatest Years, Vol. 2*, *Lord of Lords* would be her last record for Impulse. The label referred to as "The House That Trane Built" didn't renew the widow Coltrane's contract. "I think that the Coltrane archives worked in her favor," Ed Michel said. "When her contract was not renewed, there was a shift in the makeup of the executives at the top of ABC Records, replacing Jay Lasker's guys, which included me."[7] No doubt, ABC looked at her albums as little more than loss leaders; her male counterparts Sanders, Shepp, John Klemmer, Gato Barbieri, Michael White, and Marion

Brown would all linger at the label another two years. Without the archives of her late husband serving as cover, would Alice have ever been offered a recording contract in the first place, much less the opportunity to record some of the most singular music of the late 1960s and early 1970s? Considering how few other female artists had major recording contracts, the answer would be a firm "no."

Turiya played only a handful of shows, including two weekends at the famous Lighthouse on Hermosa Beach. Murray Adler remembered the hour drive down to South Bay. "She put the same effort into her recordings as she did the live music. We would just go there," he said. "My work with her was when she was playing harp. Her harp playing was so free. I didn't really know what she was doing. I would imagine there was a form to it, but I could not follow it. I did not know. When she played, it was just like when she wasn't playing. Very faintly, she emanated this goodness, this pleasantness."[8] On January 31, Turiya returned home to Detroit to perform at the Ford Auditorium.

While Turiya was now without a recording contract, her music continued to radiate and find sympathetic listeners beyond the narrow confines of jazz, stretching to soul, pop, and rock, and into other fine arts. A newspaper feature with Aretha Franklin had her pick some of her favorite albums, from Marvin Gaye's *What's Going On* to the Four Tops' *Nature Planned It* to *World Galaxy*. Yet the accompanying text failed to connect Alice back to Detroit's Black community. A feature on Motown superstar Stevie Wonder found the fellow Detroit native "rapping about Alice Coltrane and Transcendental Meditation...and the vibratory cycle of E-flat."[9] Alvin Ailey's "Cry" became part of the repertoire and continued to expose modern dance audiences to the catharsis of "Something About John Coltrane" on a near-nightly basis.

Her music reached the rock world as well. During the peak months of the Summer of Love, a friend in San Francisco had turned guitarist Carlos Santana onto *A Love Supreme*, handing him the album and a joint. And while he admitted not connecting to it right away, Santana soon realized the urgency of fusing his music with spiritual intention, his solos transferring that questing, soul-levitating quality of John Coltrane into a rock setting. A searing performance at Woodstock and his 1970 multiplatinum album *Abraxas*[10] made him a star. A few years on, Santana was deep into meditation along with other jazz-rock guitarists like Larry Coryell and John McLaughlin, and had also adopted an Indian guru of his own, Sri Chinmoy.[11]

In the spring of 1973, Santana had "maybe the biggest realization of my spiritual dream—going from being a dishwasher to meeting the widow of John Coltrane and then getting to make music with her," he said, adding that she invited him to spend a week with her in Los Angeles.[12] For his new album, he recorded another Coltrane cover ("Welcome") and his own rendition of "Going Home," with Turiya providing the orchestral arrangements.

Turiya's music also found its way into opera houses, auditoriums, planetariums, and other alternative spaces around the country. In the wake of the mind altering, sensorially immersive rock concerts of the psychedelic 1960s, the light-and-film component became a draw in its own right. A group of four Seattle-based lighting and film professionals combined forces as Retina Circus, staging the backdrops for a number of bands touring through Seattle and the Pacific Northwest, from the Grateful Dead to Creedence Clearwater Revival, while also staging listening events that wove together light and music into a singular trip. In late 1971, Retina Circus presented "Journey into Outer-Inner Space," weaving flickering lights, colorful gels, abstract film, symbolic imagery, an early Moog synthesizer, and the early computer animations of John Whitney into a holistic new experience. Amid the psychedelic and progressive rock luminaries on the soundtrack, the production also prominently featured "Journey in Satchidananda," which a review said "lifts the viewer into another dimension...[and] brings the viewer full circle back to the symbolic source of oneness."[13]

That summer, another visual troupe from San Francisco, Heavy Water, took their audiovisual experience to Salt Lake City, East Lansing, Rochester, and Miami. John Hardman, Joan Chase, and Mary

Ann Mayer cut their teeth on the San Francisco rock scene, working with the Dead, Jefferson Airplane, and Santana. The program music ranged from the aforementioned rock acts to Elton John, Mike Oldfield, Parliament, Hot Tuna, and Country Joe and the Fish. The most abstract and cosmic middle sections of these light shows inevitably peaked with a selection like "Galaxy in Satchidananda" or "Hare Krishna," before returning their viewers back down to terra firma with rock selections.[14]

That same summer, Black-owned Compton radio station KJLH 102.3 FM staged a benefit concert for a Transcendental Meditation center. It was a reunion on many different levels. Alice's old collaborator Bennie Maupin was there. After stints with Miles Davis, Lee Morgan, and Woody Shaw, Maupin's early sextet studies with her had now informed his collaboration with Herbie Hancock and the Mwandishi band for a series of fascinating electronic explorations.[15] In less than three months' time, Maupin and Hancock would enter the studio with a funky newfound focus, cutting *Head Hunters*. She also reunited with their old neighbor Berry Gordy and Motown stars like Stevie Wonder, Smokey Robinson, and Syreeta. Syreeta Wright was a dulcet singer-songwriter in her own right at the label, but her albums were eclipsed by that of her more famous husband, Stevie Wonder. Their marriage had dissolved less than a year before, but both were still ardent believers in the power of Transcendental Meditation.

Bennie Maupin remembered a jam onstage featuring himself, Turiya, and Hancock. The show caught in one night how different branches of Eastern tenets all commingled and supported one another within the Black community, whether they were adherents to Vedic Hinduism, Nichiren Buddhism, or Transcendental Meditation.

Although Alice was no longer with Impulse, the label repackaged selections from her catalog for *Reflection on Creation and Space (A Five Year View)*. Longtime jazz critic Bob Rusch reviewed the compilation: "I was unimpressed with the quality of her writing…[and] have never been able to really appreciate Ms. Coltrane's music and that goes back some fifteen years."[16] Leonard Feather, one of the *Down Beat* critics who levied the charge that the music that Eric Dolphy and John Coltrane made together was "anti-jazz," reviewed an Impulse triple bill of Coltrane/Klemmer/Barbieri at L.A.'s Palladium: "Having admired Ms. Coltrane since way back in her days with Terry Gibbs, I cannot believe that what was heard Friday—grinding, aimless lines on organ, repetitious arpeggios on harp—represented her ultimate goal."[17]

Soon after the TM benefit concert, Turiya received an invitation to be an honored guest at the Transcendental Meditation Teacher training course being held at Haile Selassie International University. It was situated in Alemaya, approximately a ten-hour drive from the capital of Addis Ababa in Ethiopia. Upon her arrival, she fulfilled yet another desire of her late husband. Both had long dreamed about traveling not just to India but also to Africa. "He liked to draw an analogy between mankind and his horn," Turiya said:

> One group might represent the upper register, another the mid-range, and yet another the deeper notes, but it took all to make the whole. Due to this desire for unity and his exposure to a world in which things were more often bitter than sweet, he had a great concern for "the plight of his people" and, during the last months, expressed a desire to go to Africa, "to check everything out."[18]

Now her feet were on African soil, and she stayed in Africa for several weeks as she oversaw a teacher training course. Over a hundred students from underserved communities learned TM. "She was so regular," one attendee said. "Yet you knew right away there was something special about her." Another said that when she performed at the center, her music "was a light portal through sound. She was this beautiful African woman and I definitely recognized her Mother energy. I strongly felt that I knew her as a Guru in a past lifetime."[19]

Events like the informal jam sessions that would transpire with Satchidananda at IYI or on their travels through India also occurred here in Africa. One monsoon-heavy night, Turiya and Syreeta took shelter in a lecture hall with a rickety, out-of-tune piano. But Syreeta's angelic voice and Turiya's touch on the piano transformed the room:

> She played and we were looking at each other with mouths open and eyes wide. Everything shifted. Then Syreeta and Mrs. Coltrane did their thing together and we were paralyzed. I mean we couldn't applaud, we couldn't do anything. We just sat there. It was magical... And when we came out of the hall the rain had stopped and it was the most beautiful night sky I had ever seen.[20]

Another fine collaboration awaited her in October, as she reunited with her old roommate Joe Henderson once more, adding piano, harp, tamboura, and harmonium on an ambitious suite of music he had composed for the four primary elements of "Fire," "Air," "Water," and "Earth." The resultant album, *The Elements*, was a kinetic slice of spiritual jazz that unfortunately escaped sales or acclaim back when it was released but has since gone on to become a highly esteemed and collectible record.

In March 1974, Turiya performed with Carlos Santana and John McLaughlin on a night at the Kabuki Theater in San Francisco. The performance was billed as "an evening of spiritual music," with acoustic sets from McLaughlin, Santana performing on harmonium with his partner, and long, winding solo turns on organ and harp by Turiya. With Reggie Workman and Leon Ndugu Chancler, she delivered a trio version of "Africa" that veered as close to organ soul-jazz as anything in her catalog, taken at a delectably unhurried pace, unlike her husband's original. The headlining trio then joined forces for a version of "A Love Supreme."

At that same time, Devadip Carlos Santana and Turiya Alice Coltrane commenced work on a collaborative album. "She opened her house to me and I spent close to a week with Turiya," Santana said. After the kids went to bed, they would work on music and meditate together until the wee hours. Near the end of that week, Santana recounted a fascinating meditation:

When you meditate at three in the morning, the first half hour is like being on a plane flying through turbulence. Your eyes are red, you know it's dark all around you, you're trying to stay awake, and you're shaking. Then all of a sudden things get really smooth...I could see a beautiful flame in the candle that was burning it was like a flame inside the flame. So in my minds eye I went into it, as I had done many times before. But this time I began to feel the presence of somebody in the room besides Turiya. It was John Coltrane. Then he materialized in my vision. He was looking right at me—and he was holding two ice-cream cones, each of which had three scoops![21]

In the meditation, he could see Turiya enter the vision from the corner of his eye and hear her encouragement to take a taste. He wondered how she could know what was happening inside his own meditation. When he took a lick of the ice cream, John said: "Good, huh? Well, that's a B-flat diminished seventh chord."

Despite her serious, introspective air, Santana remembered that she also liked to laugh and have fun. The legendary Cuban percussionist Armando Peraza "would tell a story, and we'd crack up, then Turiya would say something that made us all laugh even harder," Santana said. "Everyone thinks of Alice Coltrane as being a serious, deeply spiritual person who was somehow close to the divine and was not allowed to joke around, but she loved to laugh and have fun."[22] One time, she giggled like a little kid in the back of his limousine as she played him her favorite song at the time, Ben E. King's slinky mid-1970s cut "Supernatural Thing." They also bonded over a shared love of Aretha.

Whether or not that meditative scoop of celestial ice cream inspired him or not, Santana soon had some new pieces and Turiya came up with arrangements to augment them, "symphonic oceans of sound, tides flowing in and out," as Santana described them. Turiya was still without a record deal and "basically, Columbia told us, 'Go and have fun.'" Santana convened his bandmates, bassist Dave Holland, and drummer Jack DeJohnette, while Turiya tapped Murray Adler to be concertmaster. "I want to play music like Turiya plays...infinite waves of sound," Santana said.²³

The sessions yielded *Illuminations*, an outlier even in the spiritually informed recordings of that decade. In much the way that she deployed orchestral strings to amplify her late husband's horn on *Infinity*, she now added these immense waves to Santana's piercing guitar tone. And her organ was every bit the sonic equal of his axe. "My favorite moment on the whole album came right after I finished that solo on 'Angel of Sunlight,'" Santana said. "Suddenly Turiya blasted off like a spaceship, playing that Wurlitzer, bending the notes with her knees and Jack and Dave and I all looked at each other like we were hanging on for dear life. It was one of the most intense things I ever heard her play."²⁴

Released in September 1974, *Illuminations* occupied some no-man's-land between heavy rock, spiritual jazz, raga, and modern classical, not quite settling into one thing. Now it could baffle rock critics as well as jazz critics. In *Down Beat*, Wayne Shorter and Joe Zawinul—then riding high on the critical and commercial success of their fusion group Weather Report, discussed it in the magazine's "Blindfold Test," picking out Santana but not Coltrane. Zawinul commented: "It was kind of unnatural sounding to me, the way the strings were written... sounded like a background to a movie about animals, a documentary."²⁵ Eugene Chadbourne quipped it should have been titled "The Worst of Alice Coltrane and Carlos Santana."²⁶ Rock critic Robert Christgau, never a fan of Santana, wrote: "Mrs. Coltrane contributes background music barely worthy of 'Kung Fu.'"²⁷ It was the first Santana album not to go gold and even the guitarist himself called it "career suicide."²⁸

But it's the rare occasion to hear Coltrane in the context of hard rock. Her harp was mere garland on albums by Laura Nyro and the Rascals, but now she was grappling intently with an outright shredder whose platonic ideal was John Coltrane. "Angel of Air" and "Angel of Water" slotted right into the Heavy Water repertoire of Santana and Pink Floyd, and her music continued to ripple outward, picked up by those properly attuned to it.

A handful of dedicated listeners could be found out in San Francisco, perhaps none as zealous as husband and wife Franzo and Marina King. The Kings were jazz fans going back a decade and loved to share new discoveries with friends and neighbors. In the mid-1960s, the couple began playing new jazz albums on a stereo setup they had in their garage. "Maybe less than a dozen brothers and sisters would come together every week," Franzo King said. "Everybody would bring a new album. We'd put the music on and start testing our ears and our knowledge." An airing of *A Love Supreme* seemed too beholden to the church to really capture King's imagination at first: "I wasn't really that impressed! I didn't even want to listen to the album." But then the Kings were able to experience Coltrane live one night out in North Beach. As Franzo recalled:

> It was as though he was speaking in tongues and there was fire coming from heaven—a sound baptism. That began the evolutionary, transitional process of us becoming truly born-again believers in that anointed sound that leaped down from the tone of heaven out of the very mind of God, stepped from the very wall of creation and took on a gob of flesh, and we beheld his beauty as one that was called John.[29]

Transformed, the Kings were determined to turn their listening club into something more devotional. They moved to a storefront in the working-class neighborhood of Visitation Valley, taking the mantle Yardbird Temple Vanguard Revolutionary Church of the Hour.[30] Now King believed John Coltrane to be Christ incarnate, that *A Love Supreme* doubled as a full prayer service. The couple themselves would adopt the honorifics His Eminence Archbishop Franzo W. King, D.D., and the Most Rev. Supreme Mother Marina King. The music of Coltrane could catalyze even the most ardent nonbelievers to true belief.

By 1971, the Yardbird Temple Vanguard Revolutionary Church had changed its name to the One Mind Temple Evolutionary Transitional Church of Christ, usually shortened to One Mind Temple. Working with their Black Panther neighbors, the Kings had established their Free Food Program, serving the dropouts, homeless, burnouts, and runaways who otherwise would go hungry on the streets. And while people would gratefully be eating a warm healthy meal, sometimes the temple would spin great jazz records, mostly the 1960s work of John Coltrane.

A nineteen-year-old attendee at the Temple named Carl Hickson had been coming around for a few months in 1973, helping out as needed. "I was very happy to find a vegetarian place that made really good food and was playing the music of John Coltrane in the background," he said. Soon, he was helping them to serve others in the community. Hickson grew up in a small upstate New York town but felt "a really deep fire to understand what's real" that drew him out west. Hickson didn't have a steady job or a place to call home, spending his time between church crash pads and the One Mind Temple.

One night, Hickson was clearing away the last of the dishes at the communal tables when the music that had been playing in the background suddenly zoomed into the foreground of his mind. "Now, as if for the very first time, I heard it," he testified:

> The celestial sound gently embraced me then it shook me to the core! It was otherworldly. Ethereal. Cosmic. I placed the stack of dishes on the floor. As if pulled by a tractor beam I walked over to the stereo and picked up the album jacket. With my eyes glued to the cover I slowly sat down on the wood floor in a clumsy cross legged position. Pulsating celestial music flowed from the speakers. Staccato organ music danced between the sound of violin strings like children joyfully crossing a stream—jumping from one rock to another.[31]

Literally floored by "Hare Krishna," off *Universal Consciousness*, Hickson forgot all about the stack of dirty dishes behind him and submitted to the music. He opened the gatefold and grew even more enchanted: "She was seated in a cross legged meditation posture and light was passing through her body. An orb of light at the top of her spine and the back of her head wordlessly conveyed the idea of enlightenment," he said. "The music, the artwork, the words, all spoke to my inner being. Deep in my heart, I knew, *she knew*! This being had attained transcendental levels of consciousness. She had been to the mountain top."[32] Hickson was determined to meet this person in the flesh.

Swami Satchidananda's sixtieth birthday celebration was booked for December 22 at the Wilshire Ebell Theatre in Los Angeles, with guests such as Linda Ronstadt, Sally Kirkland, acoustic guitarist John Fahey, and Coltrane. Hickson made his way south to L.A. and bought the biggest bouquet of flowers he could find. "Tall and slender, about 5'8", smooth skin, a blend of ebony and mahogany that gave her a royal complexion, Mother Turiya walked with a grace and elegance I had never seen before," Hickson recalled. She played keyboard and harp and also directed a full string section: "It was a joy to watch her cue the conductor and the string section with movements of her head or eyes. Every now and then she would turn and bestow a radiant smile on the musicians and they would light up!"[33]

After the concert, Hickson made his way backstage. The hallways beckoned with a mix of sandalwood incense and fresh flowers and soon Hickson was face-to-face with the artist behind *Universal Consciousness*:

> On one level she was a kind, down to earth, motherly soul. Yet, behind the petite, feminine form, I could sense the power of an immense spiritual being. It was palpable. There was a divine presence in the room. Like the skin is a permeable link between the outer world and the inner body, Mother Turiya's physical form was a bridge between the terrestrial and the celestial.[34]

Hickson knew he had found his guru. It was not Swami Satchidananda, who had received oblations and been celebrated for hours onstage. His guru was Turiya.

PART 4

Swamini Turiyasangitananda

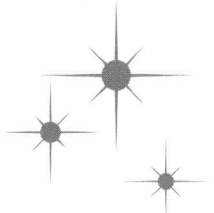

CHAPTER TWENTY

A Prophetic Song

LESS THAN A YEAR LATER, PURUSHA HICKSON WAS BACK AT THE long wooden table that the One Mind Temple used for its Free Food Program, along with seven other students. He likened the past few months to Dorothy from *The Wizard of Oz*, swept up in a spiritual whirlwind, and now he was reading the manuscript that Turiya had written and would self-publish two years later as *Monument Eternal*. "Even today I feel a wave of energy as I recall that first reading," he wrote:

> Mother Haqq [aka Marina King], the wife of the Bishop, spontaneously threw her hands up in the air and exclaimed, "The Christ!" She was referring to Swamini, and using the word Christ in its literal sense, meaning 'anointed one.' Mother Haqq's heartfelt assertion reflected what we all were feeling. Swamini was an authentic yogi of the highest order and *Monument Eternal* was a soul stirring confirmation...Shortly before the reading began, Mother Turiya shared that she was a Swami.[1]

By 1975, Turiya had reached a new plateau. She and the kids were now fully acclimated to life in sunny California. Miki was a full-blown teenager, John Jr. turned eleven, Ravi ten, and Oran was now eight years old. Her kids were quickly growing up and becoming more independent, able to take care of themselves. "I had reached a point where most of my duties as a householder were fulfilled," she said. "It gave me the time to want to see, to want to strive, to want to devote quality time, because you know, the work of a woman is so full. I mean it's sometimes twenty-four hours. So once that was reduced, I had additional time that I could apply to the path, and that's what I've been doing."[2]

Back in Woodland Hills, Turiya began to devote even more of her time to her spiritual practice, meditating into the wee hours daily. Her practice of sannyas—the ascetic practice of renouncing the material aspects of life, of detaching from identification of the body and self—intensified. "It started with taking the sannyas, that was a total mystical experience," she said. "It was God's deliverance of his anointed mercy on me."[3]

Being on the West Coast also meant that travel to India was slightly more direct, and she spent the beginning of the year in southern India. On this trip, Turiya was planning to visit with Sri Sathya Sai Baba, the figure whose picture she had seen moving just a few years before on her previous visit to the East. In her meditation before her flight, "she asked the Lord how she should view Sai Baba. The Lord revealed to her in meditation, 'He is to be viewed like a Christ.'"[4] Soon after, Turiya embarked on a solo journey through India, landing in Mumbai before continuing on to to the bustling city of Bangalore farther south. From Bangalore, she traveled three more hours to reach the remote village of Puttaparthi, where the ashram of Sri Sai Baba was located. She stayed for over a month.

She returned to the United States and in March performed two nights with Rahsaan Roland Kirk and Pharoah Sanders at Carnegie Hall. Future avant-garde jazz trumpeter Roy Campbell Jr. worked as an usher and used to sneak his friends in, one of whom was his bandmate Renee Botofasina: "For nearly two years, I attended the 'University of Carnegie Hall.' I saw every single show I ever wanted to see in *life* at Carnegie Hall. Roy would get me in. Everybody from Shirley Bassey to Sir Georg Solti and the Chicago Symphony Orchestra to Gil Scott-Heron to James Taylor, *everybody*."[5]

Botofasina was born in Brooklyn and came from a musical family. But while she was still an infant, her mother had a complete nervous breakdown and tried to kill herself by putting her head in the oven. Were it not for Renee's older sister, who quickly got a neighbor, they might not have gotten out alive. "That was the last time I was in the same house as my mother," she said. Instead, Botofasina wound up a foster child at a private agency, "a horrific way to grow up."

Her love of music gave her a path, and she found herself mentored by the likes of Mary Lou Williams when she was first starting out. By the late 1960s, she was a full-blown hippie, going to see "every blues player still alive and Black and all those white guys in England trying to sound like Black guys. We had a residence at the Fillmore East almost every single night." But Botofasina was not a jazz fan at all, and seeing Alice Coltrane at Carnegie Hall left her decidedly unimpressed: "She entered the stage barefoot, carrying an incense stick and speaking very softly. She did not engage the audience in conversation; she simply played. Personally, I did not understand her music, nor her lifestyle."[6]

Around that same time, Alice Coltrane heard from Warner Brothers Records. "I had been approached by Bob Krasnow, who I knew from Blue Thumb, who was now at Warner Bros., about coming over there with four of my Impulse! artists, of whom Turiya was one," Ed Michel said. "But that sort of fell apart, and she was the only one signed. Bob Krasnow was responsible for signing her to Warners, and he certainly didn't lack in imagination. But record companies always keep a sharp sense of what is 'commercial' and what gets exposure on the air."[7]

Turiya herself was hesitant to sign. "I got a call from a record company offering me a contract, I did not want to take it because the Lord had pointed me in the direction of spiritual activity, which would involve everything—initiations, service and whatnot," she said. "And then it was disclosed to me that I could do both spiritual and musical work. So for five years I executed that contract, and when it was finished, I didn't make another album."[8]

Originally, she had hoped to record a four-night run in July held at San Francisco's Keystone Korner, but according to Ed Michel, such recordings never happened. On one of those nights, a woman named Carol Adams was in attendance[9] along with a few of her friends:

> A tall, thin woman glided on stage with hands demurely folded. She walked to center stage. She bowed respectfully to the audience, exuding a natural composure. Her quiet demeanor reflected a breathtaking inner beauty. She took her seat at the organ. Watching the white-robed figure play the organ, artistically concentrated yet detached, I sensed an impression of someone partially present, yet partially in another realm. The audience seemed mesmerized with her sacred offering. After a period of timelessness that transported the listener to an inner dimension of beauty and bliss, the music ended.[10]

Still floating high from the music (the venue had banned smoking and alcohol sales for the night), Adams went backstage to express her gratitude. As she moved closer in the queue, the air became indelibly charged:

> The pure spiritual energy surrounding her felt like the amazing atmosphere of the higher elevations on a mountaintop. For me, the joy of meeting this unique person made a profound impact on my spirit. I anticipated that I would go from an enchanted state of bliss back to my regular consciousness. However, my spirit remained elevated; my soul could only sing in joy and jubilation. Feeling and experiencing the soul's bliss left a lasting impression in my life. The profound impact of meeting someone so blissfully aligned with divine energy became a major milestone in my life... I wondered if she had always been that way. Did divine grace always light up her smile?[11]

In Coltrane's own writings, there had been divine grace. On June 11, 1975, an entry in *Divine Revelations* read: "On this great day, a prophetic song and divine promise were made that told of the dawning of a new day under the *Avatarship* of Sri Sathya Sai Baba. The prophetic song [and] the divine promise...consisted of many sacred revelations and experiences that would transpire in the future."[12]

The extreme, life-threatening austerities and tapasyas that Turiya endured were unguided, like ascending a Himalayan mountain with neither torch nor guide. Trusting completely what she heard within as the voice of God, she undertook an arduous, life-threatening task. As she put it herself, it had been "a sacrifice...within an inch of her life." She had emerged on the other side, a chrysalis turned luminous butterfly. A Black woman from the working-class neighborhoods of Detroit had attained enlightenment and God-Realization. As Adams explained it: "Although she did receive a mantra from...Swami Satchidananda, the Lord alone directed Turiya through the moments of pain and suffering to the glorious day of highest attainment. That day concluded her tests and trials."[13]

Typically, a Hindu swami is ordained by a swami within a parampara, a lineage, so being ordained via divine edict would be an uncommon occurrence.[14] Even Satchidananda wasn't aware of Alice becoming a swami until many years later. Coltrane described how this miraculous transformation out in the suburbs of Los Angeles came about: "I received my initiation following meditation. I had a revelation about what would take place. I would be initiated through Divine Grace."[15] She had been told to wear a white dress, and when that divine day came, a vibrant new color emerged:

> I remember that Lord Ram poured the color into the white clothing worn for initiation. The orange hue that He created came down from above, softly and ethereally. It was truly magnificent to witness the Lord materializing color into the clothing so completely that a heavenly light began to radiate and flow into the periphery shining with the color of a summer's evening sunset. It was a divine honor and blessed privilege.[16]

Along with the new saffron color of her garments, she heard the Lord "call me Turiyasangitananda, which means the bliss of God's divine music."[17] Along with her new name, the feminine honorific of *Swamini* was also bestowed. Her work and mission were revealed to her, as well as the directive to start her own ashram in California.

Alice Coltrane was now Swamini Turiyasangitananda.

She left a note on the fridge announcing her new name and her kids fell out laughing.[18] "We were challenged trying to pronounce a word with so many letters and eventually John Jr., Ravi, Oranyan, and I—and even my mother broke down laughing with our attempts to say it right," Michelle recalled. "What did we know? We were teenagers, energetic and running around. We did not yet know the depth of our mother's journey ahead."[19] Later, Turiyasangitananda detailed a dialogue between her and Lord Sri Rama in her meditation:

> "Several persons in this country (USA) are inquiring amongst themselves as to 'how does an American black, Christian lady become an East Indian *swamini?*'" "It matters not whether public inquiry and opinion are favorable or unfavorable; one's country and nationality are of no underlying criterion. If one has dedicated his life in devotion to God, he can be selected to become a candidate for initiation into the renounced order of *sannyas*."[20]

In August, work began on her first album of new material in over three years. Recording at Burbank Studios, some twenty-nine players were assembled for the sessions. Ed Michel served as producer, Baker Bigsby was engineer, and Murray Adler was first violinist/concertmaster. "I generally preferred to record everybody at once, because the music was elastic and soloists responded to the whole environment," Michel said. "This was contrary to what was preferred when recording pop projects."[21] Michel even played wind chimes.

For Bigsby, he was always impressed by Turiya's demeanor in the studio. "Even though her brain was wandering around in the ether and heavens or whatever, her feet were planted firmly on the ground," he said. "So she's a real practical mother. She seemed to be really a practical down-to-earth person."[22]

Eternity, her Warner Brothers debut, is both more polished and more eclectic than her prior albums. On the mid-August recordings of "Spiritual Eternal" and "Spring Rounds," there's something decidedly Californian about her use of strings and orchestrations, which are cinematic in their sweep, able to be Technicolor-bright as a Hollywood soundtrack, the bracing dissonance of her later Impulse albums mostly buffed away. Stravinsky gets recast again, this time with a piece from *The Rite of Spring*. "Wisdom Eye" presents Turiya's mature harp style in the solo spotlight for the first—and only—time, a serene three-minute stream.

On the album's centerpiece, "Om Supreme," she debuted an all-too-rare rare turn on Fender Rhodes and her first chorale arrangement. It was also the first piece to feature vocals since her days in the Premiers,[23] but in featuring only organ and voice, it also reflected the kinds of chanting she was already leading at her Vedantic Center. The melody has its roots in the bhajans, with her providing a new vocal line on top, memorializing how the Supreme Lord instructed her to move to the west: "When I called you to California / you knew I would meet you in California." Michel brought in professional singers for the session, yet their polished delivery and enunciation stands in stark contrast to her future choir pieces. What it lacks in raw energy and the ecstatic feel of gospel music (as well as her later work with bhajans) it makes up for in its curious amalgam of Anglican and Indian vocals: There's a blissed-out feel to the back half of the piece as the six vocalists chant in Sanskrit.

Eternity's other bold move is "Los Caballos." Out in the rugged landscapes of Woodland Hills, Michelle Coltrane had become taken with horseback riding and took up dressage. "She bought a ranch house with a barn and the guy that worked with Trigger, Hollywood people were out this way," Michelle Coltrane said. "It was close but not too far away. Boys would be on BMXs and girls would meet in fields on their horses."[24] At one point, the family owned multiple horses: Chico, Bart, Loose, Joker, Peppers, Leo, and Camelot Diamond Coltrane. Her mother became enchanted by the elegant magnificence of these beasts, their strength, intelligence, and beauty.

Turiya was also fascinated by the rhythms of their hooves on the ground, creating a song that replicates "its walk, trot, jog, on up through the extended cantor, and hand-gallop."[25] Her Wurlitzer is set to whinny, mixing growling low-end jabs with high-frequency runs as bright as a meteor shower. Santana percussionist Armando Peraza added clopping congas to the backbeat, while Carlos Santana guested on timbales (called "A Friend" on the album credits). There's a definite Latin feel, but as is her wont, she speeds up and slows down throughout, a spicy rubato. The mid-1970s might have been when jazz began to dabble in disco beats, but "Los Caballos"—like its titular subject—gallops down the path less traveled. At the very bottom of the record cover, in small print, she signed off as Turiyasangitananda.

Later that same year, Turiya returned to the recording studio, this time at the Record Plant, ostensibly to play harp on one of the greatest albums—not just of the 1970s but the twentieth century—a universally acclaimed, diamond-selling masterwork. Not that she played a single note on Stevie Wonder's *Songs in the Key of Life*.[26] But since Stevie was a fan of her music and friends with Marilyn, he extended the invite:

> She was asked to play the harp on "If It's Magic." Minnie Riperton was also there in the studio and people were basically partying and having fun. And [she] was there for like a whole week. She asked the Lord: "Why? Can I go? Why am I here?" And He said it was to place something in [Stevie's] mind subconsciously, to have some kind of energy subconsciously placed in his mind from her being there. Swamini said to me directly—not that I understood her at the time—she said: "I know what he wanted, he wanted that *F*."[27]

Despite the shared Detroit upbringing of Coltrane and Wonder, having a teetotaling Swamini seated in a studio with a pop star and loads of friends and hangers-on partying and getting loose must have made for an incongruent sight.[28] Botofasina said, "Swamini was also making the point that Minnie Riperton, the people who were like partying and all that, they didn't know how close they were to leaving their body."[29] After a week or so, Turiyasangitananda again asked the Lord if she still needed to be present in the studio and was informed that she could leave.[30]

Originally, Turiya established her Vedantic Center at the One Mind Temple, traveling to San Francisco every few weeks to give readings and lectures. Seven others studied during that time. Hickson was in attendance as often as possible, as was Adams, who noted Turiya's gentle grace toward all she encountered. "She greeted the higher, divine Self of each person she met," she wrote, likening her to Mother Teresa and St. Francis of Assisi. "She expressed that her intent as she met each person was to receive them as the Lord receives them. Instead of seeing human flaws and character defects, these holy beings perceive the spark of divinity."[31]

Hickson saw in Turiya's example an empathy to the progressive social movements of the day, an intersectional meeting between the Black Liberation Movement and the Women's Liberation Movement (not to mention freedom from the oppressive, regressive patriarchy of Western religions). "In meditation she was told to 'shatter' two of the prevailing myths of our time," Hickson said. "The first, 'Black people could not be leaders, teachers, and gurus.' The second, 'Women could not be leaders, teachers and gurus.' And shatter them she did!"[32]

At the end of the year, Hickson and Adams received initiation. He was given the spiritual name *Purusha* and she was given the name *Shankari*. Hickson recalled the anticipation of the day before:

> I meditated with Swamini during the early morning hours of December 20th, one day before our initiation. The light in the meditation room was dimmed and had a soft orange hue. The scent of sandalwood incense lingered in the air... during this first meditation, it felt like being enveloped by a soft, rose colored cloud—like being in a lucid dream. I couldn't see Swamini but I could sense her presence.[33]

Swamini Turiyasangitananda ushered in 1976 in South India but was back in the United States by the end of the month, as she went out to Burbank to record a duet with Charlie Haden. When Haden first extended the invitation, Turiya demurred, saying she was no longer performing on harp, but Haden finally convinced her to join him on a piece written especially for her, "For Turiya." As Haden remembered: "I thought I had ascended into heaven, the way she played it. It was so magnificent."[34]

In late February, she performed at the Beacon Theatre in New York as part of Warner Brothers' big rollout package of their roster, conquering the Big Apple under the banner "California Soul." The weekend-long event featured the likes of the Staple Singers, Ashford and Simpson, Dionne Warwick, Graham Central Station, First Choice, Leroy Hutson, and the Impressions, the label's pop side, paired to their light and airy jazz roster: David Sanborn, Al Jarreau, Pat Martino, Miroslav Vitous, and guitarist George Benson. Benson was on the precipice of releasing *Breezin'*, a triple-platinum smash that would forever affect the expectations of the rest of the WB jazz roster.

Onstage at the Beacon, her music stood apart: "The most informal music of—and in many ways the most honest—was provided by Alice Coltrane's quartet. Mrs. Coltrane and her musicians exuded a quiet strength that was conspicuously absent from the rest of the program."[35] Renee Botofasina was back in the crowd, still trying to figure out this music. "It was an odd pairing opening before George Benson's set," she said:

> My focus was myopically visceral. I was listening for certain known musical patterns and she was playing in a universe I was yet to explore. She came out in a sari. I just didn't get it. I only got a little crack. I heard her playing more piano and you could tell that she had a lot of chops, technique and all that. But still, her approach to solo was so far outside of... it was so much more open than bebop, where everybody was trying to solo. She was a very capable musician, but still, I didn't get it.[36]

Eternity came out that spring and she performed a few concerts in support of the album. *Down Beat*'s three-star review compared her to her late husband ("She certainly has never demonstrated the capacity for organic creativity that John did"), questioned "her insistence that everything be permeated with cosmic significance," and concluded: "It's all very smooth, but it's also rather emotionless, devoid of warmth."[37] Another review concluded: "She will remain a minor-league avant-garde jazz figure, because she exercises without consistency or reason."[38] Elsewhere, other reviewers were more forgiving. One wrote: "Drawing its inspiration from several worlds of experience, *Eternity*, like its creator, is a complex entity."[39] Another esteemed: "The total effect of her music is a very unearthy and far out sound, as if it's pulling you out into space."[40]

A reporter in Toronto detailed the ironic sight of Alice Coltrane, draped in a sheer saffron robe, seated unperturbed amid the ambient lavishness of the Cole Porter Suite at the Waldorf Astoria, stating: "'All my work, my music, is really just an extension of myself'... [while] oblivious to the dozens of record company executives running around the hotel's halls worrying about her. She might just as well have been meditating in the lower foothills of the Himalayas for all she seemed aware or cared about the activity around her." The piece went on to describe *Eternity* as "a luxurious album full of lush textures and shifting harmonies... You can feel her quiet hand at work everywhere."[41]

Just a few months later, Turiya recorded *Radha-Krsna Nama Sankirtana*. While credited for five of the six compositions on *Eternity*, *Radha-Krsna Nama Sankirtana* exclusively featured traditional Hindu chants set to music. In the wake of George Benson's *Breezin'*, Warner Brothers was no doubt hoping for something that could sell, yet the quiet strength of her presence—what Ed Michel called her "will of tungsten"—would be neither hurried nor bent. As he recalled: "What I remember is waiting for her to come up with a title, with the record company screaming at me to get an answer ('It's holding up the damn release!'), while she patiently waited for her meditation process to give her the answer."[42]

And after the experience of working with professional singers on *Eternity*, she brought her students from the Vedantic Center into the Record Plant on August 5 to record "Govinda Jai Jai," "Prema Muditha," and "Hare Krishna." "Govinda Jai Jai" again features Turiya on Fender Rhodes, leading a boisterous kirtan with eleven voices—including those of Shankari, Purusha, and the Kings—blending together into an ecstatic whole. Compared with the zero-gravity iteration full of body-tingling strings that appeared on *Universal Consciousness* just five years prior, this version of "Hare Krishna" is much closer to what one can hear chanted in subway stations and on street corners. It also laid bare her connection to the Hare Krishna movement.

In 1965, the year before Conrad Rooks purchased an airline ticket for Swami Satchidananda to visit America, another Indian spiritual teacher also crossed the Pacific Ocean, albeit in far less accommodating environs. Then sixty-nine years old, the man born Abhay Charan—now known as Abhay Charanaravinda Bhaktivedanta Swami Prabhupada—had recently taken sannyas. At the behest of his guru, Srila Bhaktisiddhanta Sarasvati Thakur, he endeavored to travel to the West—even at his advanced age—to spread his teachings. He could only secure passage on a cargo ship, though, undergoing an arduous thirty-five-day sea voyage where he suffered two heart attacks and barely arrived alive in Boston Harbor. He then made his way to the Lower East Side in New York City, where he began to teach the Bhagavad Gita in Tompkins Square Park and led kirtan with chants of the Hare Krishna mantra. Ten months after landing, Prabhupada established the International Society for Krishna Consciousness (ISKCON).[43]

At this point, Turiya's Vedantic Center was sympathetic with a small network of other like-minded, Eastern-oriented groups, from the One Mind Temple in San Francisco and the Transcendental Meditation center in Los Angeles to ISKCON. In the liner notes, she thanked Prabhupada and Bhagavan Sri Sathya Sai Baba.

She remained close with Swami Satchidananda and still spoke of him as a "gentle leader and selfless servant of humanity,"[44] but she was no longer his student, but rather his equal.

Swamini began to experience mounting tensions at the One Mind Temple. It soon came to a head sometime in 1976. "Ramakrishna had a good heart. Nevertheless, he was having a harder and harder time accepting instruction from Swamini," Hickson said, primarily because Turiya was a woman. "Ramakrishna was bumping into a fierce enemy—himself." During one lesson that Turiyasangitananda was giving, she suddenly found herself being accosted by an onslaught of hostile questions from the King family. "It wasn't the questions themselves that was so startling, but the sarcasm and dissatisfied energy behind them," Hickson said. "I was stunned."[45]

As was Turiya, who quickly took her leave and made her way out of the temple, never to return. But as she was at the front gate, Hickson walked up to her, went to his knees, "and bowed with my forehead touching her feet. I stayed there awhile. Swamini bent over and with her arms encouraged me to stand up. I was at peace... As I stepped back, Shankari stepped forward and knelt at Swamini's feet as well."[46] Hickson and Adams would soon relocate to Los Angeles to live and study at the Vedantic Center, which would now be relocated to the neighboring house in Woodland Hills.

Radha-Krsna Nama Sankirtana offered an intimate glimpse into what the early days of the Vedantic Center would have sounded like. It also gives its listeners a glimpse into what it might have felt like in the pews during her earliest days as church organist at Mt. Olive, those places of worship in Detroit. With her organ driving the music, her students sang with great fervor and devotion.

That intimacy extends to two other pieces on the album, wherein Turiyasangitananda thanked "the students who played tamboura and drums," who—in an example of nonattachment—were in fact her own children. A brief yet gorgeous version of "Ganesha," which—according to her liner notes "is usually chanted at the beginning of any important undertaking, so that God will remove all obstacles"—features her harp accompanied on tamboura by her daughter Sita, now on the verge of turning sixteen. The side-long "Om Namah Sivaya" presents her in duet with Arjuna John Coltrane Jr., just three weeks shy of the boy's twelfth birthday.[47] It had long been one of Turiya's long-held dreams to have John's children playing this music, and now it was becoming a reality.

That year, Michelle not only performed with her mother on an album, but she also met her biological father, Kenny Hagood. When he went to reach for her hand, she recognized the resemblance in her own hands and fingers. Father and daughter would meet only a handful of times before Hagood passed away in 1989.

CHAPTER TWENTY-ONE

Monument Eternal

On New Year's Day 1977, Swamini Turiyasangitananda was on a plane to Bangalore with Sri Sai Baba: "To fly on the plane with Baba is a cosmic flight and a truly unforgettable experience," she wrote. "You know that you are flying; yet it is more like the earth is slowly moving beneath the plane while you are suspended in space."[1] It marked the first of three extended journeys she would take through India that year. Whenever the message was conveyed to her, Swamini immediately began preparations for the transpacific flight.

Released in January 1977, *Radha-Krsna Nama Sankirtana* was mostly ignored, though one kind review applauded how her "cosmic approach can meld a gospel sound with a mantra."[2] The album otherwise received the harshest reviews of Coltrane's career. *Down Beat* gave the album no stars, calling "the virtual nonexistence of a tonal base and clarity… not worthy of serious consideration." The review compared it to "Hare Krishna chanters out in the street," while Alice's playing revealed "a singular lack of technique." The evisceration continued with the most damning—and unadulterated—glimpse into how the jazz establishment viewed her after all these years:

> If Alice had been the wife of a Detroit auto worker, she'd obviously be a nonentity. Yet the lineage lives on, not only in her but in offspring Sita

and Arjuna John... The tyke(s) might have potential, but when playing behind mother's one chord buzz little rhythmic input is needed... What a pity then that this rich liturgy has been subjected to the designs of a sincere, but virtually talentless lady who married the right man.³

The critical grousing, the carefully worded yet still blatant misogyny, the insinuated unworthiness of her as a "Coltrane," the subtle disrespect of her as a wife/musician/mother, and the accumulated animus in the mainstream jazz world had finally reached its ugly nadir.

Yet it's on *Radha-Krsna Nama Sankirtana* that we get our first long look at where Turiya would be going for the rest of her recording career: the fruitful fusion of ancient bhajans to the Black American gospel tradition. In these centuries-old chants to God, she found a way to wed the antiphony of these bhajans with gospel, yoking both to the improvised spirit of jazz. Shanti Morris said:

> For me, she brought a kind of jazz element to traditional chanting. Whether or not that's actually true, for somebody who can analyze musical styles, I don't really know. But for me, I love really rocking out, devotional chanting. To this day she is one of my favorite all-time people. If I heard anywhere that she was leading a kirtan, then I would go in a second. Because she brought something different to that. There are places in India you can go where people really rock out and really chant, and still her chanting is different. It's that and some other element. Which is her, you know, uniquely her. Which is phenomenal, in my opinion.⁴

Berkman traced the earliest English adaptations of Indian bhajans back to the arrival of guru Paramahansa Yogananda in the early 1930s. At his Self-Realization Fellowship, the bhajans were presented to a Western audience in a more docile and churchlike setting, framing them as liturgical hymns. Prabhupada's revolutionary ecstatic chanting of the bhajans transformed them in the eyes of the West.⁵

Turiya sent Prabhupada a copy of the album and the two began a correspondence. One letter began: "My dear Turiya, Please accept my blessings. I have listened to your new record album...and am very pleased with your chanting. You have become transcendental."[6]

During that time, Purusha Hickson lived next door to Swamini's family home in Woodland Hills. Being that close to his guru and spiritual teacher was eye-opening. He saw her not only as an enlightened teacher but someone who could just *be* in the world. Her grace was evident in her every interaction, whether dealing with a young kid, a spiritual seeker, or a record industry executive. "Living next door...not only allowed me to see Swamini on a regular basis, but also to see her in different roles and contexts," Hickson said. "I saw her as a loving mother who patiently balanced her children's need for discipline and their expanding desire for independence. She was an astute business woman overseeing Jowcol Music."[7]

Her house was on a quiet side street away from the main road; the backyard was a hushed open space and a wonderful place to sit in meditation or to practice yoga. "It had plum trees, peach trees, and a luscious concord grapevine that draped over and through the fence that separated Swamini's house and the center," Hickson said. "Students created a large garden which yielded a colorful and generous variety of vegetables."[8]

Swamini herself did not practice yoga, but she gave him a copy of Satchidananda's book on yoga and he began to practice diligently. He also witnessed the rigors of Swamini's spiritual practice up close:

> She spent significant portions of every day dwelling in this transcendental state. Sometime after midnight, after the children had turned in and the house became quiet, she would begin to meditate. Her meditation cave was her bedroom. Her meditation seat was a sturdy orange chair fortified with armrests. She would sit through the early morning, through the sacred Brahmamuhurta time, and take rest for a couple of hours between 6 am and 8 am. The bed in her bedroom was seldom used.[9]

The spiritual life is a rigorous and ascetic discipline. Waking before dawn's light to meditate for hours was de rigueur. Initiates would practice both japa meditation (rapidly repeating a holy name) and mantra meditation (a slow recitation of a holy phrase) and record each in notebooks. Study classes were held multiple nights a week, as Hickson, Adams, Jayalakshmi Moss, and other students studied foundational Hindu texts like the Bhagavad Gita and the *Ramayana*, as well as the teachings of Sai Baba and Swami Sivananda. Swamini also instructed the class to read the works of Theosophical Society co-founder Madame Blavatsky; *The Light of Asia*, Sir Edwin Arnold's 1879 narrative poem about the life of Gautama Buddha that first introduced the tenets of Buddhism to a Western audience; and *Monument Eternal*. As Adams recalled:

> She cautioned aspirants to avoid using an academic approach to study spiritual literature. Wisely, she advised students to discern the spiritual message instead of focusing on literal meanings. Like all noble guides, she emphasized that learning requires heeding as well as hearing. During the Wednesday evening classes, Swamini presented students with a question to assess the understanding of inner meanings. To each brave response, she graciously replied, "That's *part* of the answer."[10]

When it came time for her to deliver her satsangs each Sunday, Adams said that Swamini would first meditate in deep silence, listening to the Lord's message and only then convey it to the others. "However, there were no prepared notes," she said. "Even the Sanskrit verse from *Bhagavad Gita* that she cited each week was never read."[11]

Being able to practice and learn to recite a Gita passage in its original Sanskrit is not impossible, but certainly it would be a difficult, time-consuming effort, especially for a native English speaker. Which wasn't the case for Swamini. The anecdote brings up a common theme with regard to her knowledge and ability to acquire new skills in the blink of an eye. Bennie Maupin marveled at her ability to transcribe a piece after hearing it once. Terry Gibbs was wowed by how quickly she picked up the vibraphone. In the span of just a few months, Alice Coltrane went from having a harp land on her doorstep to concertizing on it, a feat other harpists might spend years of practice to replicate. She oversaw the building of a home studio and learned the ins and outs of recording and engineering all on her own, not to mention establishing her own record label. Rather than attend Juilliard or study composition with an established teacher, she picked up transcribing and arranging on the fly. To say nothing of her elevating to the level of a swamini by divine edict, rather than by a spiritual teacher. A few of these skills could be credited to just being an enthusiast and honor roll student who loved learning. But taken together, it's a breathless amount of knowledge to seemingly acquire overnight. Especially by a woman raising four young kids on her own.[12]

On May 5 and 6, Turiyasangitananda entered Burbank Studios with her Vedantic Center students to record four more traditional bhajans for her next album, *Transcendence*.[13] While Swamini deeply appreciated Hindi chants, it had not been her intention to record them for a general audience. "I follow directives from the Supreme," she told Adams:

> This is the Lord's work. I see that He has selected a time for people, who have appreciated and been inspired by our music over the years, to observe another dimension of it. There may not be any words in the English language to truly describe this. However, one becomes immersed in the glory of the Names—the soul is enlivened. It is uplifted when hearing the Names of the Lord. People should open their hearts to experience the chanting. Let it permeate within. Experience its truth. One need not be a musician, nor of a certain age. Hearing the chanting of the Holy Names will produce spiritual good. The sound itself allows the spirit to soar and be transported to higher realms of divine consciousness.[14]

Nine months on from the recording of *Radha-Krsna Nama Sankirtana*, these bhajans leaned further into the American gospel tradition.[15]

"She used to tell us to chant from the heart and not worry about mispronouncing names; that if you are calling to god, god will know who you are calling to," Hickson said. "Even when we were chanting in Hindu, she said you don't have to sound Indian; just give it that universal feeling."[16]

Turiya explained how she perceived the overlap between her Baptist upbringing and Hindu faith:

> When I was learning the bhajans, I heard more the gospel influence from them! They maybe could have been scholastic or in a more contemporary style, but they weren't. They were really strongly gospel, and I liked that. I wondered about it, and even inquired in my meditation, and I was told, "Do not change it, you do not have to imitate India, you do not have to try and sing like Subhalakshmi, let everyone sing in the way that comes from their heart." That's how the sound developed.[17]

Two weeks later, she went to the Village Recorder with Ed Michel to record two more pieces bearing devotional Indian titles, but with her credited as composer. Coltrane played harp on these dates while Murray Adler helmed a string quartet. Where her Impulse-era blend of harp and strings could be turbulent and fierce, punctuated by dissonant stabs, "Radhe-Shyam" is a serene reverie, a musical portrayal—in her words—of "the Supreme One and the enjoyment manifestation of His energy." The string arrangements on the title track hearken back to her *Lord of Lords* arrangements.

On May 20, Turiya returned to the studio one last time to record "Vrindavana Sanchara." A solo piece, it featured her layering harp, tamboura, tambourines, and wind chimes to sublime effect. "Vrindavana Sanchara" also seemed to anticipate her return trip to India, as it was an homage to the garden groves of that Indian city she would soon visit in person.

If one were to sit out in their backyard to take in the sounds of dawn, such gentle movements would find a soundtrack in Turiya's graceful playing. These four minutes hint at a new form of music that favored less structured musical traits. The adjectives that had been used to disparage Coltrane's music over the past ten years—wispy, subdued, content, pretty, going nowhere—were now a cherished attribute. This was music that could assist in meditation, music that heightened attention, music that could align chakras, music that could abet astral projection, music that could promote healing. In a decade's time, this music would all be labeled "New Age," but a few other folks out in California had already begun to explore this new area in earnest; keyboardists Steven Halpern and Michael Stearns, jazz flautist-turned-progenitor Paul Horn, flautist Joseph "Iasos" Bernardot, harpist Joel Andrews, and New York zither player Edward "Laraaji" Gordon all began to record and self-release their intrepid inner voyages at this time. They often preferred to release their music on cassette, which meant not getting up out of a seated lotus position to flip a record over. "Vrindavana Sanchara" would also mark the last time Turiya entered a big studio to record her own music for the next few decades.

Swamini made a second trip to India in June, traveling through northern India, visiting Vrindavan in Uttar Pradesh (where Lord Krishna lived five thousand years ago). Adams accompanied her to many holy places and various temples: "All of these sacred sites were seen and profoundly appreciated by Swamini. The pilgrimage to the Krishna Balaram Mandir, however, presented the blessed opportunity for her to also have audience with Srila Prabhupad, her spiritual brother."[18]

Since establishing ISKCON in the mid-1960s, Prabhupad had circled the globe dozens of times before returning to India near the end of his mortal life. In the early days of the Vedantic Center, Turiya strengthened her bonds to ISKCON and the Sai Baba Center, visiting the ISKCON temple in New York City. She insisted on going to India in the heat of the summer, as an ISKCON member recalled: "People tried to dissuade her from going, saying it would be too hot. But she insisted. 'No, I must see Srila Prabhupada now.' It was as if she knew that he would soon be departing."[19] Less than six months after her visit, Prabhupad would indeed pass on.

On July 24, the Jagannatha Chariot Festival took place at noon in Golden Gate Park. Alice Coltrane was the fair's special guest and she brought her Vedantic Center singers to the site to perform. The annual event featured huge carts rolling through the park with over ten thousand folks in attendance, reenacting the traditional Hindu ritual. Adams was one of the singers:

> Although overcast skies and cold temperatures prevailed, and required everyone on the program to wear winter coats, most enthused participants remained unaffected by weather conditions. When it was our turn to sing, we moved forward and eagerly took our places. Swamini accompanied the bhajans on the organ, with her usual fervent energy and bhava feeling, as if it were a clear, sunny day...As if to share in the joy of the occasion, the sun emerged from the clouds to smile blessings of sunshine upon everyone present.[20]

Monument Eternal was self-published later that year in a small run of two thousand copies. Small ads for the book ran in the back pages of *Down Beat* and in Black newspapers around the country. Copies appeared at health food stores, New Age shops, or the kinds of Afrocentric bookstores and foldout tables you could find along 125th Street in Harlem. Roy Campbell picked up a copy and immediately called his old friend. "I left New York and was in Sacramento, pregnant," Renee Botofasina said. "I was getting too much pressure from my management, who wanted me to get an abortion to focus on my career. Roy told me I should get Alice Coltrane's book."[21]

While the concerts Botofasina saw in New York failed to move her, the book—all fifty-three pages of it—was utterly transformative:

> I read it in one hour. Once I read that book, I went back to the bookstore and I ordered fifteen more copies because I wanted to give it to all my

friends. When I read that book, transcendental things began to happen. I wanted to write about her. I wanted people to know about her spirituality. I was not interested in dissecting her music. Zero interest. Zero. That was not my quest.[22]

Botofasina pitched a story on Alice Coltrane's spiritual side. By that time, Adams served as Swamini's secretary and responded to her, asking for a list of questions in advance. "Swamini related to Shankari that she saw me offering obeisances in her meditation," Botofasina said. "I didn't know *what* she was talking about."[23]

The revelations to be found in *Monument Eternal* remain stunning decades later. Stylistically, it's closer to another small, profound book, Paramahansa Yogananda's *Autobiography of a Yogi*, first published in 1946. The rainbow-covered booklet barely mentions her jazz music career, her iconic husband, or her travels to India. There's little in the way of regular biography. In its pages, Turiyasangitananda matter-of-factly details making a doctor recoil in horror at the sight of her blackened right hand, the nuances of various astral planes, her ability to hear trees sing, and what occurs when one experiences supreme consciousness. One passage in *Monument Eternal* details the sort of extreme spiritual learning Turiya underwent during the period of intense tapas:

> I had to memorize a whole tract...of some unfamiliar subject matter. Upon learning it, I had to mentally repeat it several times around at rates of speed up to approximately three hundred words per minute. After this was accomplished, I had to reverse the whole process, going counter-clockwise, and mentally repeat it backwards at the same rate of speed.[24]

What Swamini is discussing in this instance are passages written in Sanskrit, a language that is considered by historians to be a "dead language," one not spoken in everyday use with no native speakers, for well over a hundred years. Where she learned to speak (and write) Sanskrit out on Long Island or in the suburbs of Los Angeles needlessly confuses the matter. She wasn't just learning a passage in Sanskrit, but instantly learning it both forwards and backwards at a superhuman speed. Which doesn't seem to be humanly possible. Which instead makes us question our own level of understanding.[25]

"In *Monument Eternal*, it said the level of consciousness that one achieves through God realization, understanding that where you go—beyond liberation, beyond salvation, beyond self-realization—all the way to the pinnacle," Botofasina explained:

> It transcends all levels of genius. *You* don't know what genius is, *I* don't know what genius is. And I don't know what it means to transcend all those levels of genius. But to really understand that consciousness expansion, she said it took her almost six months to be able to even *talk* to people. Six months to bring the consciousness back down.[26]

Rather than look at Turiya's remarkable learning as a result of study that beggars belief, Botofasina believes that Swamini had instant access to whatever human learning was available, a cosmic archive of human knowledge available to her at a transcendental level:

> You and I are both talking from a perspective that we don't really know because neither one of us are God-Realized. The whole idea is once you're given this energy, then you realize that you can be as expanded as possible because the being, the source of it, is the same being that creates cosmos and universes and the sky and the sun and the moon that moves the human body, that has all these working parts, the gift of a wind instrument within a human body...Do you understand? We have no understanding.

Alice Coltrane turned forty that August. Less than a week later, John Coltrane's mother, Mrs. Alice Gertrude Blair Coltrane, passed away at age seventy-nine. In November, Alice Coltrane prepared for a return trip to the East Coast for a joint concert with John McLaughlin at the

Beacon Theatre as part of a few concerts around the release of *Transcendence*. She hadn't been to New York City in three years and brought a trio featuring Reggie Workman on bass and Michael Carvin on drums.

A *New York Times* feature dedicated ample space to McLaughlin and Coltrane. She explained her exploration of the bhajans to writer Robert Palmer: "These chants are very, very old. Sanskrit is the Holy Language. It's said that the Supreme Lord spoke in Sanskrit to beings that existed before the creation of the universe. People think that language belongs to India, but it belongs to every place, just like the sun shines on every place."[27] She also hinted that her time as a performing artist might be winding down: "My life as a musician was very fulfilled by being with John Coltrane."

As the Christmas holiday season neared, Swamini Turiyasangitananda made her third pilgrimage to India that year, to visit with Sai Baba again. "For the first three weeks, she and other Sai devotees accompanied Bhagawan Sai Baba to and from Bombay to Bangalore, as well as to the city of Madras," Adams said. "During the remaining weeks, she remained in Puttaparthi to receive Baba's divine darshan."[28]

CHAPTER TWENTY-TWO

Highest Song of Bliss

SWAMINI TURIYASANGITANANDA BEGAN THE NEW YEAR IN PUTtaparthi. Early in her visit, she was concerned that her orange color sari might be a distraction from Sai Baba's own orange garments, about appearing "equal to You in any way; visibly or otherwise." Baba reminded her of her night of initiation, when that special saffron color was poured onto her white clothing so that it glowed with a heavenly light. "Ram does not want you to change anything," he said.[1] Turiya stayed at the ashram for over a month, but when her departure date neared, he bid her to stay in India for longer.

Her trip stretched into spring. In an entry dated March 10, 1978, she wrote: "All of the auspicious mysteries of life can be found in India. All of the hidden, esoteric secrets of life, death, and reincarnation are here. And all knowledge of the sacred sciences, and the locations of the most powerful, electrical, magnetic energy fields are here."[2]

But she was back in the United States by April, headlining a concert on Sunday, April 16, at the University of California–Los Angeles campus, as part of a special series titled "Women in Jazz." Since the *Eternity* recording dates, she had been working exclusively with her children, her string quartet, and Vedantic Center members in the studio, but she convened a trio featuring Reggie Workman on bass and Roy Haynes on drums. The format hearkened back to her high school days fronting a classic jazz piano trio as well as her first two albums. The concert would allow Alice Coltrane to come full circle and conclude her commercial recording career.

While she had signed a five-album deal with Warner Brothers, her first three albums for the label failed to make much of a dent. "I think Turiya moved ahead with her own sense of what she wanted to do," Ed Michel said. "I also think that was a different direction than what Warners expected when they signed her." Whereas her label mates were pushing further into the slick sounds of fusion and pop, she had gone diametrically in the opposite direction, not covering R&B hits du jour, but rather songs that were thousands of years old. Her cosmic winds were never going to be *Breezin'*. "[Warner Brothers] wanted out," Michel said. "But she wouldn't go for a less than a full number of recordings, so the double album was the answer." A location recording truck was pulled up to the venue, Baker Bigsby engineered the session, and Michel set up recording equipment in UCLA's Schoenberg Hall. But it was no ordinary live concert date. While her previous Warner Brothers albums drew from traditional bhajans, this performance featured many of Turiya's new originals. Compositions like "Affinity," "One for the Father," "Prema," "Krishna," and the title track had no previous studio recording otherwise.

"That was just a special evening," she remembered:

> The people, all the elements, everything was in place somehow. The music, the musicians, just the atmosphere. It was so interesting because, to me, at some levels it was higher than a concert audience. It was like a gathering of people who give something that we also receive. And we also give to their receptivity, what they're there for. So it was like that sharing, that giving, that just kept reverberating and encompassing the whole evening... Audiences do become part of the music in their own way. They're breathing it with you, they're living it through with you, they're receiving what you experience or perceive, but also they give. And then you find out you're not just playing a solo, you're not playing for

yourself, it's for everybody. We talked earlier about John's idea: it's for all people for all the time, for the universe itself, for God. Sometimes people put themselves very deeply into sound—so deep into it that they give up everything. It's like they renounce everything at that moment just to live those moments of music. And that I've seen several times.[3]

Renee Botofasina was invited to the concert by Coltrane herself. "I had started saying her spiritual name," she said:

"Turiya" being the fourth state of consciousness, the highest state of consciousness. San, I think, translates that into "high." Gita is "song." Nanda is "bliss": "The Lord's highest transcendental song of bliss." What stuck with me was that I felt I should say her name. So I started saying "Turiya Sangitananda" in my room. And as I said it, I had a kind of a cosmic experience. The walls felt like they were, like, vibrating.[4]

The walls at Schoenberg Hall might have also felt like they were vibrating when Coltrane was seated at the Wurlitzer. When she concertized on it, it kindled memories of playing with her late husband, invoking the formidable force of his saxophone through its keys. That vibration carried forward in the decade after his death into the present moment. "What I found is a sound that matched his," she said:

When I played the Wurlitzer organ with the synthesizer up on the top, you could pick his vibration out like anything. It's not a saxophone or a piano, but the vibration is like Coltrane's sound. I still think there's that unity, that sharing, the light and the spirit of what he gave. It's me at a moment. Not me trying to further a legacy, I have no interest in doing that. It's a landmark thing.[5]

Her soloing on "Transfiguration" and "Affinity" in particular are some of the most passionate and intense she ever put to wax. You can hear someone in the audience shout their enthusiasm on the latter piece.

But it's on the performance of "Leo," the lone John Coltrane piece she performed that night, that it all turned transcendent.

Of all the late compositions her husband put to tape in the waning months of his life on Earth, few pieces resonated with her like "Leo." In the album liner notes, she wrote that "Leo" is "a direct reflection of the cosmic strength, life force, and power of spiritual energy. The music transmits spiritual vibrations from a mass of Consciousness the way in which a sun transmits light, heat and energy to a universe."[6]

The *Los Angeles Times* review reported that roughly a quarter of the audience left but the reporter himself was overwhelmed by the power of "Leo," noting that "the peculiar quality of the organ-stop she chose conjured up the timbre of [her late husband's] tenor saxophone with eerie accuracy."[7] Still seated in the audience after others had walked out, Botofasina again felt like she wasn't connecting to the music, despite the chanting of "Turiyasangitananda" she had been doing at home:

> I didn't quite understand the music, but I decided to use a different approach to seeking a way to understand it. She was playing "Leo" by John Coltrane. I was like, "Oh, my God. I don't understand it! Let me just try to sing along as she plays." So as I sang along, you know, as she's playing… [imitates the melody] Well, doggone it. I mean, my head… it almost exploded! I thought the song lasted fifteen minutes. After they recorded it, they found that it was forty-one minutes long! It was a very transcendental time.[8]

Botofasina rushed backstage to gush: "I was completely out of my gourd with happiness and craziness, telling her, 'Oh, you're playing just like a horn!' And she was just very quiet and calm. I mean, she was *so* tolerant of me. I mean, she was changing out of the clothes she had been performing in and she just took the time to talk to me."[9] The concert was a success by any artistic measure, but there was one last detail for Turiya: She wanted to add strings to "Prema." Michel was adamantly opposed, but he knew that she would not be swayed. "Prema," the hushed gem of the performance, repurposed the vocal melody from "Om Supreme" and placed it in a new setting, with a string quartet overdubbed a few days later. This time, Michelle Coltrane's violin lessons paid off and she performed as a member of the string quartet.

In May, Coltrane did a brief book tour for *Monument Eternal*. There was a signing at The Tree of Life, a small New Age bookstore located in the heart of Harlem at 125th Street and Lenox, where actress, poet, and activist Ruby Dee came out to speak with her. Later that month she traveled to San Francisco, where she did a book signing in Oakland at Cody's Books and performed at a benefit for radio station KPOO[10] with Charlie Haden and Billy Higgins at Glide Memorial Church.

Botofasina drove up from Sacramento and took her infant son to the book signing for a blessing for her newborn:

> She put her hand on his forehead and then she said to me—not that I understood what she was talking about—she said: 'His third eye opened.' O-*kaaay*. I was told that she was giving a class once a week on *Monument Eternal* and I wanted to be in that class, I wanted to find out what that was about. I had to make a decision: God or music industry? And I decided on God. And based on that, I think God really saved my life.[11]

In June, the *Oakland Post* ran a feature on Coltrane, describing her as a "tall, lean reed-like musicologist...[who] wears no make-up, and her thick head of hair is worn shoulder length and simply. Her facial appearance is more that of an East Indian than an American Black." She explained the use of *Turiyasangitananda*, that she was basically the same person but with a different name, using a metaphor she had used previously to differentiate piano and harp: "It's like seeing the sunrise, bright, beautiful in the morning and in the evening you see a sunset, another aspect of the same thing. The sun is no less, it's the same thing."[12]

She spoke at length about John Coltrane's meditation practice, that "it was a stimulus for his music to reach the levels that he reached," that her music is "the will of the Supreme Being. Music has always been connected to the dedication of God, either, be it avant-garde or church music. The Supreme Being is actually using me and my music... to the glorification of God." Even establishing the Vedantic Center, she maintained, was not her idea, but rather followed upon instructions from the Lord, "where spiritually interested people could come and try to advance themselves through meditation, selfless services, charity." She then urged readers "to be concerned about your spiritual nature because you are basically spirit... you are soul... The soul does not know sorrow... it does not know old age or death and that is so natural." Her last quote offered a rare glimpse into her perspective on life from her vantage: "I don't really know sad moments. There's always something that can stand improvement on the material plain [sic] but my instructions were to be transcendent to pain or to change or chaos because that's what it is out there. You live with an awareness of change because that's what the external life is all about."[13]

In August, Coltrane again performed for the Festival of the Chariots that took place on Venice Beach. And on her forty-first birthday, Turiyasangitananda entered in *Divine Revelations* that Lord Rama allowed several astral projections to take place: "I was projected into four different locations at once, including one outside of the country. Later that evening, there were the ordinary kinds of singular projections to a mile away, or hundreds of miles away into the home of relatives. Of those who were asleep, one could hear and view their dream world."[14]

A column in the Black-owned weekly newspaper *Los Angeles Sentinel* argued in its headline: "Alice Coltrane: 'More' Than Mrs. John Coltrane," calling her "a highly evolved, integrated and innovative musical mind." Her Warner Brothers albums in particular had staying power:

> Alice Coltrane's art emanates from both musical and religious grounds. Refusing to mark a division between the two, her music speaks a spiritual language common to all peoples... Orthodox evaluations fall by the wayside when confronted with the profound creativity of Alice Coltrane.

She is a remarkable woman: intelligent, talented, imaginative, a seeker in the best sense of the word.[15]

In Black newspapers—or when female journalists wrote about Alice Coltrane—there was a level of sympathy and understanding that the mainstream press otherwise never afforded her.

Take lauded jazz critic Bob Blumenthal, who filed a column claiming "there has never been an abundance of female instrumentalists," and that even by that point in the late 1970s "there has not been a significant increase in the number of female performers the last few years." Blumenthal added: "My problem has been to find the jazz woman who, solely on the basis of musicianship...has revealed the originality and deep creativity to warrant inclusion among the jazz elite." In twenty paragraphs of bloviating, Blumenthal struggled to name any women artists beyond Mary Lou Williams, Carla Bley, and Toshiko Akiyoshi. He then turned his attention to Alice, validating the one album Ornette Coleman did arrangements for, before using a Chick Corea quote to prove his point: "What dawned on me before I knew it was Alice was the fact that it was a woman playing. I couldn't tell so much by the way she struck a single note or a phrase, but how she embroidered the piano; her lacework reminded me of a woman crocheting some very hip clothing."[16]

Besides Corea's own cringeworthy sexism, using a quote to support your thesis that features not one, but four metaphors for sewing and clothes (i.e., "woman's work") to describe a woman's playing is at best mean-spirited, but he's not done yet:

> How often has it been said that if Alice Coltrane's name were still Alice McLeod, she would be an unknown? She is the most notorious example in jazz of a woman who, because of her husband, gained exposure out of proportion to her talent. The suspicion that her presence did much to terminate McCoy Tyner's partnership with John Coltrane has only been fueled by rumors that she was reluctant to approve the posthumous

release of Trane's work recorded before their marriage. To many listeners, she is the Yoko Ono of Jazz.[17]

Blumenthal kept right on going with what reads like a misogynistic take on Alice:

> The greatest indictment against Alice Coltrane, however, is that much of her music is overblown, simplistically exotic and stagnant (especially when she plays harp). I once heard the pre-Coltrane Alice McLeod in concert with Terry Gibbs, where she played Bud Powell-ish piano and joined in an occasional vibes duet with the leader. Her unremarkable sense of rhythm and willingness to go along with Gibbs' show-biz routines have always made it easier for me to see Alice Coltrane as a performer with little originality and an appreciation for a good act.[18]

Reducing Alice to an untalented performer who connived her way into her husband's life and then immediately broke up her husband's band to get ahead as an artist herself was how the jazz establishment saw her—and would continue to see her—well into the twenty-first century. A parenthetical aside from Blumenthal *almost* gets to the heart of the matter: "It's notable, by the way, that a large number of the jazz women with national reputations are not black."[19] Here, a white male critic almost acknowledged the three strikes that a Black female artist would face in America. But ultimately, Blumenthal just *wished* there was a way for a woman to "create a distinctly feminine approach to jazz"—that was not sewing—that might somehow one day appeal to him. A woman's work truly is never done.

Botofasina and her infant son Surya relocated to Los Angeles later that year. "The first night I got there, I immediately drove over to Woodland Hills where the class was and rang the wrong doorbell. A lady's voice said: 'Oh, you want next door.' Many years later, Swami reminded me that I came to *her* door. 'Your soul came directly to the guru.' Because I rang her doorbell, not even knowing it was her!"[20]

Botofasina turned her back on the world for the more spiritual endeavors at the Vedantic Center and soon received her spiritual name, *Radha*:

> I was a single mom. I had a child who was barely a year old and she just began to instruct me, tell me how to be a better mom, and also how to really open myself up to spiritual life. It was really hard, because I was living with people I didn't know who I felt I had nothing in common with. They weren't artistic or anything you know. They all spoke *really* soft, like: "Why you moving so slow? Golly, I'm moving at light speed over here!" I stopped playing music. I just did other things. I worked as a nurse's aide. I started a health food company under her direction. I just concentrated on my son. She told me, "You really shouldn't have put that piano down." But I didn't care. All I wanted to hear about was God. The only thing that mattered to me was I loved to hear her speak about God.[21]

During the 1960s and 1970s, there were an influx of alternative churches, Eastern temples, and small new denominations sprouting up like mushrooms, as well as an assortment of grifting gurus, cult leaders, suspect healers, eye-of-the-pyramid schemes, and spiritual scammers to be had all up and down the West Coast. Right around the same time that the King family began to preach the gospel of St. John Coltrane, a minister from the Midwest set up shop a few blocks west of One Mind Temple. Jim Jones originally preached an iteration of Christianity that was anticapitalist, antiwar, and antiracist, drawing many Black members of the Oakland community to his Peoples Temple.

But as his temple continued into the next decade, Jones became paranoid and delusional, a controlling cult of personality. As news of his "miraculous" healing began to be debunked as elaborate hoaxes in the press and the temple received increased scrutiny from the IRS and the U.S. government, Jones decamped to Guyana with hundreds of his followers to settle a new utopia, Jonestown. But in November 1978, the group committed a gruesome mass suicide that resulted in over nine hundred deaths.

There was something fundamentally different about Swamini Turiyasangitananda and her message. In her heart, Botofasina knew it was the right choice for her and her son. "Turiyasangitananda was the entire package," she said:

> Totally mystical, but not like "head in the clouds." With Swamini, it was completely different. We got to witness that. We lived next door to her for five years in the center and that was incredible. She was such an incredible mom. She had three boys who would get on Rollerblades and jump over garbage cans and stuff. They were just boys. She would get on the bike, she would take them for bike rides. They respected her. Their word was, "What Ma says, goes." Her energy was such that she just understood it all. Everything had meaning. Super strong person. She walked the walk.[22]

When the Oakland reporter asked her about the greatest moment in her life, Turiya was unequivocal in response: "The realization of God. That's greater than everything." Musical work fulfilled, she would now focus solely on her spiritual work. Christmas approached and Turiya Sangitananda returned to Prasanthi Nilayam in Puttaparthi to bask in Sai Baba's presence. She carried a harp with her. "I used to always bring a small Troubadour harp with me to India," she said:

> This harp, with a few technical adjustments, could become somewhat comparable to a concert grand harp. For that evening, a beautiful Nativity scene was to be prepared and everyone finalized all requirements for the program to take place on time. The instrument was sent early to the mandir and placed in position for good accessibility. I found out later that Baba had arrived early and had "blessed" the little harp by playing a few arpeggios on it.[23]

CHAPTER TWENTY-THREE

Turiya Sings

A FEW WEEKS AFTER SHE TURNED FORTY-TWO, TURIYA SANGITAnanda described her meditation:

> On this fine day, Lord Rama allowed me to enter the astral worlds. The atmosphere was dense and the sky was quite dark. I went to a mountain top that had numerous spark formations and several fires burning on the perimeters. Nearby, a circle of seven fires began to greatly conflagrate. When the temperature became extreme, the Lord appeared in the most blessed aura of cool moonlight. In His presence, the flames quieted down, and eventually burned completely out. Thereafter, He let my spirit soar high above the mountain. Upon arriving at another astral elevation, the Lord stood before me and said, "You should remain here at least for one year. I can provide on earth an identical facsimile of you. Not anyone there shall know the difference."[1]

Was there a facsimile of Swamini at the Vedantic Center in Woodland Hills at the time? Or is that asking the wrong question? Trace the life of Alice Coltrane through her music and you ultimately face a rupture or else a steep ascent to now understand her beyond her role as a pianist, composer, wife, daughter, and mother and instead as a guru and spiritual teacher to her community. For the handful of devotees who attended the center, who lived on the premises, who studied in her weekly Wednesday study class, there is a bit more insight.

"It's hard to explain this in terms that Western people—maybe even Eastern people—would understand," Radha Botofasina said. "When one reaches the state of God-Realization, that's the pinnacle of all human birth. Oftentimes when beings reach that state—after God knows how many eons of evolution—they are given the option of taking human birth to come back and help others."[2]

Every Wednesday, as study of the Bhagavad Gita or other holy texts would end, students could ask Swamini any question to deepen their own understanding. Botofasina remembered one question: with a U.S. population of over two hundred million people (circa 1980), how many God-Realized beings were in the United States? "She told us three. Two were male and one was female at that time." In *Monument Eternal*, she wrote about having the veil lifted and how she could recall all of her past lives: "She told us directly there were some things she couldn't put in the book. The Lord said don't put them in because people would probably have a hard time understanding it."[3]

What's already in *Monument Eternal* was so astonishing that it almost beggared belief. She discussed her past lives, one as a woman who "died during a successful effort to save the life of a child," another as a woman who passed "due to a pneumonic condition." But in one past life she was a boy "in the family of Ptolemy and Cleopatra in Alexandria" in ancient Egypt. "One of the highest experiences of my existence occurred about 500,050 years ago, during the Dvapara Yuga, the period of time which was before this Kali Yuga," she wrote, mentioning our present stage of the world that Hindus believe is the fourth, shortest, and worst of the four yugas[4] (world ages). "I received transcendental Vedic knowledge direct from the mouth of Bhagavan Lord Sri Krishna." Later she added: "I often pondered many many days and nights over returning to this relative plane and witnessing it on the level of the ordinary human being again... by my own vote, I elected to come back to this earth."[5]

Concepts like reincarnation and past lives are spiritual conceits most regular people and Christians can understand, if not quite find tactile examples of in their own lives. More profound are the stories that arise from her deep meditations and direct dialogues with the Lord. One passage in the book feels particularly futuristic and fantastical:

> Many of the celestial musical instruments can be played without the use of hands or any physical contact whatsoever. Your mind, your heart, is your only approach to them. Your thoughts open up the many avenues of sound and expression on these wonderful instruments. Practically every night, I was permitted to play a "psaltery"...while the floor and walls vibrated from the force of it. The Lord said: "Only four souls in this creation have seen it. You will be the fifth one"...When hearing the names, I found them all to be outstanding ones. They included two musicians and composers (Handel and Bach), Sri Aurobindo (an all-informing source of the universe), and the fourth name was found to be the most outstanding one of all; it is the name of the great prophet and Savior, Jesus Christ.[6]

On one level, it's easy to conceptualize a psaltery—a stringed instrument similar to the harp—that has been strummed and plucked in some form or another going back millennia. A *divine* psaltery that makes the walls quake from the vibration is a more intense imaginative leap to make, but it is a concept common enough to folkloric tales. But a psaltery whose strings have only been seen by two great Western composers, an Indian philosopher and yogi, Jesus Christ, and yourself? That is a profound vision on an entirely different plane of thought.

At the same time, this concept that Swamini conveyed of a musical instrument that is otherwise impossible to learn by playing it with your hands or body, only by approaching it with your heart, is at once out of this world but also wondrous to imagine.

Alice Coltrane somehow wound up in the quotable section of the newspaper during that time, slotted between comedian Tim Conway and former senator Eugene McCarthy: "Most music is only meant for a certain group of people. It depends upon your development. Not just musically but in everyway. When your mind and soul express a need for higher things—more challenging things—then you will be able to get out of any musical experience everything the artist is trying to convey."[7]

It might scan as elitist at first glance, but she suggested something deeper that music had to offer to our souls. A harp blessed by the Avatar Sri Sai Baba, a psaltery played only with your heart, a music that speaks to higher, more challenging spiritual realms, returning to Earth to help others, this all became Swamini's focus in the years after her jazz career drew down. "I couldn't devote time really until the '80s," she said. "I mean, I could read about spirituality and go hear lectures, things like this, however, I still had the children to raise. And there was no way I could not do my duty, because God wants us to be dutiful and fulfill our responsibilities and not sit before the Lord in meditation and leave those responsibilities to someone else."[8]

By 1981, Marilyn McLeod was settled in her home on the other side of her sister's two homes, with a bustling career as a songwriter at Motown. Her credits ranged from Junior Walker tunes to Diana Ross's smash hit "Love Hangover."[9] The Vedantic Center was one door over but nearly filled to capacity, with some families living on the premises. Gardens were planted and tended to by students, and there were also family nights with bhajans being sung. Swamini would decamp to India for weeks at a time.

In addition to all of that, Swamini Turiyasangitananda had a houseful of teenage boys to wrangle. Rather than her eleven-syllable honorific, "I called her mom," Ravi said. "That seemed to work for me."[10] She was no longer being called to make commercial recordings, so the music being played was just for herself, for God. Michelle recalled waking up to "hearing this beautiful harp music playing at dawn, when your eyes are still closed and ears open first [to hear this] beautiful, tranquil, heavenly music."[11]

Now the Coltrane boys would come home from a long day at school to find the home often filled with chanting students and their mother at the keyboard, dressed in vibrant saffron-colored saris, robes, or salwar kameez, that color signifying her spiritual ascendancy and renunciation of the material world. "She played music in the house every day," Ravi Coltrane recalled. "And I'd come home from school and she'd be at the piano or the organ you know playing these quiet sort of hymns."[12]

She didn't often play their father's records, much less her own. "I was not playing very much of our music at home," she said. "I really believe their interests sort of developed in a lot of their own appreciation and their own concerns. It wasn't something that I encouraged in any form or something that I insisted on that they must live up to a name or to a tradition or something like that."[13] If they were going to carry on the family tradition, they would have to come to it via their own interests. As they grew older, their curiosity about music led their mother to gently encourage "their natural heritage. They're born into a tradition here that's theirs. What would be more appropriate?"[14]

Arjuna John Jr. had become a star athlete at El Camino Real High School, playing tight end his senior year, an integral part of that team's playoff run. Arjuna had physically blossomed his senior year, now six feet, two inches and 210 pounds of muscle, and USC had already offered him a football scholarship, though he was also a natural in basketball. He was the spitting image of his father and exuded a similar sense of calm. Hickson remembered how "he embodied the presence of a spiritual warrior,"[15] and that the boy's love of music was burgeoning.

He had played drums on his mother's album but now had taken up bass, just like his late Uncle Ernie. "Basically, because of his character, I suggested it," Coltrane said. "For his character, that instrument somehow suits his personality. He played on the football team, so there needed to be something to match that personality and he had an affinity for the instrument."[16]

Meanwhile, Ravi had picked up clarinet and joined the school marching band, in part "because he would be able to attend all the football games," his mother said. "He didn't want to miss out on that." Oran came to the alto saxophone much later, but now the three Coltrane boys began to practice together, with their father's instruments all around them. "Three days a week they practice, so I'm right there," she said. "So you know, it's quite beneficial."[17]

Every once in a while, Baker Bigsby said he would still get calls from Turiya. "Anytime she wanted to record, she'd call me up," he said.[18] He was working out of Westlake Audio at that time and he recalled that she'd record cassettes of bhajans to hand out to her students to help them with chanting and meditation.

One day in late spring, Turiya called him up and Bigsby arranged "a little home studio in Tarzana." In her meditations, Swamini had received a direction for the music and in a single fifteen-hour session at Redwing Studios, she laid over a dozen bhajans to tape. And rather than record the chants with the Vedantic Center students en masse, she used a new vocalist for the session: herself. "It was just her and her Hammond organ and I thought it was wonderful, because her voice and that wooden-sounding Hammond organ just kind of worked together in an organic way that was just fantastic," Bigsby said.[19]

Purusha Hickson recalled that one summer morning in the wee hour of four A.M.:

> Swamini brought each student their own copy of a cassette tape she had recorded. The recording was fascinating. There were several chants on the cassette. I recognized the Sanskrit words and I recognized the organ but I had no idea who was singing. It was a haunting, moving, unadorned sound. Lo and behold it was none other than Swamini.[20]

The songs were also familiar to Ravi, having heard them played at the house on a daily basis, though the vocalist wasn't: "I remember being 16 at the time hearing it and asking, 'Mom, is that you?'"[21]

On October 17, she booked another date with Ed Michel producing the session and brought her boys with her. She played piano, John Jr.

was on bass, Ravi played soprano, Oran played alto, and Billy Higgins was on drums. They recorded four songs written by their father: "Blues Minor," "The Promise," "Africa," and the opening section from *A Love Supreme*. "This was something Turiya wanted to do," Michel recalled. "It was definitely a Mom & the Kids situation. John played bass and had strong, impressive, big sound!"[22] These family tapes have never been released, but they served as a demo to shop around to potential labels.

Later that week, Turiya sued the One Mind Temple Evolutionary Transitional Church of Christ for illegally using John's name and image "without family sanction...misrepresenting us and infringing on copyright laws." According to her, One Mind Temple's belief in Coltrane "is not so much a true belief as it is exploitation," she alleged. "[John] never set himself up as a minister of God or a Christ figure. I'd know—who could be more close to the man than his own family? He never met these people and would never have agreed with them...I don't think the Lord raised up John Coltrane to be any kind of minister."[23] The last straw was when they used the sacred poem he wrote for *A Love Supreme* to raise donations for the church. She asked for $7.5 million in damages in the lawsuit. (The case was ultimately dropped.)

She made her third recording of the year that December, appearing on pianist Marian McPartland's syndicated radio program, *Piano Jazz*. Perhaps they crossed paths in the hallways of the Jazz Loft, when Alice lived on the fifth floor and McPartland was in the building to study composition with Hall Overton, but both women had navigated the shifting sands of midcentury jazz. The longest-running cultural program on NPR, *Piano Jazz* not only gave flowers to living legends in the exquisite jazz piano tradition (like Eubie Blake and Teddy Wilson) but also allowed McPartland to correct the historical record by highlighting many neglected female players: Mary Lou Williams, Barbara Carroll, Hazel Scott, Patti Brown, Joanne Brackeen, Norma Teagarden, and Alice all appeared in the first four years of the program.

In this national broadcast, the stunning arc of Alice's musical life gets traced, moving from classical music to her husband's most iconic compositions to her own poignant and eloquent late works. The episode opens with "Transfiguration." Originally an eleven-minute, Wurlitzer organ–powered starburst on *Transfiguration*, she delivers a succinct solo piano version here, full of those liquid, cascading runs that recall her style in the last Coltrane quintet. Next she plays "Prema," the pinnacle of Alice's late works, telling McPartland that it translates as "divine love." Shorn of the strings on the album version, this stunning, intimate version reveals the aching beauty, the shifting moods and majesty of the composition. "Oh Alice, that's *gorgeous*," McPartland gushes at the end. "I hear all these different influences, you even play in the treble like the harp. The way you voice the chords it almost sounds like the harp. It has a lot of a kind of religious feeling to it."

Sandwiched around a dramatic read of "One for the Father" are the women duetting on two of John's compositions, "Miles' Mode" and "Giant Steps." The latter is perhaps the lone instance of Alice performing her husband's classic, as it had long been out of his repertoire even before the two met at Birdland. The two women handle its dizzying changes with grace while also tracing its every contour. Talking about John's piece, Alice is demure: "I'm not an authority on this music, I'm really just one who *appreciates* this kind of giving."

McPartland then surprises her guest with a Chopin prelude. Within the first notes, Alice recognizes it as Opus 27 and the two render a beautiful, nuanced version. Her reads on Dvořák and Stravinsky used electric organ and strings, so it's the lone chance to hear the unadorned classical pianist side of Alice's playing. After McPartland's solo take on "Naima," they conclude the broadcast with another of John's minor-key compositions, "Blues Minor," from his Impulse debut, *Africa/Brass*. After the many years she performed "Africa" in concert, it's a rare glimpse of another song she transcribed off that record back in 1961 but had never performed previously.

That episode of *Piano Jazz* began making its way out to affiliates in early 1982. By then, Swamini Turiyasangitananda was back in India, though she would return home in February, opening for Ornette

Coleman at the Westwood Playhouse on February 25.[24] That same month, the city of Detroit shut down Northeastern High School, long ranked as "Detroit's worst high school." Alice was listed as one of the school's alumni, along with Berry Gordy and future Motown stars like Martha Reeves, Mary Wells, and several of the original Supremes.

That year, another singer appeared at the Vedantic Center doors. "With a larger than life aura, Nina Simone, the world renowned pianist, singer and cultural icon walked through the front door of Woodland Hills, accompanied by two assistants," Hickson recalled. "She came for refuge. She was granted shelter, a safe place, a spiritual place where she could heal and gather herself and then take off again."[25]

While it's uncertain if Simone and Coltrane had ever met professionally on the jazz circuit in the 1960s, the two women had much in common. Simone had Black and Native American heritage, her father also drove a truck for a living, and she also took up European classical piano from a young age. When she attended Juilliard, she also lived in the 140s up in Harlem. But Simone tasted the heights and scrutiny of stardom in the 1960s and suffered more than one nervous breakdown in the intervening decades. She described it as being "in a state where I was half outside myself, observing my peculiar behavior from a safe distance... At the same time wave after wave of tiredness broke over me and I felt like any minute I would fall asleep for a hundred years."[26]

A biographer noted that "in the early '80s, as her condition deteriorates, it becomes almost impossible to track the chronology of Simone's different residences," but she definitely spent some time in Los Angeles.[27] "She was first brought by a couple of students because they knew somebody in her circle and they knew that she was having a very heavy-duty mental breakdown," Radha Botofasina said:

> It was very obvious she had some kind of mental issues going on. And Nina Simone's mother was a Methodist preacher and so what Swamiji did was she went to the organ and she started playing "There's a Balm in Gilead" to get Nina to remember her roots. You know, the spirituals

are strong and they have energy. And then she spoke very gently to her, encouraged her not to take the pills. Swamiji gave the instructions to go ahead and get an apartment [for her] and, you know, paid for the apartment and everything for Nina to be in there while she was just trying to figure herself out.[28]

Simone thanked Alice in her 1991 biography but never talked about her stay at the center, though she did attend a few services during that time, as Hickson recalled: "One Sunday while leading kirtan Swamini hit a deep soulful chord and Nina spontaneously jumped up and started dancing. I was playing the *mridunga* drum and was so surprised that I stopped playing, Nina turned to me and rapidly said, 'Come on come on don't stop!' I immediately resumed playing and Nina went into a beautiful holy dance."[29]

Chapter Twenty-Four

A New Sun

In the spring of 1982, the bhajans that Swamini Turiyasangitananda had recorded earlier in the year were pressed in a small run of cassettes, made available by mail order or for sale at the kind of bookstores that also carried *Monument Eternal*. It was titled *Turiya Sings* and credited to Alice Coltrane. *Turiya Sings* marked the first music Coltrane had made since withdrawing from public life and leaving her recording career. Nine bhajans were selected[1] and Turiya went back to add scored strings and layer upon layer of gossamer synthesizer. "She took those tunes and added parts to some of it," Baker Bigsby said.[2]

In the years since she had withdrawn from being a performing artist in the public eye, a new cottage industry had sprung up. Artists left out of the music industry had instead turned to self-releasing their own music. Much in the same manner that John and Alice Coltrane had envisioned Coltrane Records to release their works without interference or input from marketing executives, this new generation of artists could control everything, from recording and production to cover art and the music within. These privately issued New Age tapes might not always make it to the display racks at major record stores, but they could be found in bookstores, healthy grocery stores, and other alternative spaces, an air of carob powder, nutritional yeast, and sandalwood about them. One of the most influential drivers in the field was the three-hour radio program *Hearts of Space*,[3] created in 1973 by Stephen Hill as a late-night show on KPFA in Berkeley. As the 1980s progressed, it became a lucrative industry. Hill himself was a fan of her work and was supportive of her new release. In text that accompanied the original cassette, Hill called it an "ambrosial mantra," adding: "She draws you into an interspace of deep peace and knowing."[4]

Turiya Sings offers up Turiya's most direct musical statement to date. She was in complete control, from performing to self-releasing the music within. "Jagadishwar" opens with lush, airy strings right out of a dream, its light pink clouds paired with the earthy tones of the Hammond. A hymn to Lord Krishna, it states (in Sanskrit): "You are dear to devotees who chant bhajans of Your holy names." The added strings are sweet and at times as saccharine as a Hollywood score, but when Turiya's voice enters—deep, oaky, resonant—it creates a stunning amalgamation. Neither masculine nor feminine, her voice and the lower register of the organ bring forth a dramatic, devotional, almost mournful essence to the piece, while the strings add a high, ethereal essence. It's a speedball of sound that's ancient and futuristic, confectionary and anthemic.

Already an early adopter of electronic instrumentation, by the 1980s Turiya herself was enchanted by all the possibilities that the new technology afforded her. "When I started playing electronic instruments, I said, 'This is an addition!'" she said. "It doesn't take you away from your original instrument or anything like that—this adds to the sound, the capacity, the dimension of the music."[5]

Her voice and organ reach an even deeper register on "Jai Ramachandra," eliciting the kind of bass vibrations that you can imagine making the walls quiver. "Victory to Ram who destroys worldly ties / Victory to Ram who gives delight," she intones in Sanskrit, her delivery such that it feels forlorn, even while offering up such praise to God. The whooshing synthesizers and strings again make the bhajan feel weighty and gossamer, an effect that carries through on the tape. It's hard in English to convey such seemingly opposed properties: bittersweet, oxymoronic. It's similar to Michelle Coltrane's descriptor of "Goin' Home": "It's happy and sad, whatever that emotion is."[6]

"*Turiya Sings*—the way that it's orchestrated around her voice—you can't touch that. You can't touch that at all," said Surya Botofasina. Still a toddler living at the Vedantic Center at the time of its recording, he nevertheless remained in awe of the end result decades later. "It's a life-defining collection of sounds. That's why you can listen to even the most like low-quality rips of it and be like, 'Yeah, that touched every single part of my heart,' because the essence is all that matters."[7]

Turiya Sings's profundity rests on eliciting that sensation: heavenly and earthy, woody and synthetic, haunted and blissed-out, conflicted yet resolved, containing these diametrical opposites wholly within itself. Baker Bigsby and Ravi Coltrane have stated that they prefer the original, unadulterated versions of these bhajans,[8] but there's something singular about the original cassette version of *Turiya Sings*. Remove the jazz legacy of John Coltrane; the audacious, unrivaled albums Turiya released as a solo artist in the realm of spiritual jazz in the early 1970s; the more polished albums she made in the late 1970s; take all of that catalog away, and there remains an argument to be made about the genius of *Turiya Sings* as a standalone work. In the world of New Age and electronic music, if she had only released that one tape, obscure and rare as it remains to this day, her legacy would be secured, its beauty and spiritual message undiluted and undiminished by the subsequent decades. It's the sound of a soul in direct commune with the divine, revealing that duality to be an illusion, all united as one in God.

Around the time that *Turiya Sings* was prepared for release, Swamini Turiyasangitananda also began work on a book titled *Endless Wisdom*, also published that spring.[9] She returned to Northern California for a book signing and concert of chanting at the Shared Visions bookstore in Berkeley. A feature in the *Oakland Tribune* noted that "Coltrane is a wonderful combination of ethereal spirituality and down-to-earth personality. She seems at complete peace and full of joy, yet very much a human being to whom one could talk." In the story, she credited both the tape and book to enacting directives from the Lord, including the very act of singing:

> I had intended to give a classical tape recording to students at the Vedantic Center because they had arranged a banquet for me, but then I received a divine directive not to do that, but to make a tape of devotional music, my Sanskrit chants with English translations, using Western instrumentation. It was quite a wonderful directive, and quite challenging. Now that I have done this, I would like to do more music like it. It seems that, even above instrumental music, vocal music is the highest expression of devotion. Instruments can make sounds, but they cannot pronounce the names of God.[10]

As for writing *Endless Wisdom*: "I also believe there is always a need for the divine word, for this guidance through the ages. People do need it, and many of the old books are often taken for granted rather than for what they contain." She then reinforced that she did not believe, present, or propagate the notion that hers was the only answer, or the only path to reach God: "It's not to promulgate this particular way or path. And it's the same with the center. If students find that there is another path they must take, they pursue it. People must seek and find the path for themselves. The same is true of this book. It is not meant to be the answer to change people's lives, but a sharing of wisdom."[11]

A feature in the Berkeley paper mentioned "disgruntled jazzophiles" walking out of the talk while a hundred others—"young women in white who knew all the chants and sang along"—crowded onto the store's carpet. "Robed in bright orange, a steady stream of admirers and worshippers approached her, all dropping to their knees and many bowing to the ground before her," it reported. "Even in the most droning passages of music…echoes of Ms. Coltrane's gospel roots could be heard." The piece also noted that had the jazz fans stuck around, they would have been hit with "a monumental organ solo that could have made their heads spin with visions of Sun Ra and John Coltrane himself."[12]

A May 5 entry in *Divine Revelations* depicted a most fantastic vision:

> In this meditation, I was in Egypt in the Nile Valley at Giza. I entered a great pyramid. After standing awhile inside, I observed the brick formation of a wall that was designed to conceal the opening of a passageway to a secret, underground chamber. Slowly, a panel opened in the wall exposing a stairway that led to the door of the chamber. I walked downstairs; Baba was there. He told me that Jesus will be here soon, and to "go inside." Inside the dimly-lit room, there was an array of ancient vessels, Egyptian relics, and several stringed, musical instruments. When the music of the harp began, Jesus Christ suddenly appeared. He was standing tall and radiant like the demigods. At this point, Christ placed something into my hand. I offered great thankfulness and appreciation. Upon opening my hand, I found a most beautiful, crystal scarab. It had an energy field that vibrated in consonance with the harp's sound waves that were mystical like India and mysterious like Egypt.[13]

That summer, Coltrane and her sons began to rehearse in earnest for an upcoming concert. Arjuna John Jr. was soon to turn eighteen, Narayana Ravi sixteen, and Ramlal Oran was now fifteen. All three boys were growing by leaps and bounds in their confidence, and their mother felt that it was time to perform live. Arjuna's growth on the bass was pronounced, yet another instance of the young man excelling at whatever he put his intention toward. "He was a super athlete," Radha Botofasina recalled. "Very charismatic, whatever he said his brothers followed."[14] While still young, Surya remembered the eldest Coltrane brother "as such a graceful, charismatic, and funny person. Just a superstar. He had a lot of what you would now call swag."[15] His mother could sense that "he had all the ability to be a great musician. He thought very highly of his father and he was beginning to listen and understand his music."[16]

Longtime jazz critic Leonard Feather visited the family for a late July story in the *Los Angeles Times*. He noted that the living room in

Woodland Hills was almost exactly as it was in Dix Hills, the room festooned with the same Persian rugs and exotic instruments that John had bought during his travels. "It's almost like walking into the same house," Alice said. "We have that same white piano, as well as the concert grand. Over there is the koto [John] brought from Japan; those are his bagpipes, and this is a begena, an Ethiopian harp." Matter-of-factly, she discussed the time soon after his death in 1967:

> There were instances, at a time immediately after he left the body, when he did actually return to me in spirit form; there were communications, conversations, and you know what that does to you? There is no real grief. You can't harbor sorrow for someone you know has existed. We don't observe the visible now, yet we never see the last of him. He's always here, always among us, although in another state of existence. It's very beautiful.[17]

She described the upcoming Coltrane Family concert as being dedicated to John's music. Oran said that he only knew his father through the home movies the family had: "I really wasn't interested in music. That came to me gradually as I heard more of my father's records." Ravi admitted that "Giant Steps" was still too hard for him, but that the brothers had been working on "Africa" and "A Love Supreme." Like their father, their mother noted: "They don't like to be confined or restricted in any way... There was a time when it was just 'I wanna play football' or 'I want to race cars,' but now it's more crystallized. They seem to have a natural skill, a feeling—and I'm not just speaking as a partial observer, I'm telling you objectively."[18]

Alice talked about how in performing with her children, she might soon devote more time to their music and a little less time to the Vedantic Center. She also recounted her continuing conversations with John in the afterlife, noticing in their talks that he was often holding an alien instrument, like a soprano, but much longer:

I asked him, "Do you think about Earth life?" He said, "Not much." I said, "Do you consider that you might prefer living on Earth as opposed to your life in the afterlife?" And he said, "No, I wouldn't prefer living on Earth." So I said, "Really? Not with all the acceptance, the recognition, the fame?" His reply was, "I prefer the spirit life to the way life is on Earth."[19]

At article's end, Alice Coltrane smiled at the thought of John's pride in his teenaged sons: "It's really wonderful. When we're having a rehearsal here, it's just like their father is living again."

Purusha Hickson attended the July 31 concert at Royce Hall on the UCLA campus and noted the audience applause for them: "She looks like a lioness being followed by three lion cubs." He added: "A rainbow of wonderful possibilities awaited—then the unimaginable happened."[20]

On August 5, Turiya recorded a meditation:

Baba said to me: "Gird up; prepare yourself for a year of greater works, higher tasks, and the encumbrance of austere tests and trials. In view of all of these, We will be standing beside you, strengthening you as you proceed along the rough roads and winding *mayic* paths of this transitory world." In the forthcoming days and months, some of the worst visions and experiences occurred with practically everything that *maya* could produce in terms of illusion masked as reality, desecrations on the sacredness of spiritual life, and misrepresentations of the truth surrounding rebirth, death, and immortality.[21]

In the early morning hours of Saturday, August 7, John Jr. and a friend were returning home. Too tired to drive, Coltrane asked his friend Derrick Traylor to take the wheel of his brand-new car, even though Traylor didn't yet have his license. As they wound their way through the hills, the car veered across the road and smashed head-on into a parked car. Traylor suffered head and abdominal injuries but was otherwise in stable condition. John Jr. was killed instantly.[22] He had just graduated from high school. It was less than three weeks until his eighteenth birthday.

Later that morning, Purusha Hickson walked next door to start his daily chores in Swamini's yard: "As I got closer to the house, Swamini emerged through the kitchen's sliding doors," he recalled. "It was the first and only time I ever saw Swamini look slightly disheveled. 'No karma yoga today,' she softly said. Swamini gave me a gentle smile, turned around and slowly walked back inside."[23]

When Swamini informed Shankari Adams of the car accident, she was stunned. "It was as if my ears would not hear or process what was being said. I will always remember that somber imagery," she said:

> Yet she remained composed, even as she proceeded to the mortuary to make funeral arrangements... Relatives, friends, neighbors, and John's devastated classmates all arrived at the funeral home in a state of shock. As the parent of John Jr., it was she who spoke words of comfort, and stood by as a pillar of strength. Her calm presence consoled everyone, especially the boy's three distraught siblings.[24]

The entire community was devastated. Swamini could know great details about the ancient past, could glean knowledge of future events, and knew that one day this too would come to pass. In much the same way that Turiya made the ultimate sacrifice in her tapasya, suffering third-degree burns on her right hand (and nearly losing use of it altogether), she again made a sacrifice unfathomable to most other human beings.[25] Radha Botofasina recalled:

> She told us. She said that when she had children, the Lord said that one would be going back. She knew that from the time they were babies. Then she said, when they came to the door to let her know, she said to us that she still had the human heart in there. The human heart would have some kind of response. Swamini told us directly that he was standing

right there next to them in a white sweater. He had been given the option of either remaining in that 17-year-old body as an invalid or going out the body. He chose to leave the body.[26]

The following Sunday, Swamini wrote a song for Arjuna, "A New Sun." Botofasina remembered the words:

"A new sun has arisen in the sky / It's the same sun with the same name and the same sign." She wrote that song and asked me to sing it. So I sang it and then she asked me to sing it again. And I started having an emotional sobbing response to it. She was okay with that. When we went to the home to see him laid out, she had him on a table with garlands and flowers all over. He was going to be cremated. People were wailing and crying. One of the students had a little son, maybe 2½, he was just playing and rolling. She indicated that that's the way people should respond to death, in terms of equilibrium. She was always the example of complete surrender to the will of God.[27]

A month after his passing, her meditation revealed to her that Arjuna reincarnated and had been born again to a member of their community.[28] As her students and Vedantic members grieved, they could look to Swamini and see that she too had suffered: as a spouse, as a mother, as a guru. Yet still she gave herself fully to the Lord's divine will. Radha Botofasina said it was for her the ultimate example of detachment: "She referred to her children as 'the son,' 'the daughter.' As human beings, we are attached to 'my.' It's a responsibility given to you by the Lord. We do the best we can. It's a double blessing to understand something outside of ourselves to lay down our lives for. But at the same time, you're willing to do this, but you have to understand it's not yours."[29]

In the studio, in concertizing with the children, in grief, in business dealings, in maternal loss, in weekly spiritual guidance in Woodland Hills, in everyday interactions, in world travel, Turiya maintained a level demeanor that came across in almost every interview and conversation with those that knew her intimately. Adams said, "Swamini always maintained equanimity whether recording in the studio, performing on stage, greeting the media, or enduring the unexpected challenges associated with travel. She had no separate persona from one setting to another. Her demeanor remained centered, efficient, and pleasant regardless of circumstance."[30]

That September, Turiya gave a spoken introduction and accompanied Indian master shehnai player Ustad Bismillah Khan on shruti box at Chicago's Orchestra Hall.[31] During these months, other entries in *Divine Revelations* featured Lord Sri Rama saying: "Depend upon Us, be strong; suffer for Us" and "Walk patiently, ever courageously onward for Us." In one meditation, she recounted playing harp in one of Krishna's Heaven worlds, gifted with a necklace of rubies in gold by the Lord.[32]

And then in the middle of December, Swamini was astrally projected—not up into some heavenly realm, but to the nearby hills:

> I was taken to a large expanse of land on 48 acres in Southern California. The area is mountainous with a valley that has many Oak and Sycamore trees throughout the landscape. There is a stream coursing through the canyon. Deer and other creatures go there each day. The surroundings looked very familiar. It was Chumash Native American land. While walking on the land, I knew that I had been there before; and as a matter of fact, I was reminded of the divine prophecy that Baba had given regarding the reemergence as an ashram.[33]

In the waning days of 1982, she closed on the property, purchased for $1.3 million. The Supreme Lord had called her to California a decade before and now she would establish an ashram there.

CHAPTER TWENTY-FIVE

Each Second an Eternity

A MOTHER'S HEART SUFFERED AND THE CHILDREN GRIEVED. "It created such a fissure," Ravi said. "A shockwave went through all of us. But my mother was the glue that held it all together."[1] Ravi graduated that spring from El Camino but postponed a decision on college. Mourning and adrift, he wasn't even sure if music was his calling anymore. He picked up a string of menial jobs, just punching a clock and going to work.

Meanwhile, Swamini diligently set about establishing the Shanti Anantam Ashram in Chumash Pradesh[2] in neighboring Agoura Hills. Or "The Land," as she and her students would lovingly call it. Located twelve miles away from Woodland Hills, it was an easy fifteen-minute drive from the family home to the forty-eight acres of rustic land, surrounded by neighboring horse ranches. Three mobile homes arrived by February and the Vedantic Center families were ready to move. Radha Botofasina recalled:

> The day we left for the ashram, one medium-sized moving truck came and gathered up all the people and their possessions. There were three different houses. Nobody had any possessions. We didn't have a couch. I had a rocking chair, that was it. We slept on the floor. Our clothes were negligible. Shankari and I were a house together, because we were both

Brahmacharinis; we had taken vows of celibacy. We were also both single parents. She had her daughter Janardani, who was a year older than Surya.³

It was an El Niño year and on the drive over, Hickson remembered that "the sky took on a dark and ominous mood. We were greeted with howling winds and a torrential downpour." The gentle stream that traversed the land? It was now a raging river. And the dirt road that ran parallel to it was now viscous mud. When the moving truck got hopelessly mired in it, the families resorted to unpacking in the driving rain and carrying it all uphill. When Hickson woke up the next day, the storm seemed like a bad dream: "Sunlight was streaming through the mighty oak and sycamore trees. The morning light revealed a green wooded valley fortified by magnificent mountains on both sides... We could hear the flowing water and when we listened deeply—we could hear the stillness of the valley itself."⁴

After life in the suburbs of the Valley, the rough, wild mountain land was a test for the young community. Trees and underbrush had to be cleared, permanent housing had be constructed, the dirt road that instantly turned to mud when it rained had to be paved, and a run-down old building on the land needed to be torn down so that a mandir could be erected in its place. What's more, more torrential rains had destroyed the original concrete bridge on the land.

And the person who conceived of a new design for the bridge was Swamini herself. As Hickson noted, while she had "no engineering skills, no contractor skills, no building skills, and no architectural drawing skills... she had a connection with the Source of all engineering, building, and architecture." The resultant design was enacted and it held for decades.

For the kids, the raw land was a source of endless wonder and play. Surya was not yet five when they moved out there:

> The beautiful thing about being on such a large parcel of land is that there's a lot to do. There's a lot to explore in a safe environment. We

spent a lot of time in the creek. I would go to the creek and try to catch a crawfish or frogs and skip rocks. Someone put up a basketball hoop. My best friend and I set up a backyard baseball stadium. People were getting rid of some old doors and my mom let us use them, like our own version of the Green Monster in Boston. We tried to make a tall fence out of them. Making a bow and arrow is awesome and being able to shoot it at a tree was great! There was a lot of that kind of imaginary play.[5]

With the Summer Olympics taking place in L.A. in 1984, that Olympic spirit soon spread to the ashram. More and more families were arriving and Surya's mom recalled: "We had a summer program here for the kids, where they could do videography, really creative things. You get twenty kids together, creating a phony Olympics, using the land for them to run around and ride on skateboards. One kid is the 'studio guy,' another kid is the pretend anchorman, stuff like that, using ironing boards as surfboards. They just had a blast."[6]

From the first day of first grade, Surya Botofasina knew he wasn't like the other kids at his school. "I had a weird name and was eating tofu," he said. "I got made fun of for my name, for my skin, for the food that I ate since I was vegetarian." When the class sang songs, he wondered why they were all in English and not in Sanskrit:

It was very obvious early on that we were different. Growing up in Agoura as an African-American young man, I knew that that was also a different experience. The ashram was very diverse and it had a lot of African-American individuals and a lot of other folks. It was not uncommon for me to look at The Ashram and see people that shared a heritage with myself. But when I went to school, it was very clear that I was amongst a different set of numbers when it came to those who shared my heritage. We weren't raised to react in certain ways that some of our peers did. We didn't have the liberty to speak to our parents in the way that our peers were able to; It probably was a good thing.[7]

In September 1984, Alice Coltrane returned to New York City for the first time in seven years and played two shows at Carnegie Hall with saxophonist Sam Rivers, bassist Reggie Workman, and drummer Rashied Ali. As she told Robert Palmer, "I have heard reports of people saying: 'Oh, she wouldn't be available for concerts, she's just involved with her spiritual group.' But people always know where to find me when they're putting together a benefit concert." She also talked about seeing musicians in India who "play in or near the temples and aren't necessarily interested in recognition from the rest of the world… I'll always be striving to make my own music transcendental in that way, and in other ways."[8] A trio with Reggie Workman and Roy Haynes performed on John Coltrane's birthday in Philadelphia. The next month, she returned to Detroit for the first time in years, where she reconnected with drummer Roy Brooks and Workman for a performance at the Detroit Institute of Art.

Back home, Swamini would be at the ashram multiple times a week. She conducted classes studying the Bible and the Bhagavad Gita on Wednesday nights with the adults. But Sunday was the main day at the Shanti Anantam Ashram. For young Surya, "it all revolved around Sunday. That was the day when time was not able to be calculated by the measurements that we use today."[9]

The Sabbath would begin with the kids getting dressed in their Sunday best, usually white clothes that wouldn't stay white till lunchtime. First they'd attend Bal Vikas—translated as "blossoming of the child" in Sanskrit—the iteration of Christian Sunday school as first ideated by Sri Sai Baba and taught by parents at the ashram. "We'd go to Sunday school and have assignments like meditate for five minutes or read this story, or question and answer," Surya recalled. "Or maybe we'd do activities or some sort of play that would exemplify human values."

As Bal Vikas wound down, the kids would join their parents in the recently erected mandir, where kirtan and the singing of bhajans would have already commenced in anticipation of Swamini's arrival. Time would grow increasingly pliant, as songs "could last twenty minutes, easy," Surya said. But what is an hourly sense of time as measure for antiphonal exaltations to the Eternal Lord that stretch back centuries?

Yet rather than make the bhajans hew toward her jazz or classical stylings, Swamini reconfigured them to make them more readily approachable to her devotees:

> Her instrumentation, arrangements, and harmonic foundations are comparatively simple; they consist of keyboard, vocals, and hand percussion, with simple pentatonic melodies set over conventional chord progressions. To facilitate group singing, bhajan melodies tend to be antiphonal in nature and quite simple, falling within forms of raga and tala accessible to most amateur singers.[10]

Soon Swamini herself would approach, most times driven out to the land by her sister Marilyn. Surya remembered it clearly:

> It would be an early afternoon arrival. She had this maroon Lincoln-Continental and you could hear the music blasting from her car. Inevitably, less than a minute later, her car would pull around and the bhajans would be blasting at a nice volume level. Whether she was driving, her son, or sister was driving, she'd get out and she had on her distinct orange robe and that's when the day *really* began. That's when time wasn't a factor any longer. There would be a moment of pause and then she would turn on the organ and the takeoff would begin! At first the music just felt good, it felt unique.[11]

For the adults in the room, chanting felt just as transformative. "The bhajans started with a traditional format: We sang each line four times returned to the top and began a new round and each round the tempo increased," Hickson said. "Finally, we would get to the last line and Swamini would stay with those lyrics. She might change melodies, harmonies, tempos, or change keys or all of the above! It didn't matter if two people were present or two thousand, Swamini brought it every

Sunday."[12] As chanting continued, there would be a marked shift in the energy within the temple that everyone else could feel, with the handheld percussion and chanting intensifying:

> During kirtan, Swamini's inner consciousness door opened and she was also able to amplify and sustain the divine energy flow until others' inner doors opened as well. Swamini was fully absorbed, almost in a trance state, simultaneously orchestrating the chanting and driving it with celestial melodies and harmonies. I was playing the mridanga drum and trying to stay with Swamini's dynamic rhythms. It felt like the temple was percolating; soon the sacred waters of devotion started to boil over.[13]

Swamini herself was well aware of the dilation of time, the increasing pressures, the transformative energies swirling around the mandir. The chanting would continue and "the air itself seemed to be supercharged with divine energy," Adams recalled. "There appeared to be no difference between the total bliss of that moment and the experience of heaven." To which Swamini noted:

> As I am playing the organ, sometimes I am not even in this mandir! My soul is elevated awhile, then it ascends higher, and there is this on-rushing force of the *pranas* (life-breath) and the consciousness rises and pierces the crown chakra. Sometimes the human heart must yield to the pressure. On the journey to meet God, there are times when each second is like an eternity of worship; that is what is known as spiritual realization. What I mean by spiritual is that the music is directed toward the Supreme Being—the Source of all life, all beings, and all existence. The least I can do is offer the music back to the Supreme One.[14]

And then the Wurlitzer would gently drift back down toward silence, and everyone in the ashram would slowly return to Earth. "After that we would eat," Surya said. "It had a potluck family meal aspect. People knew how to make some wonderful vegetarian food, so of course it was only natural that I go around and sample each home's dish."[15]

In her many years of meditation, Turiya had received many inner directives from the Lord, acquiring knowledge in any number of areas, from learning harp, string arrangements, singing, and writing a book to learning Sanskrit and designing a concrete bridge. But in 1985, she received a challenging new directive: create a devotional television program.

Outside of going to see the film *Gandhi* in the theaters, Turiya hadn't much engaged with popular film or television, but she soon set about learning the medium. "She was unfamiliar with the techniques of visual programming, yet she immediately began her assignment," Adams said. "She researched the technical aspects of television production, secured a local studio, and contracted a highly qualified cinematographer with years of experience."[16] Writing a book or playing music can happen as a solo endeavor, but working in a visual medium like television or film required more participants with technical expertise. Swamini was guided to cameraman Bill McCloud, who had recently won an Emmy for his work on the television show *Benson*. Students helped to build sets.

The intention behind the program was to showcase the ashram's devotional music, Swamini's sermonizing and organ work, and creative visual imagery in a setting far beyond the fences of Agoura Hills, so that it might touch others out there, presenting it all in such a way so as to "depict universal harmony and peace among the various spiritual paths... the program's imagery of light and sound did portray the eternal soul, who has realized God and dwelt in the joy of an eternal, absolute relationship with God."[17] By the end of December 1985, a TV listing at two A.M. appeared in the *Los Angeles Times*: "Eternity's Pillar Alice Coltrane, with devotional music and meditation."

The first week in 1986, *Eternity's Pillar* began to air on KTTV Channel 11 at midnight. An early episode opened with Swamini's face transposed against a twinkling backdrop of stars and blinking Christmas lights as the bhajan "Keshava Murahara" played in the background. There was a low-angle shot of three pillars and a voiceover: "It attests that truth that the biblical teachings of the West and the esoteric wisdom of the East are harmonious, are universal, and are in one accord."

An extremely slow fade-in leads to Swamini playing organ against a cloth backdrop, her hair gently blowing from a nearby fan. She talks of the Supreme Lord and everlasting God and then plays "Let Us Praise God Together," an old spiritual.[18] There are extreme close-ups of a crystal lotus incense holder, smoldering incense, and her playing piano in her living room, a veena and sitar glimpsed against the wall behind her. The segment ends with a globe spinning slowly against a star field. She reads from her own book *Endless Wisdom*, then recites the Lord's Prayer, soon after joined by voices reciting it in German, Spanish, Hindu, until it's a jumble of prayer against a drawing of a flower with five religious symbols around it, including the Christian cross, the Islamic crescent moon and star, and the *om* symbol. Another sermon is paired with video images of solar flares and a Happy New Year 1986 message. In a halting cadence, Swamini then addresses her television audience directly: "After prayer and meditations are over, I like to chant the holy names of God." Watching an old episode, one can't help but notice Swamini speaking with a curious accent that appears to have no distinct origin. Which was her intention. In a Q&A sent out as a public response, she answered the question: "Why does Swami speak with an accent?" as such: "The accents appears [sic] to present itself when speaking of God."[19]

In the paper, Coltrane called "this program quite unlike any other shown on television. It presents devotional music, wisdom and meditation in an ecumenical context, thereby promoting universal harmony and peace." Serving as Center spokesperson, Shankari Adams added: "Swamiji has undertaken the television ministry in a willing response to the Lord's directive to 'share God's light.'"[20]

But in this, Swamini and the Vedantic Center were not alone. In the 1980s, many ministers and evangelists began to take to the airwaves to spread the message of God, their range extending far beyond the pulpit. In the greater Los Angeles area, you could tune in to see sermonizing from the likes of early televangelist personalities like Dr. Gene Scott, Jan Crouch, Puerto Rican astrologer Walter Mercado, and the like.

Stuart Swezey was an L.A.-based concert promoter who booked punk shows out in the Mojave Desert with alternative acts like Sonic Youth, Meat Puppets, and the Minutemen. He also ran an alternative bookstore and had taken an interest in video collages. Scanning local television stations in the wee hours, he stumbled upon *Eternity's Pillar*. "The music reminded me of that kind of old-school Paramahansa Yogananda–type yoga and spirituality of an earlier time on the West Coast," Swezey said. "But then Alice was also doing part-gospel, part-Hindu chanting, and it was just *out there*. I just appreciated it as something really original. The only person I could possibly compare [it] to was Korla Pandit."[21] In the latter part of the decade, Swezey would collage footage from the show into an influential underground VHS tape series, *AMOK Assault Videos*.

The show would run for a few years, with estimates that some twenty-four episodes were made during that time. The tapes weren't properly archived at the station, according to Bigsby. "The television station actually lost those tapes," he said. "They were aired. They got lost."[22]

CHAPTER TWENTY-SIX

The Coltrane Legacy

Ravi Coltrane was a bag boy at the local supermarket, and his manager saw potential. "He promoted me to frozen foods, or something like that," Ravi said. "[He] said I would someday make a good manager because he started out as a bag boy, too."[1] Realizing that his path might lead deeper into the cold case, Ravi quickly enrolled in the Cal Arts music program. That same spring of 1986, an anti-apartheid protest took place in Oakland, with over a thousand protesters marching. Folk singer Richie Havens (a friend and mentor to Radha Botofasina and a guest on a lost episode of *Eternity's Pillar*) and Coltrane both performed in solidarity with the protest.[2]

A protest concert might appear at odds with Turiya's focus on spiritual concerns, but worldly detachment is not the same as disengagement. She greatly respected the work of Dr. Martin Luther King Jr. and Malcolm X, while always keeping a universal perspective on human conflict. So while she often hewed to her late husband's example of not being overtly political, she was nevertheless engaged to combat injustices happening elsewhere. One entry in *Divine Revelations* read: "America is a country whereof invaders from other lands brutally fought with Native American Indians and nearly drove them into obscurity... [purgatory] shall remain filled with these perpetrators until the fullest extent of retribution has been undergone."[3] In another passage, Lord Sri Rama discussed South Africa: "Indigenous people have had to endure with the false sovereignty, oppressive racial superiority, and the bondage of apartheid imposed upon them by invaders onto that land. Mark ye well these words: In the forthcoming years, the ivory towers of apartheid and its self-appointed, unlawful government shall crumble."[4]

At the ashram, Swamini hosted several Peace Days, inviting priests and clergy from various other faiths in the area to combine forces and work toward a greater good for their communities. Much like the artwork from *Cosmic Music* or the emblem on *Eternity's Pillar*, she was steadfast in her belief of a universal force for good, using religious symbols regardless of denomination. As Satchidananda had always preached, and what Swamini herself echoed: "Truth is one. Paths are many."[5]

The Shanti Anantam Ashram community continued to grow. Shankara Antero, brother of Radha Botofasina, and his wife, Ana; daughter Enid, eleven; and son Miguel, six, had moved from Pasadena the summer before, bringing the number of adults living on The Land to twenty-three. A core group of about a dozen kids of all ages lived there now, riding the bus to Woodlake or White Oak Elementary and back every day. The school bus stopped at the bottom of the hill on Triunfo Canyon Road and the kids walked the short distance into the compound. These kids also helped around the ashram. Surya remembered being responsible for sweeping the bridge and road. There were always leaves to rake, sidewalks to sweep, or a wheelbarrow full of dirt and pulled weeds to dump. It was an idyllic terrain for the kids, according to Radha Botofasina: "Kids growing up, they could go into any house on the land, anyone and everyone was 'Mom So-and-So' or 'Pappa So-and-So,' that was it. No doors were locked or anything like that."[6]

One Tuesday afternoon, April 8, Miguel got off the school bus and started walking down the dirt road that led to the ashram. The community that day was in a buoyant mood, having recently completed a balloon payment on a loan for the property. Everyone looked forward to a celebratory dinner with Swamini at a local Indian restaurant, and Ana volunteered in Westlake getting things ready for the feast. But Miguel never reached home.

"When the word came that he was missing, that he hadn't been seen since the bus dropped him off, we started a huge manhunt for him," Radha Botofasina said.[7] Students, neighbors, and police scoured the land well into the night. Night fell fast and the search continued. Seven hours later, his body was found hidden in the brush right off the road. He had been sexually assaulted and stabbed dozens of times.

As the manhunt continued and the property was combed over for any clues or evidence, the ashram community was visibly shaken, the mood somber. Adults now accompanied the kids home from the bus stop, watching over them as they played in the woods. "The community was devastated and my family was blown apart, my physical family was blown apart," Botofasina said of the tragedy, her voice still emotional at the memory of that day. "The fallout from that just got worse and worse, relatives wailing and screaming on top of each other. The only person my sister-in-law really wanted to see was Swamini. Swamini came down to the cottage and offered so many kind things. Anything they needed she was there for them, always beyond any kind of generosity."[8]

Botofasina's brother and sister-in-law were able to sit in meditation with Swamini for hours at a time as they grieved. "Five-hour meditation with Swamini was like something you'd never experience," she said. Proximity to Swamini during this time allowed them to do something powerful: "They would sit there and they would go into the state where they could see their son, be able to talk to him, and all kinds of things."[9] At the service held at a Westlake chapel, Swamini addressed the audience: "This little boy touched our hearts in a way that won't be forgotten." She also told the crowd that she had been in contact with Miguel since his death: "The boy told me very lucidly... 'I'm very happy in heaven.' Let not this event destroy our faith and trust in God."[10]

Regardless, the grief over the gruesome tragedy was too much for the family to endure. The Anteros moved from the ashram, with

Swamini helping the bereaved every step of the way. But within six months, their marriage ended. Miguel's murder went unsolved for decades.

In meditation that December, the Lord spoke to Turiya:

> I will show you the sun itself in a direct way that is not possible for human beings... Within seconds, the Lord elevated me above the sun. Immediately, I became greatly aware of the massive volume of the sun. When I considered what would the enormous weight be, the Lord said that scientists on earth calculate upon the weight of the sun, when in reality, the sun is weightless.[11]

In the early part of 1987, Swamini began to record more bhajans, using a new synthesizer. Michelle recalled accompanying her mother to Guitar Center and as she tinkered around on the keys, a crowd gathered: "Now people are following us, listening, because wow, she's really playing something beautiful," she said, and when they got to the Oberheim OB-8, "by then it was like the Pied Piper, there's a crowd around her as she's hitting the buttons. She left the store with that one."[12]

Most of the recordings that would constitute her second ashram tape, *Divine Songs*, followed the same template as *Turiya Sings*, the music just as mysterious, edifying, and profound. Bhajans like "Keshava Murahara" and "Rama Guru" dated back to *Eternity's Pillar*, the former serving as the opening music for the program. With Swamini's layered vocals, shimmering chimes, and the soaring portamento of the OB-8, each number again suggested the earthy and the celestial. The OB-8's portamento especially appealed to her mother, Michelle said. "She referenced that to what the universe sounded like to her... it's reminiscent of the Om or the breath. It just has a very spiritual overtone."[13]

Swamini even used the harp for perhaps the most enigmatic song in her entire catalog, "Er Ra." Featuring just harp and her voice, "Er Ra" stands apart from all the other ashram tape material in that it is technically not a bhajan. Instead of singing in Hindi, Swamini sings in ancient Egyptian, one of the earliest known written languages (dating back to 3200 BCE) and long since considered a dead language with no native speakers for hundreds of years. "No one could understand it except for some academic Egyptologists," Bigsby explained. "That's an early Egyptian language that doesn't exist anymore."[14] Just what is being sung or how Swamini would have attained knowledge of that language remains unknown, unless it was yet another skill set she attained from the Supreme Lord. Or as Surya hinted: "'*How* does she know that language?' Well, that's a good question now, isn't it?"[15] Perhaps it's in homage to the Sun God of ancient Egypt, or an iteration of that celestial harp music she heard deep within a pyramid during one of her prior meditations.

About half of the other bhajans on *Divine Songs* feature the students from the Vedantic Center. "The big deal for me was when she was going to the studio," Surya said. "We would order from my favorite vegetarian restaurant, Follow Your Heart in Woodland Hills. I just remember being blown away at the studio, by the console, the tape machine, the two-inch tapes."

Bhajans like "Om Shanti" and "Madhura Manohara Giridhari" featured the students and a string quartet, led by Swamini's harp and organ. Baker noted Surya's interest in the console and let him do a punch-in during one take. "That was like the biggest deal for me ever when he let me do like my first punch-in," Surya said. "I messed it up! And Baker ate it. He took it for me: 'Oh sorry, that was my fault.' Anyone who has eyes knew it was *my* fault and Swamini *of course* would have known."[16]

Sessions took place at Rumbo Recorders, a studio in Canoga Park about a half-hour drive from Swamini's home. While she and her students were recording *Divine Songs* in Studio B, another L.A. group was camped out in Studio A: Guns N' Roses. "I remember Rumbo was where they were recording... I'd hear them and see them hanging out,"[17] Surya recalled. They were laying down the songs that would become their 1987 debut, *Appetite for Destruction*,[18] which would go on to sell thirty million copies worldwide.

The year 1987 also marked the thirtieth anniversary of John Coltrane's passing[19] and the widow Coltrane decided it was the right time to take her sons out on tour. Ravi was studying music at Cal Arts and Oran had graduated from high school, so concerts were presented during that summer in London, the Netherlands, and Japan, with more concerts staged in the United States and Poland later that fall. Despite the intervening decades and the waning of jazz as an influence, the ardor for John's music had never diminished.

"It's very universal in many ways," she said. "Young people—it doesn't matter what their field is exactly—they are inspired by him. They hear something in it that they can relate to. That's really why I'm here, to offer this concert to his legacy, to his genius." Exposing her sons to the wide world, as well as allowing them to dig deeper into their own heritage, was also important. When asked about his father's legacy, Ravi was demure: "The music is very pure. It started out that way and time doesn't have a major effect on him."[20] At a concert that fall, a reviewer noted: "Ravi, in particular, seemed to summon up past images, with a stance and a look that was eerily similar to that of his father."[21]

The Coltrane family returned to New York City to perform on what would have been John's sixty-first birthday. Fittingly, "Homage to John Coltrane: A Spiritual Legacy" was presented within the gigantic expanse of the Cathedral of St. John the Divine in upper Manhattan. Reggie Workman helmed the first part of the program, dedicated to John's music. With Andrew Cyrille on drums and Marilyn Crispell on piano, an array of saxophonists appeared: Oliver Lake, Dewey Redman, Frank Lowe, Arthur Thames, and Oran.

Robert Palmer made a case for the "cosmic music" of that last Coltrane band with Alice, arguing that they "are journeys, beginning with lyrical, peaceful themes, erupting into textural turbulence that intensifies in force, then winds down, returning the listener gradually to the music's lyrical starting point." Of that time period, Alice remembered listening to recordings of Tibetan bells and their resonance in the family home, how her husband drew on Eastern philosophy in his last years: "That music is like a mosaic of sound and energy. It wasn't anything other than an expression of the colors and varieties of sound, and how they interweave and complement each other. A number of people were quite confused by that, but if the same people look at paintings with a variety of colors and textures, they're pleased."[22]

For the second half of the concert, Alice Coltrane appeared with Workman and Ali as rhythm section, Oran on saxophone, while cornetist-composer Butch Morris conducted a sixteen-piece string ensemble. The night was plagued by sound problems, from poorly mic'd strings to Alice's organ levels fluctuating in the mix. Which was too bad, as the concert included rare performances of "Lord of Lords" and "Goin' Home," the latter featuring gospel singer David Peaston. Live reviews of the concert raved about Peaston, with Palmer feeling "it was the concert's emotional high-point."[23]

The family next traveled to Poland for the twenty-ninth International Jazz Festival in Warsaw, where they performed alongside the likes of the Sun Ra Arkestra, Chick Corea, the Tony Williams Quintet, and Art Blakey. Billed as "The Coltrane Legacy," they performed at the magnificent Sala Kongresowa, a 2,880-seat theater at the Palace of Culture and Science that had been constructed in the midst of the Cold War. Alice played some of her husband's compositions that didn't often pop up in her concertizing, like "Lonnie's Lament" and "Song of the Underground Railroad."

Slawomir Kulpowicz, a sympathetic Polish artist who also used bhajans in modern settings, opened the show and also played "Prema." Swamini was touched by the performance: "I could not help but notice the deep, devotional spirit in his sound. It was a momentous occasion for all present—a profound joy to hear the Holy Names of God chanted in a building that had been constructed under the rule of Stalin."

Kulpowicz and two thousand of his countrymen in turn were stunned by Coltrane's concert, especially the nine-minute harp solo midway through the set:

When Swamini played, the ethereal, all-pervading sound filled the hall with divine power. In fact, throughout one of Swamini's harp solos, the harp appeared to move and sway along with her. It seemed to merge with her, and its ethereal sound charged the very air with spiritual energy. The audience was deeply moved by the pure, divine sounds that transcended all other music previously heard in that hall.[24]

Filmed and broadcast on Polish television, the concert can still be found online. Outside of the heavily edited *Black Journal* live footage shot back in 1970, it's the lone instance of an Alice Coltrane concert being recorded in its entirety. It gives us a rare glimpse of her onstage: the intention on her face, her lips pursed in deep concentration, her graceful glissades, the radiance of her smile during a particularly joyous run. A close-up of Alice and the harp strings also reveals the deep scar tissue on her right hand. It's just a passing glimpse but an ever-present reminder of the great sacrifice made.

Returning to Los Angeles after the concert, Coltrane next appeared on *For Members Only*, a local television show focused on African American history hosted by longtime DJ/columnist/historian Tom Reed, discussing John Coltrane's legacy and an upcoming three-day festival created in his honor. The first annual John Coltrane Festival was staged that November, with three days of concerts stretched across three L.A. neighborhoods, culminating in a performance in Griffith Park with Charlie Haden, Albert "Tootie" Heath, and actress Marla Gibbs (at the height of her post-*Jeffersons* fame).

At the festival, Surya was shocked to realize that there were people out there who knew about his guru's late husband: "All these people showed up and I was like, 'People know who John Coltrane is??' I'd see people come up to her with such reverence. That's when I started to see that John Coltrane was on the Mt. Rushmore of influential jazz musicians, the godfather of the avant-garde movement of jazz."[25]

The next year of the festival, Joe Henderson, soul singer-turned-reverend O. C. Smith, Richie Havens, and more participated. By the time of the fourth iteration, the jazz landscape in Los Angeles was quickly shifting. The city's primary jazz station, KKJZ, had changed formats, and the festival itself brought in Carlos Santana to headline alongside Coltrane, bringing in more of a rock audience.

The end of the decade presented another shift for Swamini. In the jazz world, she remained Alice Coltrane, widow of John Coltrane and keeper of her late husband's legacy. She still managed the catalog, the reissuing of his albums on compact disc, and his intellectual property.[26] Public performances would occur during the annual John Coltrane Festivals, but his music was emphasized. She concertized rarely beyond that time of year, always prioritizing instead the music he had composed rather than her own. In a feature for *Ebony*, she talked about his presence still being there with her. "I can't miss him, he's here, I feel him here, I see him physically in my room while I'm in a transcendental state," she said, though she also said it had been nine years since she last spoke to him in that state, thinking that he had since been reincarnated. "I know people don't understand or believe what I'm saying. All I can say to them is to meditate and find out for themselves."[27]

By 1988, *Eternity's Pillar* production was also winding down. Even on the cassettes that were sold only at the Vedantic Center, she increasingly ceded the foreground to the students, while she focused on the keyboards and arrangements. Increasingly, more and more time was spent nurturing the ashram, to the point where upward of fifty families were now living on the land or active members in the ashram community. Her travels to India happened more frequently, for longer durations.

Shankari Adams recalled one of her Sunday talks: "Music is an accessory-ornamentation. I can leave it totally, if God's Name cannot be written on it. Music has to serve God's purpose. When music cannot glorify God, I do not have any interest in it."[28] If that suggests an increasingly monastic life away from music, it would be a misconception. If you were inclined to see Alice Coltrane play music, the Shanti Anantam Ashram opened its gates to the public every Sunday. "In the '80s and the '90s, you could have gone there, introduced yourself casually to Swamini, and requested a conversation," Surya Botofasina said. "That's what cracks me up about like 'Oh, she was musically *inactive* for twenty-seven years.' Actually, I think she was her most musically active—if you want to call it that—as far as a weekly public musical experience. She played all the time."[29]

In 1988, radio host Dolores Brandon produced "The Evolution of Alice Coltrane," a dedicated two-hour radio program broadcast over Pacifica network stations WBAI (New York) and KPFK (San Francisco). Brandon herself called it "the most concentrated tribute to Alice Coltrane ever heard, an unabashed radio fan letter from me to her."[30] At a time when her entire catalog languished out of print and the jazz press had all but written her off, it boldly argued for the validity and genius of her own music. On it, Coltrane spoke about preparation for a concert. "When the performance begins, I don't think about technical concerns at all, I concern myself only with the performance that's going out to the audience, with what they are going to receive," she said. "I do get very deeply engaged spiritually in the music. Music is a spiritual language for me. Today music is a spiritual language and I'm expressing, articulating deep feeling and deep experience in life, in spiritual life, in God."[31]

She traveled to India twice in 1989. In spring, she wrote in *Divine Revelations* that "when I was undergoing austerities...Mother Mary had sent to me a written, divine communication in her own handwriting. It was her gracious decision to read it to me. She kindly related her acknowledgment of one's attainment on the clef of the staff of spiritual life."[32] On a second trip that August, Swamini's plane landed in Kolkata. Two Catholic sisters boarded, along with an elderly nun holding a rosary. "Looking at her, especially her eyes, I recognized that I knew her as a Christ-like being from the past," she said. "She also appeared to recognize me. We conversed for a time."[33] On that commercial flight in India, Swamini Turiyasangitananda met Mother Teresa.

CHAPTER TWENTY-SEVEN

The Divine Fragrance of a Dedicated Life

When Baker Bigsby's phone rang, he would pack up a mobile recording unit and truck it out to Agoura Hills. He would record the bhajans in situ, knowing the importance of capturing that fervent energy and knowing they would get the studio treatment later. "They sang live so they're not necessarily balanced that well," he recalled. "That's why she would bring the singers into the studio and add new voices to the existing voices to strengthen the chants. It was like half live/half studio." Sometimes, they would record at other home studios around the valley. He recalled one session in Malibu, with a studio right off the kitchen. "Ants were coming in the back door and crawling along the wall," he said. "I needed to get rid of them and asked Turiya, 'How does that square with the sanctity of all life?' She said 'You ask the ants twice to leave nicely. And if they don't...you can do whatever you want to 'em!'"[1]

Surya Botofasina fondly remembered such recording sessions, as he got to witness close-up how Swamini would conduct from the organ bench, or arrange a vocal arrangement on the fly, directing the students with a wave of her hand. "During the time, the only thing that mattered to me was to be around her," Surya said, echoing the sentiments of many at the ashram during that time. "I just wanted to hear her speak and hear her play and ask her questions about music. She was the equivalent of the loving grandmother, that matriarch of a whole family that everybody looks to."[2]

Surya learned to play during Bal Vikas, studying the melodies that accompany the text of the Bhagavad Gita. "There would be a keyboard set up in our small classroom and she would teach us the book," he said. "And as the only person in our class who played, I would literally lean out of the way when she would play something and I had to learn it that way. It comes by once, try to get it or jot it down."[3]

The ashram also boasted a powerful new vocalist, Panduranga John Henderson. Henderson began his career singing with Ray Charles, before shifting his priorities elsewhere, living at the ashram with his wife, Mirabai Henderson. Released in 1990, *Infinite Chants* fades in with "Sita Ram," the ashram singers already at a lather with Swamini's portamento on the Oberheim soaring high above the mix. Just when it seems the piece couldn't possibly go any higher, Panduranga's R&B-honed, gospel-powered voice enters, the melisma teasing out the Sanskrit, transforming the chant and pushing the ecstatic music to another level.

"Om Rama" also opens midchant. Swamini's organ supports the group, her left hand laying down plangent chords while the portamento suggests an extraterrestrial craft descending upon the ashram. Just as it appears the entire room is going to achieve liftoff and leave Bigsby's mics behind on Earth, Swamini downshifts, Panduranga's voice moves to the foreground, and we're now in the midst of a hand-clapping, foot-stomping prayer meeting. Like *Infinite Chants* suggests, each of the recordings of the nine bhajans starts midchant, meaning it could have gone on for just a few seconds before or an entire eternity before Bigsby finally hit record.

Several students from the ashram accompanied Swamini on her trip to India in 1991, including Radha Botofasina, who perceived her guru in a different light overseas. "It's completely different from Swamini in the United States," she said. "People recognized her energy immediately, a lot of them. She speaks Hindi. People would just see her—we're talking street people, babies—and they would just sense her divinity. They would touch her feet. She would say: 'No, no, no, give that to Baba, give it to Swami.'"[4]

Another student on that trip witnessed a miracle. As Swamini and the students left for Puttaparthi, their car ran over a dog in the road. Horrified, the student turned to Swamini:

She looked at me, then, referring to the dog, said, "He's okay. Turn around and see." To my utter amazement, the animal was walking along the roadside, unhurt, and unscathed, despite being hit by the car... That moment, my eyes met the guru's, in acknowledgement of this eye-witnessed miracle. I saw a vast ocean of light, wisdom, and knowingness flow from Swamini, in that brief moment that our eyes met. I was unable to hold that gaze... unable to face her Light... like one who closes his eyes to the brightness of the noonday sun.[5]

At the fifth annual John Coltrane Festival in 1991, the event widened its reach, not only highlighting young, emergent jazz players in the city but also bringing in more international artists. It resulted in an eclectic mix that most closely mirrored Coltrane's own broad tastes, even if she herself didn't perform that year. There was a classical harpsichordist playing Bach, an Indian group blending raga with fusion, singer Al Jarreau, and Polish pianist Slawomir Kulpowicz; the headliner that year was Pharoah Sanders.[6]

There was a need for unity during that time in Los Angeles. Just after midnight on March 3, 1991, a Hyundai Excel carrying three passengers led police officers on a high-speed chase through the San Fernando Valley, just about twenty miles north of Woodland Hills. When the chase finally ended, a group of eight white police officers stomped on two of the passengers, then swarmed, Tasered, kicked, and truncheoned the driver of the car, Rodney King. The overhead police helicopters roused a plumber named George Holliday from his bed. Thinking quickly, he pulled out a Sony Handycam to see what the disturbance could be.

In eighty-one seconds of video footage, King's body absorbed over fifty baton blows, numerous kicks, and Taser shocks administered punitively by the cops. In the Black communities of Los Angeles and other urban centers, violence on a Black body wasn't exactly new—or news—but as the footage circulated, first on local station KTLA and then to CNN, it became a national story and scandal, with everyone from the L.A. chief of police to the president of the United States publicly announcing disgust at the violence. The nation watched as the trial stretched through the spring of 1992. All the while, racial tensions throughout Los Angeles continued to simmer.

For seven days, the jury deliberated and then on April 29, 1992, they delivered a verdict of acquittal for all four police officers. That not-guilty verdict sparked a fuse. By nightfall, Los Angeles was burning. Stores were looted, cars were set aflame, and white drivers were dragged from their vehicles and beaten by roving groups of rioters. The city burned for six days, with over sixty deaths and $1 billion in damages, primarily to Black and Korean neighborhoods. The death, damage, and injuries even outstripped that of the Belle Isle Riots, becoming the most destructive race riot in U.S. history. Nearly fifty years after those riots roared outside her window in Detroit, Swamini saw history repeat itself.

"Swamini had us drive her into the riot area and she's seeing the devastation all around, the devastated community, and she begins to formulate a way to help," Radha Botofasina recalled. "We found some places where we could make sandwiches and take them down every single week to make sure they got down to the people in need. She did have us very much involved in the community for about three or four months after the riots on a weekly basis."[7] Months later, Brotherhood Crusade co-founder Danny Bakewell singled out the likes of Berry Gordy and Alice Coltrane as the "real unsung heroes of the riot recovery effort,"[8] donating funds to provide food, clothing, shelter, and medical supplies during that fraught post-riot time.

"Swamini would do things quietly, it wasn't ostentatious," Hickson said of her outreach programs, which ramped up in the wake of the L.A. riots. "She started the Youth Employment Program, with me as the main point person. We would hire lots of youth from the inner city in all kinds of different positions, who would actually get the chance to work during the summer and get paid while they worked with professionals. They loved it."[9]

Adams noted that Swamini was very active when it came to humanitarian and community service endeavors: clothing drives, financial support for orphanages and schools, medical supplies sent to other countries, or basic necessities given to Native American communities both in Los Angeles and elsewhere. That sort of charity, given without notice or attention or a trace of ego, makes it difficult to ascertain just how much Coltrane donated to causes, to community groups, to spiritual institutions, to individuals, to people in her own community, even within her own family. Her nephew Steven Ellison, Marilyn's grandson, remembered as a kid that:

> My aunt Alice had bailed my family out of really bad times, financially. There were some really hard times when we didn't have anything. She made it so we had something and helped us out. She always tried to find a way to be helpful, to go out of her way to help. It extended way past my family. She had a willingness to jump in, to do something. And that's why everyone wanted to do everything for her. That's why people wanted to drive her around.[10]

Outside of the Coltranes' accountant, it would be nearly impossible to know just how much she financially helped others. "Nobody knows how many rents she paid, nobody knows how many scholarships she gave out, nobody knows how many people she paid for their education, nobody knows how many conversations she had with people to help guide them in their life or job or career," Surya said. "No one will ever know those things because a true servant of divine intention is not a braggadocious individual."[11]

Walking one day at a public event in Los Angeles with her students, Swamini was approached by an unkempt, unhoused man who—in Adams's estimation—seemed mentally unbalanced. A student moved to protect Swamini, only to realize that she had drawn to a halt and looked at the man "with deep compassion. Our perspective saw a disheveled, strange-acting individual, who could have posed a possible danger. Swamini's compassionate glance, however, perceived someone longing for a kind word, a smile, or blessing of reassurance."[12]

When a modest Hindu temple opened in the San Fernando Valley, Swamini began giving Friday night religious talks to the Indian-born congregation, who didn't bat an eye at a Black woman from Detroit leading the discourse. "She has a very high scale of spiritualism and is highly respected here," Dinesh Lakhanpal, president of the Hindu temple, said. "What God wants us to do is love his creation no matter what race or creed."[13] Asked in the story if she practiced levitation, she answered yes, but only in private: "I don't encourage the development of mystical practices because it detracts from devotion to God."[14]

The sixth annual John Coltrane Festival featured Elvin Jones as the headlining act. Around that same time, Elvin had invited Ravi into his band, a cross-generational gesture that not only reminded the drummer of his former boss but introduced the son to the jazz world at large. The next year of the fest, Santana returned as headliner, with Oran Coltrane debuting on backing guitar. Alice and Miki both also performed that year.

In March 1993, Turiya visited her longtime friend and onetime guru, Swami Satchidananda, at his new compound in Yogaville, Virginia. Footage exists online of a forty-minute recital she spontaneously performed, starting with a solo harp rendition of "Journey in Satchidananda" and proceeding through a series of bhajans rendered on a makeshift keyboard setup. Around that same time, Turiya considered relocating the ashram to Yogaville at the behest of Satchidananda. Hickson was part of the entourage and said that such a move was under consideration, but it never happened. It was a dynamic that could be confusing to believers as well as outsiders: "She would make decisions that in the eyes of the business people made no sense: 'You're going to be paying more taxes' or this and that. But when she got an inner directive, *that's* what she was following."[15]

That lack of ego, of self-interest, of retaining just that thin sheath of the self, these qualities—or lack thereof—set Turiya apart. "That's why I maintain to this day the hardest thing to do was to give her a compliment," Surya remembered. "She would give it to Baba, or she would deflect. It would be gracefully done." Try to compliment her on the music and she would defer: "'It was so beautiful what you played on the organ.' 'Oh, the Lord was so kind to show me.' It would be gracefully redirected toward what she clearly considered as the source, the divine, God, however one wants to term it."[16]

An entourage from the ashram, including nine adults and seven children, convened in India with Swamini in early 1994. Surya traveled there and remembered seeing her in Mumbai and then at Sai Baba's ashram in Puttaparthi: "She gave some guidance—what to eat, what not to eat, like almost like letting us know what was happening as it was happening, like...tuned into the divine channel."

Although Surya grew up well aware of the special abilities of his guru, seeing Swamini in India revealed a greater appreciation for her uncanny connection to the divine:

> It's hard for individuals to accept that she was having direct conversations with a Supreme Unifying Being, because it sounds—in human terms—impossible. Most people equate "voices in your head" with some sort of insanity. Stevie Wonder told us to "have a talk with God," so it's not unprecedented. *He* told us to have a talk with God and we all love that song. We all have been told or have felt at some time to "follow our

intuition" of "follow your gut." But who gave you *your* intuition and *your* gut feeling? So would you rather follow your intuition and your gut feeling? Or would you rather follow the being that *gave* you your intuition and gut feeling? It's just unfortunate that some can't believe that certain people have a direct line to get that answer. It's simply a direct line. It's no different from clergy and individuals of particular faiths say that they do.[17]

During a subsequent trip, Surya also experienced for himself Swamini's power of premonition. She foretold him about an incident that would happen while he was in that foreign land and how best to negotiate it. "'There's going to be a situation and you're gonna need to know that this is what you can and can't do in that conversation with that person,'" he recalled. "An hour later, I'm in *that* situation, having *that* conversation, doing exactly what I was told to do. *Super* uncomfortable."[18]

When the other members of the ashram returned to California, Swamini stayed in India until springtime. In one of her meditations, she received a message from Lord Rama that her time on Earth was drawing to an end: "The *havan*[19] is complete; everything has been committed to flames... With your ordination day drawing nigh, We are ready to extend the designated time and secure it for a future term. Hence, it is Our decree that you do not go Home."[20] During the long spells when Swamini was not present at the ashram, Panduranga John Henderson would lead kirtan. The music hardly missed a beat thanks to Henderson's strong gospel roots.

Upon her return, Swamini received a new directive. On July 3, 1994, some eleven years after its founding in Agoura Hills, she rechristened the ashram as the Sai Anantam Ashram ("The Eternal Divine Mother Sai"). As that year drew to a close, *Divine Revelations* documented nine days of the Supreme Lord speaking directly to Turiya about myriad things: how amid the 6.7 magnitude Northridge earthquake (whose epicenter was in the San Fernando Valley) He had spared the land; that in ancient days she had "always sacrificed everything as a sacramental offering unto Me"; that the Light was within her. On the ninth day, He concluded: "The sacred flame of your devotion burns daily with the divine fragrance of a dedicated life consecrated unto Me... You are like unto the oblation, the burnt offering itself being consumed by the flames, with the exception of the remaining sheathe. And yet, you continue to sacrifice for Me."[21]

In 1995, Swamini began to compile these messages into a hardbound book. *Divine Revelations* featured a dedication to the "lotus hands of Sri Sathya Sai Baba" and the credit line read: "Inscribed by A.C. Turiyasangitananda," the divine message moving through her. That same year, the U.S. Postal Service unveiled its John Coltrane stamp and Swamini recorded her fourth and final ashram tape, *Glorious Chants*.[22]

The centerpiece of the tape is "Journey to Satchidananda," now dilated to eleven minutes and featuring a choir singing new lyrics, with a solo sung in Tamil by Sairam Iyer. The lyrics alternate between prepositions: "journey *to* Satchidananda" and "journey *with* Satchidananda." Swamini's organ playing is redolent of a church service, slow and steadfast, with the portamento from the OB-8 moving in the high frequencies like a dove in the upper reaches of a cathedral ceiling. The last lines similarly alternate: "Our journey's end is our journey home" with "Our journey home is our journey's end."

She also continued to encourage her children on their various musical endeavors, playing piano on Miki Coltrane's first album, released in 1996, and then accepting an invitation to perform with Ravi when he performed at the Texaco New York Jazz Festival in 1998. After years cutting his teeth on the jazz circuit, touring with the likes of Elvin Jones, Wallace Rooney, and Steve Coleman, Ravi released his first album as a leader on a major label, *Moving Pictures*. For the festival, he was paired with his namesake, Indian master musician Ravi Shankar, and his musician daughter, Anoushka Shankar. Alice Coltrane appeared onstage with her son for a duet on "Crescent," then joined again for a full-band version of "A Love Supreme." It was her first public appearance in New York City in over a decade.

"She sounded great and people were just raving about her," Ravi said. "Wherever I go, people will always ask about my father. But a lot of people will also ask about my mom: 'How is she doing?' and 'Is she going to record again?' I always tell her that a lot of people have been asking about you and you should do something."[23]

Chapter Twenty-Eight

Going Home

In January 2000, Alice's sister JoAnn McLeod passed away. Around that same time, Swamini divulged to some of her students what she had been told years before in her meditations, that her time on Earth had been extended.[1] With that additional time, Swamini began to focus on healing. Adams noted that "because of Swamini's proven faithfulness, the Lord granted her permission to help anyone who was suffering from ill health to reach a state of wellness."

Swamini developed the ability to absorb karmic consequences of other students and devotees, lessening their impact. Such examples ranged from serious car crashes that people were able to walk away from unscathed to the abating of cancer. In *Portrait of Devotion*, the last twenty-five pages of the book are given over to extensive personal testimonials documenting the miraculous instances of Swamini touching and healing an array of maladies: back pain, leg injuries, torn knee cartilage, infertility, multiple sclerosis, coccidioidal meningitis, abnormal growths, injured wrists, scoliosis, and class III ovarian cancer.[2]

To offset the effects of someone's deadly car crash, Swamini had to "astrally rehearse" two weeks before the accident occurred. The physical effects of taking on such karma exacted its own toll. Absorbing these illnesses might lead her to not take food for several days or to suffer paralysis in her body. She herself could exhibit symptoms of illness but not be truly sick herself.

Ravi's original plan had been to convene a dream trio, featuring Jack DeJohnette on drums and his mother on piano, but in the process of putting the two legends together, Ravi found himself unceremoniously dropped by his label at the start of the new century. Jazz was no longer seen as a viable commodity by the giant music conglomerates. But Ravi might have been even more surprised by another concert with his mother.

In May 2001, Terry Gibbs was asked to play at a bebop festival in Los Angeles. Could he quickly put a band together? His son Gerry Gibbs could handle drums, and he knew Gerry's onetime roommate Ravi could handle saxophone duties. "I don't know why, but I thought I'd call Alice and ask her if she wanted to play some bebop," Gibbs recalled. "When I asked her, the first thing she said was, 'Terry, I haven't played bebop in over thirty years.' When she didn't give me an out-and-out 'no,' I kept talking. She called me back a few days later and said she'd do it."[3]

The show—featuring mother-and-son, father-and-son, and a reunion between the two old bebop bandmates after forty years—was a big hit and Ravi was as shocked as anyone. "He had never heard those records and didn't know Alice could play that style. All he ever heard her play since he was born was mostly harp and that sounded like she was out in Regooneeville,"[4] Gibbs said. "We tore up that place. People were screaming for us. Alice and I looked at each other like 'Remember those days?'"[5]

Less than three weeks after the September 11 attacks, the seventy-fifth anniversary of John Coltrane's birthday was celebrated at the Beverly Hilton. The 1999 winner of the John Coltrane music competition, a young saxophonist named Kamasi Washington, performed, along with a bevy of old friends from Alice's life in jazz music: Bennie Maupin, George Bohanon, Kenny Burrell, and Slawomir Kulpowicz. The concert was capped by a headlining set from Gibbs. At one point, Alice and her two sons performed "A Love Supreme."

In the new century, far beyond the realms of jazz, the albums that Alice Coltrane had cut in the 1970s began to crop up in some unexpected corners. Acclaimed British rock band Radiohead released two experimental albums, *Kid A* and *Amnesiac*, pivoting away from overdriven guitars into electronic washes, hand percussion, and orchestral strings that member Jonny Greenwood admitted were heavily indebted to Coltrane's own arrangements.[6] Iconic Icelandic singer Björk released *Vespertine*, an exquisite intermingling of harp, electronics, and Björk's inimitable vocals that drew heavily from Alice's own idiosyncratic harp amalgams. Both albums were critically acclaimed and big sellers, establishing both as vanguard artists in the twenty-first century. From dance DJ–turned–film composer David Holmes to young electronic dance music producer Four Tet[7] to many others, a new generation began to publicly cite Alice and her fearless, uncompromising, uncategorizable music as their lodestar.

Coltrane addressed this new generation that same summer, when the California Institute of the Arts conferred an honorary PhD on her, inviting her to address the graduating class at commencement. "Years from now, you will all be wonderful musicians, and I would be proud and happy to see you, my children, from heaven," she said to the Class of 2002.[8]

Surya Botofasina never had formal musical training with Swamini, but ever so gently, she continued to nurture him on his musical path, whether it was sitting next to him as he played a bhajan in the mandir or having him perform onstage at the John Coltrane Festival. In 2002, Botofasina enrolled at a local junior college and she asked him out to a recording session for *Sacred Offerings*, credited to the Sai Anantam Ashram Young Adults and dedicated to Sai Baba:

> I walked from my junior college to the studio because I had no money. And I didn't want to tell her that I didn't have a ride. I'm just like, "I'm one-on-one in the studio with Swamini, this is the greatest day of my life!" She starts playing, starts going through the knobs, the classic

portamento, everything. And I was just like, "Oh, this is incredible. I can't believe I'm watching this. This is like watching the sky get painted!"[9]

Her grandnephew Steve was also gently encouraged to keep pursuing his passion for music. "She came over to the house, when I was still living at my Grandma's house," Ellison said. "I was making a beat and she came over and played on the beat! It wasn't anything special the beat—not one to keep—but I do remember she did do something in my studio and then dipped out real quick."[10]

In July 2002, a developer named Ash Agrawal purchased the Dix Hills property for $500,000. The old house was still standing, but according to an assessment, "the unoccupied building would need to be demolished for new homes to be constructed."[11] A clinical way to describe the birthplace of John Coltrane's *A Love Supreme*, which with each passing year and decade increasingly became a musical beacon for seekers of all persuasions. Here lay the temple, the womb for its creation, left to the elements for decades. The house sat on the market nearly two years. Demo papers were filed in the event the property sold.

A week before Swamini's sixty-fifth birthday, her friend and onetime guru Swami Satchidananda passed away. In the papers, the cause was a thoracic aneurysm at age eighty-seven.[12] He had recently traveled back to his native South India to attend a peace conference. Swamiji had returned home.

Alice Coltrane made an impromptu New York performance at Joe's Pub in November, performing two movements from *A Love Supreme*, on the occasion of Ashley Kahn's book-length meditation on the album. The *Times* called her brief appearance on that intimate stage "spine-tingling and semiprivate," adding: "Sitting at the piano with her back straight and her long fingers splayed, she was a serene and regal presence; it suddenly seemed unfair that she had withheld herself so completely from public performance for a quarter-century."[13]

Ravi's heart warmed to see the reception his mother received after so long away from the public, "the lines of people standing outside [the] dressing room just waiting to say hello or thank you after that concert."[14] At long last, Alice's albums finally began to be reissued on compact disc,[15] including classics like *Universal Consciousness* and her Warner Brothers albums.

Unbeknownst to the well-wishers, Ravi was gently encouraging his mother back into the studio, the tentative makings of a new studio album underway. Her son wasn't as concerned with having her return to the music business so much as making a personal document, a family keepsake to preserve these precious dwindling years. "I always felt like there was a gap that was widening—any idea of us being two professional working musicians at the same time was just evaporating," he said. "I wanted some document that I'll always be able to share with my kids. I don't want to have a day of regret, saying, 'I never did this with my mom.'"[16]

In January 2004, an engineer living out on Long Island named Steve Fulgoni became fascinated by the Candlewood Path property that had been listed for sale the last two years. The property was a mess: the four-bedroom brick house had long been boarded up and infested with black mold, the ornate white wrought-iron gate lay rusting against a pillar at the driveway entrance, and shrubs ran wild over the retaining walls. Only the doghouse built in the back remained intact. But the history of that house was undeniable. Fulgoni was president of the year-old Half Hollow Historical Association and together with the Huntington Historic Preservation Commission, he recommended landmarking the Coltrane Home.[17] The Huntington Town Board decreed it a historical landmark that April.

On the other side of the country, Alice Coltrane found herself in Capitol Records' legendary Studio B. Her four-year-old grandson William ran around and spun in the studio's plush swivel chairs, his grandmother sat at the piano bench in the isolation booth, and his father Ravi was seated in the control room. The final touches were being put on *Translinear Light*, Alice's first studio album on a label in twenty-six years. She decided on the title as "a basic continuation of where you are in your own life...if you are going forward then you are often sitting [with a] higher knowledge and spiritual experience, you wish to reach new vistas of understanding."[18]

Across three separate April sessions in 2000, 2002, and 2004, *Translinear Light* was assembled with an array of different groups and settings. Ravi's stated intention was to touch upon "songs of praise that would extend from the church music she had played growing up, to Negro spirituals, to John Coltrane's music, and her spiritual music," he said. "It would *not* be retro Alice Coltrane, this sort of nostalgic seventies-sounding record."[19] The originally ideated trio of himself, his mother, and DeJohnette appear on polished versions of "Sita Ram" and a spirited if succinct version of "Leo."[20] Ravi's own working group—bassist James Genus and drummer Jeff "Tain" Watts—contributes to smooth readings of "Jagadishwar," "Blue Nile," and the old spiritual "Walk with Me." Bassist Charlie Haden augments the original trio for a version of "Crescent," the limpid ten-minute title track, and a rendering of the old gospel hymn, "This Train."[21] When Alice's Wurlitzer buzzes to life on the piece, she follows the vocal line closely, as if singing herself.

Two hushed duets are the emotional highlights of the album. Haden duets with Alice on "Triloka," a sterling exchange that recalls 1976's *Closeness* duet. Oran also accompanies his mother on "The Hymn," a brief duet that twines son's lush alto tone with mom's gleaming synthesizer. It's one of Alice's favorites, as she described it: "It's all meditative, moving into higher vistas of life, it just goes straight, ever upwards, not looking back and its all beauty and all light and peace."[22] Only on the closer "Satya Sai Isha" does the ecstatic Indian spiritual of Alice's music come to the fore, Swamini joined by the Sai Anantam Ashram Singers.

That summer, Swamini received instruction to undergo a period of isolation similar to the earlier tapas of her life. All ashram and most family interactions were greatly reduced over a two-month period:

> Every known disease seemed to pass through her body. Her body weight declined noticeably, and the level of suffering she endured was intense.

Upon her return to the ashram, however, only divine radiance and bliss emanated from her being. One person marveled at the pristine purity of Swamini's energy field. She radiated the aura of light and purity seen and felt in the presence of angelic, holy beings.[23]

She recovered enough to endure an album press cycle. The critical reaction was generally positive and even Alice was pleased with how it came out. "It was Ravi's persistence that got this done," she said, adding that her two sons "should be carrying on the musical legacy. I didn't plan this. I've actually surprised myself." She also contemplated a follow-up.[24] In an interview conducted with British jazz historian Stuart Nicholson, she offered perhaps her most detailed concept of her creativity:

We appreciate our world as it is to the best of our ability and it is a little of what I try to express in the music, with intensity and depth. It comes from the heart and the spirit, sometimes not even how your mind can rationalize. It comes from the heart and it comes from the spirit and that's the major character of creative music. It really doesn't come from the brain, it comes from within. Your creating—it comes from the heart, the spirit, the soul, you're not manufacturing somebody else's plan, somebody else's blueprint, somebody else's idea that's not yours. So when you're creating that's the beauty side of art, you know? It comes from within you.[25]

Radha recalled Swamini saying something similar to her as well. "'Radha, the music is in here.' And she would point to her heart," she said. "'Music is an expression.' That was it. That's it."[26]

In early 2005, Swamini returned to India with some of the Sai Anantam community, including Ellison. He fondly recalled how special Sunday was for him, even as a kid: "As soon as you arrive it's just so quiet. There's a little mandir that everyone would go into...all different races, and I really liked seeing that. As a kid, I was like, 'Oh wow, everyone's getting down.'"[27] As he grew up, his appreciation for his auntie's music deepened, both on record and on Sundays at the mandir. For him, he likened it to a Jedi master. "Imagine being around Yoda and then Yoda's in a light saber battle. That's what it felt like," he said. "This person's so small and frail, suddenly just playing very intensely and fierce. It would blow me away every time. It's like, 'Where did it come from?' You'd know *where* it comes from, but still."[28]

Traveling to India was a culture shock for him. "Out the gate, the smell is crazy," he said. "It's like the funk of ages! It was also just shocking in the sense of seeing how positive people were and how happy people were with very little. You could tell the people had a different disposition about it. It was a very humbling experience." His grandmother and auntie arrived a few days later and they traveled to Puttaparthi, where he filmed their travels: "It was really interesting to see the level of respect people had for her and that people would travel to come see her and speak with her. It was really awesome just seeing how my aunt went into that space humbly."[29]

He also recalled:

I remember being young and going: "Why do people make such a fuss about Auntie?" People would come over and kiss her feet. And I kept thinking, "But this is Auntie!!" I understand it now. I understand why people would treat her as they did. She was incredible.[30]

Hickson also made the trip. "Swamini's physical body was frail, but her will and inner strength were indomitable," he said. "I suspected that she was following an inner directive to be present when Baba gave his discourse and engaged in the miraculous lingam ceremony."[31]

Swamini described the trip "as a wonderful gift from the Lord... Each day seemed to be orchestrated by Baba, so that something auspicious took place at every juncture." The day she left: "When Baba passed by, he looked as he did in the 1970s; there was no flaw, blemish, scar, or wrinkle... All one could feel was infinite timelessness. Time stood still... We could see the waves, like an oceanic flow, moving and radiating out from Him to encompass one and all."[32]

That November, Swamini began to prepare for a brief U.S. tour in support of *Translinear Light*. She played a small show at House of Blues and Prince, the iconic '80s rock star, clad in all-white, came to pay his respects to her. A few weeks later, the Town of Huntington officially purchased the Coltrane Home and set about renovating the property. Fundraising monies began to pour in to help restore the home.

A four-date tour was booked for the new year and on February 16, Alice Coltrane performed at Royce Hall with her son, Ravi. A bootleg of the concert can be found online and finds her exploratory spirit wholly intact. Pieces like "Translinear Light," "Crescent," and a reading of "A Love Supreme" recall the luminous expansiveness of *Transfiguration*, mother and son both free to push the music as far as possible while keeping its inherent beauty intact.

Essence magazine's editor-in-chief Susan L. Taylor profiled Alice Coltrane that fall, and the two women discussed at length John Coltrane, the occluded history of women as mystics and spiritual leaders—from Hindi figures like Anasuya, Sita Devi, Sarasvati, and Mirabai to Joan of Arc and Mother Mary—and meditation. "You just need to set aside 15 minutes a day to be still," Coltrane said. "Just as it is fire's nature to burn, it is meditation's nature to heal, to bring peace and uplift you beyond your worldly environment and transport you to a higher plane." At article's end, "Sister Alice" is asked to address Black women directly: "Go within. God is working on the inside. Just go into the sanctuary of your heart, offer your prayers and your worship there."[33]

In September she played Ann Arbor and then New Jersey, with a quartet featuring Ravi, Charlie Haden, and Roy Haynes. One article gushed: "Her music of the '70s makes so much more sense today, in the post-avant-garde world, than it ever could in the moment of creation... Her music was always a singular experience—wild, chaotic and beautiful as the mind of God."[34]

In addition to the tour, Alice also began working out of Oran's home studio, conceptualizing an ambitious project titled *Sacred Language of Ascension*.[35] The title a nod to both her late husband's divisive work and the act of ascension itself, it was to be her most grandiose project to date, utilizing strings and choir. The project was conceived with Dr. James J. Hurtak, a double PhD holder with a master's in theology, a figure whose personal website described him "as a social scientist, futurist, remote sensing and space law specialist."[36] He provided text composed of lines in Sanskrit, Aramaic, Hebrew, and English.

Carlos Santana was a fan of Hurtak's writings and connected the two, while Ravi helped her use a computer notation program to arrange the orchestrations. "We sat up for hours on this stuff," he said. "It was a really nice feeling to see that in her because I remember so much of that growing up, seeing her work hour after hour on a musical project."[37] Oran recalled that "when she put her hands on the keyboard, it was like somebody shooting a beam of light through your chest."[38]

"The atmosphere of chanting the Holy Names, even in the studio, was so elevated that during one session, Swamini glanced up and recognized two, divine, astral beings present," Adams said. "They must have been attracted there by the moving and soulful melodies resounding throughout the airwaves."[39] In her estimation, *Sacred Language of Ascension* was Swamini's most profound creation.

The piece premiered at the New Jersey Performing Arts Center on October 22. After the first set—which featured versions of "Sita Ram," "Jagadishwar," and "Africa" performed with Ravi, Haden, and DeJohnette—Dr. Hurtak came out to introduce two movements of *Sacred Language of Ascension*, describing his musical partner as a woman who "expresses planetary humanity in its oneness... [making] music for the emergent spirituality of the 21st century."[40]

A twenty-piece orchestra, a seventeen-member choir, and a tabla player joined the jazz group in an audacious assemblage. Reviews ranged from calling it "aesthetically dicier territory"[41] to "the evening's weakest moment."[42] One lamented that the multimedia presentation of PowerPoint-style "presentation of images from around the world... included war refugees, hunger victims, Sept. 11 stills of the World Trade Center towers and spiritual leaders like Gandhi and MLK Jr.," which obfuscated the catalytic and cathartic qualities of her work: "By chasing the racing spiritual conviction of her music, we become aware of our ability to change who we are."[43]

Alice Coltrane finished the tour with a concert at the San Francisco Masonic Auditorium. During the performance of "Leo," a review noted that "she produced a relentless cacophony of sounds on the organ that ranged from wailing sirens to fingernails screeching down the blackboard."[44] As the concert ended, the crowd spontaneously began to chant "A Love Supreme."

The brief tour done, Ravi turned his attention to what might come next. "By that Masonic Hall gig I felt like, 'Yeah! Now it's time. She's ready; we're ready,'" he said. New shows were booked for 2007, "and I remember also saying to my mom, 'We should record this music.' We had talked about possibly going back and re-recording those pieces. We couldn't overdub string and horn arrangements onto the pieces she had already recorded, so we were in the process of discussing what to do."[45]

That second week in the new year, Alice was admitted to the hospital because of fluid buildup in her lungs. Marilyn was there at her bedside with Michelle. "I was in the bed with her and she would like drift off, like just close her eyes and then she'd wake up and then she'd close her eyes again," she said. "And then when she woke up this last time, she started kind of laughing, she said, 'Oh, I see Swami... he was at the train station.' She was smiling and kind of giggling and stuff. And at that time I just said: 'Oh yea, ok.'"[46]

Ravi checked in from New York. "When she was in the hospital, I asked, 'When and where are we gonna record these strings? Are we gonna do it in New York? Are we gonna do it in Los Angeles? We could do it in February...'" But by Friday, her condition had worsened. "Later, after I started thinking about it... there used to be a song about, 'get ready for the train,' or something like that," Marilyn said. "And when I thought about that I said maybe that's what she was talking about... I just think she was happy about the whole thing. She said, 'You know, I saw Baba. He was at the train station.' That's the last thing that I remember that she said to me."[47] Just after noon that Friday, the breath left Alice Coltrane's body for the last time. The attending physician reported "respiratory failure," while Adams called it "Mahasamadhi," the act of an enlightened being consciously departing their body.

A "Celebration of Ascension" took place a few days later. "We were at the same funeral home as we were with John Jr.," Ravi said, recalling his mother's poise when his brother had passed some twenty-five years before: "She left us unexpectedly, so it was almost the same feeling in the room. All the people that my mother had touched, so many of them were there. I found myself emulating her that day. I was comforting those in attendance, and I had a little smile on my face. I was distraught and devastated, but in that moment I found her strength."[48]

There were readings from the Bhagavad Gita and Psalm 23 and renditions of hymns like "Blessed Assurance" and "I Heard the Voice of Jesus Say." The hymn "Going Home" was performed by Ravi and Charlie Haden. "That's a family song," Ellison said. "When someone passes, 'Going Home' is the song we play at the funeral. When my mom died, we played it for her. When my Auntie Alice passed, we played that one. This is that journey through that astral life, the next place."[49] Alice Coltrane was going home.

Epilogue

Early one Sunday morning on the first day of June 2008, a spark came to life amid the asphalt shingles on a backlot at Universal Studios. Workers had used a blowtorch to repair a roof and while the shingles seemed to have cooled, by the time a security guard noticed something amiss, the entire rooftop was already ablaze on New England Street, the name of the set featuring colonial-styled buildings for film and TV. It jumped to a New York City backdrop, then to the courthouse used for the film *Back to the Future*.

The fires then leapt from New York City to the King Kong Encounter, the animatronic ride at the Universal Theme Park where trolleys roll past the giant ape destroying everything around him. Flames gobbled up that robotic ape and kept growing. And just before dawn, the fire spread to Building 6197, a featureless, corrugated metal, 22,320-square-foot warehouse tucked into one corner of the theme park. Workers knew it as the "video vault," holding physical tapes of long-running TV series like *Law & Order* and *The Office*. The flames began to feast on the celluloid and acrid green-black smoke plumed upward in the early dawn.

Despite its nondescript name, the warehouse housed one of the most vital repositories of American culture. Randy Aronson, who served as senior director of vault operations at Universal Music Group (the world's largest record company), was responsible for overseeing a 2,400-square-foot corner of the warehouse, which stored master recordings from the UMG catalog, including analog tape masters from over a half century of music recording. As Aronson arrived on the scene, he could feel the intense heat and see it melting the parking lights on the nearby fire trucks. "It was like watching molten lava move through the building, just a huge blob of fire that flowed and flowed," he later said. A spokesman for UMG said the label suffered no loss, but Aronson knew better: "It was like those end-of-the-world-type movies. I felt like my planet had been destroyed."

Even the most conservative estimates put the damage at over 175,000 recordings lost in the fire, the catalogs of American music masters instantly rendered to ash: Chuck Berry, Billie Holiday, Buddy Holly, Louis Armstrong, Duke Ellington. Nearly eleven years after the fire, with UMG still not forthcoming just what was in the ashes, writer Jody Rosen brought to light some of the true damage of the fire: "Most of John Coltrane's Impulse masters were lost, as were masters for treasured Impulse releases by Ellington, Count Basie, Coleman Hawkins, Dizzy Gillespie, Max Roach, Art Blakey, Sonny Rollins, Charles Mingus, Ornette Coleman, Alice Coltrane, Sun Ra, Albert Ayler, Pharoah Sanders and other jazz greats."[1]

As a last resort, firefighters bulldozed the building so as to collapse the metal warehouse. The shelves and tape reels were a final offering that at last extinguished the fire. Barely a year after her passing, Alice's music—and all the preservation efforts she had made in her lifetime to keep her late husband's legacy alive—turned to ash.

"Metaphysically—fire symbolizes transformation," Purusha Hickson said. "Physical fire has a dual nature: it can destroy and it can also purify."[2] And yet, even as the master tapes of her and John's music literally turned to ash, Alice Coltrane's music began to radiate outward. Singer-songwriters, metal bands, R&B acts, electronic music producers, DJs, jazz newcomers, young bands, and experimental artists all began to namecheck her.

Steve Ellison rued the missed opportunity to record with his auntie. "Before she passed, I asked her to play harp on my first album," he said. "And she went, 'Okay, if you get my harp fixed, I'll do it.' But the only harp repair was on Long Beach, so it never happened." Instead, Flying

Lotus sampled "Blue Nile" for a piece titled "Drips//Auntie's Harp" on his acclaimed 2010 album, *Cosmogramma*.[3]

In March 2011, Sathya Sai Baba was admitted to the hospital he had helped build in Puttaparthi, Sri Sathya Sai Super Speciality Hospital. Initially, his condition stabilized, but in April, he suffered multiple organ failures and passed away on April 24 at age eighty-four. That same month, the nonprofit music public broadcasting internet radio station Dublab[4] in Los Angeles posted a special show[5] dedicated to music culled from the ashram tapes. Slowly, online music blogs began to post MP3 files made of Alice's ashram tapes, introducing a new generation of listeners to music that had previously only been available if one were to visit the Sai Anantam Ashram grounds.

When 2012's Super Storm Sandy made landfall on Long Island, the Coltrane Home suffered roof and exterior damage and significant flooding. In the weeks after, the home's interior bloomed with black mold, requiring the insides to be gutted once again. As the water and moisture and mold receded, the restoration work began anew. As of this date, the house is still undergoing renovation work and hopes to one day serve as both a museum and performance space.

Retired police detective John Laurie was watching the evening news one night in March 2015 when a story about a man extradited from Idaho on suspicion of killing a young boy in the early 1980s caught his attention. When they posted the mug shot of Kenneth Rasmuson, a chill went through Laurie. "That was his suspect," he thought to himself.

Despite having retired from the sheriff's department twelve years earlier, he immediately placed a phone call to the cold case unit, asking them to dig out the evidence files from the unsolved murder of Miguel Antero. "Take it to the lab and just run it through," he said. "I'm convinced this is our suspect."[6] Over twenty-eight years later, the man responsible for abducting and murdering Antero en route to the ashram was finally arrested and sentenced to life without parole.

In the spring of 2017, David Byrne's Luaka Bop released *World Spirituality Classics 1: The Ecstatic Music of Alice Coltrane Turiyasangitananda*, a compilation of music culled from Alice's ashram tapes.[7] The reviews were, well, "ecstatic," and a new generation of music listeners, unbeholden to the history of jazz and the confines of genre, tuned in. The compilation sold upward of thirty thousand copies and as a result, the Sai Anantam Singers, featuring a group of ashram members with Surya Botofasina serving as musical director, performed around the country and throughout Europe as well. Performances in New York City and in downtown Los Angeles were sold-out affairs and were well received.

Even as these concerts were taking place, the land from which these bhajans originated was on the market. The Coltrane family put the Agoura Hills property up for sale and the remaining members of the ashram still living and tending to the grounds began to make their way off "The Land." In December 2017, the property was sold. Almost a year later, the Woolsey fires would burn every extant structure on the property to the ground.

In a November 17, 2018, post to Facebook, Sita Michelle Coltrane wrote: "My mother told me that there are no coincidences in life, only incidents. We can make our own plans, but God has a spiritual path and a divine order that will be followed. For over 30 years, the ashram was a haven and a home for community members and devotees of my mother's spiritual practice. Those memories live in my heart and the hearts of many, eternally." Miraculously, while the mandir itself burned, its white stone staircase remained wholly intact. (For his 2024 solo album, Surya Botofasina is pictured seated on the steps.)

Alice Coltrane's music and message continued to spread. One night spent at New York's annual Winter Jazz Fest in 2025 made that evident. Every January, hundreds of jazz artists—legends and newcomers alike—converge on the boroughs of Manhattan and Brooklyn for a week's worth of concerts, each venue bill a mini-festival in and of itself. In the span of three sets at three different venues, I could witness the influence of Alice.

Harpist Brandee Younger and her trio played in the East Village and in the past, Younger has served as harpist for several Coltrane memorial concerts. There was even an Alice cover performed on her own harp, that Lyon & Healy harp finally restored. At the legendary Bitter End, a French-Guadaloupean up-and-comer named Sophye Soliveau rendered twenty-first-century gwo ka–soul with a strong voice and formidable harp chops, reimagining its strings in a setting more amenable to a Roberta Flack or Alicia Keys. One block over at Le Poisson Rouge, the New York–born, Tamil Nadu–raised vocalist Ganavya mesmerized a crowd with little more than a bowed bass and harp, her astonishing voice front and center. The intention of her every breath and gesture shoots directly to the heart, an unadorned openness that makes the word *performance* feel inadequate. Neither one of these performances was an overt homage to Alice Coltrane, but her spirit was present nevertheless in all of them.

The next month, I stood in a long queue stretching multiple city blocks along Wilshire Boulevard in Los Angeles. It was the opening night of *Alice Coltrane, Monument Eternal,* an exhibition at the Hammer Museum. On streetlamps throughout the city, drivers could look up and see banners featuring that thousand-yard stare of Alice from the cover of *Journey in Satchidananda*. Gazing out over the landscape—in the world yet also poised high above it—she regarded a distant horizon we still cannot imagine.

Once inside, the throng of museumgoers included extended Coltrane family members, ashram elders, celebrities, cognoscenti, and young fashionistas alike, the museum filled to capacity to celebrate Alice. Flying Lotus delivered a highly anticipated DJ set for the opening night festivities. Old family photo albums, contact sheets from session dates, archival material from the ashram, televisions broadcasting episodes of *Eternity's Pillar*, all that and more were on display, alongside new artworks from visual artists inspired by Alice Coltrane's example. Tucked along one wall were astonishing portraits of Krishna and Rama as rendered by Coltrane herself in gold leaf, peacock feathers, and ink. I bumped into Ellison at one point in the crowd. It had been ten years since we last spoke and we both shook our heads in amazement at what had transpired since that time, to where an image of his auntie now fluttered with the wind on every streetlamp in the city.

※

Just how that sea change occurred remains unanswered in some regards. There has been an uptick in an appreciation of jazz, but Alice's music still doesn't slot easily into that descriptor. There doesn't appear to be a greater appreciation of Hindu chanting either. Reading a profile on an internet rap artist, a snatch of dialogue sticks out. It's about the distinct sensation of our present moment, what the writer calls "post-reality," where everything seems to be in flux, to where reality itself feels unreal. It could speak to our post-COVID society, to the moment where misinformation floods in from every corner of the internet. One

Epilogue

doesn't have to look around in 2025 to see that the world doesn't appear to have become any more peaceful, more spiritually attuned. If anything, the threat of racism, ignorance, violence, cruelty, and injustice feels as ever present as before. Can this world, this reality, ever really change? What is real? And what is illusion?

While in California, I visited with Radha and her family at their home in Canoga Park. Photographs of Swamini and Sai Baba adorn nearly every wall. She pulled out a family album of her wedding day, presided over by Swamini herself at the ashram. The colors remain so vivid. Radha's husband enthusiastically spoke about a form of meditation he was trying out, imagining the divine spark of God inside our heart. As he breathes in, he imagines this light growing stronger, brighter, larger, until it pops like a flashbulb. The speed of light itself is an illusion, he said, because God is already everywhere.

The day after the exhibit opening, I meet with Baker Bigsby at his hotel. He's wearing his "Alice at the Hammer" tee shirt with a Grammys jean jacket on top. He has a shoebox of cassette tapes for me, including copies of the four ashram tapes. I'm stunned at the gift. He reminisces about that time in his life. When I ask if he misses Swamini, he responds: "She's with me, always." I can see his eyes brim with tears and feel them well up in my own eyes. He then adds: "She's with me still. As far as her method of worship, I didn't prescribe to that. But I believed in the lady, she had my back and was my friend."

The next day, I drive out to see Purusha Hickson in Thousand Oaks. I smile when I see the street sign leading up to his apartment that reads *McCloud*, a small reminder of Swamini's presence. When he realizes that the sun will be setting soon, he urges me to drive out to "The Land" before it gets too dark.

The sun is already behind the mountains when I reach Agoura Hills. There's no other sound of traffic. The white stone entrance to the ashram has begun to crumble but is still intact. With only my phone flashlight, I walk to the back entrance of the property and slowly make my way down to the original ashram grounds. In the darkness, I can just make out the steps and stone foundation that had once been a cottage and home for one of the ashram families.

An owl hoots in the darkness. The gentle trickle of the creek is louder now because of the recent rains. I'm acutely aware of the air all around me, alive and present. The wet grasses gleam and sparkle as the light passes over them. I find a small stone that seems to glow in the night and keep it with me, a small token of this sanctuary and the benevolent being that was once in our midst. As all the features of the landscape slide into the oblivion of darkness, I'm struck by the sense that the cosmic music and divine spirit of Alice Coltrane feels more real than ever. With every tactile trace of her life, her music, her ashram all returned to dust, that spark is now free to rove the Earth.

Acknowledgments

This book would be impossible without the love of my family and the families that surround us: the Fitt family, the Trimmier family, the Wiatrek family, the Harris family, the Augusta-Huynh family, the Klein family, the Stevens family, the Enuha-Collins family, the Lightfoot family, the Swift family, the Riehl-Hartsough family, the Muttreja family, the Hatch-Miller family, the Harriott family. Thank you to the HCES community.

My deepest gratitude and appreciation to Radha Botofasina, Surya Botofasina, and the Botofasina family. Your insight, stories, and generosity over the past decade made this endeavor come to life. My sincere thanks and gratitude to Purusha Hickson and Baker Bigsby. Special thanks to Carlos Niño, who early in the process suggested that the book should focus on the people who personally knew Swamini Turiyasangitananda in this lifetime.

A special thank you to Steve Ellison for always talking with me about his "Auntie" and sparking the idea that there was a profound message in this music, if only one were attuned to it.

Many thanks to Swami Premananda at Integral Yoga Institute for all her help and insight.

Sincere thanks to Vishnu Wood, Tulsi Reynolds, Bennie Maupin, Jack DeJohnette, Archie Shepp, George Bohanon, Kirk Lightsey, and Terry Gibbs. Thanks to Ed Michel, Rudy Tucich, Mark Stryker, Sam Stephenson, Herb Boyd, Angela Dews, Kay Crow, John Hardham of the Heavy Water Light Show, and Val Wilmer. Thank you, Terry Riley. Thanks to Yale, Eric, Eliza, and the Luaka Bop team. Thanks to Mark "Frosty" McNeil, Ale Cohen, and the extended Dublab family. Thanks to the Lot Radio family.

Acknowledgments

Thank you, Ben Schafer at Da Capo, Lee Brackstone at Orion Books, and my agent Paul Bresnick. Special thanks to Mark Andrews and Charles Van Winckle at Thornton Tomasetti and to Robert Hughes and Steve Fulgoni.

Thanks to a long line of editors over the years, including (but not limited to): Mark Richardson, Brandon Stosuy, Jeremy Larson, Jayson Greene, Jeff Salamon, Hazel Cills, J. C. Gabel, Randall Roberts, Melissa Maerz, Paula Mejia, Chuck Eddy, Charles Aaron, and many others. A special thanks to Jessica Hopper, the first editor who recognized the profundity of the Alice Coltrane story back in 2015 and helped bring a story to fruition.

Thank you, Vincent Pelote and Elizabeth Surles at Institute of Jazz Studies at Rutgers University-Newark, Amy Basen and Susan Lowenberg at California Institute of the Arts, and Auburn Nelson at Schomburg Center for Research in Black Culture.

Thanks to Phil Sherburne, Nick Sylvester, Pete Swanson, Evan Woodward, Will Hermes, Ben Ratliff, Matthew McDermott and Jessica Pratt, Shahzad Ishmaily, Nadia Sirota, Alina Bzhezhinska, Brian Piñeyro, CZ Wang, Heather Leigh, Matt Merewitz, Justin Carter, Jesse Jarnow, Tyler Wilcox, Brian Shimkovitz, Andy Zax, Nate Chinen, Ashley Kahn, Adam Shatz, Joshua Abrams and Lisa Alvarado, Oren Ambarchi and crys cole. Thank you, Sita Michelle and Narayana Ravi Coltrane.

In memory of Brother Ah, John Sinclair, Philip Melnick, Kiane Zawadi, George Bohanon, Satya Kirkland, Billy Jones, Keith McIvor, Jack DeJohnette, Marshall Gause.

Notes

Chapter One: Hellfire in Paradise Valley

1. Below that headline read the other important news of the day for Detroit's Black population: "Truman Asked to Save Mrs. Ingram from Prison Term." A widowed sharecropper and mother of twelve from rural Georgia who was imprisoned after killing her white neighbor in self-defense, Mrs. Ingram—along with her teenage sons—were found guilty in a one-day trial on January 26, 1948. They were convicted by an all-white jury and sentenced to death. A postcard writing campaign on her behalf to the president of the United States had gone on for well over a year by that time, and it perhaps helped commute the sentence of that early icon of the civil rights movement.

2. "Trowbridge Student to Compete for City Spelling Championship," *Detroit Tribune*, April 16, 1949.

3. Shankari C. Adams, *Portrait of Devotion: The Spiritual Life of Alice Coltrane Swamini Turiyasangitananda* (self-published, 2016), 6.

4. Detroit Historical Society, "Paradise Valley," accessed July 11, 2025, https://detroithistorical.org/learn/encyclopedia-of-detroit/paradise-valley.

5. Gordy would later purchase the street signs from that intersection, to always remind him of where he came from. Berry Gordy, *To Be Loved: The Music, The Magic, The Memories of Motown: An Autobiography* (Grand Central, 1994), 70.

6. Gordy, *To Be Loved*, 71–72.

7. Gordy, *To Be Loved*, 71–72.

8. Gordy, *To Be Loved*, 71–72.

9. Adams, *Portrait of Devotion*, 8–10.

10. "Director Entertained," *Michigan Chronicle*, May 22, 1943.

11. Adams, *Portrait of Devotion*, 7.

12. Adams, *Portrait of Devotion*, 8–10.

13. Adams, *Portrait of Devotion*, 8–10.

14. Adams, *Portrait of Devotion*, 8–10.

15. Gordy, *To Be Loved*, 63.

16. Gordy, *To Be Loved*, 44.

17. Herb Boyd, *Black Detroit: A People's History of Self-Determination* (Amistad, 2017), 140.

18. Franya J. Berkman, *Monument Eternal* (Wesleyan University Press, 2010), 20–24.

19. Berkman, *Monument Eternal*, 20–24.

20. Boyd, *Black Detroit*, 150–151.

21. Boyd, *Black Detroit*, 135.

22. Boyd, *Black Detroit*, 152.

Chapter Two: Motor City Music

1. Franya J. Berkman, *Monument Eternal* (Wesleyan University Press, 2010), 20–24.
2. Berkman, *Monument Eternal*, 20–24.
3. Shankari C. Adams, *Portrait of Devotion: The Spiritual Life of Alice Coltrane Swamini Turiyasangitananda* (self-published, 2016), 12.
4. Adams, *Portrait of Devotion*, 12.
5. Berkman, *Monument Eternal*, 20–24.
6. Berkman, *Monument Eternal*, 20–24.
7. Herb Boyd, *Black Detroit: A People's History of Self-Determination* (Amistad, 2017), 3.
8. Berry Gordy, *To Be Loved: The Music, The Magic, The Memories of Motown: An Autobiography* (Grand Central, 1994), 71–72.
9. "War Worker Dies When Struck By An Automobile," *Michigan Chronicle* (August 11, 1945), 9, ProQuest Historical Newspapers, https://www.proquest.com/hnpmichiganchronicle/docview/2473838523/52B899943D884455PQ/.
10. Miles Davis and Quincy Troupe, *Miles: The Autobiography* (Simon and Schuster, 1990), 119.
11. Albert Murray, *Stomping the Blues* (Da Capo Press, 1989), 164–165.
12. Chicago postbop pianist Andrew Hill told writer Ben Ratliff he understood Parker's music as a refutation of the "Eurocentric" music education he had grown up with—where melody is paramount, harmony accompanies it, and rhythm is the last part to worry about.
13. Davis and Troupe, *Miles*, 67.
14. Mark Stryker, interview with author, February 2024.
15. Berkman, *Monument Eternal*, 25–32.
16. Lars Bjorn with Jim Gallert, *Before Motown: A History of Jazz in Detroit 1920–1960* (University of Michigan Press, 2001), 153.
17. Bjorn, *Before Motown*, 153.
18. Kirk Lightsey, interview with author, May 2024.
19. Kirk Lightsey, interview with author, May 2024.
20. Claire Lobenfeld, "Flying Lotus and His Grandmother Talk Being in a Family Bound by Music," Pitchfork, May 23, 2019, https://pitchfork.com/features/family-matters/flying-lotus-and-his-grandmother-talk-being-in-a-family-bound-by-music/.
21. Adams, *Portrait of Devotion*, 12.
22. Adams, *Portrait of Devotion*, 11.
23. McDougall, Clea, "Alice in Wonder & Awe," *Ascent*, Spring 2006, https://ascentmagazine.com/articles.aspx%3FarticleID=185&page=read&subpage=past&issueID=29.html
24. Adams, *Portrait of Devotion*, 13.
25. McDougall, "Alice in Wonder & Awe."

Chapter Three: Only God Can Make a Tree

1. Aretha Franklin and David Ritz, *Aretha: From These Roots* (Villard, 1999), 34.
2. Mike Hennessey, *Klook: The Story of Kenny Clarke* (Quartet Books, 1990), 69.

3. "Origins of 'Redevelopment,'" Wayne State University, accessed July 11, 2025, https://projects.lib.wayne.edu/12thstreetdetroit/exhibits/show/beforeunrest/panel4.

4. Herb Boyd, *Black Detroit: A People's History of Self-Determination* (Amistad, 2017), 161.

5. Franya J. Berkman, *Monument Eternal* (Wesleyan University Press, 2010), 25–32.

6. Berkman, *Monument Eternal*, 20–24.

7. Franya Berkman, "Divine Songs" (PhD diss., Wesleyan University, 2003), 52.

8. Miles Davis and Quincy Troupe, *Miles: The Autobiography* (Simon and Schuster, 1990), 173.

9. Kirk Lightsey, interview with author, May 2024.

10. Berkman, *Monument Eternal*, 20–24.

11. Boyd, *Black Detroit*, 166.

12. Boyd, *Black Detroit*, 166.

13. Ben Ratliff, *The Jazz Ear: Conversations over Music* (Henry Holt, 2008), 117.

14. Berkman, *Monument Eternal*, 52.

15. Berkman, *Monument Eternal*, 25–32.

16. Berkman, *Monument Eternal*, 25–32.

17. Berkman, "Divine Songs," 47.

18. Berkman, "Divine Songs," 47.

19. Berkman, "Divine Songs," 47.

20. David Lerner, "Alice Coltrane: Jazz Pianist, Inspirational Organist," *Keyboard Magazine*, November 1982.

Chapter Four: Graduation

1. Berry Gordy, *To Be Loved: The Music, The Magic, The Memories of Motown: An Autobiography* (Grand Central, 1994), 139–140.

2. Gordy, *To Be Loved*, 139–140.

3. If this quote might bring to mind that famous scene from *Mad Men*, when one of the men at the ad agency suddenly "realizes" that one of the female secretaries might have the mental capacity to write copy for them, patronizing her with the simile that it was "like watching a dog play the piano," in context it was perhaps the biggest compliment a guy could give a gal in the early 1950s. Terry Gibbs with Cary Ginell, *Good Vibes: A Life in Jazz* (Scarecrow Press, 2003), 155–156.

4. Lars Bjorn with Jim Gallert, *Before Motown: A History of Jazz in Detroit 1920–1960* (University of Michigan Press, 2001), 128.

5. Gibbs, *Good Vibes*, 168.

6. Gibbs, *Good Vibes*, 157.

7. Shankari C. Adams, *Portrait of Devotion: The Spiritual Life of Alice Coltrane Swamini Turiyasangitananda* (self-published, 2016), 14.

8. Bennie Maupin, interview with author, January 2024.

9. Franya J. Berkman, *Monument Eternal* (Wesleyan University Press, 2010), 25–32.

10. Berkman, *Monument Eternal*, 25–32.

11. Bennie Maupin, interview with author, January 2024.

12. Berkman, *Monument Eternal*, 32.

13. Mark Stryker, interview with author, February 2024.

14. Franya Berkman, "Divine Songs" (PhD diss., Wesleyan University, 2003), 52.

15. Kirk Lightsey, interview with author, May 2024.

16. Rudy Tucich, interview with author, March 2024.

17. You can hear what a night at the World Stage sounded like on *Byrd Jazz*, an album produced by future Bob Dylan and Velvet Underground producer Tom Wilson and released on his Transition label. Recorded on August 23, 1955, it captured a sextet featuring Harris on piano, Frank Gant on drums, Alvin Jackson (Milt's younger brother) on bass, Bernard McKinney (of the large McKinney clan) on the all-too-rare euphonium, and the full-length debuts of two of Detroit's greatest jazz artists: saxophonist Yusef Lateef and trumpeter Donald Byrd. The band presents an expansive fourteen-minute read of Bud Powell's "Parisian Thoroughfare," two Dizzy tunes, an upbeat take on the standard "Dancing in the Dark," and two originals from Harris, including a smoldering slow blues named for Yusef.

18. Bjorn, *Before Motown*, 118.

19. Berkman, "Divine Songs," 52.

20. Bjorn, *Before Motown*, 159.

21. In less than two years, the faux ethnographic sounds of "exotica"—as made famous by Martin Denny and Arthur Lyman—were topping the charts and brightening the moods of drunks in bars around the United States. Few artists challenged that mindset and fused Eastern modalities in a meaningful manner quite like Lateef did at the same time. His pioneering exploration inspired the likes of another saxophonist, John Coltrane, to study just how to integrate Indian and African musical systems into jazz. It's also been suggested that Lateef turned Coltrane onto the Quran and hipped him to the concept of checking out other religions beyond Christianity.

22. Dolores Brandon, "The Evolution of Alice Coltrane," WBAI, New York, 1988.

23. It wasn't uncommon at the time to have the Dvořák piece played along with "Old Folks at Home" in recitals. Whether she interloped the classical composition or not, it wouldn't mark the last time Alice took direct inspiration from the composer.

24. A few years after Alice's recital, British guitarist Tony Sheridan would record a version of the song with a pickup band he had encountered in Hamburg who called themselves the Beatles.

25. Edwin Pouncey, "Alice Coltrane: Enduring Love," *The Wire*, April 2002.

26. Tucich exclaimed with a laugh: "Eighty years later, I can still remember 'Anthropology.' We'd play some Charlie Parker, Bud Powell, Clifford Brown tunes, a Duke Jordan tune like 'Jordu.' We were just stone beboppers." There were also ballads like "Just Friends" and "I'll Remember April," also part of the canon thanks to the popular versions by Bird, Brown, Chet Baker, and the like.

27. Rudy Tucich, interview with author, March 2024.

Chapter Five: Three Guys and a Doll

1. Shankari C. Adams, *Portrait of Devotion: The Spiritual Life of Alice Coltrane Swamini Turiyasangitananda* (self-published, 2016), 15.

2. Juilliard comes up in more than one biographical background of Alice, with some suggesting she had been accepted there. A search request at Juilliard's Office of the

Registrar between 1954 and 1962 yielded no such results, though their paper recordkeeping wouldn't have archived declined or withdrawn applications.

3. Franya J. Berkman, *Monument Eternal* (Wesleyan University Press, 2010), 37.

4. Adams, *Portrait of Devotion*, 15.

5. Franya Berkman, "Divine Songs" (PhD diss., Wesleyan University, 2003), 52.

6. Vishnu Wood, interview with author, January 2024.

7. Kirk Lightsey, interview with author, May 2024.

8. Bennie Maupin, interview with author, January 2024.

9. Alyn Shipton, *Handful of Keys: Conversations with Thirty Jazz Pianists* (Routledge, 2004), 28–32.

10. Adams, *Portrait of Devotion*, 15.

11. "Alice Coltrane Interview," Stuart Nicholson, November 3, 2004, https://stuartnicholson.uk/wp-content/uploads/2017/03/Clike-Here-To-Go-To-Alice-Coltrane-Interview.pdf.

12. Terry Gibbs, "Terry Gibbs Quartet with Terry Pollard," *The Tonight Show*, October 12, 1956, YouTube, https://www.youtube.com/watch?v=T8z6fwq4ZSE.

13. Weirdest of all was an LP titled *Leonard Feather Presents Cats vs. Chicks: A Jazz Battle of the Sexes*, with Pollard helming an all-female septet.

14. Mike Wahls, "Terry Pollard Trio," *Michigan Chronicle*, October 6, 1962.

15. George Bohanon, interview with author, May 2024.

16. Keith Sterling, "Tribute Paid to Joseph T. Carter of the Premiers," *Michigan Chronicle*, April 16, 1997.

17. Vishnu Wood, interview with author, January 2024.

18. Dolores Brandon, "The Evolution of Alice Coltrane," WBAI, New York, 1988.

19. Lars Bjorn with Jim Gallert, *Before Motown: A History of Jazz in Detroit 1920–1960* (University of Michigan Press, 2001), 145.

20. Sterling, "Tribute Paid to Joseph T. Carter of the Premiers."

21. George Bohanon, interview with author, May 2024.

22. Bjorn, *Before Motown*, 105.

23. Miles Davis and Quincy Troupe, *Miles: The Autobiography* (Simon and Schuster, 1990), 225.

24. Donald Stone, "The Detroit Scene," *Down Beat* 4, no. 1 (1959): 28.

25. Bennie Maupin, interview with author, January 2024.

26. George Bohanon, interview with author, May 2024.

Chapter Six: April in Paris

1. Aretha Franklin and David Ritz, *Aretha: From These Roots* (Villard, 1999), 99.

2. Kirk Lightsey, interview with author, May 2024.

3. "Alice Coltrane Interview," *LA Record*, September 2006.

4. W. Kim Heron, "Jazz," *Detroit Free Press*, July 4, 1980.

5. Adam Shatz, "Le Jazz Hot," *New York Review of Books*, July 9, 2015.

6. Rudy Tucich, interview with author, March 2024.

7. Ashley Kahn, "The Gift: Alice Coltrane and the Harp," *We Jazz*, no. 1 (Summer 2021).

8. "Lucky Thompson," *Coda*, June 1969.
9. Quincy Jones, *Q: The Autobiography of Quincy Jones* (Doubleday, 2001), 129.
10. Jones, *Q*, 136.
11. *Down Beat*, September 22, 1966.
12. Mike Hennessey, *Klook: The Story of Kenny Clarke* (Quartet Books, 1990), 133–138.
13. Hennessey, *Klook*, 137.
14. Francis Paudras, *Dance of the Infidels: A Portrait of Bud Powell* (Da Capo Press, 1986), 65.
15. Edwin Pouncey, "Alice Coltrane: Enduring Love," *The Wire*, April 2002.
16. Mark Stryker, interview with author, February 2024.
17. Paudras, *Dance of the Infidels*, 52.
18. Alice Coltrane Turiyasangitananda, "Alice Coltrane - 'Woody 'n' You' (January 9, 1960)," 3 min., 20 sec., Facebook, July 18, 2019, https://www.facebook.com/AliceColtraneOfficial/videos/alice-coltrane-woody-n-you-january-9-1960/467202594091803/.
19. Miles Davis and Quincy Troupe, *Miles: The Autobiography* (Simon and Schuster, 1990), 246.
20. On *The Final Tour: The Bootleg Series, Vol. 6*, a recording of that Paris concert, Coltrane works over tunes like "On Green Dolphin Street" and "All of You" like he's trying to explode the songs from within. Even on the open spaces of "So What," Coltrane sounds a little confined in the changes, like he's straining to break free not just from the song, but the Earth's gravitational pull. Nearing the nine-minute mark, his overblowing and dissonance elicits a few hoots and whistles from the European audience. Davis would grow exasperated at his sideman and his long, winding, sometimes long-winded peregrinations on the bandstand.
21. "Audio by Alice Coltrane in Jazz Archive," WKCR, New York, September 23, 1971, https://www.cc-seas.columbia.edu/wkcr/archives/Jazz%20Archive/artist/Alice%20Coltrane.
22. Franya J. Berkman, *Monument Eternal* (Wesleyan University Press, 2010), 36.
23. Paudras, *Dance of the Infidels*, 81.
24. Lewis Porter, *John Coltrane: His Life and Music* (University of Michigan Press, 1999), 182–183.
25. Nick Marino, "Family of Jazz Legend Keeps His Flame Alive," *Atlanta Constitution*, November 14, 2004.
26. Shankari C. Adams, *Portrait of Devotion: The Spiritual Life of Alice Coltrane Swamini Turiyasangitananda* (self-published, 2016), 17–19.
27. Lars Bjorn with Jim Gallert, *Before Motown: A History of Jazz in Detroit 1920–1960* (University of Michigan Press, 2001), 157.

Chapter Seven: Soulsphere

1. Bennie Maupin, interview with author, January 2024.
2. Bennie Maupin, interview with author, January 2024.
3. *Kind of Blue* was already widely hailed as a breakthrough in modern jazz. Charles Mingus was pushing composition into heady new realms with *Mingus Ah Um*, which looked back to his forebears like Duke Ellington and the late Lester Young while also

conveying political commentary. Jimmy Giuffre's *The Four Brothers Sound* used the multitrack capabilities of the recording studio to startling effect. Another Texas-born reedsman, alto saxophonist Ornette Coleman, released *The Shape of Jazz to Come* at the end of 1959. Its slippery tenets about how to activate a full group improvisation without following a predetermined chord structure or rhythm—when they weren't being dismissed outright by the likes of Miles Davis and the old guard—were still worming their way into the minds of the jazz world. Even big hits, like Dave Brubeck's *Time Out*, featured tricky time signatures that weren't your standard easy-listening fare.

4. Franya J. Berkman, *Monument Eternal* (Wesleyan University Press, 2010), 38.

5. Ashley Kahn, *The House That Trane Built: The Story of Impulse Records* (Granta Books, 2006), 52.

6. Robert Northern, interview with author, 2017.

7. *Down Beat* 30, no. 15 (July 4, 1963).

8. Kahn, *The House That Trane Built*, 53.

9. Ben Ratliff, *Coltrane: The Story of a Sound* (Faber and Faber, 2007), 145.

10. Berkman, *Monument Eternal*, 39.

11. Bennie Maupin, interview with author, January 2024.

12. Robert Palmer, "The World According to John Coltrane (Full VHS 1991) DELUXE EDITION," 1991, https://www.youtube.com/watch?v=f2B2SfClFtg.

13. Berkman, *Monument Eternal*, 38.

14. Cory Weeds, "Expanding the Concept: Cecil McBee on Playing with Roy Brooks," liner notes for Roy Brooks, *Understanding*, Reel to Real, 2021, LP, 3.

15. Lauren Du Graf, "The Artist in Ascension," liner notes for Alice Coltrane, *The Carnegie Hall Concert*, Impulse, 2024, LP, 6.

16. Lewis Porter, *John Coltrane: His Life and Music* (University of Michigan Press, 1999), 271–272.

17. Kirk Lightsey, interview with author, May 30, 2024.

18. Berkman, *Monument Eternal*, 39.

19. But then again, thousands of Motown sessions over the course of his storied fifty-year career can make it all blur together.

20. George Bohanon, interview with author, May 2024.

21. Bennie Maupin, interview with author, January 2024.

22. "A Professor by Day, a Jazzman by Night," NPR, December 12, 2009, https://www.npr.org/2009/12/12/121362184/a-professor-by-day-a-jazzman-by-night.

23. Sam Stephenson, *The Jazz Loft Project* (Knopf, 2009), 3.

24. Sam Stephenson, *The Jazz Loft Project* (Knopf, 2009), 17.

25. Thelonious Monk was a frequent visitor to Overton's, and they rehearsed for months leading up to Monk's legendary big band concert at Town Hall in 1959. Monk would return again in advance of other legend-cementing performances at Lincoln Center in 1963 and Carnegie Hall in 1964. Listen to some of these tapes and you're suddenly in the room with Overton and Monk, eavesdropping as they toil over the minutiae for what would be one of the most triumphant jazz concerts of the twentieth century.

26. Stephenson, *The Jazz Loft Project*, 157.

27. Stephenson, *The Jazz Loft Project*, 185.

28. Jon Thurber, "Alice Coltrane, 69; Performer, Composer of Jazz and New Age Music; Spiritual Leader," *Los Angeles Times*, January 14, 2007.

29. If the tapes are correct, though, it also conflicts with the known dates of Joe Henderson's arrival on the New York scene. In the liner notes for his Blue Note debut, *Page One*, trumpeter Kenny Dorham wrote that Joe rolled into late summer 1962 in a sleek black Mercedes-Benz, headed directly to Birdland to see Dexter Gordon and—after fifteen to twenty choruses after being invited up on stage to blow—left Gordon looking "gassed." Did she really move into the loft that year? Was it just an extended stay? Or was it an astral projection?

30. Paul Adams, "Theatre Notes," *Michigan Chronicle*, October 21, 1961.

31. "John Coltrane at Minor Key, Detroit," Setlist.fm, accessed February 26, 2025, https://www.setlist.fm/setlists/john-coltrane-bd6b596.html?page=60.

32. Berkman, *Monument Eternal*, 39.

Chapter Eight: Always

1. Terry Gibbs, interview with author, May 2024.

2. Terry Gibbs, interview with author, May 2024.

3. Terry Gibbs, interview with author, May 2024.

4. The Metropole's bandstand was a long runway that ran behind the bar, which became handy when the club gave up on live jazz around 1965 to instead feature strippers. You can glimpse the inside of the club in the opening moments of the 1968 film *The Odd Couple*. After Felix Unger's failed suicide attempt, he stops in at the bar.

5. Terry Gibbs, interview with author, May 2024.

6. Vishnu Wood, interview with author, January 2024.

7. "Alice Coltrane Interview," Stuart Nicholson, November 3, 2004, https://stuartnicholson.uk/wp-content/uploads/2017/03/Clike-Here-To-Go-To-Alice-Coltrane-Interview.pdf.

8. Terry Gibbs, interview with author, May 2024.

9. Vishnu Wood, interview with author, January 2024.

10. Terry Gibbs with Cary Ginell, *Good Vibes: A Life in Jazz* (Scarecrow Press, 2003), 230.

11. Terry Gibbs, interview with author, May 2024.

12. Edwin Pouncey, "Alice Coltrane: Enduring Love," *The Wire*, April 2002.

13. Alyn Shipton, *Handful of Keys: Conversations with Thirty Jazz Pianists* (Routledge, 2004), 28–32.

14. Vishnu Wood, interview with author, January 2024.

15. Dolores Brandon, "The Evolution of Alice Coltrane," WBAI, New York, 1988.

16. Vishnu Wood, interview with author, January 2024.

17. Eric Nisenson, *Ascension: John Coltrane and His Quest* (St. Martin's Press, 1993), 109–110.

18. Nisenson, *Ascension*, 109–110.

19. "Terry Gibbs," *Cadence* 14, no. 9 (September 1988).

20. Gibbs, *Good Vibes*, 229.

21. Franya J. Berkman, *Monument Eternal* (Wesleyan University Press, 2010), 42–48.

22. Berkman, *Monument Eternal*, 42–48.

23. Lewis Porter, *John Coltrane: His Life and Music* (University of Michigan Press, 1999), 271–272.

24. "Terry Gibbs."

25. Page 62 of the *Daily News* for July 18, 1963, features listings for a number of events going on in the city that summer day: Mets vs. Giants at the Polo Grounds; Hootenanny '63 at Forest Hills Stadium; "A Midsummer Night's Scream" with George Kirby and Timi Yuro at the Copacabana; Lionel Hampton and his Big Band at the Metropole Café.

26. Gibbs, *Good Vibes*, 227–228.

27. Porter, *John Coltrane*, 270.

28. In J. C. Thomas's biography, he hinted at Coltrane beginning an affair with an unnamed white woman starting in May 1960, which couldn't have helped home life at all.

29. "Audio by Alice Coltrane in Jazz Archive," WKCR, New York, September 23, 1971, https://www.cc-seas.columbia.edu/wkcr/archives/Jazz%20Archive/artist/Alice%20Coltrane.

30. Berkman, *Monument Eternal*, 40–41.

31. Terry Gibbs, interview with author, May 2024.

32. Vishnu Wood, interview with author, January 2024.

33. Berkman, *Monument Eternal*, 40–41.

34. Vishnu Wood, interview with author, January 2024.

35. Berkman, *Monument Eternal*, 40–41.

36. Susan L. Taylor, "A Love Supreme with Alice Coltrane," *Essence*, September 2006, 201.

37. Berkman, *Monument Eternal*, 41.

38. Terry Gibbs, interview with author, May 2024.

39. Porter, *John Coltrane*, 271–272.

40. Terry Gibbs, interview with author, May 2024.

41. Terry Gibbs, interview with author, May 2024.

Chapter Nine: Your Lady

1. Ben Ratliff, *Coltrane: The Story of a Sound* (Faber and Faber, 2007), 86.

2. "Audio by Alice Coltrane in Jazz Archive," WKCR, New York, September 23, 1971, https://www.cc-seas.columbia.edu/wkcr/archives/Jazz%20Archive/artist/Alice%20Coltrane.

3. "Audio by Alice Coltrane in Jazz Archive."

4. "Divine Music: The Spiritual Journey of Alice Coltrane," Integral Yoga Magazine, Fall 2005, https://integralyogamagazine.org/divine-music-the-spiritual-journey-of-alice-coltrane/.

5. Ashley Kahn, *A Love Supreme: The Story of John Coltrane's Signature Album* (Viking Press, 2002), 79.

6. Kahn, *A Love Supreme*, 78.

7. Lewis Porter, *John Coltrane: His Life and Music* (University of Michigan Press, 1999), 272.

8. Dolores Brandon, "The Evolution of Alice Coltrane," WBAI, New York, 1988.

9. The interracial organization founded on the antiviolence tenets of Indian leader Mahatma Gandhi, CORE was the organizing force behind the Freedom Rides of 1961 and the Freedom Summer project of 1964.

10. "Audio by Alice Coltrane in Jazz Archive."

11. "Audio by Alice Coltrane in Jazz Archive."

12. Ashley Kahn, *The House That Trane Built: The Story of Impulse Records* (Granta Books, 2006), 53.

13. Richard Brody, "How Eric Dolphy Sparked My Love of Jazz," *New Yorker*, 2019, https://www.newyorker.com/culture/culture-desk/how-eric-dolphy-deepened-my-love-of-jazz.

14. After the Philharmonic performance on New Year's Eve, Dolphy traveled to Europe with Charles Mingus's sextet. Just before a show in Oslo, Norway, Dolphy informed Mingus that he wouldn't be returning home with them but rather staying around Europe. Like the many young Black artists who had emigrated to Paris in the decades prior, the accepting social climes of Europe beckoned to him. Dolphy was also curious about the new players emerging around Europe, but he also had plans to form new bands. Another critically misunderstood saxophonist, Albert Ayler, was also kicking about on the continent and the two planned to form a group. Dolphy was also writing a string quartet, *Love Suite*. And his fiancée, Joyce Mordecai, a classically trained dancer, was also in Paris working on a ballet.

15. Ratliff, *Coltrane*, 68.

16. Eric Nisenson, *Ascension: John Coltrane and His Quest* (St. Martin's Press, 1993), 141.

17. Porter, *John Coltrane*, 273.

18. Porter, *John Coltrane*, 209.

19. Porter, *John Coltrane*, 211.

20. Nisenson, *Ascension*, 113–114.

21. Nisenson, *Ascension*, 165–166.

22. Clea McDougall, "Alice in Wonder & Awe," *Ascent*, Spring 2006, https://ascentmagazine.com/articles.aspx%3FarticleID=185&page=read&subpage=past&issueID=29.html.

23. Porter, *John Coltrane*, 258.

24. Franya J. Berkman, *Monument Eternal* (Wesleyan University Press, 2010), 54–55.

25. Berkman, *Monument Eternal*, 48–49.

26. Brandon, "The Evolution of Alice Coltrane."

27. Kahn, *A Love Supreme*, 103–104.

28. Archie Shepp, interview with author, June 2024.

29. Porter, *John Coltrane*, 254.

30. "Audio by Alice Coltrane in Jazz Archive."

31. "How Pharoah Sanders Brought Jazz to Its Spiritual Peak," Red Bull Music Academy, May 5, 2016, https://daily.redbullmusicacademy.com/2016/05/pharoah-sanders-the-son.

32. Berkman, *Monument Eternal*, 56.

33. "Audio by Alice Coltrane in Jazz Archive."

34. McDougall, "Alice in Wonder & Awe."

35. "Audio by Alice Coltrane in Jazz Archive."
36. "Audio by Alice Coltrane in Jazz Archive."
37. Berkman, *Monument Eternal*, 53–55.

Chapter Ten: Song of Praise

1. Ashley Kahn, *The House That Trane Built: The Story of Impulse Records* (Granta Books, 2006), 124.

2. Kahn, *The House That Trane Built*, 96.

3. Shankari C. Adams, *Portrait of Devotion: The Spiritual Life of Alice Coltrane Swamini Turiyasangitananda* (self-published, 2016), 17–19.

4. Peter Goodman, "A Haven, a Home, for Trane," *Newsday* (Suffolk Edition), March 28, 2004.

5. Clea McDougall, "Alice in Wonder & Awe," *Ascent*, Spring 2006, https://ascent magazine.com/articles.aspx%3FarticleID=185&page=read&subpage=past&issueID=29.html.

6. Ashley Kahn, *A Love Supreme: The Story of John Coltrane's Signature Album* (Viking Press, 2002), xv.

7. Kahn, *A Love Supreme*, 105–106.

8. Kahn, *A Love Supreme*, 83–85.

9. Kahn, *A Love Supreme*, 99.

10. Kahn, *A Love Supreme*, 102.

11. "Thomas 77," Unity.org, https://www.unity.org/bible-interpretations/thomas-77.

12. Kahn, *A Love Supreme*, 103–104.

13. Kahn, *A Love Supreme*, 149.

14. Kahn, *A Love Supreme*, 156.

15. Kahn, *A Love Supreme*, 156.

16. Kahn, *A Love Supreme*, 156.

17. Kahn, *A Love Supreme*, 160.

18. Adams, *Portrait of Devotion*, 17–19.

19. Alice Coltrane and Erin Christovale, eds., *Alice Coltrane, Monument Eternal* (Delmonico Books, 2025), 39–40.

20. Dolores Brandon, "The Evolution of Alice Coltrane," WBAI, New York, 1988.

21. McDougall, "Alice in Wonder & Awe."

22. Kahn, *A Love Supreme*, 160.

23. To hear just what kind of white-hot magma Coltrane and Jones could conjure in duet, an archival tape from March 1965, *One Down, One Up*, finally saw release in 2005.

24. Susan L. Taylor, "A Love Supreme with Alice Coltrane," *Essence*, September 2006.

25. Lewis Porter, *John Coltrane: His Life and Music* (University of Michigan Press, 1999), 217.

26. Ben Ratliff, *Coltrane: The Story of a Sound* (Faber and Faber, 2007), 92.

27. Eric Nisenson, *Ascension: John Coltrane and His Quest* (St. Martin's Press, 1993), 192.

28. Coltrane and Christovale, *Alice Coltrane, Monument Eternal*, 28.

29. "Audio by Alice Coltrane in Jazz Archive," WKCR, New York, September 23, 1971, https://www.cc-seas.columbia.edu/wkcr/archives/Jazz%20Archive/artist/Alice%20Coltrane. Just which piece and which Catholic edifice have never been properly identified.

30. Taylor, "A Love Supreme with Alice Coltrane."

31. Nisenson, *Ascension*, 192.

32. Porter, *John Coltrane*, 273.

33. Taylor, "A Love Supreme with Alice Coltrane."

34. Adams, *Portrait of Devotion*, 20.

Chapter Eleven: Expression

1. Ben Ratliff, *The Jazz Ear: Conversations over Music* (Henry Holt, 2008), 134–135.

2. Ashley Kahn, *A Love Supreme: The Story of John Coltrane's Signature Album* (Viking Press, 2002), 133.

3. Drummer Rashied Ali was also invited to the date, but his ego prevented him from accepting "second drummer" status. He later realized his mistake.

4. Ashley Kahn, *The House That Trane Built: The Story of Impulse Records* (Granta Books, 2006), 136.

5. A. B. Spellman, liner notes for *Ascension*, Impulse, 1965, LP.

6. Spellman, liner notes for *Ascension*.

7. Spellman, liner notes for *Ascension*.

8. Ben Ratliff, *Coltrane: The Story of a Sound* (Faber and Faber, 2007), 92.

9. Kahn, *A Love Supreme*, 133.

10. Eric Nisenson, *Ascension: John Coltrane and His Quest* (St. Martin's Press, 1993), 192.

11. Nisenson, *Ascension*, 165.

12. But would John Coltrane have explored the third-eye opening effects of this chemical compound only by himself or with his partner? Alice is often described as a teetotaler who eschewed alcohol and marijuana. Would she have abstained from LSD as well? Or would she and John have been curious about its therapeutic benefits rather than the FBI-led smear campaign calling it a dangerous controlled substance? It's impossible to speculate, but no doubt LSD's ability to open "the doors of perception" to higher realms of consciousness might explain how someone deeply embedded in conservative midcentury church doctrine would find themselves deeply enamored with higher forms of human consciousness well beyond what the church preaches.

13. Dolores Brandon, "The Evolution of Alice Coltrane," WBAI, New York, 1988.

14. Nisenson, *Ascension*, 185–187.

15. Nisenson, *Ascension*, 185–187.

16. Nat Hentoff, liner notes for *Om*, Impulse, 1968, LP.

17. Nisenson, *Ascension*, 192.

18. Terry Riley, interview with author, October 2022.

19. Nat Hentoff, liner notes for *Meditations*, Impulse, 1966, LP.

20. In a pinch, Coltrane might resort to another player if the occasion arose, such as when Jones served three months' time on a drug rap, or bringing on another bassist to

augment Jimmy Garrison, or Ali to augment Jones. Not so if Tyner wasn't available. It was McCoy's job and his alone throughout this run.

21. Luke Saunders, "The Life and Times of McCoy Tyner," *Happy Mag*, March 12, 2020, https://happymag.tv/the-life-and-times-of-mccoy-tyner-in-5-essential-albums/.

22. Kahn, *A Love Supreme*, 182.

23. That Coltrane even needed a piano at this point was curious. Most "New Thing" players had long ago jettisoned the clunky thing. Coleman famously never used one in his quartet, Archie Shepp's first seven Impulse titles did without, and the major pianist of the avant-garde movement, Cecil Taylor, attacked his keys in such a way that Valerie Wilmer once described it as "eighty-eight tuned drums." Since these players weren't improvising on harmony (a holdover European musical tradition they were also rejecting), they didn't need the piano comping behind them. If anything, the piano restricted their flight and tethered them to the ground.

24. "Audio by Alice Coltrane in Jazz Archive," WKCR, New York, September 23, 1971, https://www.cc-seas.columbia.edu/wkcr/archives/Jazz%20Archive/artist/Alice%20Coltrane.

25. Franya J. Berkman, *Monument Eternal* (Wesleyan University Press, 2010), 57.

26. Berkman, *Monument Eternal*, 58.

27. Nat Hentoff, liner notes for *Live at the Village Vanguard Again*, Impulse, 1966, LP.

28. Alyn Shipton, *Handful of Keys: Conversations with Thirty Jazz Pianists* (Routledge, 2004), 28–32.

29. Berkman, *Monument Eternal*, 58.

30. Shipton, *Handful of Keys*, 28–32.

31. Shipton, *Handful of Keys*, 28–32.

32. *Coda*, July 1967.

33. It wasn't released at the time and it's now impossible to hear just how Alice sounded on that first date, as she re-recorded her piano part—and Garrison's bass part—years later. Three other pieces—"Manifestation," "Reverend King," and "Leo"—were also recorded that day and would be released years later.

34. Aidan Levy, *Saxophone Colossus: The Life and Music of Sonny Rollins* (Hachette, 2022), 465–466.

35. Levy, *Saxophone Colossus*, 465–466.

36. *Down Beat*, October 20, 1966.

37. Leonard Feather, *Fort Worth Star-Telegram*, March 6, 1966.

38. "Audio by Alice Coltrane in Jazz Archive."

39. Shipton, *Handful of Keys*, 28–32.

40. Shipton, *Handful of Keys*, 28–32.

41. Franya Berkman, "Divine Songs" (PhD diss., Wesleyan University, 2003), 122.

42. Edwin Pouncey, "Alice Coltrane: Enduring Love," *The Wire*, April 2002.

43. Shankari C. Adams, *Portrait of Devotion: The Spiritual Life of Alice Coltrane Swamini Turiyasangitananda* (self-published, 2016), 17–19.

44. Pouncey, "Alice Coltrane: Enduring Love."

45. Berkman, *Monument Eternal*, 50–52.

46. Lois Gilbert, "The Multi-Directions of Jack DeJohnette," *Musician*, November 1980, 54–58.

47. Gilbert, "The Multi-Directions of Jack DeJohnette."

48. Gilbert, "The Multi-Directions of Jack DeJohnette."

49. Nisenson, *Ascension*, 204.

50. Jack DeJohnette, interview with author, May 2024.

51. Ron Welburn, "Coltrane at Pep's," *Change* 1, no. 2, Summer 1966.

52. "Darkness," "Lead Us On," "Leo," and another attempt at "Peace on Earth" were made. A week later, the group was back to record "Call" and another take of "Leo." These tapes have never been released and are believed to be lost.

53. And the community was rapidly changing. Crown Heights shifted from ninety percent white to eighty percent Black while Park Slope went from Black to white. Activism was on the rise and the neighborhood's local assembly representative, Shirley Chisholm, was soon to become the country's first Black congresswoman.

54. Kahn, *A Love Supreme*, 189–192.

55. Lewis Porter, *John Coltrane: His Life and Music* (University of Michigan Press, 1999), 275–276.

56. Kahn, *A Love Supreme*, 189–191.

57. *Jazz Hot*, August–September 1967.

58. Kahn, *A Love Supreme*, 193.

59. Kahn, *A Love Supreme*, 183.

60. Pouncey, "Alice Coltrane: Enduring Love."

61. Berkman, *Monument Eternal*, 48–49.

62. *Down Beat*'s review was a single line: "The next day's matinee, which could well have been titled 'John Coltrane and His Children,' was heavy going."

63. Porter, *John Coltrane*, 275–276.

64. Porter, *John Coltrane*, 275–276.

65. Nisenson, *Ascension*, 210.

66. Nisenson, *Ascension*, 211.

67. "Robert Quine interview," *Buffalo News*, June 18, 2004.

68. "Burt Wilson interview," *Albuquerque Journal*, May 8, 1998.

69. Porter, *John Coltrane*, 288.

70. Over a thousand folks turned out to see the likes of the Giuseppi Logan Sextet and the Ornette Coleman Trio perform. Others like Marion Brown, Jeanne Lee and Ran Blake, and Albert Ayler all performed over the course of the summer.

71. *Jazz* 6, no. 1 (January 1967): 26–29.

72. In between that concert and two upcoming nights at the Village Vanguard, Pharoah Sanders recorded his Impulse debut, *Tauhid*, drawing on his interest in Islam, Egyptology, and the folk music he heard when they had toured in Japan.

Chapter Twelve: Seraphic Light

1. C. O. Simpkins, *Coltrane: A Biography* (Black Classic Press, 1975), 114.

2. *Down Beat* 34, no. 4 (February 23, 1967).

3. Shankari C. Adams, *Portrait of Devotion: The Spiritual Life of Alice Coltrane Swamini Turiyasangitananda* (self-published, 2016), 17–19.

4. Released in 1995 as *Stellar Regions*.

5. Released in 1974 as *Interstellar Space*.

6. "John Coltrane 1967," Wild Music-Jazz, accessed July 14, 2025, http://www.wildmusic-jazz.com/jcdisc67.htm.

7. Edwin Pouncey, "Alice Coltrane: Enduring Love," *The Wire*, April 2002.

8. Ashley Kahn, *A Love Supreme: The Story of John Coltrane's Signature Album* (Viking Press, 2002), 190.

9. Simpkins, *Coltrane*, 232.

10. Kahn, *A Love Supreme*, 198.

11. Lewis Porter, *John Coltrane: His Life and Music* (University of Michigan Press, 1999), 289.

12. Porter, *John Coltrane*, 290.

13. Susan L. Taylor, "A Love Supreme with Alice Coltrane," *Essence*, September 2006.

14. Taylor, "A Love Supreme with Alice Coltrane."

15. *Down Beat*, March 7, 1968 *Expression* review: "Mrs. Coltrane, while sounding somewhat like Tyner, does not have her predecessor's physical or musical strength, and her way of playing for Coltrane is more delicate."

16. Porter, *John Coltrane*, 290.

Chapter Thirteen: Manifestation of Cosmic Energy

1. *Newark Evening News*, July 14, 1967, https://www.npl.org/archive/wp-content/uploads/2018/09/July14.pdf.

2. Ashley Kahn, *A Love Supreme: The Story of John Coltrane's Signature Album* (Viking Press, 2002), 196.

3. "Coltrane Is Given a Jazzman's Funeral Here," *New York Times*, July 22, 1967.

4. Susan L. Taylor, "A Love Supreme with Alice Coltrane," *Essence*, September 2006.

5. "Spiritual Wealth," *Integral Yoga Magazine*, Fall 2005, https://integralyogamagazine.org/divine-music-the-spiritual-journey-of-alice-coltrane/.

6. Shankari C. Adams, *Portrait of Devotion: The Spiritual Life of Alice Coltrane Swamini Turiyasangitananda* (self-published, 2016), 20.

7. Adams, *Portrait of Devotion*, 22.

8. Lewis Porter, *John Coltrane: His Life and Music* (University of Michigan Press, 1999), 293.

9. Darlene Donloe, "Living with the Spirit and Legacy of John Coltrane," *Ebony*, March 1989.

10. J. Krishnamurti, *The Book of Life* (HarperOne, 2002), 54.

11. Franya J. Berkman, *Monument Eternal* (Wesleyan University Press, 2010), 67.

12. "Audio by Alice Coltrane in Jazz Archive," WKCR, New York, September 23, 1971, https://www.cc-seas.columbia.edu/wkcr/archives/Jazz%20Archive/artist/Alice%20Coltrane.

13. She began to refer to John as "the Father" or by the Sanskrit word for "compassion," Ohnedaruth, a name he adopted in the last months of his life.

14. Edwin Pouncey, "Alice Coltrane: Enduring Love," *The Wire*, April 2002.

15. W. Royal Stokes, *Living the Jazz Life* (Oxford University Press, 2020), 157.

16. Alyn Shipton, *Handful of Keys: Conversations with Thirty Jazz Pianists* (Routledge, 2004), 25–32.

17. Ashley Kahn, *The House That Trane Built: The Story of Impulse Records* (Granta Books, 2006), 186.

18. *Jazz and Pop* 7, no. 9 (September 1968): 14.

19. That same Sunday, just a bit farther north in Harlem, a new religious composition by Mary Lou Williams, *A Mass for the Lenten Season*, was sung by the Young People's Choir and the entire congregation at eleven o'clock Mass at St. Thomas the Apostle Roman Catholic Church, 118th Street and St. Nicholas Avenue.

20. "Coltrane's Widow to Share His Legacy of Jazz Works," *Newsday*, April 12, 1968.

21. "Coltrane's Widow to Share His Legacy of Jazz Works."

22. Probably the full title of the piece "Manifestation."

23. When I asked Jack DeJohnette what he remembered from that date, he replied: "Gosh no, I didn't do that. Only time I played with them was in Chicago. How my name got on there I don't know."

24. *Down Beat*, May 16, 1968.

25. *Jazz and Pop* 7, no. 9 (September 1968).

26. Pouncey, "Alice Coltrane: Enduring Love."

27. *Jazz and Pop* 7, no. 9 (September 1968): 14.

28. *Jazz and Pop*, 7, no. 9 (September 1968): 14.

Chapter Fourteen: IHS

1. Alice played harp on a recording session for Roland Kirk. Kirk was a blind jazz multi-instrumentalist. Kirk had mastered a way to play multiple horns (and some invented ones) all at once, making him a one-man frontline and a force of nature. He also eschewed the label of "jazz," considering his sound to be "black classical music." Kirk had befriended Coltrane on the jazz circuit, and there's also a chance that Kirk and Alice had crossed paths one night at a Jazz Loft jam session. Trombonist Dick Griffin was asked to arrange a recording date and brought Alice in, giving her the chords and letting her expand on them.

2. In the October 31, 1968, issue, a live review raved: "He has done more than any other individual to provide outlets for Detroit musicians," equating Farrow with the likes of Barry Harris. The jazz scene had been in decline in the wake of "urban renewal" and the ascendancy of Berry Gordy's Motown imprint, but if someone were to look for a direct correlation between Detroit jazz and Motown, it could be found in the ranks of Farrow's band. Pianist Teddy Harris served as musical director for Aretha Franklin and the Supremes, while trumpeter Herbie Williams was a member of the Funk Brothers house band. In three years' time, baritone saxophonist Tate Houston would take the iconic solo on Marvin Gaye's "What's Going On." That night, Farrow—stomping out time with his heel and guiding the group—"left them begging for more . . . Seldom have I seen such genuinely enthusiastic response from a Detroit concert audience."

3. *Coda*, December 1969.
4. *The Province*, January 31, 1969.
5. *The Province*, February 21, 1969.
6. Archie Shepp, interview with author, June 2024.
7. *Jazz and Pop* 7, no. 9 (September 1968): 14.
8. Alice Coltrane, *Monument Eternal* (Vedantic Book Press, 1977), 17–30.
9. Coltrane, *Monument Eternal*, 19.
10. Coltrane, *Monument Eternal*, 21.
11. Coltrane, *Monument Eternal*, 11–12.
12. Radha Botofasina, interview with author, July 2024.
13. Shankari C. Adams, *Portrait of Devotion: The Spiritual Life of Alice Coltrane Swamini Turiyasangitananda* (self-published, 2016), 22–23.
14. Coltrane, *Monument Eternal*, 15–18.
15. Coltrane, *Monument Eternal*, 29.
16. Coltrane, *Monument Eternal*, 21.
17. The description of the fourth stage is curious in hindsight, in that it seemed to echo the title of Alice's early composition "Soulsphere." One wonders if in some way it referenced this concept, even if subliminally.
18. Coltrane, *Monument Eternal*, 19–20.
19. Coltrane, *Monument Eternal*, 25.
20. Coltrane, *Monument Eternal*, 19–20.
21. Coltrane, *Monument Eternal*, 22.
22. Coltrane, *Monument Eternal*, 18–19.
23. Coltrane, *Monument Eternal*, 30.
24. Adams, *Portrait of Devotion*, 26–27.
25. Coltrane, *Monument Eternal*, 24.
26. Adams, *Portrait of Devotion*, 26–27.
27. *Chicago Tribune*, January 23, 1969.
28. *Los Angeles Times-West Magazine*, March 16, 1969.
29. These were three important Indian teachers whose teachings had begun to disperse throughout the West in the wake of the radical Immigration and Nationality Act of 1965, which abolished the restrictive—and racist—quotas on people immigrating from Asian and African (i.e., non–Northern European) countries.
30. Alice Coltrane, liner notes to *Huntington Ashram Monastery*, Impulse, 1969, LP.
31. Curiously, it slipped out with almost no notice from the mainstream press, and few notable reviews appeared in my research. One asked: "Full of bubbling contentment, pretty music, but is it jazz?"
32. Ben Ratliff, *Run the Song: Writing About Running About Listening*, Graywolf Press, 2025, 67.
33. Ashley Kahn, "The Gift: Alice Coltrane and the Harp," *We Jazz*, no. 1 (Summer 2021).
34. In the liner notes, she also admitted to mentally chanting "Jaya Jaya Rama" throughout the album.

35. David Lerner, "Alice Coltrane: Jazz Pianist, Inspirational Organist," *Keyboard Magazine*, November 1982.

Chapter Fifteen: Mantra

1. Sita Bordow and Joan Wiener Bordow, *Sri Swami Satchidananda: Apostle of Peace* (Integral Yoga Publications, 1986), 44–45. This story is not exactly correct. Ramu's wife, unhappy in an arranged marriage, left Ramu and their children behind for another man. In those days, a wife leaving her husband and children was shocking and considered shameful, so the tight-knit community considered her dead. Ramu was surprised by his own sense of calm, and his attention turned to the welfare of his children.

2. The name Satchidananda is a combination of three Sanskrit words: "Sat" (existence or truth), "Chit" (Consciousness or pure Awareness), and "Ananda" (bliss). Together, they express the experience of the Absolute—eternal existence, pure Consciousness, and divine bliss.

3. It was later rechristened Sri Lanka in 1972.

4. In Ceylon, he served communities in practical ways—giving health and wellness talks to tea plantation workers struggling with alcohol issues, introducing yoga to the police force, and fostering interfaith understanding by bringing together Christians, Hindus, Muslims, and Buddhists in a spirit of unity.

5. Bordow and Bordow, *Sri Swami Satchidananda*, 218.

6. Bordow and Bordow, *Sri Swami Satchidananda*, 233.

7. Vishnu Wood, interview with author, January 2024.

8. Vishnu Wood, interview with author, January 2024.

9. Tulsi Reynolds, interview with author, April 16, 2024.

10. Michele Kort, *Soul Picnic: The Music and Passion of Laura Nyro* (St. Martin's Griffin, 2003), 110–111.

11. Just check out your local yoga class and see who gravitates toward the practice.

12. Vishnu Wood, interview with author, January 2024.

13. Tulsi Reynolds, interview with author, April 16, 2024.

14. Edwin Pouncey, "Alice Coltrane: Enduring Love," *The Wire*, April 2002.

15. Sri Swami Satchidananda, "The Woodstock Opening Address," Swamisatchidananda.org, accessed August 20, 2025, https://swamisatchidananda.org/life/woodstock-guru/swami-satchidanandas-woodstock-address/.

16. The day after the festival drew to a close and its stragglers made their way back to New York City, Alice's old schoolmate Bennie Maupin and musical collaborator Jack DeJohnette were called to a recording session by John Coltrane's old bandleader, Miles Davis, going down at Columbia Studio B. There they began playing in loose-knit groups of upward of thirteen musicians, laying down the exploratory, seeking sounds that would soon be trimmed and edited into *Bitches Brew*, a landmark fusion of acoustic jazz, electric instrumentation, and studio wizardry. The rigors that had codified jazz fully dissolved in the wake of that album.

17. A. C. Turiyasangitananda, *Divine Revelations* (Avatar Book Institute, 1995), 17.

18. Pouncey, "Alice Coltrane: Enduring Love."

19. Pouncey, "Alice Coltrane: Enduring Love."
20. Pouncey, "Alice Coltrane: Enduring Love."
21. Kent D. Smith, "Trane's Jazz Echoes Inspire His Widow," *Newsday*, May 11, 1970.
22. Pouncey, "Alice Coltrane: Enduring Love."
23. Pouncey, "Alice Coltrane: Enduring Love."
24. Vishnu Wood, interview with author, January 2024.
25. Susan L. Taylor, "A Love Supreme with Alice Coltrane," *Essence*, 2006.
26. Stan Lathan, "Black Journal: 26; Alice Coltrane," Smithsonian Institution, 1970, https://nmaahc.si.edu/object/nmaahc_2012.79.1.16.1a.
27. Lathan, "Black Journal: 26; Alice Coltrane."

Chapter Sixteen: Journey on the Ship of Satchidananda

1. Tulsi Reynolds, interview with author, April 16, 2024.
2. Tulsi Reynolds, interview with author, April 16, 2024.
3. Ed Michel, email interview with author, 2024.
4. Ed Michel, email interview with author, 2024.
5. Leonard Feather, liner notes for Alice Coltrane, *Ptah, the El Daoud*, Impulse, 1970, LP.
6. Feather, liner notes for *Ptah, the El Daoud*.
7. Edwin Pouncey, "Alice Coltrane: Enduring Love," *The Wire*, April 2002.
8. "Galaxy in Turiya: Alice Coltrane with Strings," California Festival, accessed February 28, 2025, https://www.cafestival.org/excursions/alice-coltrane/.
9. Ed Michel, email interview with author, 2024.
10. Feather, liner notes for *Ptah, the El Daoud*. For most of his mature recorded output, John Coltrane eschewed the trend of quoting other songs in his own solos, favoring total individual creativity, making this one of the few recorded instances where Alice would have referenced an older song within her own improvisations. The bittersweet blues "Parker's Mood" was originally cut by Parker in 1948, the vocals written five years later by King Pleasure. Pleasure was one of the stylistic touchstones for the Premiers, so it stands to reason that even if that modulation occurred only in the opening seconds of the song, Alice would have been deeply familiar with Pleasure's particular rendition. It offers a fascinating glimpse into Alice and her ability to draw on her many influences and distill it down to its essence. An autobiography across eight minutes. One can hear the Hastings Street blues, God's question as queried during Mt. Olive services, the Flame Show Bar sophistication of the Premiers, the levity of John's compositions like "Alabama" and "Peace on Earth," with Alice refracting it all through the prism of Indian thought.
11. Incidentally, Bartz had taken over Shorter's role in Miles Davis's group around this time.
12. "Galaxy in Turiya: Alice Coltrane with Strings," California Festival, accessed February 28, 2025, https://www.cafestival.org/excursions/alice-coltrane/.
13. Ratna Paula Stone, "A Love Supreme," *Integral Yoga Magazine*, Spring 2007.
14. Kent D. Smith, "Trane's Jazz Echoes Inspire His Widow," *Newsday*, May 11, 1970. In the story, Alice is described mixing a four-track recording of a sextet session date featuring five tracks, which doesn't correspond to any known lineup or released album.

15. Smith, "Trane's Jazz Echoes Inspire His Widow."

16. Angela Dews, interview with author, March 2024.

17. Angela Dews, personal correspondence with author, May 18, 1970.

18. According to Ellis's daughter Melissa, executives insisted on old shows being erased and taped over. Preservation only began in 1971. Of the 130 episodes of *Soul!* produced, only 24 have been digitized.

19. Vishnu Wood, interview with author, January 2024.

20. There's no recording credit, and Ed Michel has no idea who would have recorded the set or if there's any other music from that concert.

21. *Down Beat* gave it three stars and said: "It seems incredible that a group so heavily stamped by the late John Coltrane would not be able to pull off an album, but that's just what happens here. It's not that this is not good music, because it is, but it doesn't come close to the potential of the individual players. It seems that each subdued his talents to accommodate the others. And for the life of me I don't know why." Another review said that Alice was never "a tower of strength in the rhythm section or a very inventive soloist" and called the album a disappointment "that by the end left me tense and unsettled."

22. Sita Bordow and Joan Wiener Bordow, *Sri Swami Satchidananda: Apostle of Peace* (Integral Yoga Publications, 1986), 304. In the many different accounts of this story, the exact dollar amount fluctuates wildly. In some it's $1,500, in others $3,000, and when a kirtan was hosted at the center in 2024—some fifty-four years on—the dollar amount was now $5,000. Regardless, the legend remains that Alice's check was the precise amount needed to secure the building for the institute, a gift that keeps the IYI relevant into the present day.

23. "Spiritual Wealth," *Integral Yoga Magazine*, Fall 2005, https://integralyogamagazine.org/divine-music-the-spiritual-journey-of-alice-coltrane/.

24. Tulsi Reynolds, interview with author, April 16, 2024.

25. Tulsi Reynolds, interview with author, April 16, 2024.

26. Franya J. Berkman, *Monument Eternal* (Wesleyan University Press, 2010), 66.

27. Nathaniel Friedman, "'If You're in the Song, Keep On Playing': An Interview with Pharoah Sanders," *New Yorker*, January 12, 2020, https://www.newyorker.com/culture/the-new-yorker-interview/if-youre-in-the-song-keep-on-playing-pharoah-sanders-interview.

28. Tulsi Reynolds, interview with author, April 16, 2024.

29. There are many examples, but Tony Scott's clarinet and sitar duets on *Music for Yoga Meditation* remains a favorite.

30. Shankari C. Adams, *Portrait of Devotion: The Spiritual Life of Alice Coltrane Swamini Turiyasangitananda* (self-published, 2016), 74.

31. Lao Tzu, *Tao Te Ching*, chap. 11.

32. Michel's notes mention two takes of "Journey" and three of "Shiva," as well as notes for two recordings, "Leo" and "The Sun," that remain unheard/unissued and are presumed to be lost.

33. Some state that what drew Alice to Swami Satchidananda was a shared connection. After the loss of her husband, Alice Coltrane became disillusioned with worldly life and turned to full-time spiritual seeking. Though Swamiji's calling began in early childhood, the failure of his marriage and the lack of fulfillment in various business in which he had

been engaged led him to renounce worldly pursuits and dedicate himself entirely to spiritual life. For both, the search for higher truth became their life's focus, drawing them toward a profound connection with the divine.

34. Dolores Brandon, "The Evolution of Alice Coltrane," WBAI, New York, 1988.
35. Brandon, "The Evolution of Alice Coltrane."
36. Angela Dews, "Alice Coltrane," *Essence*, December 1971, 61.

Chapter Seventeen: Universal Consciousness

1. Franya J. Berkman, *Monument Eternal* (Wesleyan University Press, 2010), 78.
2. Thankfully, IYI students diligently shot color 16mm film documenting Satchidananda's return to India, portions of which are viewable online.
3. Integral Yoga Institute, "THE 1970 WORLD PEACE TOUR Part 4," YouTube, 2018, https://www.youtube.com/watch?v=nCIOVc9L7rw.
4. A. C. Turiyasangitananda, *Divine Revelations* (Avatar Book Institute, 1995), 18.
5. In Hindu tradition, it is associated with the goddess Parvati, who undertook extreme austerities in her devotion to God.
6. "Spiritual Wealth," *Integral Yoga Magazine*, Fall 2005, https://integralyogamagazine.org/divine-music-the-spiritual-journey-of-alice-coltrane/.
7. Radha Botofasina, interview with author, July 2024.
8. Joe H. Klee, "Record Reviews," *Down Beat*, May 27, 1971, 20.
9. Tulsi Reynolds, interview with author, April 16, 2024.
10. Also on the bill: Lloyd McNeil, Byard Lancaster, and the New Black Edition with Sunny Murray.
11. Tulsi Reynolds, interview with author, April 16, 2024.
12. Joe H. Klee, "Carnegie Hall Live Review," *Down Beat*, April 15, 1971.
13. Archie Shepp, interview with author, June 2024.
14. Archie Shepp, interview with author, June 2024.
15. *Down Beat* called her versions of "Africa" and "Leo" "some of the finest improvisational music that's been played since Trane checked out in 1967."
16. Jurebu Cason, "Heard and Seen," *Coda*, June 1971, 42–43.
17. Turiyasangitananda, *Divine Revelations*, 23–24.
18. The sound of her young sons making a racket throughout the entire interview is tiring/triggering for most parents (including this one). It's a testament to Alice's patience and gentleness as a mother to have conducted such an interview and not raise her voice once or be stern in any way.
19. "Audio by Alice Coltrane in Jazz Archive," WKCR, New York, September 23, 1971, https://www.cc-seas.columbia.edu/wkcr/archives/Jazz%20Archive/artist/Alice%20Coltrane.
20. Berkman, *Monument Eternal*, 80.
21. "Audio by Alice Coltrane in Jazz Archive."
22. Angela Dews, "Alice Coltrane," *Essence*, December 1971.
23. Shankari C. Adams, *Portrait of Devotion: The Spiritual Life of Alice Coltrane Swamini Turiyasangitananda* (self-published, 2016), 74.
24. Berkman, *Monument Eternal*, 80.

25. Berkman, *Monument Eternal*, 80.
26. Dolores Brandon, "The Evolution of Alice Coltrane," WBAI, New York, 1988.
27. Tulsi Reynolds, interview with author, April 16, 2024.
28. No recording like that has ever surfaced, though Jarvis was credited with bells and percussion on the *Universal Consciousness* sessions, along with Ali and DeJohnette. Might Alice have originally conceived the music with Shepp or another saxophonist in mind and then changed direction?
29. Archie Shepp, interview with author, June 2024.
30. Phil Elwood, "Alice Coltrane, Sun Ra Leave Audience Cold," *San Francisco Examiner*, April 24, 1971, 10.
31. "Frank Lowe," *Cadence* 8, no. 1 (January 1982): 7.
32. Just ask La Monte Young's old bandmate, violinist Tony Conrad, who with fellow violist John Cale had expanded the drone potential of these strings in the 1960s.
33. In the liner notes, Alice wrote that her "sound is reminiscent of spherical harmony."
34. Ed Michel, email interview with author, 2024.
35. Turiya Aparna (Alice Coltrane), liner notes for Alice Coltrane, *Universal Consciousness*, Impulse, 1971, LP.
36. "Galaxy in Turiya: Alice Coltrane with Strings," California Festival, accessed February 28, 2025, https://www.cafestival.org/excursions/alice-coltrane/.
37. She still hoped to return to the East but also wanted "to view Egypt, Africa, and the Holy Land." In just a few paragraphs, Alice name-checked the likes of El Daoud, Kali, Swami Sivananda, the Universal Mother, Jesus Christ, Zoroaster, Isis and Osiris, the Tao, the half-monkey deity Hanuman, nineteenth-century Iranian religious figure Bahá'u'lláh, Mary and Joseph, Indian philosopher Sri Aurobindo, and others. In mentioning Ohnedaruth, she wrote he is "situated near a point in space where stands a mammoth Colossus of Three Worlds, [and] will sound the valorous hymn to the dead in war." Turiya Aparna (Alice Coltrane), liner notes for *Universal Consciousness*.
38. Turiyasangitananda, *Divine Revelations*, 30.
39. Judith Jamison with Howard Kaplan, *Dancing Spirit: An Autobiography* (Doubleday, 1993), 132–136.
40. Jamison, *Dancing Spirit*, 132–136.
41. Clive Barnes, "The Dance: Judith Jamison's Triumph," *New York Times*, May 5, 1971.
42. Tulsi Reynolds, interview with author, April 16, 2024.
43. Tulsi Reynolds, interview with author, April 16, 2024.
44. "Across the Water," *Lincoln (NE) Star*, October 17, 1971.
45. Richard Seidel, "Caught in the Act," *Down Beat*, November 11, 1971.
46. Ashley Kahn, *The House That Trane Built: The Story of Impulse Records* (Granta Books, 2006), 228.

Chapter Eighteen: Galaxy in Turiya

1. Angela Dews, interview with author, March 2024.
2. Angela Dews, "Alice Coltrane," *Essence*, December 1971, 61.
3. "Galaxy in Turiya: Alice Coltrane with Strings," California Festival, accessed February 28, 2025, https://www.cafestival.org/excursions/alice-coltrane/.

4. "Galaxy in Turiya."

5. "Spiritual Wealth," *Integral Yoga Magazine*, Fall 2005, https://integralyogamagazine.org/divine-music-the-spiritual-journey-of-alice-coltrane/.

6. "At Home with the Coltranes, Listening to Stravinsky," NPR, July 19, 2012, https://www.npr.org/2012/07/19/157060981/at-home-with-the-coltranes-listening-to-stravinsky.

7. Alice's name appeared on the cover along with Angela Davis, Huey Newton, Curtis Mayfield, and Billy Paul. The magazine also featured a naked centerfold in the "Brother's Choice" section of the magazine.

8. Rhetta Nickerson, "Alice Coltrane," *Soul Illustrated*, Summer 1972, 48.

9. "Audio by Alice Coltrane in Jazz Archive," WKCR, New York, September 23, 1971, https://www.cc-seas.columbia.edu/wkcr/archives/Jazz%20Archive/artist/Alice%20Coltrane.

10. Edwin Pouncey, "Alice Coltrane: Enduring Love," *The Wire*, April 2002.

11. Tulsi Reynolds, interview with author, April 16, 2024.

12. Baker Bigsby, interview with author, September 17, 2024.

13. Nadia Sirota, email interview with author, May 30, 2023.

14. Pouncey, "Alice Coltrane: Enduring Love."

15. Not to mention the subsequent horror movies that also use these effects in their soundtracks for frightening effect.

16. Ed Michel, email interview with author, 2024.

17. *Down Beat* 39, no. 10 (May 25, 1972).

18. *Calgary Herald*, November 10, 1972.

19. A. C. Turiyasangitananda, *Divine Revelations* (Avatar Book Institute, 1995), 39–40.

20. *Detroit Free Press*, March 21, 1972.

21. There exists a radio broadcast of this set that's utterly fascinating. Alice's group that night features Frank Lowe on saxophone, John Blair on violin and leading a string section from the New England Conservatory, and a tabla player/percussionist. No bassist or drummer. Without a true rhythm section, the set has a curious floating, unmoored pacing, led by Alice's otherworldly bass tones on the Wurlitzer. The set draws from *World Galaxy* and features rare performances of "Galaxy in Turiya" and an expansive read of "Galaxy in Satchidananda."

22. "Audio by Alice Coltrane in Jazz Archive."

23. Ed Michel, email interview with author, 2024.

24. Ed Michel, email interview with author, 2024.

25. She was also not satisfied by her own playing on that early date, re-recording her piano part as well as replacing Jimmy Garrison's bass with a new track put down by Charlie Haden.

26. Ed Michel, email interview with author, 2024.

27. Murray Adler, interview with author, June 1, 2023.

28. "Galaxy in Turiya."

29. There's a bootleg of the Berkeley show featuring her group augmented by the presence of two sons of famous Indian sarod master Ustad Ali Akbar Khan: Aashish on sarod and Pranesh on tabla. She performed three of John's pieces but only one of her own, a

particularly blistering version of "Journey" with her on organ. She switches to harp to engage with the classical Indian performers at one point, a furious repartee, before returning to organ. A live review by Philip Elwood in the *San Francisco Examiner* on May 22, 1972, stated it was a "generally unsatisfying demonstration of the confused state of today's avant-jazz expressions" and that Coltrane's accompanists were "consistently more substantial and exciting in their contributions than their leader…I found her own instrumental contributions to be shallow and inexpertly performed."

30. "Oral History of Jazz Harpist and Pianist from the U of I Leonard Feather Collection," University of Idaho, accessed December 10, 2024, https://www.lib.uidaho.edu/digital/coltrane/items/alice_13.html.

31. "Oral History of Jazz Harpist and Pianist from the U of I Leonard Feather Collection."

32. Susan L. Taylor, "A Love Supreme with Alice Coltrane," *Essence*, September 2006, 201.

33. Ed Michel, email interview with author, 2024.

34. Ed Michel, email interview with author, 2024.

35. "Galaxy in Turiya."

36. Turiya Coltrane, liner notes for Alice Coltrane, *Lord of Lords*, Impulse, 1972, LP.

37. Turiya Coltrane, liner notes for *Lord of Lords*.

38. Turiya Coltrane, liner notes for *Lord of Lords*.

39. Ed Michel, email interview with author, 2024.

40. Pouncey, "Alice Coltrane: Enduring Love."

41. Franya J. Berkman, *Monument Eternal* (Wesleyan University Press, 2010), 87.

42. Turiya Coltrane, liner notes for *Lord of Lords*.

43. "Galaxy in Turiya."

44. Ed Michel, email interview with author, 2024.

45. Pouncey, "Alice Coltrane: Enduring Love."

46. Ed Michel, email interview with author, 2024.

47. Michael Beckerman, "The Real Value of Yellow Journalism: James Creelman and Antonín Dvořák," *Musical Quarterly* 77, no. 4 (1993): 749.

48. "Seventy Negro Spirituals," Alexander Street, accessed December 1, 2024, https://search.alexanderstreet.com/preview/work/bibliographic_entity%7Cbibliographic_details%7C356841.

49. Turiya Coltrane, liner notes for *Lord of Lords*.

50. "Galaxy in Turiya."

51. Pouncey, "Alice Coltrane: Enduring Love."

Chapter Nineteen: Angel of Sunlight

1. Bob Blumenthal, "Infinity" review, *Boston Phoenix*, October 10, 1972.

2. Edwin Pouncey, "Alice Coltrane: Enduring Love," *The Wire*, April 2002.

3. *Commercial Appeal* (Memphis), November 26, 1972.

4. *Boston Globe*, November 24, 1972.

5. *Michigan Chronicle*, July 7, 1973.

6. *Winston-Salem Journal*, November 19, 1972.

7. Ed Michel, email interview with author, 2024.

8. Murray Adler, interview with author, May 2023.

9. Gwen Evans, "Stevie's Wonderlove at Hinterland," *Sun Reporter* (San Francisco), March 10, 1973.

10. It was even recorded at the same West Coast studio that John and Alice used in 1966.

11. McLaughlin and Santana even released a duo album in homage to Chinmoy, titled *Love Devotion Surrender*. It featured a cover of "A Love Supreme" with guitar pyrotechnics and driving Latin rhythms.

12. Carlos Santana with Ashley Kahn and Hal Miller, *The Universal Tone: Bring My Story to Light* (Little, Brown, 2014), 348.

13. Ed Jeffords, "Imagery Production Scores Big Here," *Tacoma News Tribune*, November 10, 1971, 41.

14. Programs would feature her music sandwiched between Jefferson Airplane and the Grateful Dead, or else Yes and Pink Floyd.

15. Not to mention the group's adherence to the tenets of Nichiren Buddhism.

16. *Jazz Digest* 2, no. 8 (August 1973). Decades later, Rusch was sued for sexually abusing three twelve-year-old girls at the private school he taught at, so his ability to assess an adult female musician might be biased. Priscilla DeGregory, "Three Women Accuse Ex-Private School Teacher of Sexual Abuse: Suit," *New York Post*, July 30, 2020, https://nypost.com/2020/07/30/three-women-accuse-ex-private-school-teacher-of-sexual-abuse-suit/.

17. Leonard Feather, "3 Groups in 'New Directions,'" *Los Angeles Times*, November 6, 1973.

18. Purusha Hickson, *Journey to Turiya: One Yogi's Path to the Transcendental Teachings of Swamini Turiyasangitananda* (Stretch 4 Success, 2024), 16–17.

19. Hickson, *Journey to Turiya*, 16–17.

20. Hickson, *Journey to Turiya*, 16–17.

21. Santana, *The Universal Tone*, 349–351.

22. Santana, *The Universal Tone*, 365–366.

23. *Down Beat*, June 6, 1974.

24. Santana, *The Universal Tone*, 365–366.

25. Wayne Shorter and Joe Zawinul, "Blindfold Test," *Down Beat*, May 8, 1975, 25.

26. *Calgary Herald*, December 6, 1974.

27. Robert Christgau, "Devadip Carlos Santana/Turiya Alice Coltrane," accessed July 14, 2025, https://www.robertchristgau.com/get_artist.php?id=4779.

28. Chris Heath, "The Epic Life of Carlos Santana," *Rolling Stone*, March 16, 2000, https://www.rollingstone.com/music/music-news/the-epic-life-of-carlos-santana-89485/.

29. M. H. Miller, "The Canonization of John Coltrane," *New York Times*, December 3, 2021, https://www.nytimes.com/2021/12/03/t-magazine/john-coltrane-church.html.

30. In *A Love Supreme: 50 Years of the Coltrane Church*, Rev. King lists the various names: "the listening clinic, to the Yardbird Club, to the Yardbird Temple, to the Yardbird Temple Vanguard Revolutionary Church of the Hour, to the One Mind Temple Evolutionary Transitional Body of Christ, the Saint John Will I Am Coltrane African Orthodox Church."

31. Hickson, *Journey to Turiya*, 43–44.
32. Hickson, *Journey to Turiya*, 43–44.
33. Hickson, *Journey to Turiya*, 46.
34. Hickson, *Journey to Turiya*, 46.

Chapter Twenty: A Prophetic Song

1. Purusha Hickson, *Journey to Turiya: One Yogi's Path to the Transcendental Teachings of Swamini Turiyasangitananda* (Stretch 4 Success, 2024), 52.
2. Clea McDougall, "Alice in Wonder & Awe," *Ascent*, Spring 2006, https://ascent magazine.com/articles.aspx%3FarticleID=185&page=read&subpage=past&issueID=29.html.
3. McDougall, "Alice in Wonder & Awe."
4. Shankari C. Adams, *Portrait of Devotion: The Spiritual Life of Alice Coltrane Swamini Turiyasangitananda* (self-published, 2016), 84.
5. Radha Botofasina, interview with author, October 2015.
6. Radha Botofasina, interview with author, October 2015.
7. Ed Michel, email interview with author, 2024.
8. McDougall, "Alice in Wonder & Awe."
9. There is some discrepancy on which concert Adams might have attended. In her book she says it was 1975, but she told the *New York Times* the concert was in Berkeley, which would have been in 1972.
10. Adams, *Portrait of Devotion*, introduction.
11. Adams, *Portrait of Devotion*, introduction.
12. A. C. Turiyasangitananda, *Divine Revelations* (Avatar Book Institute, 1995), 86.
13. Adams, *Portrait of Devotion*, 28.
14. When a divine edict ordaining occurs, it's mostly by wandering mendicants, who don orange robes and live their lives as renunciates.
15. "Spiritual Wealth," *Integral Yoga Magazine*, Fall 2005, https://integralyoga magazine.org/divine-music-the-spiritual-journey-of-alice-coltrane/.
16. Turiyasangitananda, *Divine Revelations*, 122.
17. "Spiritual Wealth."
18. Britt Robson, "Universal Consciousness: The Spiritual Awakening of Alice Coltrane," Red Bull Music Academy, May 3, 2016, https://daily.redbullmusicacademy.com/2016/05/universal-consciousness.
19. Thulani Davis, liner notes for *Turiya Sings: Kirtan*, Impulse, 2021, LP.
20. Turiyasangitananda, *Divine Revelations*, 87.
21. Ed Michel, email interview with author, 2024.
22. Baker Bigsby, interview with author, September 17, 2024.
23. Her old Premiers bandmate and boyfriend George Bohanon also arranged horns on the session date.
24. "Galaxy in Turiya: Alice Coltrane with Strings," California Festival, accessed February 28, 2025, https://www.cafestival.org/excursions/alice-coltrane/.
25. Turiyasangitananda, liner notes for *Eternity*, Warner Bros., 1976, LP.
26. Alice Coltrane is thanked for her "time and kindness" along with 150 other names.

27. Radha Botofasina, interview with author, July 2024.

28. Radha Botofasina further explained: "I was like, 'What does she mean he wanted that F?' When I actually started learning 'If It's Magic,' every time we'd go to this F chord, instead of playing it as a regular F, I would put this thing in position and make it look like an F minor with an extra thing on it, so it kind of had this heart-wrenching type of thing. I said, 'Oh, that's what she was talking about!'"

29. By August of the next year, Riperton would receive a breast cancer diagnosis and undergo a mastectomy, passing away from the cancer on July 12, 1979, at the young age of thirty-one.

30. Ultimately, the harp part was performed by another Detroit legend who also dated back to Coltrane's early days on the scene, Dorothy Ashby, who rendered a beautiful performance on "If It's Magic." Ashby's services were in demand during that era, playing on albums by Bill Withers, Earth, Wind & Fire, and Minnie Riperton.

31. Adams, *Portrait of Devotion*, introduction.

32. Hickson, *Journey to Turiya*, 59.

33. Hickson, *Journey to Turiya*, 55.

34. Nate Chinen, "Recalling the Music and the Spirit of a 'Mother of Many,'" *New York Times*, May 19, 2007.

35. Robert Palmer, "California Soul Ends 4-Night Run," *New York Times*, March 2, 1976.

36. Radha Botofasina, interview with author, October 2015.

37. *Down Beat*, November 4, 1976.

38. *The Post-Star* (Glens Falls, NY), August 7, 1976.

39. *Los Angeles Sentinel*, May 13, 1976.

40. *New Pittsburgh Courier*, April 24, 1976.

41. Peter Goddard, "A Gentle Coltrane Extension," *Toronto Star*, May 22, 1976.

42. Ed Michel, email interview with author, 2024.

43. A 1966 *New York Times* article noted the groups of young people who had gathered for the group chant. It was the dawn of "Krishna Consciousness" and the Hare Krishna movement in the United States. And like Satchidananda, Prabhupada also enjoyed a certain cultural cachet with big rock acts like the Grateful Dead and Big Brother & the Holding Company performing at his festivals. Even the Beatles were fans, with George Harrison going on to produce an album by the Radha Krishna Temple and a single that hit #11 on the UK charts.

44. Alice Coltrane, *Monument Eternal*, Vedantic Book Press, 1977, 33.

45. Hickson, *Journey to Turiya*, 73–74.

46. Hickson, *Journey to Turiya*, 73–74.

47. The organ-drums duet doesn't quite recall his father's charged duets with Rashied Ali on *Interstellar Space* so much as the gentle, nurturing, familial sense of play captured by Ornette Coleman with his then-ten-year-old son Denardo playing drums on the 1966 album *The Empty Foxhole*.

Chapter Twenty-One: Monument Eternal

1. A. C. Turiyasangitananda, *Divine Revelations* (Avatar Book Institute, 1995), 106.

2. *Hartford Courant*, February 27, 1977.

3. *Down Beat*, July 14, 1977.

4. Franya J. Berkman, *Monument Eternal* (Wesleyan University Press, 2010), 79.

5. Such Hindu chanting has become very popular as well. A number of American artists with Sanskrit spiritual names have robust careers: Krishna Das, Ram Das, Jai Utal, and Ma Chetan Jyoti. Krishna Das videos on YouTube can top twenty million views.

6. Satyaraja Dasa, "Highest Song of Bliss: Alice Coltrane and the Maha-Mantra," Back to Godhead, accessed December 20, 2024, https://btg.krishna.com/highest-song-of-bliss-alice-coltrane-and-the-maha-mantra/.

7. Purusha Hickson, *Journey to Turiya: One Yogi's Path to the Transcendental Teachings of Swamini Turiyasangitananda* (Stretch 4 Success, 2024), 82.

8. Hickson, *Journey to Turiya*, 99.

9. Hickson, *Journey to Turiya*, 84.

10. Shankari C. Adams, *Portrait of Devotion: The Spiritual Life of Alice Coltrane Swamini Turiyasangitananda* (self-published, 2016), 35–36.

11. Adams, *Portrait of Devotion*, 37.

12. Michelle Coltrane also said that in addition to her mother learning to write in Sanskrit, she was also a gifted visual artist in rendering portraits of jazz artists like Dizzy Gillespie in pastels. A recent exhibition on Alice Coltrane at the Hammer Museum featured two lovely drawings of Krishna and Rama that she rendered.

13. Students who provided backing vocals and hand percussion included Brahmajyoti Lee, Chitsukhananda, Christine Soricelli, Dharmadhyaksa Dasa, Mahashakti Williams, Mangalananda Dasa, Mukunda Dasa, Purushattama Hickson, Rasangi Dasi, Saieshwar Roberts, Shankari Adams, Jagajivana Dasa, Sarada Devi King, and Sita Coltrane.

14. Adams, *Portrait of Devotion*, 74–75.

15. Foregrounding the powerful church-steeped vocals of students Mahashakti Williams and Sarada Devi King. Swamini's turn on Fender Rhodes for "Ghana Nila"—with Williams and Brahmajyoti Lee handling lead—is a particularly soulful gospel highlight, giving praise to Lord Krishna (aka "the child of the Yadavas, the blue-bodied Lord," as she explains in the liner notes).

16. Britt Robson, "Universal Consciousness: The Spiritual Awakening of Alice Coltrane," Red Bull Music Academy, May 3, 2016, https://daily.redbullmusicacademy.com/2016/05/universal-consciousness.

17. Clea McDougall, "Alice in Wonder & Awe," *Ascent*, Spring 2006, https://ascentmagazine.com/articles.aspx%3FarticleID=185&page=read&subpage=past&issueID=29.html.

18. Adams, *Portrait of Devotion*, 85.

19. Dasa, "Highest Song of Bliss: Alice Coltrane and the Maha-Mantra."

20. Adams, *Portrait of Devotion*, 80.

21. Radha Botofasina, interview with author, July 2024.

22. Radha Botofasina, interview with author, October 2015.

23. Radha Botofasina, interview with author, October 2015.

24. Alice Coltrane, *Monument Eternal*, Vedantic Book Press, 1977, 24–25.

25. Perhaps you can organize in your mind a way to recite an overly familiar text or song backward—"Happy Birthday" or "The Star-Spangled Banner"—but any attempt will make you understand the difficulty in reorienting a linear mind. Now try to say something backward at three hundred words a minute. Now try to sing "Happy Birthday" in a foreign language backward at that same speed. The mind will surely reel.

26. Radha Botofasina, interview with author, July 2024.

27. Robert Palmer, "East and West Meet in Jazz at the Beacon," *New York Times*, November 4, 1977, 64.

28. Adams, *Portrait of Devotion*, 85.

Chapter Twenty-Two: Highest Song of Bliss

1. A. C. Turiyasangitananda, *Divine Revelations* (Avatar Book Institute, 1995), 121–122.

2. Turiyasangitananda, *Divine Revelations*, 127.

3. Edwin Pouncey, "Alice Coltrane: Enduring Love," *The Wire*, April 2002.

4. Radha Botofasina, interview with author, October 2015.

5. Pouncey, "Alice Coltrane: Enduring Love."

6. Turiyasangitananda, liner notes for *Transfiguration*, Warner Bros., 1978, 2 LPs.

7. Harvey Siders, "Alice Coltrane in UCLA 'Women in Jazz' Concert," *Los Angeles Times*, April 19, 1978, 97.

8. Radha Botofasina, interview with author, October 2015.

9. Radha Botofasina, interview with author, October 2015.

10. A review of that concert referred to her as Coltrane-Turiyasangitananda and mistakenly reported how she had "probed various Far Eastern spiritual cults," then likened her flowing improvisations "to Indian raga, but there is no strong solo instrument such as John's soprano or tenor sax to break the monotony or otherwise guide the ensemble." The review also added that Coltrane-Turiyasangitananda had performed a spiritual at the request of her mother: "She announced her mother had asked her to play in a recent conversation. Her mother died many years ago, she commented—but the organ solo was a very lovely rendition." Philip Elwood, "Two (Boggling) Faces of Jazz," *San Francisco Examiner*, May 22, 1978, 28.

11. Radha Botofasina, interview with author, October 2015.

12. *Oakland Post*, June 11, 1978.

13. *Oakland Post*, June 11, 1978.

14. Turiyasangitananda, *Divine Revelations*, 131.

15. *Los Angeles Sentinel*, September 21, 1978, B4A.

16. Bob Blumenthal, "Singing the Blues for Lost Jazz Women," *Chicago Tribune*, October 22, 1978.

17. Blumenthal, "Singing the Blues for Lost Jazz Women."

18. Blumenthal, "Singing the Blues for Lost Jazz Women."

19. Blumenthal, "Singing the Blues for Lost Jazz Women."

20. Radha Botofasina, interview with author, October 2015.

21. Radha Botofasina, interview with author, October 2015.

22. Radha Botofasina, interview with author, October 2015.

23. Turiyasangitananda, *Divine Revelations*, 134.

Chapter Twenty-Three: Turiya Sings

1. A. C. Turiyasangitananda, *Divine Revelations* (Avatar Book Institute, 1995), 147.

2. Radha Botofasina, interview with author, October 2015.

3. Radha Botofasina, interview with author, October 2015.

4. Yugas last 432,000 years (1,200 divine years). Our present kali yuga phase will end in approximately 426,875 years.

5. Alice Coltrane, *Monument Eternal*, Vedantic Book Press, 1977, 42–43.

6. Coltrane, *Monument Eternal*, 48–49.

7. *Detroit Free Press*, May 4, 1980, 19.

8. Clea McDougall, "Alice in Wonder & Awe," *Ascent*, Spring 2006, https://ascentmagazine.com/articles.aspx%3FarticleID=185&page=read&subpage=past&issueID=29.html.

9. Marilyn also played keyboards and co-produced a band called Mighty Fire and arranged and produced the disco/funk/rap-adjacent group Flakes. Judging by that band's two album covers, there might have been some serious partying going on. One cover featured a silver spoon holding up corn flakes sprinkled with a white powder, and another had mounds of white flakes.

10. Anastasia Tsioulcas, "By Any Name, Alice Coltrane Turiyasangitananda Was a Force," NPR, May 21, 2017, https://www.npr.org/sections/therecord/2017/05/21/529124610/by-any-name-alice-coltrane-turiyasangitananda-was-a-force.

11. Ashley Kahn, "The Gift: Alice Coltrane and the Harp," *We Jazz*, no. 1 (Summer 2021).

12. Tsioulcas, "By Any Name, Alice Coltrane Turiyasangitananda Was a Force."

13. "Oral History of Jazz Harpist and Pianist from the U of I Leonard Feather Collection," University of Idaho, accessed December 10, 2024, https://www.lib.uidaho.edu/digital/coltrane/items/alice_13.html.

14. "Oral History of Jazz Harpist and Pianist from the U of I Leonard Feather Collection."

15. Purusha Hickson, *Journey to Turiya: One Yogi's Path to the Transcendental Teachings of Swamini Turiyasangitananda* (Stretch 4 Success, 2024), 132.

16. "Oral History of Jazz Harpist and Pianist from the U of I Leonard Feather Collection."

17. "Oral History of Jazz Harpist and Pianist from the U of I Leonard Feather Collection."

18. Around this same time, Bigsby recorded another album by a famous religious woman, Tammy Faye Bakker's *The Lord's on My Side*. Baker Bigsby, interview with author, September 17, 2024.

19. Baker Bigsby, interview with author, September 17, 2024.

20. Hickson, *Journey to Turiya*, 107–108.

21. Ravi Coltrane, liner notes for *Kirtan: Turiya Sings*, Impulse, 2021, 2 LPs.

22. Ed Michel, email interview with author, 2024.

23. "Musician's Widow Sues Church for Using Husband's Name," *Roanoke Times and World-News*, October 22, 1981, 9.

24. "Listings," *LA Weekly*, February 25, 1982.

25. Hickson, *Journey to Turiya*, 105–106.

26. Nina Simone with Stephen Cleary, *I Put a Spell on You* (Da Capo Press, 1991), 110.

27. Alan Light, *What Happened, Miss Simone?* (Crown Archetype, 2016), 216–220.

28. Radha Botofasina, interview with author, July 2024.

29. Hickson, *Journey to Turiya*, 105–106.

Chapter Twenty-Four: A New Sun

1. Other bhajans were recorded at that session that have not been officially released, including "Om Namah Sivaya," "Nam Kaho Bolo Re," "Vrindavana Radhe-Shyam," and "Yashoda Nandalala."

2. Baker Bigsby, interview with author, September 17, 2024.

3. At one point, Alice rendered a more synth-heavy version of *Turiya Sings* for the program that has never been officially released. Some estimate there are four slightly different versions of *Turiya Sings*.

4. Stephen Hill, liner notes for *Turiya Sings*, Avatar Book Institute, 1982, cassette.

5. Elzy Kolb, "Spiritual Coltrane," *The Record*, September 2006.

6. "Galaxy in Turiya: Alice Coltrane with Strings," California Festival, accessed February 28, 2025, https://www.cafestival.org/excursions/alice-coltrane/.

7. Surya Botofasina, interview with author, December 2024.

8. *Kirtan: Turiya Sings* is Ravi's approved version of the tape using the early version of the recording, without the voices, synthesizers, and strings.

9. In the early 1980s, she also printed up a series of little folios and pamphlets with titles like *Bouquet of Divine Wisdom, Devotional Music & Chanting, Infinite Truths, Spirituality in the Family*, and *Peace of Mind*. Some can be seen in the recent exhibition at the Hammer Museum in Los Angeles.

10. "Alice Coltrane Follows a Divine Path," *Oakland Tribune*, April 22, 1982, 37.

11. "Alice Coltrane Follows a Divine Path."

12. Derek Richardson, "Coltrane Still Shares a Powerful Vision," *Berkeley Gazette*, April 30, 1982, 23.

13. A. C. Turiyasangitananda, *Divine Revelations* (Avatar Book Institute, 1995), 191.

14. Radha Botofasina, interview with author, July 2024.

15. Surya Botofasina, interview with author, December 2024.

16. "Jazz Great's Son Killed," *Los Angeles Times*, August 10, 1982, 13.

17. Leonard Feather, "To John Coltrane's Family, His Spirit Is Very Much Alive," *Los Angeles Times*, July 31, 1982, 18.

18. "Oral History of Jazz Harpist and Pianist from the U of I Leonard Feather Collection," University of Idaho, accessed December 10, 2024, https://www.lib.uidaho.edu/digital/coltrane/items/alice_13.html.

19. Feather, "To John Coltrane's Family, His Spirit Is Very Much Alive."

20. Purusha Hickson, *Journey to Turiya: One Yogi's Path to the Transcendental Teachings of Swamini Turiyasangitananda* (Stretch 4 Success, 2024), 132.

21. Turiyasangitananda, *Divine Revelations*, 194.

22. "Jazz Great's Son Killed."

23. Hickson, *Journey to Turiya*, 133.

24. Shankari C. Adams, *Portrait of Devotion: The Spiritual Life of Alice Coltrane Swamini Turiyasangitananda* (self-published, 2016), 54–56.

25. In her book, Adams reported other instances where Swamini would "absorb karmic consequences of persons destined to leave this earth life," detailing head-on car collisions where students only suffered mild shock and abrasions rather than certain death. "One auto impact was so forceful that she had to astrally rehearse for two weeks in advance, to prepare for it," she wrote.

26. Radha Botofasina, interview with author, July 2024.

27. Radha Botofasina, interview with author, July 2024.

28. Adams, *Portrait of Devotion*, 54–56.

29. Radha Botofasina, interview with author, July 2024.

30. Adams, *Portrait of Devotion*, 57.

31. "Ustad Bismillah Khan* – Live Shehnai Performance at Chicago Orchestra Hall on September 25, 1982," Discogs, accessed July 14, 2025, https://www.discogs.com/release/9730662-Ustad-Bismillah-Khan-Live-Shehnai-Performance-At-Chicago-Orchestra-Hall-On-September-25-1982.

32. Turiyasangitananda, *Divine Revelations*, 195–199.

33. Turiyasangitananda, *Divine Revelations*, 203.

Chapter Twenty-Five: Each Second an Eternity

1. Alice Coltrane and Erin Christovale, eds., *Alice Coltrane, Monument Eternal* (Delmonico Books, 2025), 36.

2. "Eternal Peace ashram in the Chumash province" approximately, paying homage to the indigenous people who lived on the land centuries before.

3. Radha Botofasina, interview with author, July 2024.

4. Purusha Hickson, *Journey to Turiya: One Yogi's Path to the Transcendental Teachings of Swamini Turiyasangitananda* (Stretch 4 Success, 2024), 142.

5. Surya Botofasina, "Sai Anantam Ashram Memories," liner notes for *The Ecstatic Music of Alice Coltrane Turiyasangitananda*, Luaka Bop, 2017, 2 LPs.

6. Radha Botofasina, interview with author, July 2024.

7. Botofasina, liner notes for *The Ecstatic Music of Alice Coltrane Turiyasangitananda*.

8. Robert Palmer, "Alice Coltrane's First Concerts Here in 7 Years," *New York Times*, September 21, 1984.

9. Botofasina, liner notes for *The Ecstatic Music of Alice Coltrane Turiyasangitananda*.

10. Franya J. Berkman, *Monument Eternal* (Wesleyan University Press, 2010), 102–104.

11. Botofasina, liner notes for *The Ecstatic Music of Alice Coltrane Turiyasangitananda*.

12. Hickson, *Journey to Turiya*, 179.

13. Hickson, *Journey to Turiya*, 179–181.

14. Shankari C. Adams, *Portrait of Devotion: The Spiritual Life of Alice Coltrane Swamini Turiyasangitananda* (self-published, 2016), 72–73.

15. Botofasina, liner notes for *The Ecstatic Music of Alice Coltrane Turiyasangitananda*.

16. Adams, *Portrait of Devotion*, 76–77.

17. Adams, *Portrait of Devotion*, 76–77.

18. This spiritual became widely known after publication in *The Second Book of Negro Spirituals* (1926), compiled by the brothers James Weldon Johnson and Rosamond Johnson. The tune gained further popularity through a variety of choral arrangements; it can be found in many hymnals dating after 1955, when it was published in the *American Presbyterian/Reformed Hymnbook*.

19. Coltrane and Christovale, *Alice Coltrane, Monument Eternal*, 123.

20. "TV Series Planned," *Los Angeles Sentinel*, January 9, 1986, C10.

21. Stuart Swezey, interview with author, September 2024. Born John Roland Redd, Korla Pandit was Liberace before Liberace and had a TV show. Korla played organ and also had a television show in 1949. It wasn't known at the time, but Pandit was a Black man who couldn't get success because of racial discrimination at the time. So instead, he used makeup and a turban to pass as a "mysterious" Hindu personality.

22. Four episodes were made available for streaming on the Criterion Collection channel and screened as part of the Hammer Museum's Alice Coltrane exhibition in early 2025. Miraculously, the Coltrane family archive recently turned up an additional thirteen episodes, some seventeen episodes in total, set for release as *Eternity's Pillar*, a two Blu-ray disc set from the Exotic Material imprint in the UK.

Chapter Twenty-Six: The Coltrane Legacy

1. Francis Davis, "Songs of the Father," *Philadelphia Inquirer*, September 22, 1996.

2. Kathy O'Toole, "UC Shantytown Nails Apartheid," *Oakland Tribune*, April 1, 1986.

3. A. C. Turiyasangitananda, *Divine Revelations* (Avatar Book Institute, 1995), 189.

4. Turiyasangitananda, *Divine Revelations*, 218.

5. Shankari C. Adams, *Portrait of Devotion: The Spiritual Life of Alice Coltrane Swamini Turiyasangitananda* (self-published, 2016), 58.

6. Radha Botofasina, interview with author, July 2024.

7. Radha Botofasina, interview with author, July 2024.

8. Radha Botofasina, interview with author, July 2024.

9. Radha Botofasina, interview with author, July 2024.

10. Bob Pool, "Slain Boy Eulogized as Police Seek Clues," *Los Angeles Times*, April 13, 1986, 32.

11. Turiyasangitananda, *Divine Revelations*, 235.

12. Alice Coltrane and Erin Christovale, eds., *Alice Coltrane, Monument Eternal* (Delmonico Books, 2025), 40.

13. Surya Botofasina, "Sai Anantam Ashram Memories," liner notes for *The Ecstatic Music of Alice Coltrane Turiyasangitananda*, Luaka Bop, 2017, 2 LPs.

14. Baker Bigsby, interview with author, September 17, 2024.

15. Surya Botofasina, interview with author, December 2024.

16. Surya Botofasina, interview with author, December 2024.

17. Botofasina, liner notes for *The Ecstatic Music of Alice Coltrane Turiyasangitananda*. In this quote, Surya remembered it being during the *Use Your Illusion* sessions, but the band didn't record at Rumbo for those album sessions.

18. It would be hard to imagine two albums more diametrically opposed than these: one an homage to God, the other to drugs, violence, paranoia, and sex. Axl Rose even took a groupie into the studio, her orgasm audible on "Rocket Queen."

19. And the fifth anniversary of John Jr.'s passing.

20. "Alice Coltrane—Interview (Jazz Jamboree, 1987)," YouTube, https://youtu.be/Gk6SLbAnbDE.

21. *Los Angeles Times*, September 1, 1987.

22. Robert Palmer, "Jazz: Coltrane Tribute," *New York Times*, September 25, 1987.

23. Palmer, "Jazz: Coltrane Tribute."

24. Adams, *Portrait of Devotion*, 80.

25. Botofasina, liner notes for *The Ecstatic Music of Alice Coltrane Turiyasangitananda*.

26. Because of the profanity and drug use in the film, in 1989 she denied director Spike Lee's request to title his next film *A Love Supreme*. Instead, he went with *Mo' Better Blues*.

27. Darlene Donloe, "Living with the Spirit and Legacy of John Coltrane," *Ebony*, March 1989.

28. Adams, *Portrait of Devotion*, 82.

29. Surya Botofasina, interview with author, December 2024.

30. Dolores Brandon, "The Evolution of Alice Coltrane," WBAI, New York, 1988.

31. Brandon, "The Evolution of Alice Coltrane."

32. Turiyasangitananda, *Divine Revelations*, 254.

33. Adams, *Portrait of Devotion*, 87. Interestingly enough, their birthdays are one day apart in August.

Chapter Twenty-Seven: The Divine Fragrance of a Dedicated Life

1. Baker Bigsby, interview with author, September 17, 2024.

2. Surya Botofasina, liner notes for *The Ecstatic Music of Alice Coltrane Turiyasangitananda*.

3. Surya Botofasina, interview with author, December 2024.

4. Radha Botofasina, interview with author, July 2024.

5. Shankari C. Adams, *Portrait of Devotion: The Spiritual Life of Alice Coltrane Swamini Turiyasangitananda* (self-published, 2016), 91.

6. Don Heckman, "A Long, Slow 'Trane Festival," *Los Angeles Times*, October 1, 1991.

7. Radha Botofasina, interview with author, July 2024.

8. Ron Russell, "Bakewell Vows to Continue Shutdown of Non-Black Work Sites," *Los Angeles Times*, July 24, 1992, 30.

9. Purusha Hickson, interview with author, 2024.

10. Steven Ellison, interview with author, February 2025.

11. Surya Botofasina, interview with author, December 2024.

12. Adams, *Portrait of Devotion*, 50–51.

13. "Black Woman Swami Adds a Uniqueness of Valley's 1st Hindu Temple," *Los Angeles Times*, May 25, 1992.

14. "Black Woman Swami Adds a Uniqueness of Valley's 1st Hindu Temple."

15. Purusha Hickson, interview with author, 2024.

16. Surya Botofasina, interview with author, December 2024.

17. Surya Botofasina, interview with author, December 2024.
18. Surya Botofasina, interview with author, December 2024.
19. A stone crucible used for fire sacrifice in ceremonies.
20. A. C. Turiyasangitananda, *Divine Revelations* (Avatar Book Institute, 1995), 299.
21. Turiyasangitananda, *Divine Revelations*, 307–313.
22. In addition to the students serving as choir, the tape also showcased two new singers. Mumbai-based vocalist Sairam Iyer had performed one year at the John Coltrane Festival, before being invited to the recording. His voice rises to the fore on the opening bhajan, "Nataraja," his powerful, dramatic delivery perfectly harmonized with Swamini's synthesizer work. And Turiya first encountered Sandhya Sanjana in Poland back in 1987 and invited her to perform on these bhajans, her voice arresting on the concluding piece, "Hara Siva."
23. Fred Jung, "A Fireside Chat with Ravi Coltrane," *Jazz Weekly*, accessed July 14, 2025, https://www.jazzweekly.com/interviews/coltrane.htm.

Chapter Twenty-Eight: Going Home

1. Shankari C. Adams, *Portrait of Devotion: The Spiritual Life of Alice Coltrane Swamini Turiyasangitananda* (self-published, 2016), 141.
2. Adams, *Portrait of Devotion*, 114–139.
3. Terry Gibbs with Cary Ginell, *Good Vibes: A Life in Jazz* (Scarecrow Press, 2003), 231.
4. Gibbs, *Good Vibes*, 232.
5. Terry Gibbs, interview with author, May 2024.
6. "Alice Coltrane," BBC Radio 3, January 20, 2001, https://citizeninsane.eu/interconnex/alicecoltrane.html.
7. In the *Guardian*, Four Tet cited *Journey in Satchidananda* as his favorite album: "The cover looked cool so I bought it. Then I went home and went, 'Oh my God.' It was what I had been looking for all my life: heavy rhythmic elements combined with melodic complexity…The album has a sense of madness to it, and I think it proves that if you make a bold move people will understand it." *The Guardian*, December 12, 2003, 77.
8. Adams, *Portrait of Devotion*, 151.
9. Surya Botofasina, interview with author, December 2024.
10. Steven Ellison, interview with author, February 2025.
11. Peter Goodman, "A Haven, a Home, for Trane," *Newsday* (Suffolk Edition), March 28, 2004, 89.
12. Obituary, *Los Angeles Times*, August 25, 2002, 124.
13. "Jazz Listings," *New York Times*, October 20, 2006.
14. Ashley Kahn, *The House That Trane Built: The Story of Impulse Records* (Granta Books, 2006), 281.
15. Unfortunately, albums like *World Galaxy*, *Lord of Lords*, and *Huntington Ashram Monastery* only saw CD release in Japan. In the United States, they were released as two-for-one comps.
16. Kahn, *The House That Trane Built*, 281.
17. Peter Goodman, "A Haven, a Home, for Trane," *Newsday*, March 28, 2004, 90.

18. "Alice Coltrane Interview," Stuart Nicholson, November 3, 2004, https://stuartnicholson.uk/wp-content/uploads/2017/03/Clike-Here-To-Go-To-Alice-Coltrane-Interview.pdf.

19. Kahn, *The House That Trane Built*, 281.

20. Especially considering that Alice's final album statement was a white-hot forty-one-minute version of it.

21. Also known as "This Train Is Bound for Glory," it was first documented in the early 1920s, then became part of the lexicon thanks to a popular recording by Sister Rosetta Tharpe in 1939.

22. "Alice Coltrane Interview."

23. Adams, *Portrait of Devotion*, 66.

24. *Billboard*, October 14, 2004.

25. "Alice Coltrane Interview."

26. Radha Botofasina, interview with author, July 2024.

27. Surya Botofasina, "Sai Anantam Ashram Memories," liner notes for *The Ecstatic Music of Alice Coltrane Turiyasangitananda*, Luaka Bop, 2017, 2 LPs.

28. Steven Ellison, interview with author, February 2025.

29. Steven Ellison, interview with author, February 2025.

30. Steven Ellison, interview with author, 2014.

31. Purusha Hickson, *Journey to Turiya: One Yogi's Path to the Transcendental Teachings of Swamini Turiyasangitananda* (Stretch 4 Success, 2024), 207. At Maha Shivaratri, a Hindu festival dedicated to Shiva held every year, Sai Baba would cough up a golden, oval-shaped object called a *lingam*.

32. Adams, *Portrait of Devotion*, 109.

33. Susan L. Taylor, "A Love Supreme with Alice Coltrane," *Essence*, September 2006.

34. Carlton Wilkinson, "A Love Supreme for Alice Coltrane," *Asbury Park Press*, October 15, 2006.

35. To date, this music has not seen release. It's an outlier in Coltrane's discography, a dense lyrical work in four languages that would be difficult to navigate without a libretto. It sounds and feels like a liturgical recording, like what you would buy at the end of Mass at a church. Hurtak's benedictions are always in the foreground, bringing to mind what Coltrane would have sounded like as a church organist, comping to accompany the pastor's sermon. Yet the downside is that it also relegates Coltrane's music to the background. Underwhelming on disc, in concert, her son Ravi Coltrane has performed evocative renditions of this music that reveal the true profundity of this final work.

36. "Dr. J.J. Hurtak and Dr. Desiree Hurtak: Social Scientists and Explorers of the Future," accessed November 28, 2024, https://hurtak.com/.

37. Mark Stryker, "Alice Coltrane Makes a Rare Appearance on Stage," *Detroit Free Press*, September 22, 2006.

38. Botofasina, liner notes for *The Ecstatic Music of Alice Coltrane Turiyasangitananda*.

39. Adams, *Portrait of Devotion*, 78.

40. Ben Ratliff, "Communing with the Astral, Spiritual and Tuneful," *New York Times*, October 24, 2006.

41. Ratliff, "Communing with the Astral, Spiritual and Tuneful."

42. Ratliff, "Communing with the Astral, Spiritual and Tuneful."

43. Carlton Wilkinson, "Smallest Band Delivers During Alice Coltrane Show," *Asbury Park Press*, October 22, 2006.

44. Jim Harrington, "Fans Share 'A Love Supreme' with Alice Coltrane and Son," *Oakland Tribune*, November 7, 2006.

45. Bill Milkowski, "Ravi Coltrane: Digging Deeper," *Jazz Times*, March 1, 2009, https://jazztimes.com/features/ravi-coltrane-digging-deeper/.

46. Botofasina, liner notes for *The Ecstatic Music of Alice Coltrane Turiyasangitananda*.

47. Botofasina, liner notes for *The Ecstatic Music of Alice Coltrane Turiyasangitananda*.

48. Alice Coltrane and Erin Christovale, eds., *Alice Coltrane, Monument Eternal* (Delmonico Books, 2025), 37.

49. Andy Beta, "Cover Story: Flying Lotus Confronts Death," Fader, October 1, 2014, https://www.thefader.com/2014/10/01/flying-lotus-youre-dead-interview-cover-story

Epilogue

1. Jody Rosen, "The Day the Music Burned," *New York Times*, June 11, 2019, https://www.nytimes.com/2019/06/11/magazine/universal-fire-master-recordings.html.

2. Purusha Hickson, *Journey to Turiya: One Yogi's Path to the Transcendental Teachings of Swamini Turiyasangitananda* (Stretch 4 Success, 2024), 272.

3. The title itself stems from Ellison mishearing one of her recorded discourses: "Once this earthly experience is over, we won't be wearing our costumes anymore, playing parts in this 'cosmic drama.'" Chris Martins, "Flying Lotus Rising," *LA Weekly*, May 13, 2010, https://www.laweekly.com/flying-lotus-rising/.

4. The resident DJs there, like Mark "Frosty" McNeil, Carlos Niño, and Zach Cowie, all helped to spread the word about the ashram tapes even further.

5. Mark "Frosty" McNeil, "The Ashram Tapes of Alice Coltrane," Dublab, April 7, 2011, https://www.dublab.com/archive/rbma-radio-saved-from-the-fire-the-ashram-tapes-of-alice-coltrane-by-frosty/.

6. Ryan Parry, "EXCLUSIVE: Man Who Killed My Son 30 Years Ago Must Face the Death Penalty—Father Speaks Out as Sex Murder of Miguel, Six, Who Vanished After School Is Finally Solved," *Daily Mail*, November 3, 2015, https://www.dailymail.co.uk/news/article-3301156/Man-killed-son-30-years-ago-face-death-penalty-father-speaks-cold-case-review-finally-solves-sex-murder-six-year-old-Miguel-Antero-vanished-school.html

7. On the album's cover, there's a young girl in a neon pink dress, seated to Swamini's right. Her name is Amala Ratna Zandile Dlamini and she lived on the property for only a few years before her family relocated. Some years later, she found pop superstardom as Doja Cat.

Index

A&R Studios, 106
ABC Records, 192, 274
Adams, Pepper, 54, 60–61
Adams, Shankari
    background of, xi, xviii
    books by, xviii, 373
    recollections of, 20, 29–30, 49, 59, 84, 182, 199, 202–203, 290–291, 295, 298–299, 304–305, 308–309, 311, 340, 342–344, 348–351, 361, 367–368, 373, 384
Adderley, Cannonball, 70, 74
Adderley, Nat, 99
Adler, Murray, 263, 266, 275, 280–281, 292, 306
"Affinity," 314–316
"Africa," 225, 244, 279, 329, 338, 382
Africa/Brass (John Coltrane), 89–91, 104, 106, 110–111, 123–124, 149, 224, 330
The African Methodist Pocket Hymn Book (Allen), 17
"Afro Blue," 111, 129
Agrawal, Ash, 376
"Ah! So Pure," 39
Ailey, Alvin, xviii, 251–252, 275
Aja (Steely Dan), 265
Akiyoshi, Toshiko, 319
"Alabama," 118–119, 129, 188, 234
Alcindor, Lew, 204
Alexander, Mary, 176, 183
Alhambra Theater, 77
Ali, Rashied
    Alice Coltrane and, 189–191, 204–205, 225, 227, 230, 249, 346, 359

early years of, 143
    John Coltrane and, 143, 156–161, 166, 169–176
Alice Coltrane, Monument Eternal (exhibition), 389–390
Alice Coltrane Quartet, 242–252, 296
Alice McLeod Trio, 56–57
Allen, Richard, 17
Allen, Steve, 62–63
"Altruvista," 174
"Always," 111–112
American Federation of Musicians, 24
Amnesiac (Radiohead), 375
AMOK Assault Videos (tapes), 351
Amos 'n' Andy (radio program), 11
"Anastasia," 66
Anastasia (film), 66
Anderson, Eddie "Rochester," 11
André 3000, xx
Andrews, Joel, 307
"Andromeda's Suffering," 267
"Angel of Air," 281
"Angel of Sunlight," 281
"Angel of Water," 281
"The Ankh of Amen-Ra," 249
Antero, Ana, 354–356
Antero, Enid, 354
Antero, Miguel, 354–356, 388
Antero, Shankara, 354–356
"Anthropology," 57
Appetite for Destruction (Guns N' Roses), 357
Archie Shepp–Bill Dixon Quartet (Shepp and Dixon), 148

Armstrong, Louis, 23, 144, 386
Art Blakey & the Jazz Messengers, 60, 120
Ascension (John Coltrane), 150–151, 154–155, 161, 171, 243
Ashby, Dorothy, 68, 186, 204
  Dorothy Ashby Trio, 68
Ashford and Simpson, 296
Astaire, Fred, 193
Atlantic Records, 82–83, 88
Atmosphères (Ligeti), 267
Austin, Will, 84–85
Autobiography of a Yogi (Yogananda), 130, 146, 309
Ayler, Albert
  Alice Coltrane and, 232
  death of, 235
  early years of, 98, 120, 143
  John Coltrane and, 120, 143, 148, 156, 161–162, 181, 386
  soundtrack by, 150
Ayler, Don, 161

Bach, Johann Sebastian, 40, 44, 77, 130, 269, 325
Back to the Future (film), 385
Baker, Chet, 38, 78
Bakewell, Danny, 366
Baraka, Amiri, 142–143
Barbieri, Gato, 274, 278
Barneke, Wally, 221
Bartz, Gary, 222, 224
Basie, Count, 34, 386
"Battle at Armageddon," 249
"Battle Hymn of the Republic," 18
Beach Boys, 238
Beacon Theatre, 296–297, 310–311
Beat (Brooks), 94
Beatles, xiii, 152, 265
Beckett, L. C., 131
"Been on a Train," 251
Beethoven, Ludwig van, 40, 44, 77, 170
Belafonte, Harry, 47, 106
Belle Isle Riots, 14–16, 23, 30, 35, 69, 117, 184, 366–367

Benson (TV show), 349
Benson, George, 296–297
Berg, Alban, 123
Berger, Daniel, 167–168
Bergman, Ingrid, 66
Berkeley University, 264
Berkman, Franya
  background of, xi, xviii
  books by, xviii
  recollections of, 17, 21, 26, 37, 43–44, 51, 81, 92, 101, 107, 128–129, 162–163, 184, 302
Berlin, Irving, 111
Bernardot, Joseph "Iasos," 307
Berry, Chuck, 386
Best of John Coltrane: His Greatest Years, Vol. 2 (John Coltrane), 274
Bhagavad Gita, 155–156, 187, 214, 298, 304, 324, 346, 364, 384
Bhatnagar, Shyam, 219
Bible, 16–17, 40, 131–132, 140, 346
Bigsby, Baker, 259–260, 292, 314, 328, 333, 335, 351, 357, 363–364, 391
Birdland, 24, 48, 101, 106–112, 129, 136, 138, 173
Birth of the Cool (Miles Davis), 74
Björk, 375
Black Arts Festival, 224–225, 244–245
Black Arts Repertory Theater/School, 143
Black Bottom, 5–6, 11, 13–18, 35–36, 69, 73–74
Black Journal (TV show), 359
"The Black Liberation Movement Suite," 224
Blackextravaganza, 242
Blackwell, Ed, 242, 253
Blair, John, 248
Blair, William, 127
Blake, Arthur "Blind," 22
Blakey, Art, 60, 120, 359, 386
Blavatsky, Madame, 97, 304
"Blessed Assurance," 384
Bley, Carla, 319
Bley, Paul, 147

Blue Bird Inn, 46–47, 57, 60, 64, 70–71, 74, 79
Blue Moods (Miles Davis), 96
"Blue Nile," 223, 227, 378, 387
Blue Note, 105, 222, 224
Blue Train (John Coltrane), 71
"Blues Minor," 329–330
Blumenthal, Bob, 273, 319–320
Bohanon, George, 64–69, 71–72, 92–95, 98–99, 374
Bohemian Club, 60
Bono, xix
"Boogie Chillen," 22
Boone, Pat, 66
Borges, Jorge Luis, 91
Botofasina, Radha Renee
  early years of, xx, 288–289, 294–296, 308–310
  recollections of, xvii–xviii, 199, 241, 288–289, 294–296, 308–310, 315–317, 320–324, 337, 340–341, 343–345, 353–355, 364–366, 379, 391
  son of, xx, 320
Botofasina, Surya
  early years of, xx, 320, 335–337
  mother of, xx, 320
  recollections of, 335, 337, 344–349, 357, 360, 362–364, 370, 375–376, 388–389
Boulanger, Nadia, 76
Bowles, Thomas "Beans," 74
Boyd, Herb, 12, 14–15, 22
Boyton, Eunice, 3–4
Brackeen, Joanne, 329
Brand, Julius, 248
Brandon, Dolores, 362
Brazil, Joe, 71, 155
Breezin' (Benson), 296–297, 314
The Brian Lehrer Show (radio program), xx
The Bridge (Rollins), 104
"Bring Back My Bonnie to Me," 55–56
Brody, Richard, 123
Brooks, Roy, 66, 93–94, 346

Brown, Devora, 67
Brown, Jack, 67, 69
Brown, Marion, 149–151, 174, 274–275
Brown, Patti, 329
Buddha, Gautama, 191, 304
Buffalo State University, 244–245
Building 6197, 385–386
Burbank Studios, 292, 296, 305
Burleigh, Harry, 270
Burrell, Billy, 37
Burrell, Kenny, 26, 35, 37, 53–54, 61, 374
Byrd, Donald, 35, 37, 60, 78
Byrds, xix, 90
Byrne, David, xx, 388

Café Au Go Go, 230
Cal Arts, 353, 358
California Institute of the Arts, 375
Calloway, Cab, 68
Campbell, Roy Jr., 288, 308
Capitol Records, 377
Carnegie Hall, 54, 189–190, 210, 242–244, 288–289, 346
Carroll, Barbara, 47, 329
Carter, Betty, 34, 143, 172
Carter, Jesse, 65, 67–68
Carter, Joe, 65, 67–69, 71–72
Carter, Ron, 204–205, 220–223
Carvin, Michael, 311
Cass Technical, 26, 38, 53, 64, 186
Cavaliere, Felix, 211, 220
Cavalleria rusticana (opera), 39
Cayce, Edgar, 97
"Celebration of Ascension," 384
Center for African Culture, 176
Chadbourne, Eugene, 260, 281
Chambers, Paul, 35, 37, 53–54, 61, 70
Chancler, Leon Ndugu, 279
Change (magazine), 166
Chariot Festival, 308, 318
Charles, Ray, 89, 256, 364
Charles, Teddy, 96

Index

Charlie Parker with Strings (Parker), 249
Chase, Joan, 276
Chatham, Rhys, 231
Cherry, Don, 98, 156, 222
Chidananda, Swami, 204, 206
"Chim Chim Cher-ee," 148
Chinmoy, Sri, 276
Chopin, Frédéric, 37
Christgau, Robert, 281
Christmas and the Beads of Sweat (Nyro), 225–226
Christy's Minstrels, 55
Church of God in Christ, 18, 29, 41–42, 84
Clapton, Eric, xix
Clark, Sonny, 37–38, 96
Clarke, Kenny "Klook," 25, 34, 78–79
Classic Quartet, 154–164, 224, 234, 257, 261–264, 268. *See also* John Coltrane Quartet
Closeness (Haden), 378
Coast Recorders, 160, 261
Cobb, Jimmy, 70
Cobo Hall, 160
Coda (magazine), 196, 245
Cole, Nat King, 113
Coleman, Ornette, 80, 91, 98, 119, 148–150, 162, 182, 228, 248, 253–257, 319, 330–331, 386
Collegiate Jazz Festival, 108
Collins, Addie Mae, 117
Collins, Mabel, 131
Coltrane, Alice
  albums by, xii–xv, xvii, xix–xx, 156, 191–192, 196–197, 203–205, 222–224, 228, 231–233, 238, 241–242, 247–254, 258–261, 266–277, 281–284, 290–294, 297–299, 301–302, 305–307, 311, 313–314, 318–319, 330, 333–335, 356–357, 364, 368–369, 371, 377–378, 381–383, 390
  ashram tapes by, 356, 363–364, 371, 387–388, 391
  astral projections of, 29–31, 200–203, 213
  birth of, 3–4
  books by, xvii–xviii, 198–199, 202, 230, 287, 290–291, 304, 308–310, 317–318, 324, 333, 335–337, 342, 350, 353–354, 362, 370–371
  chants and, 126, 150, 155, 188, 205, 250, 260, 293, 297–306, 311, 316, 327–328, 334–351, 363–364, 371, 382–383, 390
  childhood of, 3–22, 28–31
  as church pianist, 20–22, 28, 38, 55–57
  death of, xvi–xviii, 383–384
  depression of, 184–185, 197–206, 209–213, 242
  early years of, 3–31, 33–43, 49–71, 73–85, 87–113
  education of, 3–4, 19–20, 28, 38–43, 47–52, 59
  exhibition honoring, 389–390
  final years of, 378–384
  first recording by, 67–68
  first solo concert by, 189–191
  first solo recording by, 174
  first writing credit, 94–95
  funeral for, 384
  going home, 373–384
  healing others, 373–374
  Hinduism and, xvii, 155–156, 173, 187–188, 211–235, 250, 276–278, 288–295, 298–311, 324, 346, 350, 353–357, 364–375, 380–381, 384
  home studio of, 174, 186–187, 190, 204, 220–223, 226–231, 248, 255–257
  honoring, 375–377
  illness of, 378–379, 383–384
  jam sessions and, 93–94, 98–100, 220–221, 277–279
  John Coltrane and, 80, 83–84, 99–113, 117–177
  legacy of, 353–362
  lost recordings of, 386
  marriages of, 75–82, 121–177

Index

meditation and, 9, 132–133,
  137–142, 150–153, 176–177, 183–185,
  195–203, 216–217, 239–253,
  257–258, 264–271, 277–284,
  288–309, 317–328, 337–350,
  355–361, 370–384
musical style of, xii–xx, 80–81, 87–88,
  91–95, 102–108, 157–174, 185–193,
  195–198, 220–231, 242–270, 302
in New York City, 59–61, 98–99
out-of-body experiences of, 29–31,
  200–203, 213
in Paris, 75–82
quartet of, 220–231, 242–252, 296,
  306, 313–317, 357, 374, 381
riot recovery and, 366–367
spiritual name of, xiv–xviii, 179–284,
  287–384, 388–392
spirituality of, xiv–xviii, xxi, 127–133,
  139–163, 173, 179–284, 287–311,
  313–351, 353–392
suffering of, 184–185, 197–206,
  209–213, 230, 245, 291, 340–343,
  378–379
tours and, 65–71, 101–108, 113,
  122–123, 159–162, 165–172,
  237–248, 252–254, 261, 264, 275,
  278–280, 288, 310–311, 313–317,
  330–331, 346, 358–360, 381–383
see also Turiya; Turiyasangitananda
Coltrane, Alice Gertrude Blair, 122, 145, 310
Coltrane, John
  albums by, xii–xiv, xix, 71, 80–83,
    88–91, 104–112, 123–124, 129, 135,
    138–142, 147–156, 161, 167–171, 174,
    177, 182, 187–188, 191–192, 196,
    224, 241, 243, 261–264, 273–275,
    282, 329–330, 376
  Alice Coltrane and, 99–113, 117–177
  death of, 177
  early years of, 38, 70–85, 87–113
  final years of, 150–177
  funeral for, 181–182
  Hinduism and, 155–156, 173
  home studio of, 174
  honoring, 360–361, 365, 368–369, 374
  illness of, 176–177
  jam sessions and, 98–100, 154–155
  legacy of, 353–362
  lost recordings of, 386
  marriages of, 109, 121–177
  meditation and, 132–133, 137–142,
    150–153, 176–177, 317–318
  musical style of, xii–xiv, xxi, 70–71,
    80–84, 88–92, 107–112, 118–176,
    196, 234, 358
  postage stamp of, 371
  quartet of, 80, 108–112, 136–164, 224,
    234, 257, 261–264, 268, 273
  quintet of, 102, 160, 171–175, 330
  spirituality of, 127–131, 138–145,
    152–156, 171, 173
  tours and, 80, 83, 112–113, 122–125,
    154–155, 161–162, 165–172
Coltrane, John Jr.
  birth of, 136
  death of, 340–343
  early years of, 136, 138, 143, 154, 174,
    202, 255, 287, 292, 300–302
  playing music, 300, 327–329, 337–339
Coltrane, Michelle
  albums by, 371
  birth of, 82
  early years of, 75–76, 82, 87–88, 94, 99,
    103–104, 121, 136–144, 174, 202,
    255–259, 287, 293, 300, 326
  playing music, 300–302, 317, 368, 371
  recollections of, 75–76, 103–104,
    144, 223–225, 255–256, 259, 263,
    271–274, 292–293, 326, 334–335,
    356, 383–384, 388
Coltrane, Oran
  birth of, 174
  early years of, 174, 202, 255, 287, 292, 358
  playing music, 264, 327–329, 337–339,
    358, 368, 374, 378
  recollections of, 292, 382
  tours and, 358–360, 368

438 Index

Coltrane, Ravi
  albums by, 371
  bands of, 378
  birth of, 154
  early years of, 154, 174, 202, 255–257, 287, 292, 326, 353, 358
  playing music, 327–329, 337–339, 358, 368, 371–372, 374, 378–379, 381
  recollections of, 141, 255–257, 292, 326, 335, 343, 353, 376–377, 382–384
  tours and, 358–360, 368, 381–383
Coltrane, William, 377
Coltrane Family concert, 337–339
Coltrane Home landmark, 377, 381, 387
"The Coltrane Legacy," 359
Coltrane "Live" at the Village Vanguard (John Coltrane), 108, 129, 169, 174
Coltrane Records, 175, 191–192, 333
Columbia Records, 280
"Come Dance With Me," 65
Community College of Philadelphia, 242
Connor, Bull, 117
Conway, Tim, 325–326
Cook, Junior, 61
Cooke, Sam, 40
Coolidge, Calvin, 205
Copland, Aaron, 146
Corea, Chick, 98, 319, 359
Coryell, Larry, 276
"cosmic music"
  concept of, 181–193, 195–196, 204, 232, 253, 266–267, 271, 358, 392
  cosmic energy and, 181–193, 267
  description of, xix–xx, 181–193, 195–196
Cosmic Music (Alice and John Coltrane), 191–192, 261
"Cosmic Music" concert, 189–191, 222
Cosmogramma (Ellison/Flying Lotus), 387
Cotton Club Review, 68
"The Creator Has a Master Plan," 204
"Crescent," 372, 378, 381
Crescent (John Coltrane), 123
Crispell, Marilyn, 358

Crosby, David, 90
Crouch, Jan, 351
"Cry," 251, 275
Cry (Ailey), xviii
Cyrille, Andrew, 358
Cyrus, Miley, xxiv

Dandridge, Dorothy, 68
"Darn That Dream," 74
Dave Brubeck Quartet, 105
Davis, Art, 138, 148–149
Davis, Miles
  albums by, xi–xiii, xix, 70, 74, 80, 96
  bands of, 37–38, 70, 74–75, 80, 96
  early years of, 24–25, 34, 37–38, 46
  musical style of, xi–xiii, 70, 80, 92, 105, 144
  tours and, 80, 83, 125
Davis, Sammy Jr., 47, 68
Davis, Steve, 82–83
Davis Sisters, 67
Decca Records, 186–187
Dee, Ruby, 317
"Defunk Brothers," 93
DeJohnette, Jack, 164–165, 189–191, 249, 280–281, 374, 378, 382
Denny's Show Bar, 67
Detroit Free Press (newspaper), 56
Detroit Tribune (newspaper), 3–4
Dews, Angela, 226–227, 255–256
"Diana Grande Valse de Concert," 39
Dillard, Gladys Wade, 27–28, 38–40, 51
Divine Revelations (Alice Coltrane), 230, 290–291, 318, 337, 342, 353–354, 362, 370–371
Divine Songs (Alice Coltrane), 356–357
Dixie Hummingbirds, 40
Dixon, Bill, 147–148
Dizzy Gillespie and his Orchestra, 34–35. *See also* Gillespie, Dizzy
Dolphy, Eric, 102, 104, 108, 120, 123–124, 129, 144, 188
Dorsey, Tommy, 40, 46
Douglas, Alan, 219

Douglass, Frederick, 55–56
Down Beat (magazine), xviii, 71, 77–78, 90, 161, 174, 196, 241, 243, 253, 260, 277–278, 281, 297, 301–302, 308
Drake, Nick, xix
"Drips//Auntie's Harp," 387
Dublab, xv, 387
Duncan, Edmondstoune, 39
Dvořák, Antonín, 55, 270
Dylan, Bob, 140, 152, 252

"E Minor," 174
"The Eagle Stirreth Her Nest," 40–41
Earth Groove (Pran Nath), 219
Ebony (magazine), 361
Eckstine, Billy, 28, 68, 111
economic downturns, 69–70
The Ecstatic Music of Alice Coltrane Turiyasangitananda (Alice Coltrane), xx
Edwards, Altevia "Buttercup," 77, 81–82
Einstein, Albert, 111, 130, 170
El Nutto (Gibbs), 108
The Elements (Henderson), 279
Ellington, Duke, 23, 108, 138, 144, 159, 182, 219, 253, 386
Ellison, Steven, xiv–xvi, 367, 376, 379–380, 384, 386–387, 390. *See also* Flying Lotus
Endless Wisdom (Alice Coltrane), 335–336, 350
"Er Ra," 356–357
ESP-Disk', 147–148
Essence (magazine), 255–256, 381
Eternity (Alice Coltrane), 293–294, 297–298, 313
Eternity's Pillar (TV show), 349–351, 353, 356, 361, 390
Evans, Bill, 35, 70, 92, 96, 243. *See also* Lateef, Yusef
"The Evolution of Alice Coltrane," 362
Expression (John Coltrane), 177, 187
Extensions (Tyner), 224

"Fables of Faubus," 119
Fagen, Donald, 140
Fahey, John, 284
The Family Album (Gibbs), 108
Far Cry (Dolphy), 104
Farrell, Joe, 98
Farrow, Ann Johnson, 4–5, 8–9. *See also* McLeod, Ann Johnson
Farrow, Ernest "Ernie"
  bands of, 60–61, 70–71, 74–75, 93, 101
  birth of, 5
  death of, 210
  early years of, 4–5, 8, 10, 18–20, 27, 51
  music of, 18–20, 27, 36, 47, 55, 59–61, 70, 108, 196
Farrow, Harold Clifford, 4–5, 8, 23
Farrow, Margaret, 4–5, 8, 10, 20, 52
Farrow, Mia, 238
Faubus, Orval, 119
Feather, Leonard, 107, 161, 264, 277–278, 337–338
"Finis," 65
Finnegans Wake (Joyce), 170
The Firebird (Stravinsky), 256–257, 268–269
First Choice, 296
Fisher, William Arms, 271
Fisher Theatre, 56
Fitzgerald, Ella, 23, 35
"500 Greatest Albums of All Time," xx
Five Spot, 80, 122, 148
Flack, Roberta, 389
Flame Show Bar, 23, 45–46, 68, 73
Flanagan, Johnson, 28
Flanagan, Tommy, 27–28, 35, 38, 51, 65–66
Fleetwood Mac, 265–266
Flying Lotus, xiv–xv, 386–387, 390. *See also* Ellison, Steven
Folkways, 125–126
For Members Only (TV show), 360
"For Turiya," 296
Ford Motor Company, 13, 22, 26
Fortune Records, 67
Foster, Frank, 157

Foster, Stephen, 55
Four Freshmen, 65
Four Tet, 375
Four Tops, 275
Franklin, Aretha, 33–34, 41, 73, 256, 275, 280
Franklin, C. L., 33–34, 40–41
Free Jazz (Coleman), 150
Freedomways (journal), 140
Friday, Bob, 56
"A Friend," 294
Fulgoni, Steve, 377
Fuller, Curtis, 35, 60, 120
Fuqua, Charles, 68

"Galaxy Around Olodumare," 259
"Galaxy in Satchidananda," 277
"Galaxy in Turiya," 259
Gandhi, Mahatma, 130, 238
"Ganesha," 299–300
Garner, Errol, 113
Garrett, Donald, 154–155, 165
Garrison, Jimmy
   Alice Coltrane and, 174, 187, 189–191, 195, 227, 242–245, 248–250
   early years of, 108, 124, 135
   John Coltrane and, 108, 124, 135, 138, 159, 161, 167–168
Gaye, Marvin, 275
Genius + Soul = Jazz (Charles), 89
Gensel, John G., 182
Getz, Stan, 78, 80, 96, 99, 182
Ghost Stories (radio program), 11
"Giant Steps," 330, 338
Giant Steps (John Coltrane), 80, 83, 88
"Gibberish," 63
Gibbs, Gerry, 374
Gibbs, Marla, 360
Gibbs, Terry
   albums by, 105–108, 158
   early years of, 46–48, 278, 320
   quartet of, 62–64, 101–108, 112–113, 157, 207, 374
Giddins, Gary, 161

Gillespie, Dizzy, 23–25, 34–35, 46, 60, 66, 74–76, 104, 386
Gilmore, John, 148
Ginsberg, Allen, 152
Giuffre, Jimmy, 96, 147
Gleason, Ralph J., 89
Glorious Chants (Alice Coltrane), 371
"Goin' Home," 271, 276, 335, 359, 384
Gold Room, 99–100
Goldsmith, George, 93
Gordon, Edward "Laraaji," 307
Gordy, Berry
   early years of, 5–6, 9–11, 22, 27, 45–46, 68
   record labels of, 74, 94, 277, 331
   riot recovery and, 366–367
Gospel Hymns and Sacred Songs (Moody and Sankey), 18
Gospel Pearls (hymn book), 18, 21
"Gospel Trane," 195
"Govinda Jai Jai," 298
Graham Central Station, 296
Grand Bar, 103, 107
Granz, Norman, 35, 80
Grateful Dead, 90, 276–277
Green, Al, 46
"Greensleeves," 105–106
Greenwood, Jonny, 375
Grieg, Edvard, 40
Griffin, Chuck, 251
Griffin, Johnny, 61
Grimes, Henry, 98
Grubbs, Juanita "Naima," 109, 112, 118, 121, 127–130, 141, 145, 183
Guns N' Roses, 357

Haden, Charlie, 98, 228, 266, 273, 296, 317, 360, 378, 382, 384
Hagood, Alice
   divorce of, 82
   marriage of, 75–82
   in Paris, 75–82
   returning to Detroit, 82–83
   see also Coltrane, Alice

Hagood, Kenny "Pancho"
   addiction and, 79
   Alice McLeod and, 74–76
   divorce of, 82
   marriage of, 75–82
   in Paris, 75–82
   quartets and, 34
   returning to Detroit, 82
Hagood, Michelle, 75–76, 82. *See also* Coltrane, Michelle
Haile Selassie International University, 278
Haizlip, Ellis, 227
Half Note, 122, 136, 138, 140, 143
"Half Steps," 174
Hall, Jim, 96
Hall, Rex, 49–50
Halpern, Steven, 307
Hamilton, Chico, 72
Hamilton, Dave, 68
Hammerstein, Oscar II, 83, 259
Hampton, Lionel, 34, 76
Hancock, Herbie, 222, 277
Handel, George Frideric, 325
Hanna, Roland, 52
Haqq, Mother, 287
Hardman, John, 276
Hardy, Janet, 39–40
"Hare Krishna," 250, 277, 283–284, 298, 314
Harris, Barry, 27, 35, 37, 51–53, 57, 61, 93, 107
Harrison, George, xiii
Hartman, Johnny, 68, 108
Hassell, Jon, 231
"Hastings Street," 22
"Have You Met Miss Jones," 28
Havens, Richie, 353, 360
Hawkins, Coleman "Hawk," 50, 160, 386
Hayes, Louis, 60
Haynes, Roy, 96, 247, 313, 346, 382
Hayworth, Rita, 79
Head Hunters (Hancock), 277
Hearts of Space (radio program), 334

Heath, Albert "Tootie," 360
Heavy Water, 276–277, 281
Hebb, Bobby, 227
Heckman, Don, 99
Hencken, George E., 95
Henderson, Joe, 61, 67, 71, 98, 172, 189–191, 220–223, 279, 360
Henderson, John, 364, 370
Henderson, Mirabai, 364
Hendrix, Jimi, 259
Hennix, Catherine Christer, 231
Henry Swing Club, 22
Hentoff, Nat, 126
Heraclitus, 153
Herman, Woody, 46
Hickson, Purusha
   background of, xi, xviii, 283–284
   books by, xviii
   recollections of, 283–284, 287, 295, 298–299, 303–304, 306, 328, 331–332, 339–340, 344, 347–348, 367, 369, 380, 386, 392
Higgins, Billy, 317, 329
Hillyer, Lonnie, 54, 66
Hobby Bar, 84–85, 87
Holiday, Billie, 23, 46, 386
"Holiday for a Graveyard," 182
Holland, Dave, 280–281
Holliday, George, 366
Holly, Buddy, 386
Holmes, David, 375
Holst, Eduard, 39
"Homage to John Coltrane: A Spiritual Legacy," 358
Hooker, John Lee, 22–23
Hootenanny My Way (Gibbs), 105
Horn, Paul, 238–239, 307
Horne, Lena, 47
House of Blues, 381
Housing Act, 35
Hubbard, Freddie, 71, 120, 123, 149, 223
Huntington Ashram Monastery (Alice Coltrane), 204–205

Hurtak, James J., 382
Hutson, Leroy, 296
"The Hymn," 378

"I Heard the Voice of Jesus Say," 384
"I Want to See You," 195
"I Want to Talk About You," 111–112
"If It's Magic," 294
"IHS" ("I Have Suffered"), 205–206
Illuminations (Alice Coltrane and Carlos Santana), 281
"Impressions," 111
Impressions (band), 296
Impulse Records, 89–90, 108, 129, 144, 175, 187, 192, 196, 214, 220, 233, 262, 270–278, 289, 330, 386
"India," 124
Infinite Chants (Alice Coltrane), 364
"Infinity," 190
Infinity (Alice Coltrane), 262–264, 273–274
Ink Spots, 23, 68
Inside (Horn), 239
Integral Yoga Institute (IYI), 207, 210–215, 220, 228, 242, 258, 278
International Jazz Festival, 359
International Jazz Quartet, 71
International Society for Krishna Consciousness (ISKCON), 298, 307–308
Interstellar Space (Alice Coltrane), 249
"Isis and Osiris," 228
Ithaca College, 242
Ives, Charles, 123
Iyer, Sairam, 371

The Jack Benny Show (radio program), 11
Jackson, Alvin, 37
Jackson, Ira, 56–57
Jackson, Mahalia, 40
Jackson, Milton "Bags," 26, 34–35, 37, 104
Jackson, Oliver, 71
Jackson State College, 225
"Jagadishwar," 378, 382
"Jai Ramachandra," 334

"Jail Bait," 67
Jamerson, James, 74
James, Rick, 140–141
Jameson, Judith, 251–252
Jarreau, Al, 296, 365
Jarvis, Clifford, 242, 247–248, 250
"Jaya Jaya Rama," 205
Jazz (magazine), 172
Jazz & Pop (magazine), 192
Jazz at the Philharmonic, 35
Jazz Composers Guild, 147
Jazz Gallery, 173
"jazz loft," 93–99, 170, 172, 239, 329
Jazz Mood (Lateef), 61
Jazz Workshop, 94, 136, 166, 171
Jefferson Airplane, 277
The Jeffersons (TV show), 360
Jeffries, Edward, 12
Jenkins, Leroy, 248
Jewels of Thought (Sanders), 222
Joe's Pub, 376
John, Elton, 277
John Coltrane Festival, 360–361, 365, 368–369, 375
John Coltrane Memorial Concert, 253, 389
John Coltrane Quartet, 80, 108–112, 136–164, 224, 234, 257, 261–264, 268, 273. *See also* Classic Quartet
John Coltrane Quintet, 102, 160, 171–175, 330
"John Henry," 105
Johnson, Ann K., 4–5. *See also* McLeod, Ann Johnson
Johnson, Margaret, 59
Johnson, Marv, 74
Johnson, Robert, xix
Johnson, Ziggy, 68
Johnston, Dewey, 149
Jones, David, 243
Jones, Elayne, 259
Jones, Elvin
  Alice Coltrane and, 224, 368, 371
  early years of, 37, 46, 54, 82–83, 93, 96, 104, 108, 125

John Coltrane and, 82–83, 108, 125, 135, 138, 143, 149, 155–160, 165–168, 253
Jones, Hank, 34–35, 37, 46
Jones, Jim, 321–322
Jones, Quincy, 76–77, 89, 106
Jones, Thad, 35, 37, 46
Jordan, Sheila, 122
Jost, Ekkehard, 160
"Journey in Satchidananda," 231–233, 243, 276, 368–369
Journey in Satchidananda (Alice Coltrane), xii–xiv, xix–xx, 231–233, 241–242, 247–249, 368–369, 390
"Journey into Outer-Inner Space," 276
"Journey to Satchidananda," 371
Jowcol Music, 303
Joyce, James, 170
"Juanita," 55–56
Juilliard School of Music, 25, 51, 59, 91, 263, 331
Julia, Raul, 211, 220

Kabuki Theater, 279
Kahn, Ashley, 75–76, 89–90, 121, 135, 376
Kalin, Victor, 182
Kalisch, Joan, 248
Karma (Sanders), 204, 222
Kennedy, John F., 118
Kent State University, 225
"Keshava Murahara," 350, 356
Keyboard Lounge, 68
Keys, Alicia, 389
Keystone Korner, 289
Khan, Aly, 79
Khan, Hazrat Inayat, xxi, 130
Khan, Ustad Bismillah, 342
Kid A (Radiohead), 375
Kilmer, Joyce, 39
Kind of Blue (Miles Davis), xiii, 80
King, Ben E., 280
King, Franzo, 282–283, 298–299
King, Marina, 282–283, 287, 298–299

King, Martin Luther Jr., 112, 117–118, 121, 142, 188, 217, 235, 353
King, Rodney, 365–366
Kirk, Roland, 98, 167–168, 288
Kirkland, Sally, 211, 229, 284
Klein's Show Bar, 57, 60
Klemmer, John, 264, 274, 278
Kofsky, Frank, 109, 171
Kramer, Kumar, 242–243
Krasnow, Bob, 289
Krishna, 390
Krishnamurti, J., 130, 153, 184
Krupa, Gene, 102
Ku Klux Klan, 13, 117
Kulpowicz, Slawomir, 359, 365, 374
Kulu Sé Mama (John Coltrane), 155, 174

Lake, Oliver, 358
Lake Forest College, 264
Lakhanpal, Dinesh, 368
Lao Tzu, 232
"Largo," 270–271
Lasker, Jay, 274
Last Poets, 219, 248
Lateef, Yusef, 26, 35, 53–61, 70–71, 91–96, 127, 160, 176, 207, 243
Laurie, John, 387
Law & Order (TV series), 385
Lawson, Hugh, 53, 60, 71
Le Blue Note, 77–79, 82
Leary, Timothy, 153
Leitch, Donovan, 238
Lemon Gospel Chorus, 42
"Leo," 227, 244, 316, 378, 383
Lesh, Phil, 90
"Let Us Praise God Together," 350
Lewis, Juno, 155, 165
Lewis, Ramsey, 99
Liberace, 48
Life (magazine), 13, 210
Ligeti, György, 260, 267
Light of Asia (Arnold), 304
Light on the Path (Collins), 131
Lightfoot, Gordon, 141

Lightsey, Kirk, 27–28, 38, 52–54, 64, 73, 93–94
Lincoln, Abbey, 140
Lincoln Center, 120, 160–161, 176
Liszt, Franz, 37
Little, Booker, 89
"Little Boy, Don't Get Scared," 65
Live at Birdland (John Coltrane), 112, 129
Live in Japan (John Coltrane), 170, 263
Live in Seattle (John Coltrane), 154
"Living Space," 263–264
Lloyd, Charles, 164
Logan, Giuseppi, 147
London House, 113
London Symphony Orchestra, 253
"Lonesome Mood," 65
Longhorn Jazz Festival, 166
"Lonnie's Lament," 359
"Lord, Help Me to Be," 187–188, 190
"Lord of Lords," 265–268, 359
Lord of Lords (Alice Coltrane), xiv, 265–271, 273–274, 306
Los Angeles riots, 366–367
Los Angeles Sentinel (newspaper), 318
Los Angeles Times (newspaper), 316, 337–338, 349
"Los Caballos," 293–294
Love, Josephine, 27, 51
Love, Mike, 238
"Love Hangover," 326
"A Love Supreme," 139, 167–168, 182, 258, 260, 279, 338, 372, 374, 381, 383
A Love Supreme (John Coltrane), xiii, 135, 138–142, 147, 149–150, 154, 167–168, 182, 196, 241, 275, 282, 329, 376
"Lovely Sky Boat," 195
Lowe, Frank, 140, 248, 253, 257–259, 358
Luaka Bop, xx, 388
Lyon, Charles "Little Willie," 14–15
Lyrichord, 125

"Madhura Manohara Giridhari," 357
Mahal, Taj, 204
Mahler, Gustav, 259
Makeba, Miriam, 106
Malcolm X, 118, 136, 142, 234–235, 353
"Manifestation," 187–188
"Manifestation of Cosmic Energy," 190
"Mantra," 190, 223
Martha (opera), 39
Martino, Pat, 296
Marx, Harpo, 145
Mary Poppins (film), 148
Mascagni, Pietro, 39
Massey, Cal, 89, 166–168, 172, 175, 182, 224
Massey, Zane, 168
Mathis, Johnny, 68, 102
Maupin, Benjamin "Bennie," 50, 60, 71, 87–95, 100, 277, 374
Max, Peter, 208–209, 211, 258
Mayer, Mary Ann, 276–277
McAlister, Melani, 131
McBee, Cecil, 54, 93, 98, 230–231, 234–235, 242–245
McCann, Les, 99, 136
McCarthy, Eugene, 326
McCloud, Bill, 349
McCoy Tyner Plays Ellington (Tyner), 138
McGuinn, Roger, 90
McKie's, 122
McKinney, Bernard, 93
McKinney, Harold, 37
McKinney, Ray, 37, 93
McKinney, William, 37
McLaughlin, John, xiii, 276, 279, 310–311
McLeod, Alice
  astral projections of, 29–31
  birth of, 3–4
  childhood of, 3–22, 28–31
  as church pianist, 20–22, 28, 38, 55–57
  divorce of, 82
  early bands of, 56–57, 65, 71–72, 79, 93
  early years of, 3–31, 33–43, 49–71, 73–85, 87–113
  education of, 3–4, 19–20, 28, 38–43, 47–52, 59

first recording by, 67–68
first writing credit, 94–95
graduation of, 56, 59
jam sessions and, 93–94, 98–100
John Coltrane and, 80, 83–84, 99–113, 117–177
marriages of, 75–82
musical style of, xii–xx, 80–81, 87–88, 91–95, 102–108
in New York City, 59–61, 98–99
out-of-body experiences of, 29–31
parents of, 3, 8–10
in Paris, 75–82
returning to Detroit, 62–63, 82–83
tours and, 65–71, 101–108
see also Coltrane, Alice
McLeod, Ann Johnson Farrow, 3–4, 8–11, 17–18, 122, 154, 261
McLeod, Jackie, 4, 8, 10
McLeod, JoAnn, 4, 8, 10–11, 38, 373
McLeod, Marilyn, 4, 8, 10–11, 28, 64, 184, 256, 326, 347, 367, 383–384
McLeod, Solon, 3–4, 8–11, 172
McNair, Denise, 117
McPartland, Marian, 47, 329–330
McPhee, Joe, 143–144
McPherson, Charles, 54, 66
Meditations (John Coltrane), 156, 171
Mendelssohn, Felix, 40
Mercado, Walter, 351
Messiaen, Olivier, 76, 123
The Methodist Pocket Hymn Book (Allen), 17–18
Metropole Café, 102
Michel, Ed
  early years of, 220–223
  recollections of, 221–223, 248, 260–270, 274, 297, 314–317, 328–329
  recording studios and, 220, 233, 243, 260–261, 265, 289–293, 306, 314–315, 328–329
Michelot, Pierre, 79
Michigan Chronicle (newspaper), 8, 36, 38, 52, 55–56, 65, 68, 99, 122

"Miles' Mode," 330
Milestones (Miles Davis), 70
Mingus, Charles, 46, 96, 119, 386
Minor Key, 82–83, 100, 109
Minton's Playhouse, 24
Mr. Kelley Lounge, 94
Mitchell, Billy, 46
Mitchell, Joni, 141
Mitchell, Red, 61
Modern Jazz Quartet, 105, 127
A Monastic Trio (Alice Coltrane), 196–197, 203–204
Monk, Thelonious, 25, 34–35, 74, 152, 160, 187
Monument Eternal (Alice Coltrane), xvii–xviii, 198–199, 202, 287, 304, 308–310, 317, 324, 333
"Mood Indigo," 65
Moody, Dwight Lyman, 18
Moore, O. D., 3
Moran, Pat, 101
Morehouse College, 173
Morelli, Frank, 93, 99
Morgan, Lee, 71
Morgenstern, Dan, 143
"Morning," 61
Morris, Butch, 359
Morris, Robert, 64
Morris, Shanti, 302
Moses, J. C., 161
Moses, Robert, 35
Moss, Jayalakshmi, 304
Mother Teresa, 199, 295, 362
Motown label, 74, 93–94, 256, 275–277, 326, 331
Mt. Olive Baptist Church, 4, 8, 17–21, 28–29, 38–43, 51, 55, 59, 65, 132, 261
Moving Pictures (Ravi Coltrane), 371
Mozart, Wolfgang Amadeus, 40, 130
Mulligan, Gerry, 61
Murray, Albert, 24
Murray Body Corporation, 13
Musgnug, Roy, 186–187

"My Favorite Things," 83, 157, 161, 164, 169, 258
My Favorite Things (John Coltrane), 83, 88, 90
"My Old Kentucky Home," 55–56
The Mysticism of Sound and Music (Khan), 130

"Naima," 169, 330
National Association for the Advancement of Colored People (NAACP), 13–14, 68
"Nature Boy," 148
Nature Planned It (Four Tops), 275
Neti Neti (Not This, Not That) (Beckett), 131
New Bethel Baptist Church, 33–34, 40–41, 73
New Jersey Performing Arts Center, 382
"New Sun," 341
"New Thing," 80, 147–148, 151, 159, 164–165, 189
New World Symphony (Dvořák), 270–271
New York Eye and Ear Control (Ayler), 150
New York Times (newspaper), xviii–xix, 191, 252, 311, 376
New York University, 173
Newport Jazz Festival, 109, 169, 176
Newsday (newspaper), 226
Nicholson, Stuart, 379
Nielsen, Carl, 196
Nirvana, xiii
Nisenson, Eric, 105, 126, 152–153, 165, 170
Nola Studios, 101
Northern, Robert, 89
Norton, Caroline, 55–56
"Now's the Time," 57, 63, 102
"Number One," 174
Nyro, Laura, 211, 225–226, 242, 244, 251, 281

Oakland Post (newspaper), 317
Oakland Tribune (newspaper), 335
"Oceanic Beloved," 190, 195

The Office (TV series), 385
"Ogunde," 174
"Oh Allah," 249
"Ohnedaruth," 187
Olatunji, Michael Babatunde, 173, 176
Old Beachcomber, 69
"Old Folks at Home," 55
"Old Rugged Cross," 140
Oldfield, Mike, 277
Olé (John Coltrane), 124, 149
Olympia Theatre, 80, 109
Om (John Coltrane), xii–xiv, xix, 152, 155, 187–188, 261
"Om Namah Sivaya," 300
"Om Rama," 364
"Om Shanti," 357
"Om Supreme," 293, 317
On the Corner (Miles Davis), xi–xiii, xix
"One for the Father," 314, 330
One Mind Temple, 282–283, 287–288, 295–299, 321, 329
"Oop-Bop-a-Da," 74
Orchestra Hall, 342
Overton, Hall, 96

Packard Motor Company, 13, 26
Palace of Culture and Science, 359
Palestine, Charlemagne, 231
Palladium, 278
Palmer, Robert, xix, 311, 346, 358–359
Pandit, Korla, 351
Paradise Theater, 23, 27
Paradise Valley, 3–16, 18–23, 31–36, 45, 69, 73–74
Parker, Charlie "Yardbird," 24–25, 35–38, 48–51, 60, 63, 74, 104, 162, 262
Parks, Rosa, 63
Parliament, 277
Paudras, Francis, 78–79, 81–82
Payne, Cecil, 167
"Peace on Earth," 160, 170, 196, 263
Peaston, David, 359
Penderecki, Krzysztof, 267
Pep's, 138, 166

Peraza, Armando, 280, 294
Pershing, John, 8
Peterson, Oscar, 80, 113
Pettiford, Oscar, 79
Philadelphia Daily News (newspaper), 102
Philadelphia Jazz Society, 227
Philharmonic Hall, 120, 160–161, 176
Philpot, Hellen, 19
Philpot, Ruby, 19–20
Piano Jazz (radio program), 329–331
Pike, Bobby, 102
Pinelawn Memorial Park, 182
Pink Floyd, 281
Pitchfork, xx
The Planets (orchestral suite), 39
Plantation Club, 23
Plays (John Coltrane), 148
Plugged Nickel, 164
Pollard, Terry, 19–20, 47–52, 57, 62–64, 84–85, 99–104, 244
"Polly Wolly Doodle," 105
Porter, Lewis, 93, 109, 122, 139, 170
Portland State University, 264
Portrait of Devotion (Adams), 373
Powell, Bud, 25, 57, 65, 76–85, 94, 99, 102, 105, 107
Powell, James, 136
Prabhupada, Swami, 298, 302–303, 307–308
Pran Nath, Pandit, 219–220, 229–231
"Prema," 298, 314, 316–317, 330, 359
Premiers, 65–71, 92, 108
Presley, Elvis, 79
Presley, Priscilla, 79
Prince, 381
"The Promise," 329
Prysock, Arthur, 68
"Ptah, the El Daoud," 222
Ptah, the El Daoud (Alice Coltrane), 222–224, 228
Purushottamananda, Swami, 239

Quine, Robert, 171
Quran, 54, 127

Ra, Sun
   Alice Coltrane and, 232, 248, 254, 270, 359
   early years of, 130–131, 143
   John Coltrane and, 130–131, 147–148, 166, 386
Rachmaninoff, Sergei, 44, 267
Radha-Krsna Nama Sankirtana (Alice Coltrane), 297, 299, 301–302, 305
"Radhe-Shyam," 306
Radio City Music Hall, 173
Radiohead, 375
Rama, 390
"Rama Guru," 356
Ramayana (text), 304
Ransom, Delores, 42, 44
Rasbach, Oscar, 39
Rascals, 211, 220, 242, 244, 281
Rasmuson, Kenneth, 387
Ratliff, Ben, 118, 150
The Real Book (songbook), 28
Rebbilot, Pat, 220
Record Plant, 257, 294, 298
Red, Sonny, 71
Red Clay (Hubbard), 223
Redman, Dewey, 358
Redman, Joshua, 148–149
Redwing Studios, 328
Reed, Tom, 360
"Reet Petite (The Finest Girl You Ever Want To Meet)," 68
Reeves, Dianne, 41
Reeves, Martha, 331
Reflection on Creation and Space (A Five Year View) (Alice Coltrane), 277
Reich, Steve, 91, 96
Reid, Irene, 136
"Reminiscing About Dear John (for John Coltrane)," 224
"Resolution," 138
Retina Circus, 276
"Reverend King," 187–188
Revolution in Jazz, 147

Reynolds, Toby "Tulsi"
  early years of, 210–212
  playing music, 220, 229–232, 242–243, 248–250
  recollections of, 210–212, 215, 219–220, 229–231, 234, 242–243, 248–253, 258
Richmond, Trevor, xxiv
"Right On, Be Free," 251
Riley, Ben, 221, 266
Riley, Terry, 155–156, 187–188, 195, 219, 231, 257
Rimsky-Korsakov, Nikolai, 40
Riperton, Minnie, 294–295
The Rite of Spring (Stravinsky), 256, 293
Rivers, Sam, 346
Roach, Max, 25, 119, 140, 172, 182, 386
Robertson, Carole, 117
Robeson, Paul, 39
Robinson, Smokey, 68, 74, 277
Rodgers, Richard, 83, 259
Rogers, Ginger, 193
Rogers, Sinclair, 69
Rolling Stone (magazine), xviii, xx
Rolling Stones, 140, 266
Rollins, Sonny, 37–38, 78, 104, 122, 130, 160–161, 386
Ronstadt, Linda, 284
Rooks, Conrad, 208, 211, 298
Rooney, Wallace, 371
Roosevelt, Eleanor, 6
Roosevelt, Franklin Delano, 15, 163
Rosen, Jody, 386
Ross, Diana, 326
Royce Hall, 339, 381
Rudd, Roswell, 98
Rumbo Recorders, 357
Running Fox, Chief, 9
Rusch, Bob, 277
Russell, Arthur, xix

Sacred Language of Ascension (Alice Coltrane), 382–383
Sacred Offerings (Sai Anantam Ashram Singers), 375

Sai Anantam Ashram
  ashram tapes, 356, 363–364, 371, 387–388, 391
  location of, xiv–xvii, xx, xxiv–xxv, 343–349, 392
  renaming, 370
  see also Shanti Anantam Ashram
Sai Anantam Ashram Singers, 375, 378, 388
Sai Baba Center, 307
Sai Baba, Sathya, xvi–xviii, 240, 288–311, 313, 322–326, 342, 369–375, 380–384, 387–391
St. Gregory's Rectory, 166–167
St. Peter's Lutheran Church, 181–182
Sala Kongresowa, 359
Salzedo, Carlos, 186
San Francisco Examiner (newspaper), 260
San Jose State College, 264
Sanborn, David, 296
Sanders, Pharoah
  albums by, 204, 222
  Alice Coltrane and, 187–191, 196, 204, 209, 220–234, 242–245, 261, 270, 274, 288
  early years of, 148–151
  John Coltrane and, 149–151, 154–161, 166, 171, 174, 253, 365, 386
  recollections of, 160–161
Sankey, Ira David, 18
Santamaría, Mongo, 111
Santana, Carlos, xiii, xix, 259, 275–281, 294, 361, 368, 382
Satchidananda, Swami, xiii–xiv, xxi, 207–217, 219–235, 237–260, 276–284, 298–303, 368–376
"Satya Sai Isha," 378
Schifrin, Lalo, 106
Schoenberg, Arnold, 67, 146
Schoenberg Hall, 314–316
Science Fiction (Coleman), 253
Scott, Gene, 351
Scott, Hazel, 244, 329
Scott-Heron, Gil, 288

Search-for-a-Star competition, 56
Selflessness (John Coltrane), 261
Seventy Negro Spirituals (Fisher), 271
Shabazz, Majid, 234
Shad, Bob, 105
Shakespeare, William, 52
Shankar, Anoushka, 371
Shankar, Ravi, 173, 233, 371
Shanti Anantam Ashram, 343–347, 354, 361–362, 370. *See also* Sai Anatam Ashram
Shatz, Adam, 75
Shaw, George Bernard, 53
Shearing, George, 113
Shelly's Manne-Hole, 120
Shepp, Archie
    albums by, 148
    Alice Coltrane and, 196, 224, 227–228, 232, 241–248, 264, 274
    early years of, 129–130, 138, 143, 147–151
    John Coltrane and, 143, 149–151, 157, 172, 253
    recollections of, 129–130, 138, 143, 147–151, 196, 227, 241–248
"Shiva-Loka," 233–234, 243
Shorter, Wayne, 71, 120, 129, 139, 224, 281
Showboat, 102, 109
Sibelius, Jean, 196
Simone, Nina, 182, 331–332
Sims, Zoot, 96, 160
Sirota, Nadia, 250, 259
"Sita Ram," 250, 364, 378, 382
Sivananda, Sri Swami, 204, 208, 239, 304
Skidmore College, 264
Skies of America (Coleman), 253
Slate, John, 135
Smith, Lonnie Liston, 130
Smith, O. C., 360
Smith, Patti, 140
Smith, W. Eugene, 96–99
Snow, Michael, 150
Sojourner Truth Projects, 12
Soliveau, Sophye, 389
Solti, Georg, 288

"Something About John Coltrane," 251, 275
"Song of the Underground Railroad," 359
Songs in the Key of Life (Wonder), 294
Sonic Youth, xiii
Soul! (TV show), 227
Soul Illustrated (magazine), 257
Soul Stirrers, 40
"Soulsphere," 94–95
The Sound of Music (play), 83
"Spiritual," 129
"Spiritual Eternal," 293
"Spring Rounds," 293
Stacy, Barbara, 219–220
Stanford University, 165
Staple Singers, 296
"The Star Spangled Banner," 18
Stearns, Michael, 307
Steely Dan, 265–266
Steiner, Rudolf, 97
"Stella by Starlight," 28
Stephenson, Sam, 96
Stevenson, Jimmy, 98
Stevenson, Sandy, 98
Stewart, William, 56
Stitt, Sonny, 74
Stollman, Bernard, 147
Stravinsky, Igor, 40, 67, 77, 146, 256–257, 262, 267–270, 293
"Stravinsky: Excerpts from the Firebird," 269–270
Stryker, Mark, 25–27, 52, 79
"The Sun," 187–188, 196
Sun Ship (John Coltrane), 154, 261
Super Storm Sandy, 387
"Supernatural Thing," 280
Supremes, 331
Swallow, Steve, 97–98
Swan Silvertones, 40
Swezey, Stuart, 351

Tamla label, 74, 94
tapasya (spiritual fire), 199–204, 213–217, 230, 241, 245, 291, 309, 340–341, 378–379

Taylor, Cecil, 120, 143
Taylor, Creed, 88–89, 119
Taylor, Susan L., 381
Tchaikovsky, Pyotr, 44
Tchicai, John, 149
Teagarden, Norma, 329
Temple University, 172
Terry, Michael, 56
Terry Gibbs Plays Jewish Melodies in Jazztime (Gibbs), 106, 158
Terry Gibbs Quartet, 62–64, 101–108, 112–113, 157, 207, 374
Texaco New York Jazz Festival, 371
Thakur, Srila, 298
Thames, Arthur, 358
Thelonious Monk Quartet, 34–35. *See also* Monk, Thelonious
"There's a Balm in Gilead," 331
Thiele, Bob, 140, 155, 175, 177, 182, 192, 214
"This Train," 378
Thompson, Lucky, 34, 61, 76, 78–79
Threnody to the Victims of Hiroshima (Penderecki), 267
Time Records, 105
Timmons, Bobby, 71
The Tonight Show (TV show), 62
Tonight with Steve Allen (TV show), 62–63
Tony Williams Quintet, 359
Townshend, Pete, xiii
Transcendence (Alice Coltrane), 305–306, 311
Transcendental Meditation center, 277–278, 298
"Transfiguration," 315, 330
Transfiguration (Alice Coltrane), 330, 381
Transition (John Coltrane), 148–149, 261
"Translinear Light," 381
Translinear Light (Alice Coltrane), 377–378, 381
"The Trap of Love," 67
Traylor, Derrick, 339

"Trees," 39
"Triloka," 378
Truman, Harry, 35
Truth, Sojourner, 12
"Truth Is Marching In," 181
Tucich, Rudy, 53–54, 56–57, 60–61, 75
Turf Lounge, 102
"Turiya & Ramakrishna," 223
Turiya Sings (Alice Coltrane), xv, xvii, 333–335, 356
Turiyasangitananda, Swamini (Turiya), xiv–xviii, 179–284, 287–384, 388–392. *See also* Coltrane, Alice
Tusk (Fleetwood Mac), 265–266
Tuskegee Institute, 4
Tyner, McCoy
  albums by, 138, 224
  Alice Coltrane and, 224
  early years of, 82–83, 108, 128
  John Coltrane and, 82–83, 108, 135–138, 148–149, 156–161, 166, 253, 319–320
  recollections of, 137–138

U2, xix
UC Jazz Festival, 248
United Theatres Corporation, 56
"Universal Consciousness," 249
Universal Consciousness (Alice Coltrane), xiv, 247–250, 253–254, 283–284, 298, 377
Universal Music Group (UMG), 385–386
Universal Studios fire, 385–386, 388
University of California–Los Angeles (UCLA), 204, 313–316, 339
University of Notre Dame, 108
University of Southern California (USC), 327
Urban League, 16

Van Gelder, Rudy, 61, 89, 118, 138, 140, 149, 182, 222–224
Vaughan, Sarah, 28, 34, 46, 51, 68
  Sarah Vaughan Trio, 68

Vedantic Center, xvii, 264–265, 293–308, 313, 318–328, 331–344, 350, 357, 361
Vespertine (Björk), 375
"video vault," 385–386
Village Gate, 140, 143, 155, 172, 227
Village Recorder, 260–261, 265, 306
Village Theatre, 171–172
Village Vanguard, 108, 124, 129, 169, 174, 243
Vitous, Miroslav, 296
Von Flotow, Friedrich, 39
"Vrindavana Sanchara," 306–307

Waits, Freddie, 244–245
"Walk with Me," 378
Walker, Clarence LaVaughn, 33–34
Walker, Junior, 326
Walton, Cedar, 120
Ward, Carlos, 154, 161
Ware, David S., 169
Warner Brothers Records, 289, 293, 296–297, 314, 318
Warwick, Dionne, 296
Washington, Dinah, 46
Washington, Kamasi, 374
Watkins, Doug, 60
Watts, Jeff "Tain," 378
Wayne State University, 6, 36, 52–53, 66–67
We Insist (Roach), 119
Weather Report, 281
Webern, Anton, 123
Welburn, Ron, 166
"Welcome," 276
Wells, Mary, 331
Wesley, Cynthia, 117
West End Hotel, 60
Westlake Audio, 328
Weston, Kim, 227
Weston, Randy, 209
Westwood Playhouse, 331
What's Going On (Gaye), 275
"When Johnny Comes Marching Home," 105

"When You Are in Love," 67
White, Michael, 261, 270, 274
Whitney, John, 276
Williams, André, 67
Williams, Earl, 56
Williams, Mary Lou, 244, 289, 319, 329
Williams, Tennessee, 52–53
Williams, Tony, 359
Wilmer, Valerie, 130
Wilmore, Gayraud, 128
Wilshire Ebell Theatre, 284
Wilson, Burt, 171
Wilson, Jackie, 46, 68, 74
Wilson, Teddy, 329
Winans, David, 42
Winter Jazz Fest (New York), 389
"Wisdom Eye," 293
"Women in Jazz," 313
Wonder, Stevie, 275, 277, 294, 369
Wood, Vishnu, 209–215, 225–227, 247
Wood, William
    Alice Coltrane and, 66–67, 110, 209–215
    early years of, 60–61, 66–67, 74, 98
    recollections of, 60–61, 66–67, 102–104, 108, 110, 207–215
    Terry Gibbs and, 102–104, 108
Woodstock Festival, xiii, 212–213, 276
"Woody 'n' You," 57, 79
Workman, Reggie
    Alice Coltrane and, 225, 247, 257, 279, 311, 313, 346, 358–359
    early years of, 120, 124
    John Coltrane and, 124, 253
The World According to John Coltrane (documentary), 92
World Galaxy (Alice Coltrane), 257–261, 275
World Peace Tour, 237–239
World Scientific Yoga Conference, 229, 238
World Spirituality Classics 1: The Ecstatic Music of Alice Coltrane Turiyasangitananda (album), 388

World Stage, 52–54
Wright, Herman, 47–48, 101–102, 106
Wright, Syreeta, 277–279

Yogananda, Paramahansa, 130, 146, 204–206, 302, 309
Yogi, Maharishi Mahesh, xiii, 238, 265
Young, La Monte, 219–220, 231

Young, Lester, 51, 67, 78
Young, Neil, xxiv, 141
Young People's Choir, 20–21
Younger, Brandee, 389
"Your Lady," 118

Zawinul, Joe, 281
Zazeela, Marian, 219–220, 231
Zupan, Hari, 228